The Longest
Battle

The Longest Battle

SEPTEMBER 1944 TO FEBRUARY 1945
From Aachen to the Roer and Across

Harry Yeide

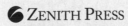 ZENITH PRESS

To those who fought.

This edition published by Zenith Press, an imprint of MBI Publishing Company, Galtier Plaza, Suite 200, 380 Jackson Street, St. Paul, MN, 55101-3885 USA.

Design: Tom Heffron and Mandy Iverson

ISBN: 0-7603-2155-8

Printed in the United States

CONTENTS

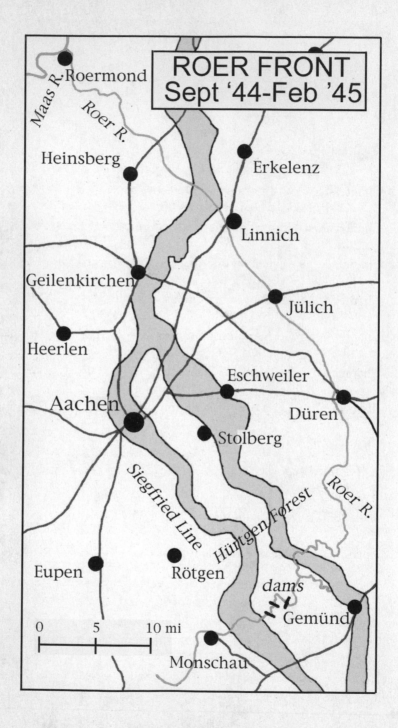

ROER FRONT
Sept '44–Feb '45

Maas R.
Roermond
Roer R.
Heinsberg
Erkelenz
Linnich
Geilenkirchen
Jülich
Heerlen
Eschweiler
Aachen
Düren
Stolberg
Siegfried Line
Hürtgen Forest
Roer R.
Eupen
Rötgen
dams
Gemünd
0   5   10 mi
Monschau

PREFACE

The battle in the West has largely moved onto German soil; German cities and villages will be battlegrounds. This fact must make our fighting more fanatical and harden every available man in the battle zone to turn every bunker, every apartment block in a German city, every German village into a fortress. . . .

FÜHRERBEFEHL, 17 SEPTEMBER 1944

N early half a year passed from the time the Roer River first became an operational objective at the division level to the day American troops swarmed across its racing waters. There were Allied strategic objectives—including the Rhine River—that were on the books for longer periods. But no other place in Western Europe featured for so long in the plans and efforts of the men who controlled the daily activities of the GIs, tankers, tank destroyer crews, combat engineers, and other soldiers who actually fought and won the war. The same might be said for the *Landsers*, *Grenadiere*, *Fallschirmjäger*, and *Panzertruppen* on the German side.

This work has some bias toward the Allied perspective. Because the Allies held the initiative, the organizational structure is built mainly on stages in their campaign to cross the Roer River. At the same time, I have tried to give fair representation and treatment to the German view of the struggle. The unequal weight in lower-level unit reports and personal anecdotes from the two sides results from having access to richer sources on the Allied experience. The reader may note that many of the accounts by German soldiers come from a collection posted at www.faem.com/mywar. The collection is unique, as far as I can tell, and coincidentally focuses on the period covered in this work. I do *not* endorse the political views expressed by the sponsors of the website.

It may not be apparent to the casual reader, but it is hard to tell exactly what happened lo these many years ago. Contemporary reports written by separate participants in any given incident are likely to differ, sometimes substantially. Later accounts introduce additional flaws of memory. The reader should be aware that the tale offered here is merely as close as the author can get.

I have elected to exclude much of the tragic battle in the Hürtgen Forest for several reasons. First, most of the Hürtgen Forest at first fell outside the mental framework of the American generals who visualized the Roer River as an intermediate objective, even though geographically the upper reaches of that river flow among the forest's brooding firs. Control over a series of dams in the heart of those woods would determine when the Americans could cross the Roer River downstream once they reached it, but there is a convincing case that this fact did not shape American operational decisions in the forest until December 1944. Second, the Hürtgen battle is a tale of military command stupidity with its own internal dynamic that deserves separate treatment. Third, that struggle has in recent decades received such attention from military historians. The reader should turn to a book-length history, such as Gerald Astor's *The Bloody Forest*, to develop some appreciation for the horror of that place.

I have generally used German unit descriptors. When there is a nearly exact English equivalent, or the German word has entered the English language, I have used the English variant (for example, panzer, grenadier). For ease of identification of almost invariably numbered formations on both sides, I have adopted the U.S. Army Center of Military History's convention and italicized nongeneric German units (for example, *3d Panzergrenadier Division*, but 1st Battalion). I have also italicized German words where appropriate. The text generally applies the phrase "assault gun" to cover a large range of turretless German armored fighting vehicles. The purist may object, but the *Sturmgeschütz* III, for example, frequently filled the tank destroyer role, whereas a Hetzer or a *Panzerjäger* IV often supported assaults. Moreover, German records often dropped the distinction.

I have taken small liberties with texts drawn from the military records and personal accounts to correct grammatical errors and spelling mistakes, and to introduce consistency in references to unit designators, equipment, dates, and so on.

September 2004

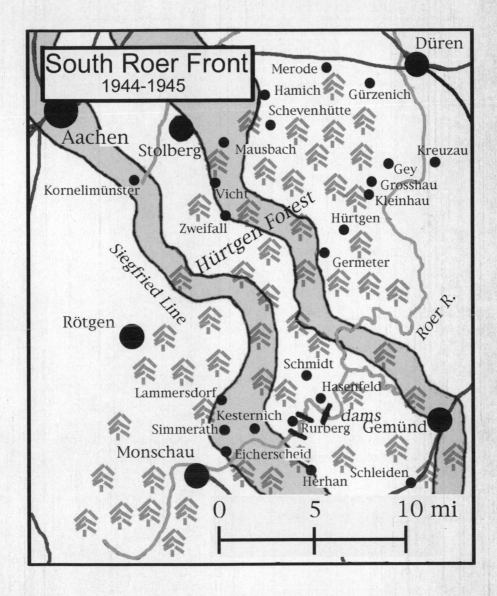

South Roer Front
1944-1945

Düren
Merode
Hamich
Gürzenich
Schevenhütte
Aachen
Stolberg
Mausbach
Kreuzau
Gey
Grosshau
Kornelimünster
Vicht
Kleinhau
Zweifall
Hürtgen
Hürtgen Forest
Germeter
Roer R.
Siegfried Line
Rötgen
Schmidt
Hasenfeld
Lammersdorf
Kesternich
dams
Simmerath
Rurberg
Gemünd
Monschau
Eicherscheid
Schleiden
Herhan

0   5   10 mi

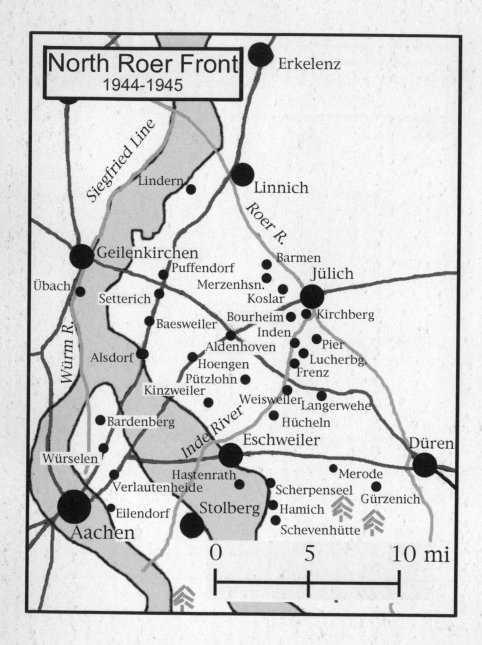

North Roer Front
1944-1945

Erkelenz

Siegfried Line

Lindern

Linnich

Roer R.

Geilenkirchen

Barmen

Jülich

Übach

Puffendorf

Merzenhsn.

Koslar

Kirchberg

Setterich

Bourheim

Baesweiler

Inden

Pier

Aldenhoven

Lucherbg.

Würm R.

Alsdorf

Hoengen

Frenz

Pützlohn

Kinzweiler

Weisweiler

Langerwehe

Bardenberg

Inde River

Hücheln

Eschweiler

Düren

Würselen

Hastenrath

Merode

Verlautenheide

Scherpenseel

Gürzenich

Eilendorf

Stolberg

Hamich

Aachen

Schevenhütte

0   5   10 mi

ACKNOWLEDGMENTS

I would like to thank my wife, Nancy, who is my destiny and makes me better in every endeavor, including this one. She helped ease me through a few trying moments.

I am grateful for the assistance of many individuals in the veterans' community. Stan Zimmerman provided his recollections of key days in his tank battalion's history. Frank Towers, executive secretary and historian of the 30th Infantry Division Association, was kind enough to review the manuscript and offer the insights of one who was there. Peter Branton and Gene Lytle, of the 104th Infantry Division Association, granted permission for the use of material drawn from veterans' accounts culled from the *Timberwolf Howl*. Gene Cocke, who runs the 26th Infantry Regiment's association, provided leads and material related to the Battle of Aachen. Thanks once again to Lieutenant Colonel Mark Reardon for providing his usual helpful material assistance.

I am particularly grateful to Tommy Maurice Löwenzahn-Nilsson, who cheerfully shared his expertise and painstaking research on the German armed forces. Eric Hammel, my editor, again provided sage counsel. I am indebted to Peter Bernotas for the courtesy permission to use images from the German wartime newsreels marketed by his company, International Historic Films, Inc. Thanks also to the webmaster at the My War website for courtesy permission to use parts of German war veterans' accounts posted there.

I would also like to thank the cheerful and efficient public servants at the National Archives and Records Administration's document, microfilm, still photo, and moving image reading rooms in College Park, Maryland. The taxpayer is getting a good deal.

CHAPTER 1

AN INTERMEDIATE OBJECTIVE

In essence, the decision emerging from the 23 August meeting [among Generals Eisenhower, Montgomery, and Bradley] resulted in a temporary shift of the main effort from the Maubeuge-Liege-Aachen axis to the plain of Flanders, a route that pre-invasion planners had blackballed as a primary axis into Germany. Yet the shift was more tactical than strategic in that it was made for the purpose of gaining intermediate objectives vital to a final offensive along the lines of the original strategic concept. It could be argued that it involved no real shift of any kind because of the broad interpretation that had come to be accorded the route "north of the Ardennes."

OFFICIAL U.S. ARMY HISTORY: *THE SIEGFRIED LINE CAMPAIGN*

At 1403 hours on September 12, 1944, a patrol from the U.S. 3d Armored Division—nicknamed the Spearhead Division—entered the Third Reich. Soon, the Sherman tanks and infantry-bearing M3 half-tracks of Task Force Doan, Combat Command A (CCA), approached dragon's teeth antitank obstacles—reinforced concrete pyramids—that formed part of the vaunted West Wall, or Siegfried Line, defenses west of Walheim. Task Force Lovelady from Combat Command B (CCB) penetrated the frontier north of Rötgen.[1] The armored spearhead was about ten miles due west of a series of picturesque lakes created by three dams on the little-known Roer River.

Oberstleutnant Tröster, commanding the *328th Ersatz und Ausbildung Abteilung (Replacement and Training Battalion)*, fired off a report to *LXXXI Corps*: "Two enemy tanks and four armored reconnaissance vehicles carrying infantry are entering Rötgen. Fourth Platoon of the security company is being driven from the south part of Rötgen. Lively firefight in Rötgen."[2] The 3d Armored Division's history recorded, "Several machine-gun nests were mopped up and an enemy staff car was destroyed."[3]

Somewhat farther north, the U.S. 1st Infantry Division advanced northeastward against growing German resistance offered by infantry, tanks, artillery, and minefields. The 18th Infantry Regiment nonetheless took Gemmenich, on the western outskirts of Aachen, and the 16th Infantry Regiment crossed the German border at 1515 hours and advanced deep into the Aachen municipal forest.[4] Aachen was the first large German city reached by American troops and was the symbolically important seat of Charlemagne's (known to the Germans as *Karl der Grosse*) First Reich.

Two days earlier, VII Corps artillery—parked in an orchard with guns elevated for maximum reach—had fired the first barrage into Germany, just to let the enemy know that the *Amis* (as the Germans called the Americans) were coming. The shells landed in the village of Bildchen, outside Aachen, which had the misfortune to be just in range.[5]

Major General J. Lawton (Lightning Joe) Collins had ordered a reconnaissance in force against the Siegfried Line in front of his U.S. VII Corps, which was in the final sprint of its race across northern France.[6] The nickname of the forty-eight-year-old Collins, which was earned as a division commander on Guadalcanal and New Georgia in the Pacific theater, was wholly descriptive. He was energetic and aggressive. Upon encountering Collins at the 12th Army Group headquarters (HQ) in August, Third Army's hard-charging commander Lieutenant General George S. Patton Jr. had told him, "You know, Collins, you and I are the only people around here who seem to be enjoying this goddamned war!"[7] VII Corps, for its part, had been in the European fighting from the start—its 1st Infantry Division had conducted the bloody D-day assault at Omaha Beach.

Anxious to maintain his corps' momentum, Collins obtained permission for his reconnaissance in force from a somewhat reluctant First Army commander,

Lieutenant General Courtney Hodges. Collins hoped he could push through the Siegfried Line before it was fully manned.[8]

Anticipating the possibility that his men might meet little opposition, Collins on September 11 ordered the 3d Armored Division to penetrate the West Wall. The division was to capture the town of Eschweiler (due east of Aachen) and wheel eastward to the Roer River—a distance of only twenty miles in total. For weeks, the Spearhead Division had been covering more than that distance in a single day. The terrain leading to Eschweiler was the only suitable ground for tank operations in the area. But a formidable double row of concrete dragon's teeth antitank obstacles barred the way, covered by fire from concrete emplacements on a ridge east of the industrial town of Stolberg.

The 1st Infantry Division—the "Big Red One"—on the corps' left, was to capture Aachen; it would be the first ground assault on a German city in more than a century. Nazi propaganda chief Dr. Joseph Göbbels promised the nation that Aachen would be the American army's Stalingrad.[9]

The 9th Infantry Division, on the corps' right, would enter the Rötgen Forest—the northern reaches of a fir-covered wilderness that would become best known to Americans as the Hürtgen Forest. The "Old Reliable Division" would then advance to Düren, a town on the east bank of the Roer River.[10] If anyone considered the fact that the 9th's advance would bypass the three Roer River dams upstream from Düren in the vicinity of Schmidt, he did not make much of it.

Thus began the American army's longest battle in Europe.

Major General Charles (Cowboy Pete) Corlett's XIX Corps, advancing on Collins' left adjacent to British forces, on September 12 established a firm bridgehead across the Meuse (Maas) River in northern Belgium and southern Holland. The corps consisted of the 30th ("Old Hickory") Infantry Division, on the right, and the 2d ("Hell on Wheels") Armored Division, on the left.

Elements of the *116th Panzer Division* (to which parts of the *105th Panzer Brigade* had been subordinated on September 9) were just appearing to the corps' front. Supported by long-range heavy artillery fire, they were able to slow the 30th Infantry Division's advance rather abruptly.[11]

Corlett had been under tremendous strain since D-day and was not in good health. He was also burdened with a red-hot temper and had managed to antagonize Hodges' and his own staffs. He would not command his corps for much longer.[12]

Hodges' First Army—which controlled VII and XIX corps, as well as V Corps, which was advancing farther south—noted in its operations report: "The 12th of September marked the approximate end of the sustained drive [across France]. . . . On this date, the enemy was fighting on his own soil for the first time since Napoleon. . . . From 13 September onward, the advances were measured by thousands of yards and by a heavy price in casualties and material for every yard gained."[13]

Collins on September 13 reiterated his instructions to the 3d Armored and 9th Infantry divisions but told the 1st Infantry Division to bypass Aachen to the south and capture the commanding high ground east of the city. There it would wait for XIX Corps to come abreast and complete the encirclement. Collins added that advancing units were not to cross the Roer River as yet, an instruction that the official U.S. Army history attributes to logistic concerns.[14]

The change in orders for the 1st Infantry Division came about after Collins discussed options with Major General Clarence (Ralph) Huebner, commanding the Big Red One. The two had known each other since their days working as instructors at Fort Benning in 1927.[15]

Huebner had led the 1st Division since August 1943, when Lieutenant General Omar Bradley sacked his predecessor, Major General Terry de la Mesa Allen, in Sicily. Bradley recognized Allen's brilliant record but deemed the division "temperamental, disdainful of both regulations and senior command."[16] Huebner, who had risen through the ranks after enlisting in 1910, believed in spit and polish and close-order drill.[17]

Huebner did not want to become embroiled in potentially costly street fighting. He suggested that by taking the high ground outside Aachen, he could dominate the city, prevent movement of German reinforcements, and remain free to assist the 3d Armored Division.

Collins at times thought Huebner overprotective of his division and inclined to push less hard if he could avoid casualties.[18] Collins nonetheless agreed that the 1st Infantry Division should bypass Aachen—and thereby unwittingly condemned his men to an unnecessary and bloody battle in

October. He wrote in his memoirs, "Later intelligence indicated that at that time Aachen was only lightly held and might have fallen to the 1st Division without a bitter fight, but there was no way of knowing this."[19]

Indeed, *Generalleutnant* Gerhard *Graf* von Schwerin, commanding general of the battered *116th* (*Windhund,* or Greyhound) *Panzer Division* and now of Aachen's defenses as of 0600 hours on September 13, had decided not to fight for the city. The general, a veteran of North Africa and the eastern front, had long viewed the war as lost and told trusted fellow officers that defending the Reich at the cost of its physical destruction would be criminal. (He has received sympathetic treatment from American and British historians. But Heinz Günther Guderian, who was von Schwerin's operations officer, became a Bundeswehr general and wrote an authoritative history of the division and criticized von Schwerin for undermining fighting spirit in the ranks at a critical time for the men and for Germany.) Von Schwerin had a history of making independent decisions in defiance of higher authority to save lives. The Knight's Cross with Oak Leaves and Swords that he had won in Russia points to motives other than self-preservation.

Confronted by scenes of civilians fleeing under Nazi Party orders—the party officials themselves had already bolted—von Schwerin countermanded the evacuation edict. On September 14, von Schwerin expected American GIs to enter the city by noon and drafted a written appeal for humane treatment of the civilian population to be given to the first American officer to enter the city.[20] He estimated that between twenty thousand and thirty thousand civilians were still in Aachen.[21]

It is a terrible irony that a German division commander who wanted to prevent unnecessary deaths among his compatriots was thwarted by an American division commander who wanted the same for his men. The Big Red One did not enter Aachen.

Von Schwerin's attempt to cede Aachen to the Americans came only days after SS chief Heinrich Himmler—just assigned the job of raising a replacement army to man the western front—had posted an order: "Certain unreliable elements seem to believe that the war will be over for them as soon as they surrender. . . . Every deserter . . . will find his just punishment. [His family] will be summarily shot."[22]

When news of von Schwerin's action reached higher authorities, Hitler ordered his arrest and trial for treason. In February 1944, after personally awarding von Schwerin the Oak Leaves and Swords to his Knight's Cross, Hitler had observed, "A pity that von Schwerin is not a National Socialist. He is a very efficient soldier!" Many senior officers, including SS general and Hitler favorite Sepp Dietrich, intervened on von Schwerin's behalf, and the Aachen business was dropped with a reprimand after von Schwerin had been transferred to a command in Italy.[23]

While Collins discussed bypassing Aachen with Huebner, the men in the 1st Infantry Division were finding the Germans around the city full of fight. The 1st Battalion, 16th Infantry Regiment, for example, reported that it "had the hell shelled out of us" and "casualties were streaming into the CP [command post]."

At 1000 hours that September 13, a German counterattack struck the battalion's Company C. One report described the action: "The enemy attacked, yelling and screaming, through the thickly wooded terrain and got right into [our] positions. One BAR [Browning automatic rifle] man was later found dead beside his gun, his magazines all empty and twelve enemy dead around his position. About 1045 hours, two light tanks were moved up and 'blasted' into the enemy with their 37mm guns and machine guns. By noon the attack had been repulsed, and twelve [prisoners of war] had been taken. During the twenty-four hours preceding, the battalion had suffered seventy-eight casualties."[24]

Because the 16th Regimental Combat Team (RCT) was making slower progress than expected, Huebner ordered the 28th Infantry Regiment to attack the points that were holding up the advance. The regiment recorded in its after-action report (AAR), "Plenty of bangalores and bazookas were called for to blast out the pillbox defenses encountered in the woods."[25]

The men had hoped that bitter fights such as those at the Normandy beachhead were behind them. The division's history noted, "The next few days on the line between Aachen and Stolberg slowly strangled that happy delusion."[26]

The 3d Armored Division, meanwhile, readied its moving steel fortresses to attack the static German ones of concrete, steel, and earth. The 3d Armored Division, along with XIX Corps' 2d Armored Division, had been exempted from a reorganization begun in September 1943 that created "light" armored divisions, which possessed one-third fewer tanks and four thousand fewer men. Instead of the common three-combat command system (CCA, CCB, and CCR) based on armored and armored-infantry battalions, the two "heavy" armored divisions retained one armored-infantry and two armored regiments. They used a two-combat command organization (conventionally CCA and CCB, although in VII Corps Collins mandated the use of the senior officer's name as the combat command's designator, to boost morale). The divisions had an authorized strength of 14,620 men, 232 medium tanks, and 158 light tanks.[27] An armored division, moreover, typically had a self-propelled tank destroyer battalion attached, which provided thirty-six additional guns.

Brigadier General Truman Boudinot, commanding CCB, recorded his outfit's first miles toward the Roer as they fought through the foremost band of defenses, called the Scharnhorst Line. A disparate collection of German units that had been hurriedly subordinated to *Generalmajor* Gerhard Müller's *9th Panzer Division* stood in the way.[28] The *9th Panzer Division* had barely beaten CCB to the spot; the lead elements of the division had arrived in the vicinity only three days earlier.[29]

On 13 September 1944 [we] contacted the Siegfried Line in the vicinity of Kornelimünster, Germany [outside Aachen at about the five o'clock position]. Two columns, each consisting of a battalion of tanks, a battalion of infantry, a platoon of engineers, and a platoon of [tank destroyers], began the advance through the Siegfried Line. Columns advanced along roads approximately 4,000 yards apart. We found the [defenses] weakly held by extremely poor troops, collected from several disintegrated divisions. In some instances, pillboxes were not manned, and at places the bands of dragon's teeth were not covered by fire.

Tactics and techniques identical to that of a stream crossing were used. Our armored infantry established a bridgehead across the band of dragon's teeth, and the engineers established a crossing.

At first, we tried to destroy the dragon's teeth by fire from our guns and found this was impracticable. The engineers next blew some of the dragon's teeth out with charges of TNT, but this was too slow a method. We finally confined the movement of all armored vehicles through the dragon's teeth to roads that passed through the lines. The engineers destroyed the steel gates that blocked the passage[s]. . . .

We reduced the concrete emplacements by placing artillery fire and the fire of automatic weapons on the apertures. The resistance was not determined, and the defenders would usually surrender after a short time. In some instances, our men were able to get up to pill-boxes and throw grenades in the apertures. After we had gotten through each band of dragon's teeth, our armored infantry would fan out and move behind pillboxes that were still manned. . . .

When moving through the several miles of [ground] between the bands of dragon's teeth, we often encountered [antitank] guns as we advanced around road bends. Since speed was so important, we spearheaded the advance of each column with a tank and took the tank losses from these guns. After the [antitank] gun had revealed itself, we operated against it in the usual way, with artillery and infantry. Our losses in tanks were fourteen mediums and two lights.

We found that the only weapons the Germans had placed in the pillboxes were automatic weapons. In every instance their [antitank] guns were outside the pillboxes and were well camouflaged. The firing compartment of the pillboxes is too small to mount their present [anti-tank] guns. They were designed to accommodate 37mm [antitank] guns, which were not used in the defense of the line.[30]

Combat Command A's Task Force Doan, meanwhile, tackled a cluster of pillboxes behind dragon's teeth northwest of Schmidthof. German mortar fire disrupted the first wave, but the infantry rallied and pressed on. Even pillbox-es that had taken direct hits from the 3-inch guns on the supporting M10 tank destroyers continued to spew death. Called upon to surrender, the Germans in one bunker yelled back, "Go to hell—we'll fight it out!" The tanks were unable to advance until the discovery of a secondary road where German farmers had filled in the dragon's teeth with dirt so they could cross the obstacles to reach their fields. After being briefly delayed when a mine-clearing tank got stuck, the M4 medium tanks pushed forward.

Several StuG III assault guns from the *394th Sturmgeschütz Brigade* (thirty-one panzers plus a company of panzergrenadiers at full strength)—which had arrived in Aachen late on September 10—and German soldiers with panzerfaust antitank rocket launchers engaged the Americans. The Shermans, which each had a 75mm or 76mm main gun depending on the tank model, had the advantage of a rapidly rotating turret, whereas the assault guns had their 75mm cannon mounted in a fixed superstructure that allowed the gun to swing only a few degrees to the left or right. The StuG III benefited from a low silhouette, and the Germans had the critical edge of firing from hidden defensive positions. At one point, Colonel Leander Doan could see seven of his M4s burning among the pillboxes.

At dusk, Doan dismounted and moved from one to another of his remaining tanks, giving orders and trying to boost morale. As he worked on into the night, his voice grew hoarse. Division artillery rained down destruction on the defenders. A platoon of reinforcement tanks arrived, and the men pressed doggedly on until almost midnight. Progress was slow and demanded a high price in blood, but CCA bashed a path through the first band of defenses.[31]

The 60th Infantry Regiment of Major General Louis Craig's 9th Infantry Division, meanwhile, approached the headwaters of the Roer River near Monschau, which lies in the forest south of Rötgen. The GIs from Lieutenant Colonel Lee Chatfield's 1st Battalion, 60th Infantry, cleared Camp D'Elsenborn, in eastern Belgium, but did not quite reach the Siegfried Line.[32]

STRATEGIC SETTING: DECISIONS OF THE MIGHTY

The troops on September 13 were some 234 days ahead of the schedule foreseen by planners of Operation Overlord, the invasion of France on June 6, 1944.[33] Allied commanders had seized the opportunities offered by the collapse of German defenses following the breakout from Normandy in late July. They had sent their men pelting toward the German border instead of stopping—per the pre-invasion plan—at the Seine River to build up supplies.

Struggle in the Allied Command Tent

As the German collapse unfolded in mid-August, British general Bernard Law (Monty) Montgomery and American lieutenant general Omar Bradley crossed swords over strategy for the campaign east of the Seine River, the first round in a tussle that would continue through spring 1945. Distrust between Monty and the Americans dated back to the Sicilian campaign in 1943, when many American officers concluded that the British general tried to relegate their forces to a sideshow while he grabbed the glory. Montgomery (promoted to field marshal on September 1) was commanding general of the 21st Army Group. Technically, he had remained Bradley's superior officer after the American 12th Army Group became active on August 1, at which time Bradley stepped up from commanding general of First Army. When General Dwight (Ike) David Eisenhower, Supreme Commander of Allied Forces in Europe, took personal command of the ground war at the end of the month, an increasingly de facto practice became formal: Monty and Bradley reported directly to Ike.

The Montgomery-Bradley feud blossomed in the atmosphere of optimism that was building in the Allied camp about an early end to the war. Dreams of leading the Allied charge into Berlin looked very realistic indeed. Ike's G-2, Major General Kenneth Strong, by the second week of August believed that the war would be over within three months. The buzz among journalists was that Monty's chief of staff foresaw victory within three weeks.[34] On August 22, the Chief of Staff, Supreme Headquarters Allied Expeditionary Force (SHAEF),

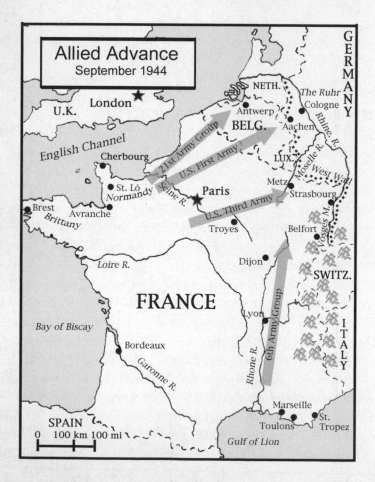

approved a cable to the Combined Chiefs of Staff stating that the headquarters no longer anticipated a single mass surrender of the German army. Instead, SHAEF expected its forces to enter a collapsing country bereft of functioning internal authority and wracked by civil war in some districts. SHAEF informed the British Chiefs of Staff on August 29 that Allied forces would reach the French-Belgian border by September 25 and the Belgian-Dutch border by October 15—goals that would in fact be achieved even sooner than that.[35]

Ike was one of the few not caught up in the wild optimism. In mid-August, he privately told his staff that he expected a German recovery in the West. On August 15, he used a press conference to warn the public that his armies still faced the task of destroying the German armies along the general line of the western border of Germany and the Rhine River.[36]

Before the invasion, Eisenhower had approved the planners' selection of the Ruhr industrial basin as a strategic objective on the road to Berlin.[37] Without the war industries there, Germany could not long support her armed forces. Montgomery now advocated making a single "full-blooded" thrust using the northern route along the coast—where his 21st Army Group was conducting operations—to the Ruhr, on the far side of the Rhine River, and from there on to Berlin. Bradley wanted to drive into Germany through the Saarland with the 12th Army Group's First and Third armies, leaping the Rhine River near Frankfurt; Commonwealth troops would conduct a secondary drive along the coast. Bradley agreed that "our primary terrain objective lay in the Ruhr."[38] SHAEF planners assessed that there were sufficient forces available to do both. The big question was logistic.[39]

Eisenhower met with Bradley and Montgomery on August 23 and explained that he was increasingly worried about logistic constraints as Allied troops drove ever farther from their supply points in Normandy. Monty argued that Eisenhower should freeze Patton's Third Army—then racing eastward just south of Paris—in place and devote all resources freed thereby to his northern drive. Ike replied that the American public would never stand for such a decision and stuck to his plan for a broad-front advance on Germany. Nonetheless, perhaps to encourage Montgomery to devote greater effort to taking the critical port of Antwerp and its approaches from the sea, the Supreme Commander instructed that the main effort would, indeed, take place in the north. He ordered a characteristically disgruntled Bradley to support Montgomery's advance on Antwerp with his entire First Army.[40]

Eisenhower had initially planned to use both the First and Third armies south of the thickly forested Ardennes. Now, he directed First Army northeastward toward the Aachen Gap to protect Montgomery's flank. The strategic objective remained the Ruhr, but American forces had just been handed a whole new set of intermediate objectives.[41] Instead of hitting the area between Aachen and Metz—held at the time by a mere eight German battalions strung out over eighty miles[42]—First Army would attack one of the strongest stretches of the West Wall.

Seemingly more obsessed with his rival Montgomery than sensitive to the huge implications of Ike's decision, Bradley could later only complain, "Monty had won the initial skirmish."[43] Montgomery, however, later snipped, "My arguments were to no avail. . . . And so we all got ready to cross the Seine and go our different ways."[44]

The 21st Army Group had liberated Brussels by September 3, and it took Antwerp the following day (although the Germans would block sea access through the Schelde Estuary for nearly two more months). On September 4, SHAEF alerted army commanders, "Enemy resistance on the entire front shows signs of collapse."[45] Hodges told his staff on September 6 that with ten more days of good weather the war would be over.[46] Dreams of quick triumph remained alive.

HITLER TRIES TO STEM THE FLOOD

In the face of the grim developments in the West, Adolf Hitler on September 4 ordered *Generalleutnant* Kurt Student, chief of the *Fallschirmjäger* (airborne/paratrooper) force, to take charge of filling the hole in German lines between Antwerp and Maastricht. Unless it was closed, British armored spearheads would have an open run to the Rhine River. Luftwaffe chief Hermann Göring that day had revealed, to an astounded army general staff, that he had six *Fallschirmjäger* regiments in training or refitting and could raise two more—plus ten thousand other Luftwaffe personnel—to use as infantry. Student rushed eighteen thousand *Fallschirmjäger* from various points around the Reich to the front and added whatever motley mix of policemen, sailors, convalescents, and sixteen year olds that he could get his hands on. Vastly outnumbered but fighting over advantageous swampy ground cut by many streams, the patchwork "*First Fallschirm (Parachute) Army*" slowed the British advance to a crawl.[47]

Also on September 4, Hitler reinstated the old Prussian warhorse *Generalfeldmarschall* Gerd von Rundstedt as commander in chief (C-in-C) of the western front. Hitler had sacked von Rundstedt on July 1. *Generalfeldmarschall* Wilhelm Keitel, chief of the Wehrmacht Supreme Command (*Oberkommando der Wehrmacht*—OKW), had queried von Rundstedt about options for dealing with the Anglo-American threat in Normandy. "Make peace, you fools," von Rundstedt had replied. "What else can you do?"[48] Hitler, evidently, had not been amused. First Army's interpretation of von Rundstedt's renewed appointment was that "the moment called for a real soldier."[49]

It certainly did. By the beginning of September, German casualties in the West since D-day amounted to more than 450,000 men killed, wounded, or captured. Losses in equipment totaled a staggering 1,300 tanks, 500 assault guns, 20,000 other vehicles, and 1,500 pieces of artillery.[50] Captured records indicate that as of early September, there were no more than a hundred panzers available along the entire western front, as compared with some 2,000 in the Allied spearheads.[51] Bradley's opposite number, *Generalfeldmarschall* Walter Model, commanding *Army Group B* (and who had also been acting as C-in-C West until von Rundstedt's reinstatement), estimated that the entire fighting strength from the North Sea to the Swiss border amounted to the equivalent of only twenty-five divisions.

Still, Model had proved himself on the eastern front to be one of the war's greatest improvisers and defensive strategists. The stocky field marshal was one of Hitler's favorites and was willing to act decisively and worry about the Führer's opinion later.[52] And one ace remained to be played: the West Wall, known to the Allies as the Siegfried Line.

The West Wall, construction of which began in 1936, ran nearly four hundred miles from north of Aachen along the German frontier to the Swiss border. The Germans had neglected the defenses after 1940, so Hitler worked furiously during the collapse in France to put together a scratch force of 135,000 men to partially rebuild and man the line. Berlin planned for a seven-week rehabilitation program; the Allies gave the Germans two weeks. On September 11, command over the West Wall passed from the Replacement Army to von Rundstedt and the Field Army.[53]

The defenses were, on average, three miles deep. The strongest portion faced Patton's Third Army along the Saar River between the Moselle and the Rhine. The second-most formidable section was a double band of defenses protecting the Aachen Gap, with the city of Aachen abutting the western band. Almost immediately behind the West Wall in this sector was the Roer River.[54]

Pillboxes in the West Wall typically had reinforced concrete walls and roofs three to eight feet thick and were generally twenty to thirty feet wide, forty to fifty feet deep, and twenty to twenty-five feet high, with at least half of the structure underground. In some areas, rows of dragon's teeth acted as antitank obstacles. In other areas, the defenses relied on natural features—rivers, lakes, forests, defiles, and so on—to provide passive antitank protection.[55]

And, as First Army had noted, the Germans would now be defending their homeland. This would have a huge impact on their fighting spirit.

FASTEST ROUTES VERSUS A WAR OF ANNIHILATION

Neither Bradley nor Montgomery believed the matter of strategy to be settled, and as the spearheads approached the West Wall the two men continued to badger Eisenhower and seek loopholes in his decision. During a meeting at Monty's headquarters on September 10, the field marshal treated Eisenhower to a tirade of growing fury. Eisenhower listened passively until the first break, when he leaned forward, put a hand on Montgomery's knee, and said quietly but firmly, "Steady, Monty! You can't speak to me like that. I'm your boss."

"I'm sorry, Ike," replied Montgomery. But he continued to plead for a single northern operation instead of a broad-front strategy.[56]

That same day, Bradley defied at least the spirit of Ike's decision when he ordered the First and Third armies to secure bridgeheads across the Rhine from Mannheim, in the south, to Cologne, a front of 150 miles.[57] Bradley's team at the 12th Army Group headquarters spent the first weeks of September cooking up a plan for executing a double envelopment of the Ruhr after closing to the Rhine along much of its length—and all the way to the Swiss border, if possible.[58]

On September 11, patrols from the U.S. Third Army made first contact with those from the U.S. Seventh Army, which only twenty-seven days earlier had landed on the southern coast of France in Operation Dragoon. The two fronts soon became one.

Eisenhower concluded by September 11 that he would have to redirect resources from forward movement to opening enough ports to sustain an invasion of the Reich. "Today our port situation could not stand a stretch of ten days of bad Channel weather," he cabled his chieftains.[59] Ike's desire to provide an adequate security zone east of Antwerp led him to silence objections from Bradley and to support Montgomery's bold plan, Operation Market Garden.[60]

Monty aimed to lay down a carpet of two American divisions and one British airborne division that would capture a chain of bridges over which his armor would run to and across the lower Rhine and thereby outflank the West Wall. Eisenhower committed his strategic reserve, the First Allied Airborne Army, to the project. He also gave Montgomery top logistic priority and increased the delivery of supplies by air to the 21st Army Group through Brussels.

On September 15, Eisenhower wrote to Bradley: "We shall soon, I hope, have achieved the objectives set forth in my last directive and shall then be in possession of the Ruhr, the Saar, and the Frankfurt area. . . . As I see it, the Germans will have stood in defense of the Ruhr and Frankfurt and will have had a sharp defeat inflicted on them. Their dwindling forces, reinforced perhaps by material hastily scratched together or dragged from other theaters, will probably try to check our advance on the remaining important objectives in Germany. By attacking such objectives we shall create opportunities of dealing effectively with the last remnants of the German forces in the West."[61]

Instead, two-thirds of the total Allied casualties on the western front were yet to fall.[62]

Market Garden, which commenced on September 17, fell just short of its goal when the *9th* and *10th SS Panzer divisions*, then undergoing rehabilitation in the area, held the Rhine bridge at Arnhem in the Netherlands against the determined efforts of the British 1st Airborne Division to capture it. The British armor did not arrive in time to turn the tide.

Proponents of the northern-thrust school, per force, assert that Eisenhower did not divert enough transport capacity from Bradley's 12th Army Group to permit Monty to engage more ground troops (there were plenty of supplies back at the Normandy coast; the problem was moving them forward).[63] Others suggest that Montgomery simply overreached. Whatever the cause, Monty's audacious crack at the northern route was over by September 26.

***

Eisenhower's subordinates and legions of historians have argued over whether Montgomery or Bradley was right. Implicit in almost every line of reasoning is the idea that Ike did not get solidly behind the correct general to lead the charge to Berlin. Instead, goes the pitch, he indecisively pursued a broad-front strategy and threw away an opportunity to end the war months earlier with a knockout punch.

Whether or not any of these might-have-beens are correct, they miss the point of Eisenhower's overall strategy: to fight a war of annihilation. Ike, in his memoirs, *Crusade in Europe*, cited the instructions he had received from the Combined Chiefs of Staff: "You will enter the continent of Europe and, in conjunction with the other Allied Nations, undertake operations aimed at the heart of Germany and the destruction of her armed forces." Eisenhower added, "This purpose of destroying enemy forces was always our guiding principle; geographical points were considered only in relation to their importance to the enemy in the conduct of his operations or to us as centers of supply and communications in proceeding to the destruction of enemy armies and air forces." It was in this context that Eisenhower wanted to take the Ruhr and Antwerp.

Eisenhower suggested that his view of war fighting had emerged in North Africa in late 1942 when he had struggled to overcome what he described as the inclination of planners to express their operational concepts solely in terms of geographical points and objectives. The key, he averred, was to gather one's strength to destroy the enemy. In truth, it had been the dire consequences of his own failure to concentrate his strength and cripple the enemy's legions, capped by the Kasserine debacle in February 1943, that had taught him this lesson.

"The problem," he observed regarding autumn 1944, "remained that of destroying the German armed forces in the field. . . ." Eisenhower wanted a sufficiently strong logistic base to provide the fuel, ammunition, and other material he would need to grind the German army to dust. And he wanted to accomplish that *west* of the Rhine River so that little would be left to defend that potentially daunting barrier.[64]

As early as August 8, with the breakout from Normandy just over a week old, Eisenhower's naval aide, Commander Harry Butcher, recorded in his diary: "Ike keeps continually after both Montgomery and Bradley to destroy the enemy now rather than to be content with mere gains of territory."[65] On August 15, Ike wrote in a letter to his wife, "The end of the war only comes with the complete destruction of the Hun forces."[66]

Ike's instructions to subordinates show he was serious on this point. On August 29, for example, Eisenhower issued a letter of instruction to Montgomery, Bradley, and other senior officers in which he stated in a concise, one-sentence paragraph (italics added): "It is my intention to complete the destruction of the enemy forces in the West, *and then*—to strike directly into the heart of the enemy homeland." He ordered his commanders to act swiftly and relentlessly and to accept risks in order to "close with the German wherever met." On September 4, Eisenhower underscored, "My intention continues to be the destruction of enemy forces, and this will be the primary task of all elements of the Allied Expeditionary Force."[67] He reiterated his point in subsequent messages. In keeping with Ike's view of proper command relations, however, he did not specifically tell his subordinates how to accomplish the mission but left implementation up to their ingenuity.[68]

The prima facie evidence that neither Bradley nor Montgomery understood the mind of Eisenhower is that neither framed his arguments to address Ike's overriding goal during the August–September strategy debates, despite his clearly stated views. Instead, they argued over a sequence of geographical points leading deep into Germany. Bradley in his memoirs would recall, "Though we sparred at this time over the pattern of attack west of the Rhine, both of us knew that this present decision would shape the later offensive east of that river."[69] Montgomery viewed a war of attrition as a side effect of the "faulty" broad-front strategy—and felt that the tight British manpower situation could scarcely bear that.[70] As late as December 7—in the midst of the bloody battle west of the Roer River—he recorded the following exchange in his diary:

> [Eisenhower] said that we must not put too much stress on the Ruhr; it was merely a geopolitical objective; our real objective was to kill Germans and it did not matter where we did it.
>
> I disagreed with this and said we would find more Germans to kill if we went for the Ruhr than anywhere else; we should also at the same time be gaining objectives towards the capture or isolation of the Ruhr and towards the attainment of the master plan [to reach Berlin].[71]

Bradley and Monty shared the argument that their strategies for penetrating Germany would eventually affect the destruction of Hitler's war machine.

They had Eisenhower's cart before his horse. Ike wanted to grapple with the German army in the West. His opposite number, von Rundstedt, was happy to oblige.

THE SCORE CARD

The U.S. First Army, advancing on the Aachen Gap, was a battlewise and powerful fighting force. Three of its divisions—the 1st, 4th, and 29th Infantry—had formed the American assault wave on D-day. Indeed, the Big Red One had first tasted action during the Allied landings in North Africa in November 1942. The rest of the divisions had learned hard-won lessons while fighting in the hedgerows of Normandy.

As of early September, First Army fielded 256,351 officers and men. It included three corps—arrayed, north to south, XIX, VII, and V—made up of five infantry divisions, three armored divisions, and three mechanized cavalry groups. The combat divisions were almost at full strength. First Army also controlled nine separate tank battalions (two of which were light); twelve tank destroyer battalions; three antiaircraft battalions (including automatic weapons and gun battalions); three field artillery observation battalions; forty-six separate field artillery battalions; three chemical (mortar) battalions; and a variety of engineer, signal, quartermaster, and other service units.[72]

On average during September, the armored divisions and separate tank battalions together fielded 1,026 medium tanks, somewhat below the authorized strength of 1,184.[73] Despite the fact that the M4 Sherman medium tank was a champion in the durability department, many of them were in bad shape after long runs across France with little maintenance. On September 10, the 749th Tank Battalion, advancing with the 8th Infantry Division, could muster only a composite platoon of five operational Shermans, all others being out of action for maintenance.[74] The 3d Armored Division's G-4 on September 18 estimated that only between 75 and 85 of the outfit's 153 tanks were battleworthy. "Many tanks could not move in high gear, others needed new engines, while still others had minor breakdowns reducing their efficiency."[75]

First Army reacted to the shortage of tanks throughout armored formations by adopting a provisional table of organization and equipment that slightly reduced the size of tank battalions in armored divisions and separate outfits from fifty-four to fifty medium tanks.[76]

***

First Army commanding general, Lieutenant General Courtney Hodges, was the only senior officer in Europe other than one corps commander to have risen from the ranks. Hodges had participated in the expedition against the Mexican bandit Pancho Villa and seen combat in World War I. He had moved up from his deputy commander's slot to replace Bradley as commanding general in First Army when the latter's 12th Army Group had been activated on August 1. Bradley, who commanded Hodges from pre-invasion preparations to war's end, described him as "a spare, soft-spoken Georgian without temper, drama, or visible emotion."[77] The official U.S. Army history pays Hodges the high tribute of calling him a "soldier's soldier." He was solicitous of the welfare of his troops. At the same time, he was a painstaking planner and tactician.[78]

First Army saw its main problem as being logistic, just as Eisenhower had feared. On September 9, First Army—which was guzzling an average of 571,000 gallons of gasoline daily—was living hand to mouth. Despite yeoman efforts using every truck available (including the famous Red Ball Express) and even air delivery in bombers, the army's three corps were 1.3 million gallons short of their basic gasoline load on September 19. The army's quartermaster instituted reconnaissance flights in light planes to spot forward-moving supply trains. Reserves of rations ran out on September 9, and the next day allocation of captured rations began. With German resistance reappearing, supply worries shifted suddenly to ammunition. First Army on September 18 for the first time requested that the Red Ball Express deliver some ammunition in place of fuel.[79]

Hodges' counterpart, *General der Panzertruppen* Erich Brandenberger, commanding general of the German *Seventh Army*, had bigger problems. Most of *Seventh Army* had been lost in the Falaise Pocket in mid-August, and Brandenberger's predecessor had been captured by British armor at his CP in Amiens on August 30.[80] Brandenberger had a huge sector to defend with few resources. As of early September, for example, *I SS Panzer Corps* had one battle-ready tank at its disposal, and *LXXIV Corps* fielded one artillery piece in full fighting order.[81]

Brandenberger had orders to hold the Siegfried Line to the last man. No up-to-date plans for a defense of the line existed, however, so he would have to improvise as he went.[82] Indeed, *Seventh Army* had to instruct its retreating divisions to reconnoiter the German defenses and make contact with whatever units were holding their assigned sector.[83] An assortment of home guard (*Heimatheer*), police, and fortress battalions (static units normally assigned to protect fixed facilities)—perhaps eight thousand troops in the entire *Seventh*

Army sector—manned the border defenses as the remnants of Brandenberger's army arrived at the German frontier. *Seventh Army* commanders grabbed retreating troops as they arrived and shoved them into the line without rest or reorganization.[84]

The fortifications of the line were outmoded and in many cases in bad condition after years of disuse. The firing embrasures were not even capable of fitting the modern MG42 machine gun, having been designed for the older MG34. Troops had to break into some of the bunkers because the keys could not be found. Brandenberger's chief of staff, *Generalmajor* Rudolf *Freiherr* von Gersdorf, went so far as to suggest, "The line actually was a hindrance as it prevented us from choosing where we would fight and tied us down to precarious positions."[85]

Brandenberger was not entirely without good news. Most corps and division staffs (and many regimental and battalion ones, as well) were still intact, and they were assigned sectors and given control over the diverse assortment of units as they became available. The system worked well enough that divisions were quickly brought back up to full strength in manpower, although equipment shortages remained a problem. Incorporation of miscellaneous units into divisions gave them support ranging from artillery forward observers to field kitchens, and they proved much less likely to crack than small outfits thrown into the line on their own.

Moreover, the underground communications system in the Siegfried Line, installed at its construction, could be quickly restored to working order. The Germans also enjoyed excellent intelligence on American movements, because they had many agents behind American lines; forest rangers proved particularly useful.[86]

Generalleutnant Friedrich August Schack was acting commander of *LXXXI Corps*, which defended a zone running from the boundary with the *First Fallschirm Army*, northwest of Aachen, south to Rötgen. Schack had five badly mauled or weak divisions—the *49th*, *275th*, and *353d Infantry* (essentially headquarters staff only in the last case), and the *9th* and *116th Panzer divisions*—with which to stop both XIX and VII corps.[87]

Schack's strength report as of noon on September 16 reveals how dire the circumstances were. The infantry divisions, relatively speaking, were in acceptable shape. The *275th Infantry Division* fielded one exhausted, four average-strength, and two fairly strong infantry battalions; eleven antitank guns; and four light artillery batteries, three of which had been attached from the *176th Ersatz (Replacement) Division* and one nabbed from retreating SS troops. Other than four hundred of *Generalleutnant* Hans Schmidt's own *Landsers* (the German "GIs"), most of the men had been culled from security, local defense, and other miscellaneous units. The *49th Infantry Division* had only five battalions, rated average-to-middle strength , and a mere three towed antitank guns. A single regiment—the *148th Grenadiers*—grouped together the surviving division soldiers; a security regiment lacking heavy weapons and officered mainly by World War I veterans had joined the division along the Meuse (Maas) River. The division had no artillery.

The panzer divisions belied the power suggested by their names. The *116th Panzer Division* reported that it had one weak, three average, and two middle-strength panzergrenadier battalions but only three Mark IVs, one Mark V Panther, one assault gun, and eight self-propelled (SP) antitank guns ready for battle. (American military terminology shortened the lengthy German model designators, hence the *Panzerkampfwagen* IV became the Mark IV; occasionally, the German nickname was used, especially in the case of the Mark VI Tiger. Germans typically referred to American tanks by their Allied nickname, such as the Sherman.) The *9th Panzer Division* had only one weak panzergrenadier battalion, plus seven panzers, five assault guns, and seven SP antitank guns. The rest of the division was still in transit to the front. The panzer divisions were in relatively good shape in terms of artillery.[88]

General der Infanterie Erich Straube's *LXXIV Corps* held the forested area from Rötgen south into the forested Eifel highland. Straube had under his command the *89th* and *347th Infantry divisions*, plus the *526th Sicherungsdivision (Security Division)*, which he broke up to fill out the infantry divisions.[89] A third corps, *I SS Panzer*, confronted Patton's men farther south. The corps consisted of the *2d SS Panzer* and *2d Panzer divisions*. Scattered among these three corps were remnants of other divisions that had been subordinated to the listed divisional staffs. A *Kampfgruppe* (battle group) from the *12th SS Panzer Division*, for example, was attached to the *2d SS Panzer Division*.[90]

PORTRAIT OF A BATTLEFIELD

The American goal was the Rhine River, yet it is the Roer River that runs through the following description of the battlefield—drawn from the official U.S. Army history—like a reappearing figure in a series of bad dreams.

[T]he Aachen Gap is a historic gateway into Germany. . . . At the border of Germany, the XIX Corps would have to cross a minor stream, the Würm River, which German engineers had exploited as an antitank barrier for the West Wall. But once past the Würm, the terrain is open plain studded by mining and farming villages and broken only by the lines of the Roer and Erft Rivers. . . .

South of the XIX Corps, the VII Corps was headed directly for Aachen and for a narrow corridor of rolling hills between Aachen and the northern reaches of the Eifel. For convenience this corridor may be called, after an industrial town within it, the Stolberg Corridor. It leads onto the Roer plain near the town of Düren (population: 45,441), nineteen miles east of Aachen. The fringe of the Eifel is clothed in a dense jungle of pines, a major obstacle that could seriously canalize an advance along this route. Communications through the forest are virtually non-existent. Within the forest a few miles to the south lie two dams of importance in control of the waters of the Roer River, the Schwammenauel and the Urfttalsperre. [There is a third auxiliary dam, the Paulushof.]

Some of the hardest fighting of the Siegfried Line Campaign was to occur in the region toward which the XIX and VII Corps were heading. It is a fan-shaped sector with a radius of twenty-two miles based on the city of Aachen. The span is the contour of the Roer River, winding northeast, north, and northwest from headwaters near Monschau to a confluence with the Würm River near Heinsberg.

The Roer River—or *Rur* to a German—was on average sixty-five to eighty-five feet wide at mean water levels, with average depths of only two to three feet. Winter flows routinely widened the stream to better than two hundred feet on average, and spring floods typically created a morass up to three thousand feet wide. At mean water levels, the river was easily fordable upstream (south) of the town of Linnich. North of Linnich, there were fords available at only a few points, and then only at low water.[91]

The Roer was not much of a river. It was not rich in legend like the Rhine. But it was destined to wash through the lives of hundreds of thousands of young American, British, and German soldiers.

CHAPTER 2

TRAPPED IN THE SIEGFRIED LINE

It was the doughboy, the tanker, and the [tank destroyer] who cracked "The Line" and broke through the vaunted defense system.

HISTORY OF THE 823D TANK DESTROYER BATTALION

The Germans would call this period the First Battle of Aachen. For the Americans, it was the opening round in the Rhineland campaign, which would drag on until March 1945.

At first, it seemed to the Americans that perhaps the Siegfried Line was not going to prove such a big deal after all.

EARLY PROGRESS AT AACHEN

As of September 14, the Big Red One faced east, with Aachen about three miles north and east of its forward positions. The weather was miserable, and the riflemen fighting mainly in thick woods were cold and wet.[1] The division that day penetrated the Siegfried Line and pushed the defenders back into pillboxes southeast of Aachen, despite numerous counterattacks.[2] The 16th Infantry Regiment's GIs pushed into Eilendorf—a substantial town due east of Aachen—by noon the next day. Their arrival was so sudden that the surprised civilians had to quickly improvise white flags with materials ranging from baby diapers to undergarments.[3] The division had accomplished its mission of seizing the high ground south and east of Aachen.[4]

In the face of this thrust, Model's *Army Group B* concluded that the fighting at Aachen was the most critical in its entire sector.[5]

TANKS AND PANZERS

The 3d Armored Division on September 14 advanced against scattered resistance between the two lines of dragon's teeth farther south of Aachen. Combat Command A aimed for the west side of Stolberg; CCB struck toward the east side. The division hoped the two commands could bypass the town and sweep on to Eschweiler.[6]

The next day, the tankers worked their way through the second band of West Wall defenses. Dismounted armored infantry now conducted reconnaissance when needed; the recon platoons had been shot up too badly.[7] Task Force Doan battled its way through a line of obstacles west of Stolberg, and at dusk the infantry took up defensive positions. Task Force Lovelady (Lieutenant Colonel William Lovelady commanding) worked its way past Stolberg to the east, and by September 16 the town was almost surrounded.[8]

What was left of *Generalleutnant* von Schwerin's *116th Panzer Division* had moved into Aachen itself by September 14.[9] A direct corps order to counterattack south of Aachen definitively ended von Schwerin's attempt to surrender the city without a fight. Reluctantly, he instructed his division to prepare for the counterattack and later reported that he had some thirty tanks and assault guns ready for action. This figure exceeds the division's contemporary strength reports but may include the *394th Sturmgeschütz Brigade*. Bolstered that morning by a batch of replacements, von Schwerin's battle-weary panzergrenadier battalions had an average strength of three hundred men. (The German army normally forwarded replacements from dedicated training battalions linked to line divisions in coherent transfer companies of between 100 and 250 men, who therefore knew their comrades and their unit.[10] The American army used an individual replacement system that typically dumped bewildered new soldiers almost straight into combat.)

Von Schwerin also had command over local flak units, which had no experience working with ground forces, as well as a hodgepodge of formations in the fortifications south of the city. He judged several battalions formed from men on furlough to be fairly reliable, but the home guard— whom he described as "old as the hills" and his men called "Santa Clauses with fowling pieces"—looked suspect. Luftwaffe personnel southwest of the city had no ground combat experience, and many men did not know how to handle their weapons.

By the afternoon of September 14, von Schwerin had moved two panzer-grenadier regiments south of Aachen to covering positions just short of the American-occupied part of the pillbox line. Local efforts to retake the bunkers gained no ground, and American pressure forced von Schwerin to concentrate on simply preventing his own line from giving way. The *116th Panzer Division's* operations officer, *Major* Heinz Günther Guderian (son of the famous panzer general), later observed, "The enemy did not break through to the town [only] because he did not continue to attack."[11]

That evening, von Schwerin was ordered to surrender command of his *Windhund Division* to answer charges regarding his effort to surrender Aachen. The *116th Panzer Division* would attack no more for now.[12]

ROOTS OF THE HÜRTGEN FOREST NIGHTMARE

The 9th Infantry Division also might have concluded on September 14 that the West Wall was not all it was cracked up to be. The division pushed through the Siegfried Line with its left wing—Colonel George Smythe's 47th Infantry Regiment—east of Rötgen. The lead GIs advanced cautiously through a drizzle that would soon become a steady downpour, but they encountered no resistance when they breached the line at 0830 hours.[13] The 47th Infantry tied into the 3d Armored Division to the north and would play a role in the central effort toward the Roer for months to come.

The 47th pushed rapidly through the first pillbox line and captured Zweifall. It encountered no more than a few isolated German troops, and by dark it had begun to penetrate the second line of bunkers. Smythe's regiment was farther into Germany than any other unit in the vast Allied armies, but this was the last day that the men had a free pass from the Wehrmacht.

By the next morning, September 15, German troops not only manned the pillboxes but launched counterattacks. One panzer-supported assault group penetrated to the kitchens, where Technician Fourth Class Clarence (Ed) Combs picked up a bazooka and knocked out a German tank. "What a man," sighed his fellows. "If only he could cook." Despite the German pressure, the regiment gained ground toward the northeast and pocketed Vicht, Mausbach, Krewinkel, and Schevenhütte.[14]

Major General Craig's two other widely scattered regiments (the 39th and 60th Infantry) were just starting to sink into the Hürtgen Forest, which, like some evil woods from an old German fairy tale, would claim so many lives.

From the first, Craig's command was unable to fight as a division; deep in the forest, even regiments became almost abstractions as individual battalions undertook largely disconnected operations.

On the 9th Infantry Division's right, Lieutenant Colonel Chatfield received orders on September 14 from the 60th Infantry Regiment for his 1st Battalion to take Monschau, Höfen, and Alzen, the latter two villages located just outside Monschau to the south. The three villages, arrayed in a two-mile-long string, formed part of the Siegfried Line near the source of the Roer River.

Chatfield planned to attack Alzen first, using firebreaks through the forest to approach unobserved. Heavy rain overnight made the ground too soft for armor to use that route, so Chatfield had no choice but to drive straight up the road through Kalterherberg to Alzen.

Company C led the advance. Making their way through sniper fire and past a large crater the Germans had blown in the road, the GIs, supported by four Shermans from the 746th Tank Battalion, advanced toward Kalterherberg. One platoon ranged between one hundred and four hundred yards ahead, and the main body of the company deployed in a column of twos on each side of the road. The Shermans were interspersed among the infantry so the lead tank could immediately support the advance platoon by fire.

Just after crossing the German frontier at 1300 hours, the men ran into small-arms fire south of Kalterherberg. Iron gates blocked the first two routes into the village investigated by Company C, but the tankers eventually found a spot where they could run through the yards of houses to bypass the obstacles. The Shermans blasted the houses while the GIs worked their way through town. Fifty Germans surrendered.

The 1st Battalion now hooked due east toward Alzen, only a mile away. Company C remained in a defensive position, because, as Chatfield later noted, he had "not a thing on the flank except Germany." Five hundred yards from Alzen, Company B encountered machine-gun fire. The company's own machine guns drove back the enemy, and the riflemen pushed through woods to a brow overlooking Alzen.

At 1830 hours, Chatfield sent Companies A and B to probe Alzen. The men had to descend a boggy hillside, cross a creek, and work their way up the slope on the far side of a little valley.

Waiting in hidden pillboxes and firing positions on the far side, *Landsers* from a replacement training regiment watched the olive-clad figures cross the open ground. The regiment (which would soon be designated the *1055th Grenadier Regiment, 89th Infantry Division*) was hardly battle-ready in a conventional sense. Many of the men were rear-echelon types with little or no infantry training. But a fair number of officers, noncommissioned officers (NCOs), and rankers were wounded veterans, and senior officers in many cases had battle-won artificial limbs. The men were well equipped with MG34 and MG42 machine guns, and the regiment even possessed a few light and medium field howitzers. The regiment was, in short, ready for battle in prepared positions such as the ones it held.

As the GIs left the cover of the woods, German officers and NCOs told their men to fire. Machine-gun bullets from pillboxes lashed the American ranks. Chatfield pulled his men back, dismayed that the defenses contained many more strongpoints than Intelligence had marked on his map.

It would take 1st Battalion three more frustrating days to work around the German defenses and enter the village.[15]

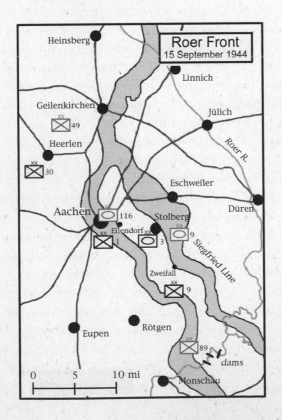

***

The 60th Infantry Regiment's other two battalions encountered vigorous small-arms and mortar fire as they pushed toward Monschau on September 15. The going was slow, but by dark the 2d Battalion occupied the quaint forest town, and the 3d Battalion held high ground south of the headwaters of the Roer River. "That placed part of the regiment over the Roer," noted the division's semiofficial history, "making the 60th the first Allied unit to cross that turbulent stream."[16] Unfortunately, for military purposes, this technicality counted not at all.

As early as September 15, *LXXXI Corps* foresaw the day when its defenses would lie along the Roer River. It thus ordered the headquarters of the *353d Infantry Division*, which only a day earlier had been told to deploy to Schevenhütte, in the Hürtgen Forest, to take charge of constructing an improved defensive line on the east bank of the river. The division was to requisition workers from local Nazi Party officials. Only twenty-four hours later, the division was ordered to turn over that task to the SS and take responsibility for the southern end of the *9th Panzer Division's* sector in the Hürtgen Forest south of Schevenhütte, roughly opposite the 9th Infantry Division's left wing. Shortly after arriving, the division was subordinated to Straube's weak *LXXIV Corps*.[17]

The German defenses in the Hürtgen and Monschau forests took full advantage of terrain obstacles such as the Roer and Laufen rivers. Numerous towns—including Schmidt, Steckenborn, Eicherscheid, Gemünd, Schleiden, Hollerath, and Losheim—were incorporated into the defenses. Defense in depth had been guaranteed by prepared positions stretching between fifteen and twenty kilometers at some points.[18] And the Germans were determined to fight for every inch in order to keep the Americans off the high ground at Hürtgen, Grosshau, Vossenack, Schmidt, and Bergstein.[19]

The *89th Infantry Division* manned the sector roughly opposite the 9th Infantry Division's right wing. The *89th Division* had been reduced almost to nothing during the fighting in Normandy and subsequent retreat across France. In addition to the replacement training regiment that became its *1055th Grenadiers*, the division had scraped together from organic personnel a second regiment—initially only of battalion size—commanded by seasoned officers. Over the coming weeks, the typical patchwork of security, Luftwaffe, and other units would be added to the division's ranks, although it refused to accept provisional units made up of stragglers, because they had proved so unreliable during the retreat.

Other than a few light field pieces, the division had no artillery, and most of its artillerymen had long ago been committed as riflemen. The *Landsers* had to rely almost entirely on bazookas and mines for antitank defenses.

The frontline in this sector remained porous for some time. Shortly after the American occupation of Monschau, a group of German military personnel on leave in the town—including several officers from the eastern front—reported to *89th Infantry Division* headquarters to ask what they should do, because their leave periods were not over. They were told to go back and finish their leave (and spy a bit while doing so); each one reported as scheduled when his leave was over, then returned to his unit. Other men arriving on leave crossed American lines and returned in one piece. The constant flow of people through the forest kept the Germans well informed as to what the *Amis* were up to.[20]

BUNKER BUSTING

An observer described one 9th Infantry Division assault on a bunker constructed of six-foot-thick reinforced concrete covered by five feet of earth: "The attacking company was able to get men on top and around the sides of the pillbox without great trouble. Bazooka shells, pole charges, and use of the flamethrower failed to dislodge the occupants, as did burning gasoline poured under the door. The ventilator was blown off and repeated charges consisting of a total of thirty-six [German] Teller mines and ten 'bee-hive' charges were placed in the hole but only effected a penetration of two-and-a-half feet. Finally, a charge of three hundred pounds of TNT was exploded in the hole, after which the occupants surrendered. The final charge did not penetrate the roof."[21]

Major Thomas Mosely Jr., S-3 (operations officer) with the 39th Infantry Regiment, in the center of the division's dispersed line, explained: "The greatest success in neutralizing pillboxes found was to send tank-infantry teams, closely supported by tank destroyers, forward toward the pillboxes, knocking out first the infantrymen dug in around the [pillboxes]. Tanks would then open up with 75s against apertures of pillboxes, forcing them shut. Flamethrowers were tried, without success. Seventy-fives, 105s, and 155s were ineffective at cracking walls or apertures of pillboxes, but concussion was sufficient usually to drive personnel out of them."[22]

FROM RECONNAISSANCE TO BATTLE

VII Corps commanding general Collins dropped the pretense of conducting a reconnaissance in force into the West Wall on September 16, when he issued clear attack orders to the 1st and 9th Infantry and 3d Armored divisions.[23] His corps held a front roughly twenty miles wide,[24] and the Roer River crossings lay between ten and twenty miles ahead. Collins had high hopes that the successes achieved thus far meant he would soon reach the object of his "reconnaissance" at the Roer.[25]

Throughout the VII Corps zone, demands for artillery support skyrocketed as compared with the pursuit phase. Assaulting troops wanted fire brought on bunkers—including self-propelled 155mm howitzers fired at pillboxes over open sights. A steady increase in German artillery activity required counterbattery fire. And as German counterattacks became more common, massed artillery fire—including corps-wide artillery "serenades"—were needed to break up the assaults. Ammunition shortages were so acute, however, that only the highest-value targets could be hit.[26]

WILD BUFFALOES STOP THE AMERICAN STAMPEDE

Oberst Gerhard Engel's *12th* ("Wild Buffaloes") *Infantry Division* detrained on September 16 in the Düren and Jülich areas along the Roer River with orders to stop any breakthrough of the outer West Wall, an issue that was moot by the time its first troops made contact with the Americans. Nor was there any hope of the division executing its orders when they were changed to holding on to the second line of fortifications.[27] Indeed, the day before, Engel had encountered an air of pessimism regarding his task when he reported to *Seventh Army* headquarters. Nonetheless, Engel had to try.

Engel, born in 1906 in Gubel, was a former adjutant to the Führer himself. He was both brave and arrogant. But this was his first combat command.

The *12th Infantry Division*—all men from Mecklenburg and Vorpommern—had earned its nickname in 1941 when it charged into Russia like a herd of wild buffaloes. The division was largely destroyed on the eastern front in July 1944, but it was reconstituted by August, with initial orders to organize as a "grenadier" division. This conversion was abandoned when an unexpectedly large number of survivors from the old division turned up; in any event, the unit transformed on October 9 into a volksgrenadier division.[28] (This has caused some confusion in any number of histories and even in German military records. Model, in a message sent to von Rundstedt on

September 8, referred to the "*12th Grenadier Division*," and *Army Group B* used that label on and off as late as October 5.[29] *LXXXI Corps* records at times referred to the unit as an infantry division even after the redesignation as a volksgrenadier formation.)

Engel's unit was no ordinary division. The Wild Buffaloes were at full strength—12,800 men, slightly larger than a standard 1944-pattern infantry division. Engel also counted on 2,000 additional men training in three dedicated battalions in the reserve army in *Wehrkreis (Military District) II*—an almost unheard of priority at this stage in the war. The *12th* had a core of seasoned officers and NCOs, but few of the replacements who filled the ranks had combat experience.

The unit had been rebuilding in Prussia when it received orders to move west as fast as possible, destination unknown—but Aachen suspected. The unit's sharp appearance restored hope to civilians as the men clambered off their troop trains, and people cheered. The first troops to arrive—from the *27th Fusilier Regiment*—boarded a convoy of waiting vehicles that included buses, civilian cars, and mail cars.[30] ("Fusilier" was a morale-boosting and unusual honorific for an infantry regiment; most other German infantry regiments had been redesignated "grenadier regiments" in 1942 for the same reason. Almost all such regiments had only two battalions, and the *27th Fusiliers* was a bit odd in that these were numbered the 1st and 3d battalions. Infantry divisions also had a separate fusilier battalion, which was available for reconnaissance or use as a reserve.)

Engel was not cheered by the rapidly deteriorating situation he found at the front. Initially, the plan had been for the *12th Infantry Division* to concentrate around Eschweiler and Würselen before heading southwest in full strength. Now, *LXXXI Corps* instructed him to commit his units as they arrived. Engel had to agree that there was no other option.[31]

If the Americans doubted the continued German will to resist, those doubts evaporated on September 16. The lead elements of two grenadier battalions from the *12th Infantry Division* made sharp contact with the Americans. A platoon of Huebner's 1st Infantry Division that had just reached the outskirts of Verlautenheide—a village outside Aachen at roughly the two o'clock position—reported that Germans were marching toward the town in a column of twos as far as the eye could see. A supporting American tank fired a half-dozen rounds into town and received five or six in return. They landed "awful close," the GIs reported, and the tank pulled back.[32]

The Wild Buffaloes ejected weak advance forces of the Big Red One from Verlautenheide. The 3d Battalion attacked through Atsch and reached the West Wall on both sides of Münsterbusch, which lies on the small Inde River due east of Aachen and halfway between that city and Stolberg. The fusiliers then attacked at Stolberg and made contact with a task force of the *9th Panzer Division*, which was still holding pillboxes there.[33]

On the American side, the 3d Armored Division's Task Force Lovelady advanced east of Stolberg toward the high ground at Weissenberg—and straight into Engel's men. The terrain was crucial for both sides, and the Germans fought back fiercely. Task Force Doan, meanwhile, attacked into such heavy fire that it gained little ground toward its objective of Schneidmühle.[34]

By evening, Engel's *27th Fusilier Regiment* held a compact front, even if organized only in strongpoints. He had made contact with the *116th Panzer Division*, on his right, but his left remained open from Stolberg south to Zweifall. He had taken charge of local elements of the *9th Panzer Division*. (Indeed, Brandenberger that day sacked *9th Panzer Division* commanding general Müller, because he did not appear to know what was happening along his front.) Three battalions of the *12th Division* light artillery, meanwhile, arrived in the Verlautenheide-Stolberg area to buttress the fusiliers. And continued bad weather protected the rest of the *12th Division* from air attack as it arrived at the front. On the downside, the infantry's indispensable friends, the assault guns, had not yet turned up. Model attached the *102d Sturmgeschütz Brigade* to compensate.[35]

COLLIDING BULLS

The Wild Buffaloes charged on September 17. The hurriedly organized counterattack mainly hit the 3d Armored Division, but it lapped over into the fringes of the 1st and 9th Infantry division zones.[36]

Task Force Doan, west of Stolberg, came under fire from Engel's *89th Grenadier Regiment* at about 0515 hours, and Lieutenant Colonel William Orr, commanding officer (CO) of the 1st Battalion, 36th Armored Infantry Regiment, soon realized that a German assault was developing. Orr called down three concentrations of artillery fire on some woods where German troops were gathering; patrols that entered the area later in the day reported heavy casualties. The attackers nevertheless almost succeeded in driving a wedge between Companies B and C and came within fifty yards of the battalion CP before a section of tanks closed the gap. Orr reported, "The enemy in this attack came in close waves, and even the more hardened of [the] machine-gunners became literally sick at the way they had to mow the line of men down." By 0600 hours, the attack was over, but patrols reported large numbers of enemy infantry still arriving.[37]

The 3d Armored Division sought to carry on with its own offensive plans regardless of Engel's counterattack. Combat Command B deployed Task Force Mills (Major Herbert Mills commanding) on Lovelady's left to take the high ground near Duffenter, which immediately dominated Stolberg from the east. Despite bringing down artillery on observed German positions, the armored infantry made little headway. The sudden appearance of a heavy German tank—identified as a Tiger but probably a Mark IV or a Panther—held up the armor. The panzer knocked out a Sherman from the nearby Task Force Lovelady; the tank went up in flames among cries for medics.

Major Mills eased an M10 tank destroyer into position on the edge of some trees to deal with the menace. The crew landed three shots, all of which bounced off the panzer. By then, the panzer's turret had rotated, and the German gunner put two rounds through the frontal armor of the tank destroyer, which killed one crewman and wounded two. The task force was stymied. For the rest of the day, Mills could only call down artillery each time the panzer nosed over the ridge to his front.[38] Task Force Hogan (Lieutenant Colonel Samuel Hogan commanding), meanwhile, was brought forward from division reserve and attacked on Lovelady's right to support the advance on Weissenberg.[39]

Meanwhile, Engel's *48th Grenadier Regiment* attacked Gressenich, in the northern Hürtgen Forest south of Werth, and retook the village. The Germans pushed on to the southwest, and after a short fight captured Krewinkel.

The grenadiers then had the good fortune to run into the flank of the 3d Armored Division attack toward Weissenberg.[40] Two German battalions struck down the road from Krewinkel to Mausbach. The 47th Infantry Regiment, in the neighboring 9th Infantry Division zone, spotted the grenadiers and called down artillery on the infantry, which broke up the assault. But one of the battalions re-formed and, just before noon, advanced east of Weissenberg. Major O. H. Carter watched in horror from the 47th Infantry Regiment's positions as the German advance surprised the men of Company E, 2d Battalion, 36th Armored Infantry Regiment, who were in an open-column formation. The Germans swooped in from both sides and took at least thirty men prisoner.[41] Only four men from Company E returned.

After bitter fighting, the Germans controlled Weissenberg and Werth, east of Stolberg, but had suffered heavy losses. The Germans also secured Mausbach, taking two hundred prisoners. Engel found his operations confounded on several occasions by civilians who had not been properly evacuated and had blundered into both the German and American lines. Commanders on both sides chose to cease firing in such instances, and precious time was lost.[42]

The *48th Grenadier Regiment* had suffered only light losses but was exhausted. Engel realized after reconnaissance that Schevenhütte, at the far left of his solidifying line, was strongly held by the American 47th Infantry Regiment. He ordered his men to dig in and hold where they were.[43]

Combat Command B's Brigadier General Truman Boudinot reported, "Although we are through the line, the resistance we are now meeting from the recently arrived *12th [Infantry] Division* is much greater than any resistance met while advancing through the line."[44]

The *12th Infantry Division* also tangled with the Big Red One west of Stolberg on September 17. Three waves of Germans rolled into the 16th Infantry Regiment during the day—the first bayonet charges the Americans had encountered—and each reached the foxhole line before being driven off by concentrated artillery, tank, and small-arms fire. Where tanks could not be brought into play, the crews from the 745th Tank Battalion dismounted their machine guns and fought beside the hard-pressed doughs, as the tankers referred to the GIs (shorthand for the still-heard term "doughboys" dating to World War I).[45] The 1st Battalion report said of the Germans, "They were well-disciplined troops and kept coming in spite of their losses."[46]

By now, the 1st Infantry Division had gained enough ground that its right flank was nearing Stolberg.[48] Fortunately for the doughboys, the *27th Fusilier Regiment's* orders were limited to improving its main line of resistance (MLR) around Verlautenheide.[49] On the other hand, for the next week the 1st Infantry Division would gain virtually no more ground as the fusiliers did just that.[50]

***

On the evening of September 17, Engel reported to *LXXXI Corps* that because of casualties, particularly in the *89th Grenadier Regiment* (one battalion lost two hundred men in the first two days of fighting), his division could no longer attack as an integrated unit. He insisted on reorganizing and bringing up his heavy weapons before launching any further attacks. On the bright side, he had established tentative contact with the friendly elements on his left, so the perilous state of the front had dramatically improved.[51]

Collins suspended the 3d Armored Division's drive to the Roer on September 18 in light of the appearance of Engel's fresh troops.[52] Nonetheless, scrumming along the division's front during the day resulted in some small gains. Diepenlinchen fell to the Americans, as did German supply dumps near Weissenberg that Engel had wanted to hold.[53]

Hans Martens was a 75mm gun platoon (*Zug*) leader in the field artillery company (*Infanteriegeschütz*, or IG) of the *89th Grenadier Regiment*. The IG company was akin to an American infantry regiment's cannon company, which had six 105mm howitzers, but the German unit had six small and readily portable 75mm guns and two 150mm pieces, all of which could engage in direct and indirect fire.[54] Martens had set up an observation post to provide cover for his regiment's ultimately unsuccessful attack to retake Diepenlinchen. He later recorded: "[T]he *Ami* attempted two counterattacks with tanks and motorized infantry. The tanks came out of the forest to our right and gained the open field. Fortunately, [none of our units was in the way]. It was time for me now to secure the open flank. Fortunately the radio connection worked well. I directed the fire to the tanks so that the infantry had to get off their vehicles. I tried hard to hit the infantry first instead of the tanks but nevertheless we achieved two direct hits on two different Sherman tanks. Both tanks didn't advance any more but served as rear-guard instead. The guns fired salvo after salvo as fast as possible. Everything that could left the barrels! . . ."[55]

General der Infanterie Friedrich Köchling on September 18 arrived at *LXXXI Corps* headquarters from the eastern front to take command from Schack (the handover occurred the next day). One of Köchling's first priorities was to execute orders from Model to extricate the *9th* and *116th Panzer divisions* from the line in order to form a mobile reserve. Indeed, Engel, too, had received an order indicating that relief of the *9th Panzer Division* was part of his mission. Soon, he and his subordinates would also have to worry about a special "Führer order" stating that commanders who lost pillboxes in the West Wall would be held personally responsible.[56]

Stolberg Holds

On September 19, the 3d Armored Division's CCA began a coordinated assault on Münsterbusch, which dominates the terrain west of Stolberg. A mixed German force consisting mainly of home guard elements, supported by guns of the *7th Flak Division* and tanks from the *105th Panzer Brigade* and the *9th Panzer Division*, defended the village. Some of the men from the locally recruited *6th Landesschütz (Local Defense) Regiment* were dressed in their World War I uniforms. (During the next twenty-four hours, Engel's *12th Infantry Division* took control over the units in this sector.)[57] Task Force Doan on the left; Lieutenant Colonel Edmond Driscoll's 1st Battalion, 16th Infantry Regiment (1st Infantry Division), in the center, and Task Force Blanchard on the right attacked up a steep, open slope against cleverly concealed defenses.

Even before the assault got rolling, a German spoiling attack supported by panzers struck Driscoll's positions at 0700 hours. Shermans from the 745th Tank Battalion and CCA helped beat off the Germans and destroyed three Mark IVs.

The Americans moved out at 1430 hours, and the troops worked their way to the western edge of Münsterbusch by dark.[58] The *9th Panzer Division* in its battle report characterized the fighting as particularly severe that day.[59]

On September 20, Lieutenant Elton McDonald, commander of a Sherman platoon from the 32d Armored Regiment—part of Task Force Blanchard—received orders to enter southwestern Münsterbusch and establish a roadblock. Early in the afternoon, the tanks moved out past a cemetery on the hillside and reached the edge of town. Fire from a well-concealed "Tiger" tank (more likely a Panther) streaked by the Shermans, and a German *Landser* with a bazooka knocked out one of the tanks in the confined space among the buildings.

The doughs from Driscoll's battalion, meanwhile, fought from house to house, supported by tank fire. Unable to evict the remaining panzers, the men hunkered down for the night.[60]

The Americans finally cleared the town the next day. All of Lieutenant McDonald's tanks dueled with the panzer for hours, but neither side scored a kill. Finally, at about 1600 hours, a bazooka team worked its way forward to a building overlooking the tank and fired three rockets at the monster. That was enough to convince the panzer commander to withdraw.[61] Nonetheless, CCA had failed to break through west of Stolberg.

Combat Command B took the high ground at Weissenberg on September 20. Task Force Mills, followed by Task Force Lovelady, immediately attempted to take Hill 287 (the Donnerberg, or Thunder Mountain) just east of Stolberg. An artillery preparation softened up Duffenter, on the right, and the objective, while smoke was laid down on the flanks. At 1600 hours, Mills attacked with his fourteen surviving medium tanks (from two companies) and fifteen light tanks—but without the infantry support he had requested. The tanks rolled across the valley in three lines, firing as they went, and reached the top of Hill 287. The smoke had shielded them from direct 88mm fire, which had been a problem all afternoon, while a platoon of supporting M10s from the 703d Tank Destroyer Battalion claimed a Tiger and a Panther knocked out near Hill 287.

The remnants of Task Force Mills could not hold the hill. Fire from the reverse slope quickly disabled seven Shermans. The survivors, who withdrew to establish defensive positions outside Duffenter, were pursued by an intense artillery barrage accurately directed from a large pillbox on the hilltop. The tankers spent the night dismounted to guard their vehicles.[62]

Task Force Hogan pushed into and through the long, narrow town of Stolberg until it reached a main intersection, at which point the German defenses held. The line in town stabilized at this intersection for the next two months.

MUTUAL BURNOUT

Both sides were exhausted. The 3d Armored Division—which eighteen days earlier had been on the banks of the Seine—noted, "Vehicles were demanding maintenance. Men were haggard with fatigue."[63] *Major* Volker, commanding the *105th Panzer Brigade* at Stolberg, reported, "When the enemy fired a smoke preparation before his attack, the men in the first line abandoned their positions and hid in cellars and the woods. Threats to shoot them were met with an indifference that soldiers who had received even a few days of rest would have never shown."[64]

On September 21, Engel concluded that the American offensive had sputtered out and would not resume until his enemies received reinforcements. American attacks were local and limited to company size. The *12th Infantry Division* had closed the hole in German lines, stopped the drive to the Roer River, and kept American artillery far enough away from important war industries in Eschweiler and Weisweiler that they could continue production free from shellfire. With the infantry firmly in place, the Germans could withdraw the remnants of their panzer divisions for refitting.[65]

The Germans had paid heavily to drain the American momentum. The *9th Panzer Division* lost nearly 900 men between September 20 and 22 alone. The *105th Panzer Brigade* had been reduced by nearly two-thirds since entering battle on September 3, and its grenadier battalion had shrunk from almost 750 men to 116.[66]

Model reported to von Rundstedt at this time that all of *Army Group B* had 239 tanks and assault guns against an estimated 2,300 enemy tanks. On the bright side, he noted that the Allies enjoyed an infantry manpower advantage of only a third, and that German morale was rising daily.[67]

Von Rundstedt told Wehrmacht Chief of Staff *generaloberst* Alfred Jodl that the requirement to defend every inch of ground would result in a war of attrition demanding a continuous flow of new units and personnel into the line. He estimated that he needed the equivalent of twelve fresh infantry divisions to hold the West Wall, backed by four proven panzer divisions to seal any breaches. His goal was to hold only long enough to attack and drive back the Allies. Von Rundstedt, as it turned out, was a pessimist.[68] He would stand his ground without the dozen fresh divisions.

On September 25, the 3d Armored Division went over to the defensive. It established a rotation system so that task forces could get some rest and turned over the Münsterbusch area to the 1st Infantry Division.[69]

A SEPARATE LOGIC IN THE HÜRTGEN

In the northern reaches of the Hürtgen Forest, the 9th Infantry Division by September 17 had established a line running from Schevenhütte south to a point east of Lammersdorf, and from there across open ground to Höfen.[70] The 4th Cavalry Group patrolled the Monschau and Buchholz forests between the 9th Infantry Division's right flank and the left wing of V Corps.[71] Straube's *LXXIV Corps* quickly discerned that only scattered armored reconnaissance elements faced the southern end of its sector, and the corps could focus its efforts on fighting in the northern third of its line.[72]

Engel's counterattack included a coup de main on September 18 against the 9th Infantry Division at Schevenhütte (just north of the boundary between *LXXXI and LXXIV corps*). At 0530 hours, the *48th Grenadier Regiment* staged a small-arms attack against part of Major W. W. Tanner's 3d Battalion, 47th Infantry Regiment. A second attack came fifteen minutes later. The attacks were designed to distract the Americans' attention toward the north. At 0600 hours, the heaviest artillery barrage ever to strike Tanner's battalion began to fall. The barrage rolled through Company L's positions toward the battalion CP near Schevenhütte, breaking phone lines and crippling radios.

The concentration stopped after fifteen minutes. Grenadiers charged the American lines from the east. The Wild Buffaloes cut off one rifle platoon and brought the howitzers of Cannon Company under fire, which forced the crews to abandon their guns and fight as infantry.[73]

Ninety men from the 2d Battalion, *48th Grenadier Regiment*, armed with flamethrowers, bazookas, grenades, and machine pistols, attacked down the road from Gressenich. The men managed to enter Schevenhütte after over-running a roadblock manned by a platoon from Lieutenant William McWaters' Company K. The Americans poured machine-gun and rifle fire into the attackers, and hand-to-hand fighting raged among the houses. A Sherman opened up at point-blank range on one group. Two German companies were largely destroyed; McWaters estimated that only fifteen to twenty grenadiers got away, whereas only two Americans were wounded. The attack had been an expensive failure for the Wild Buffaloes.[74]

The official U.S. Army history concludes that over the next two weeks, Hodges and Collins came to view the Hürtgen Forest primarily through the prism of their World War I experience in the Meuse-Argonne campaign. In 1918, a devastating German attack had struck the flank of the American Expeditionary Force from assembly areas hidden in the Argonne Forest. The Hürtgen Forest offered the Germans a similar hiding place. Hodges and Collins decided they had to clear the woods to protect the right flank of VII

Corps.[75] As a consequence, the center of gravity of the 9th Infantry Division's operations in October was at a right angle to the axis of advance toward Düren and the Roer crossings.

The results were reminiscent of the immobile trench warfare of World War I. In Collins' words, "For the remainder of September and most of October, the [9th Infantry] Division doggedly battled the German *353d [Infantry] Division* and part of the *12th [Infantry] Division* in a series of attacks and counterattacks in the thickets and mud of the Hürtgen Forest, made cold and sodden by heavy autumn rains. Neither side could make much headway. . . ."[76]

German *Seventh Army* Chief of Staff *generalmajor* von Gersdorf later remarked, "The fighting in the Hürtgen was as costly to the defending troops as it was to those engaged in the offensive. In addition to the natural difficulties of fighting in a forest, there were the added complications of poor communication, poor observation, danger from flank attacks, etc." On the other hand, the Germans realized that the Americans would not be able to exploit fully their advantages in air support, tanks, and artillery in the dense woods.[77]

The Hürtgen thus became an intermediate objective all its own, only tenuously connected to thinking regarding the Roer River drive, and operations there followed their own perverse logic. This was particularly true once V Corps took charge of the fighting in the forest's heart in late October. Collins in his memoirs states flatly that the Roer dams were not one of his assigned objectives and opines that planners from SHAEF down to his own corps failed to appreciate the significance of those dams for any drive across the Roer River.[78] Much of the vicious battle in the vicinity of the dams therefore drops from this account until the area forcefully reasserted itself in the strategic calculus in December.

XIX CORPS: SONG OF THE MEUSE

The D-day veterans of the 743d Tank Battalion, who were supporting the 30th Infantry Division doughs around them, nosed their Shermans into Maastricht on September 13.[79] Elements of the *275th Infantry Division* and two attached battalions from the *176th Ersatz Division* retreated. The Germans had not a single antitank gun, and the open terrain provided no cover from which to engage the Shermans with panzerfaust bazookas.[80]

Two days later, the 2d Armored Division, having cleared the area north of the Albert Canal, crossed the Meuse (Maas) River north of Meuse (Maas)tricht.[81]

XIX Corps was now pushing toward the major railroad center at Geilenkirchen (about twenty miles north of Aachen) with its left flank wide open. The 2d Armored Division—"Hell on Wheels"—charged forward, two combat commands abreast, each on a seven-mile front. The 99th Infantry Battalion—an unusual separate formation made up of Norwegian Americans recruited for an aborted invasion of Norway and attached to Hell on Wheels on September 16—guarded the division's left rear.

On September 17, the armor captured Sittard from the *176th Ersatz Division*, the southernmost component of *First Fallschirm Army*.[82] Lieutenant Robert E. Lee, of Company D of the 67th Armored Regiment, was helping gather prisoners when he saw a German officer reach for his pistol. Lee grabbed him and slammed him against a wall so hard that he broke the man's neck and back. Nearby, 1st Platoon from the same regiment's Company F took the division's first patch of German soil at Wehr.[83]

The 30th Infantry Division made five thousand yards on September 19 and came abreast of the 2d Armored Division. The corps now threatened Geilenkirchen from the northwest and southwest.

Generalleutnant Wolfgang Lange's fresh *183d Volksgrenadier Division* that same day arrived in Geilenkirchen and took charge of remnants of the *275th Infantry Division* as it retreated into town in some disorder before the overwhelming American surge and tied into the neighboring *49th Infantry Division*. (Following a brief rest, the *275th Infantry Division* was ordered to move to the Schevenhütte area on September 22.)[84]

The Americans could not just walk into Geilenkirchen, which was well protected by West Wall positions now full of rested troops. Instead, Corlett ordered Hell on Wheels to cross the intervening nine miles to the Roer River and establish a bridgehead. The next day, he belayed the order in view of ammunition shortages and the slow progress made by VII Corps, on his right flank. The corps settled down to wait.[85]

On September 22, the 113th Cavalry Group took over portions of the 2d Armored Division's sector, which allowed the division to regroup. Patrols from the 99th Infantry Battalion finally reestablished contact with the British Second Army on September 23, when elements of the Belgian Brigade were encountered in Maeseyck.[86]

XIX Corps had managed to gain, on average, fifteen miles east of the Meuse.[87]

COMMAND PERSPECTIVES

Eisenhower strode into the conference room at his headquarters a short distance from the famous palace at Versailles. The date was September 22, 1944. Ike had recently moved into a small annex behind the Trianon Palace Hotel from his post-invasion quarters in the seaside town of Granville. Granville had been too isolated—at least in Montgomery's opinion—to permit Eisenhower to run the war effectively. The Supreme Commander's new facilities had a bust of Luftwaffe chief Hermann Göring in the foyer, face turned to the wall.[88]

A galaxy of multistarred officers awaited Eisenhower. Present were Ike's deputy, Air Chief marshal Sir Arthur Tedder; his air and naval commanders-in-chief; commander of the American strategic air arm, Lieutenant General Carl Spaatz; senior officers from SHAEF; the two American army group commanders, Omar Bradley and Jacob Devers; and Montgomery's chief of staff, Major General Ferdinand de Guingand. Eisenhower had asked his senior officers to come to the meeting—the most important he had held since the invasion of Normandy— prepared to discuss a strategy for the conquest of the Third Reich itself. The session was the result, in part, of the disagreements between Eisenhower and Monty over the preceding several weeks regarding the best course of action. Montgomery, aware that he rubbed Americans the wrong way, deputized de Guingand to argue his case. Naturally, Monty's decision not to come rubbed Bradley the wrong way.[89]

In reality, some of the most powerful warlords in the Western Alliance could do little but tinker with decisions already set in motion. The guys on the ground were where they were because the die had already been cast.

Following the Allied war council, Bradley on September 23 informed Hodges that he would have to take over part of the 21st Army Group's sector from the British Second Army. Bradley instructed, "The principal mission of the Twelfth Army Group will therefore be to clear the area between its new boundary and the Meuse River, and at the same time push its attack on Cologne."[90] The new interarmy group line ran from Hasselt toward the spot where the Roer River joins the Würm south of Roermond.

***

The German high command had judged that the West Wall would hold if the Americans failed to break through immediately. The generals had anticipated a concentrated American thrust through the line at Aachen in mid-September. By September 25, the high command concluded that the immediate crisis had passed.[91]

During September, the Germans had managed to throw an estimated 230,000 men into the defense of the West Wall. Of these, some 100,000 formed fresh divisions. Another 50,000 came from fortress battalions, which First Army termed the "hidden reserve of the German Army."[92]

On September 25, Hitler ordered von Rundstedt to concentrate on striking back at the British in Holland, where he expected the Allies to shift their main effort for a while. He ordered most of the available panzer units in *Army Group B* to that sector.[93]

On September 27, British Ultra code breakers deciphered a message sent several days earlier directing that all SS formations—beginning with one panzergrenadier and four panzer divisions and three Tiger battalions—be withdrawn for rest and refitting.[94] First Army detected the departure of the *1st, 2d,* and *12th SS Panzer divisions*, and the *9th* and *116th Panzer divisions* from its front. The Americans conceded that "the enemy had been able to stabilize his line."[95] Model had accomplished a "miracle in the West."

CHAPTER 3

AACHEN AND BEYOND

Aachen had little military significance to either the Americans or Germans now that XIX Corps, as well as our VII Corps, could bypass it on the way to the Rhine. . . .

J. LAWTON COLLINS, *LIGHTNING JOE, AN AUTOBIOGRAPHY*

A s First Army commanding general Courtney Hodges contemplated his planned advance to the Rhine, he concluded that he lacked the resources to mount a full-fledged attack eastward and contain the city of Aachen.[1] The German high command shared this assessment, which was one reason it supported the politically motivated order to defend the city to the last man.[2] This notion, as events turned out, was wrong on one crucial count: Hodges lacked the resources to reach the Rhine even with Aachen in his pocket.

The insertion of VIII Corps between VII Corps and V Corps, a step that shortened the VII Corps front as of September 25, did nothing to ease Hodges' perceived dilemma. To take Aachen and renew the drive to the Roer, Hodges had to get XIX Corps through the Siegfried Line to complete the encirclement of the old imperial capital.[3]

On September 29, Hodges issued a letter of instruction that set the course of battle for most of October. First Army would conduct limited operations to protect the flank of the 21st Army Group and attack with its main strength through Düren, on the Roer, to Cologne, on the Rhine. The 7th Armored

Division—which began to arrive on September 26—was attached to XIX Corps along with the Belgian Brigade to assist the British. The rest of XIX Corps (reinforced by Major General Charles Gerhardt's newly available 29th "Blue and Gray" Infantry Division) was to attack on or about October 1 to penetrate the Siegfried Line, link up with VII Corps east of Aachen, and capture Linnich and Jülich, on the Roer River. VII Corps was to clear Aachen after establishing contact with XIX Corps east of the city, then seize Düren through a coordinated attack backed by all available air support. From Düren, the corps was to be ready to advance to the Rhine near Cologne.[4]

In Corlett's XIX Corps zone, the 30th Infantry Division was to break through the Siegfried Line, then hook south to form the northern jaw of a pincer movement around Aachen. Major General Ernest Harmon's 2d Armored Division was to cover its left flank; the division's attack order indicated it was to do so by reaching the Roer River. Harmon had commanded the division through its baptism of fire in North Africa and returned to his old division on September 12 from the States, where he had held orders to take command of a corps. Army Chief of Staff general George Marshall had passed along a request from Ike and Bradley that he take charge, and Harmon had accepted with only the slightest hesitation as he realized that he was sacrificing near certain promotion to lieutenant general. Hell on Wheels was well led and well seasoned.[5]

On October 1, Collins ordered the 1st Infantry Division to seize the high ground northeast of Aachen in the area Ravelsberg-Weiden-Verlautenheide and to capture the city.[6] (On October 4, Collins clarified that the division was to link up with XIX Corps in the vicinity of Würselen and only then storm the city.)[7]

As of October 1, *LXXXI Corps* had under command the *12th, 49th,* and *275th Infantry* and the *183d* and *246th Volksgrenadier divisions. Oberst* Gerhard Engel's *12th Infantry Division* was the best of the lot. Engel had anticipated Collins' order because he knew that the Donnerberg, Verlautenheide, and the Ravelsberg dominated Aachen and served as a necessary pivot point for any encirclement of the city from the south. The question was, could Engel's Wild Buffaloes hold that ground?

Replacements—many of them seasoned NCOs—had brought the division back up to full strength. Morale was high. The division had its full complement of ten assault guns. Engel had received reinforcement in the form of the *19th Flak Brigade*, which was full of fight. It had improvised its own sighting systems to allow its crews to acquire ground targets, and added measurably to the division's firepower. Engel's troops had used the relatively quiet period since about September 22 to heavily mine all logical approaches and to string barbed wire in front of their positions. Engineers had prepared a fallback MLR running between five hundred and a thousand meters to the rear, to which two-thirds of the troops would withdraw to avoid artillery fire if an attack seemed imminent. Engel worried, however, that he lacked good enough intelligence to anticipate an American assault.[8]

This would be the first major action for *Generalleutnant* Wolfgang Lange's *183d Volksgrenadier Division*, which had been activated only in September. Roughly half of the men were Austrian; the others came from various corners of Germany. *LXXXI Corps* commanding general Köchling judged that limited action so far had already demonstrated the negative consequences of the division's shortage of battle-tested officers and NCOs. Morale was good among the younger soldiers, although the veterans showed a lack of enthusiasm. The *183d* had lacked time to train as a unit, but its equipment was generally good. The division was somewhat overstrength, having an extra 643 enlisted men on the rolls.[9]

The fresh *246th Volksgrenadier Division* contained 40 percent former naval personnel and many former Luftwaffe men with only ten days of infantry training. An inspection of the division by a team from the army high command (*Oberkommando des Heeres*, or OKH) on September 20 had concluded that the division was not combat ready because personnel hardly knew one another, junior officers were green, training was inadequate, and some equipment was missing.[10] The division nevertheless had taken over the defense of Verlautenheide from Engel on September 30.[11]

Generalleutnant Siegfried Macholz's *49th Infantry Division* had recovered somewhat from its low point in mid-September. The division fielded two grenadier regiments (the *148th* and *149th*, the latter the redesignated security regiment) with six rifle battalions, three well manned and the rest of average strength. Two machine-gun battalions had arrived and been distributed among frontline units. Macholz also had received one heavy and two light artillery battalions, but he still had but a single antitank gun. Morale had recovered as positional warfare replaced retreat.

The *275th Infantry Division* was out of the line of fire during this stage of the fighting. This was just as well, because the division had been reduced to four rifle battalions, one rated weak; three antitank guns; and a single light artillery battery.[12]

LXXXI Corps by now had named a single commander with the authority to mass the fire of all corps artillery and that of the attached *766th Volksartillerie Corps*. Engel's *12th Infantry Division*, moreover, had implemented lessons learned on the eastern front and established communications links that allowed the divisional artillery commander to mass the fires of all tubes down to large mortars. Engel would credit these artillery arrangements with providing crucial support during the coming battle. (Indeed, XIX Corps medical personnel would later report that 854 of 1,221 American soldiers admitted to the 41st Evacuation Hospital between October 2 and 16 had been wounded by shells.[13])

The corps also had available the *902d Sturmgeschütz Brigade*, with nineteen battle-ready panzers. The unit had mostly veteran crews, but malaria posed a constant problem following service on Sardinia. The battered *341st Heeres Sturmgeschütz Brigade* provided another ten 105mm assault howitzers, and the peculiar *319th Panzer Kompanie (Fkl)* another four assault guns, plus twenty-three radio-controlled armored vehicles for delivering explosive charges. The *217th Sturm-Panzer Abteilung* fielded fourteen 150mm assault howitzers.[14]

The same day that First Army issued its attack instructions, Hitler ordered the transfer of the bulk of the German armor opposite Patton north to the sector opposite Hodges.[15] Hitler had thrown several fresh panzer brigades and a panzer division against Third Army in late September, but the Americans had taken a heavy toll of the attackers, and the would-be counteroffensive had sputtered out.

The Germans called the next few weeks the Second Battle of Aachen.

LEADING WITH THE LEFT

XIX Corps got the nod to kick off the Aachen operation. Even the first step looked daunting.

The Würm River is only thirty feet wide, but its steep banks and the surrounding marshy ground posed a serious antitank barrier. The east bank was generally higher than the west, and German emplacements covered all possible bridging sites by fire.

The Siegfried Line in XIX Corps' sector had been constructed to exploit the natural obstacles formed by the Würm and Roer rivers. The only exception was the stretch north and west of Aachen, where dragon's teeth made up for the absence of a natural antitank barrier. For more than 70 percent of the line's length, the embankment of a railroad running north from Aachen lay behind the Würm River. Numerous cuts and fills allowed the rail bed to run straight beside the meandering waters and also created additional antitank obstacles. Minefields, ditches, and stone walls supplemented the railroad embankment. A pillbox band roughly three thousand yards deep ran behind the rail line. The densest concentration of bunkers was just south of the confluence of the Roer and Würm rivers.[16]

The 30th Infantry Division would initially carry the spear for the corps while the 29th Infantry Division aided the assault with limited-objective attacks. On September 30, the 29th Infantry Division relieved the 2d Armored Division in the woods west of Geilenkirchen. The armor coiled, ready to pass through the 30th Infantry Division once it had established a firm hold east of the Würm River.[17]

THE INFANTRY PRIES OPEN THE DOOR

After days of artillery preparation and a substantial but generally ineffective air strike, the 30th Infantry Division jumped off at 1055 hours on October 2. While ground artillery suppressed German flak batteries, 324 medium bombers and 72 fighter-bombers tried to soften up the defenses. Few bombs fell in the target area, and prisoners who had been asleep in pillboxes at the time later reported they had not been aware that they were being bombed. As it turned out, *LXXXI Corps* had least expected the first blow to fall in this sector; to the Germans, the American center of gravity appeared to be south of Aachen. The attack ripped into the seam between the *183d Volksgrenadier* and *49th Infantry divisions*.[18]

The American infantry and supporting teams had prepared carefully. Intelligence provided excellent assessments of pillboxes and their fields of fire (but little on how many men and how much artillery waited on the far bank). Rehearsals were held using elaborate sand tables depicting the assault zone. The 117th and 119th Infantry regiments, assigned to the initial operation, made certain that everyone knew his role.

Lieutenant Colonel Robert Frankland, commanding 1st Battalion, 117th Infantry Regiment, cross-trained all personnel with tools such as the flamethrower. All of the assault personnel who had trained in England before D-day had been killed since then, and Frankland had learned that his nearest man had to be ready to fill in when a key member of the team went down.[19]

In the 117th Infantry Regiment's zone, two companies—B and C—formed Frankland's first wave, each with two platoons abreast and one in reserve. Company A was held well back; experience had shown that the Germans would paste the area just behind the assault wave with artillery to prevent the advance of reinforcements. Frankland told the assault wave to move fast to get out from under the inevitable artillery curtain.

The *330th Grenadier Regiment, 183d Volksgrenadier Division*, held the far bank. Two batteries from the attached *1183d Sturmgeschütz Brigade* were close to the point of attack, and the third battery was in reserve not far away.

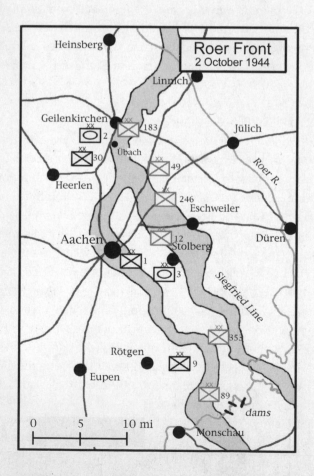

The assault wave encountered intense fire even as it advanced from the low ridge overlooking the Würm to the narrow river. Company C suffered heavy losses before getting across; the 2d Platoon was virtually wiped out by a single concentration of a dozen shells. The towering figure of Lieutenant Don Borton raced across the river and threw down his "duckboard" footbridge, yelling, "There's yer goddamned bridge!" Others followed, and many men simply waded across.[20]

Private First Class Richard Lowe Ballou served in the mortar section of Company B. He recorded the crossing of the Würm in a letter to his folks:

> We leave the town of [Marienberg], following a disappointing air-support attack. As we advanced behind our own shellfire, many thoughts skimmed through my mind. I became aware of an intense love and longing for life. "Will I make it?" pounded in my brain.
>
> We began to cross beet fields and plowed ground. Walking with my load of mortar ammunition is very difficult on this terrain. The shelling from both sides is now greatly intensified. Shells begin to drop around us in great numbers. I hit the ground as a shell lands nearby—smashing my Polaroid glasses with my helmet. I see a man heading for the rear, his hand hit by shrapnel. (He had returned to us from the hospital only two days before.)
>
> Sniper fire becomes intense as we approach some buildings to our left-front. We are sniped at from both flanks. Bullets from the buildings (now left of us). The man in front of me has a hole shot through the stock of his rifle. Bullets kick up the dirt around my feet.
>
> My squad (1st) got by that spot without casualties. Some men were lost in the 2d Squad. All but the squad leader and one man [were hit] from 3d Squad.
>
> We are pinned down by fire from the front. Mortars are set up here for the first time. From here I get a glimpse of the assault squad using flamethrowers and pole charges on the pillboxes.
>
> We gain the edge of the river. The two remaining mortars are set up on this side. Shells and sniper fire from our front make it hot. There is no footbridge at the river as had been planned. One by one,

we drop into the river and wade, waist-deep, to the opposite bank. Most of us soak our cigarettes, etc.

[Uncounted] hours at the river (climax of day's events). Sniper bullets whistle over our heads, frequently hitting the other bank. Those who try to observe over the bank are forced down. Someone up front yells for a medic. Men advancing along the opposite bank are forced into the river to wade along the edge.

Artillery barrages are more frequent. The bank gives protection from snipers—not much from shells. Tanks with bridge-building equipment approach the river from the rear. Many shells land close by. Shrapnel flies in all directions.

I start digging into the bank—many follow suit. We stop every few minutes to hug the bank as artillery lands about us. My shovel lands in the water. Someone in the rear yells for a medic. . . .

Word comes back—we prepare to advance. A shell lands in the river six or eight feet from me. We all hit the ground under the blast. A large hole is blown in the opposite bank. One man is hit a few feet back. I remember saying to myself (without a smile), "I hope that one had my name on it!"

One by one, we take our load and make a break for the railroad across the open field. Sniper fire makes it look like a mile. Forced to hit the ground—dead cow a few feet away. Halfway across, I see four or five wounded men huddled in a hollow. One by one, we make the last dash—at least a hundred yards. I keep running as bullets hit the dirt nearby.

As we reach the railroad bank, exhausted, we look back to see an airburst barrage of terrific intensity over the river.[21]

The 2d Battalion was also across. One of its main tasks was to take a pill-box near Rimburg Castle, a job that fell to Company A. Lieutenant Theodore Foote, operating on the theory that "you can't push a string, you gotta pull it," led his assault squad forward. "No prisoners on this job," he told his team. Foote ordered his BAR man to rattle away at the embrasures while the bazooka and explosives men crept close.

"Put it in low, Gus!" someone yelled to bazooka man Private First Class Pantazapulos. The round tore a three-foot hole around one firing slit. "The shot sure caused a lot of commotion," observed Gus. A pole charge followed, which was enough to finish the job, except for one man who threw out a grenade that lightly wounded Foote. "We shot him pretty quick," the lieutenant reported.[22]

The 119th Infantry Regiment's assault battalion experienced lighter resistance during the river-crossing phase. The GIs from one company quickly cleared out the nearest pillboxes, but the second company gained little ground after being pinned down by artillery fire.

Despite the fact that tanks could not get across the Würm because of soggy ground, by evening the Americans had reached Palenberg and captured nine West Wall bunkers. The Tennessee men in the Old Hickory Division had lived up to their sharpshooter reputation. Aimed fire at pillbox embrasures had claimed a remarkable number of German machine-gunners found with wounds between the eyes.

The *183d Volksgrenadier Division* counterattacked with its only available reserve—the 2d Battalion of the *330th Grenadier Regiment*, supported by a platoon of assault guns—but reported no success. Frankland dismissed the counterattack as being "of little consequence."[23]

Generalleutnant Wolfgang Lange was ordered the night of October 2 to reestablish the MLR at the Würm River. Lange was assigned three infantry battalions for the job; all were unfamiliar to him. Two came from Macholz's *49th Infantry Division* and one from *Oberst* Gerhard Wilck's *246th Volksgrenadier Division*. Lange shifted his CP to the southern (*49th*) sector, where he also committed his assault gun company. He ordered his engineer battalion—the only available reserve—to attack simultaneously from the north. Launched before dawn, the counterstroke gave the Americans a "stiff fight," but artillery stopped the German advance. Lange's engineer battalion suffered heavy losses, from which it never recovered, and casualties were high among Macholz's battalions.[24]

By nightfall on October 3, the 30th Infantry Division held a northwest-southeast line anchored at Übach, which was just north of the division boundary between the *183d Volksgrenadier* and *49th Infantry divisions*. That night inside Übach, the "lines" were only some fifty yards apart and so confused that Americans and Germans found themselves holding alternating houses along one street. The tanks of the 2d Armored Division had closed up and were waiting to go just outside of town. But Major General Leland Hobbs told Corlett thought that what they really needed was another infantry division to guarantee a breakthrough; his and Huebner's divisions were spread too thinly.[25]

ARMOR EXPLOITS THE OPENING

The 30th Infantry Division attacked at 0700 hours the next morning but made little headway. The *183d Volksgrenadier Division* counterattacked three times at Übach supported by assault guns, but it was repulsed with the help of 2d Armored Division forward elements from CCB. The combat command's deployment was slowed when German artillery fire—the guns protected from American spotter aircraft by bad weather—knocked out several vehicles on the newly built bridge assigned to the outfit.

Near Palenberg, Technical Sergeant Fred Leno, who had taken command of a 117th Infantry Regiment company after all his officers had been killed or wounded, drove off a German attack only after calling down artillery fire on his own position. One round struck Leno's observation post (OP).[26]

Brigadier General Isaac White's CCB, 2d Armored Division, began to pass through the 30th Infantry Division shortly after daybreak on October 4. Task Force 2 (1st Battalion, 41st Armored Infantry Regiment, and 2d Battalion, 67th Armored Regiment) operated on the left with orders to clear West Wall fortifications, and it divided into two columns for its attack toward the northeast. The troops had crossed the Würm the day before under fire; the Germans still held pillboxes as close as several hundred yards from the bridge thrown by engineers. Because the 117th Infantry Regiment was stalled and had not cleared Übach, the task force had to fight for its route of advance and had reached only the center of town when darkness stopped the fighting. The armored spearhead therefore was already deeply engaged before it officially attacked on October 4.

Surprisingly, German troops had evacuated Übach when the task force struck in earnest about noon. In place of volksgrenadiers, the armored doughs ran into the heaviest artillery barrage they had ever experienced. The infantry had to dash for cover in buildings and thereafter advanced with great caution.

As the day progressed, 1st (Armored Infantry) Battalion CO major E. F. Jenista fell wounded, as did his executive officer and two of his company commanders. The battalion surgeon, though wounded himself, gave aid and supervised evacuations. Surviving company-level officers scrambled to get a fix on the assault teams and reestablish command over the battalion. But they need not have worried. The assault teams were doing their jobs against the pillboxes, per orders. Indeed, one team had captured thirteen bunkers without losing a single man.[27]

The assault followed these lines: The Shermans ground forward about a hundred yards behind a creeping artillery barrage. The infantry followed another one hundred to two hundred yards behind and covered the flanks. M10s from the 702d Tank Destroyer Battalion provided over-watch while the Shermans pounded pillboxes from close range in support of the advancing riflemen, who swooped in once a bunker had been badly battered. One pillbox crew gave up after Sergeant Ezra Cook called them over the landline from a captured pillbox and told them, "We have just taken your comrades, and now we're coming after you!"

Task Force 1, also consisting of a battalion each of armored infantry and tanks, crossed the Würm and pushed out at 0800 hours. Early in the day, the task force encountered seven assault guns and knocked out three in exchange for two tanks. A German counterattack did not coalesce until about 2000 hours, by which time the Americans were within six hundred yards of Beggendorf, which lies due east of Übach. The Americans had captured a copy of the attack order and were waiting. The entire German force—some 240 men—was either killed or captured.

Task Force 2 gained fourteen hundred yards that day; Task Force 1 carved out eighteen hundred yards. The fighting cost CCB eleven tanks and a tank destroyer.[28]

The commitment of the 2d Armored Division convinced *LXXXI Corps* staff that its assessment of the American main axis of attack had been faulty. The Germans were uncertain, however, whether the Americans intended to pursue their drive eastward toward the Rhine or southward to encircle Aachen. *LXXXI Corps* concluded it would have to devote its main efforts to preventing the first scenario. Köchling ordered one light and two heavy artillery battalions to move north from behind the *12th Infantry Division* to the area opposite XIX Corps. He also instructed a Tiger battalion (the *506th Schwere Panzer Abteilung*, which had only four combat-ready tanks and had just arrived from the *First Fallschirm Army* zone), an assault gun brigade, and *Schnelles (Mobile) Regiment von Fritschen* (some fifteen hundred officers and men) to reinforce the sector.[29]

Köchling also subordinated the *246th Volksgrenadier Division's 404th Grenadier Regiment* to Lange's *183d Volksgrenadier Division*. The regiment had orders to establish a line west of Beggendorf to prevent a breakthrough by the 2d Armored Division. Lange's *343d Grenadier Regiment* was ordered south from Geilenkirchen to tie into the *404th's* left, and students from the Jülich and Düren NCO schools moved into the positions at Geilenkirchen.[30]

FALSE DAWN

The 2d Armored Division finally began to make noticeable progress on October 5 against bitter resistance. Combat Command B pushed into Beggendorf by 1630 hours, despite the *404th Grenadier Regiment's* vigorous efforts to hold the town. Brigadier General White's Task Force 1 lost eighteen medium tanks, one light tank, and three tank destroyers to intense German antitank fire. Task Force 2, still engaged in clearing pillboxes along the Würm, lost only two medium tanks. Colonel John Collier's CCA joined the fray near Beggendorf at about 1600 hours.[31]

The 30th Infantry Division, meanwhile, hooked south toward a junction with the Big Red One. A battalion each from the 117th and 119th Infantry regiments attacked out of the rubble of Übach. Changes in orders, mixing with elements of the 2d Armored Division, and heavy German shelling prevented much progress by the 117th. Moreover, fighting still flared around Übach, where the 743d Tank Battalion lost five tanks that day to direct fire from some stubbornly held barracks. At least one 702d Tank Destroyer Battalion M10 was also knocked out. With tank battles raging north of town, 2d Armored Division columns clogged the streets waiting for a clear route out.

The 119th, however, rolled two thousand yards almost due south to Merkstein-Herbach. The regiment was a third of the distance to its objective in Würselen and working straight down the rear of the Siegfried Line defenses. The next town south of Würselen was Verlautenheide, where the Big Red One waited.

The 3d Battalion, 120th Infantry—which had conducted a feint attack with two battalions on October 2 and was still on the far side of the West Wall to the southwest—now moved into the line between the 30th Division's other two regiments.[32]

Waurichen: Charge of the Light Company

On October 6, the 2d Armored Division captured Waurichen, which lies on the main Geilenkirchen-Düren road, from the *183d Volksgrenadier Division* in a most unusual manner. Combat Command B's Task Force 1 confronted a long, open stretch of ground before the objective. With Shermans leading, the Americans moved out slowly through deep mud behind a rolling artillery barrage. Artillery, mortar, and machine-gun fire pinned down the armored doughs, while antitank fire claimed twenty-one of the thirty-four tanks. The attack appeared destined to failure.

Out of conventional ideas, CCB decided to send the light tanks from Company C, 67th Armored Regiment, forward in a cavalry-style charge, hoping that their greater speed would protect them. With throttles wide open, the M5 Stuarts made an extraordinary dash to the German lines, where they overran infantry fighting positions, antitank guns, and artillery pieces. Machine guns chattered and mowed down the German soldiers who broke and ran for cover. The medium tanks and armored infantry moved up behind them.

The light tanks encountered a platoon of German assault guns. Their puny 37mm guns had little hope of even damaging the panzers, so the crews raced around the heavier foes—which had to aim by turning the vehicle—until the Germans decided to pull back. The entire venture cost only three Stuarts. Combat Command B held Waurichen against a determined counterattack preceded by a stunning artillery barrage.[33]

Combat Command A, on the division right, had in the meantime taken Baesweiler. One company of 2d Armored Division tanks and two platoons of armored infantry from CCA, meanwhile, worked with the 743d Tank Battalion and the 117th Infantry Regiment to clear troublesome defenders from the barracks near Übach.

About noon, Corlett visited Major General Harmon at the 2d Armored Division CP. The corps commander said he wanted Harmon to hold up until the circle closed around Aachen. Rather than reaching the Roer, Hell on Wheels was to dig in to hold its ground.[34]

German Fabric Begins to Tear

Köchling launched his final attempt to reestablish his line south of Übach on October 6. At 0710 hours, two battalions from the *49th Infantry Division's 148th Grenadier Regiment* struck northward and hit the 2d Battalion, 119th Infantry Regiment. The Germans gained eight hundred yards in forty-five minutes. The Americans fired until their weapons were too hot to handle, then turned to captured German weapons. "We thought we were goners," commented one sergeant, who expended twenty-two BAR clips. Men threw away souvenir German knives and pistols—which could lead to summary execution—because capture seemed imminent.

Tanks, air, and artillery saved the day. Lieutenant Walter Macht and his Sherman crew from Company C, 743d Tank Battalion, helped stem the tide by knocking out three panzers. The 1st Battalion, 117th Infantry, swung right to help out, too. After eight hours of hard fighting, the direction of movement was southward once again.

The *49th Infantry Division* had shot its bolt. Köchling was so concerned about the sector that he reinforced Macholz with an infantry battalion and some assault guns from the *12th Infantry Division* as well as an infantry battalion, a machine-gun battalion, and some antitank guns from the *246th Volksgrenadier Division*. The 30th Infantry Division was close enough to the 1st Infantry Division by now that the latter's artillery fired supporting missions for the former on October 6.[35]

October 7, observed Old Hickory's history, was a day of exploitation against a beaten and disorganized enemy. The 30th Division took more than 850 prisoners.

The key advance was that of the 117th Infantry Regiment, which cruised two miles to the outskirts of Alsdorf against light resistance from the *49th Infantry Division*. The 1st Battalion CO, Lieutenant Colonel Frankland, reported, "The troops defending Alsdorf had moved out toward us. We encountered them in wide-open terrain where our tanks could operate most effectively. Had they chosen to defend Alsdorf—a town that is difficult and complicated in its road net even when you occupy it—there could have been a helluva fight to clean them out house by house. But when we came in, it was so quiet it was scary."

Lieutenant Dewey Sandall, a rifle platoon leader, described the tank-infantry cooperation this way: "The tanks just machine-gunned the [German] boys in their holes, and when the doughs came up, it was mass surrender." Fifteen P-47s appeared and helped out by bombing and strafing a retreating German column.

Hobbs told Corlett, "We have a hole in this thing big enough to drive two divisions through. I entertain no doubts that this line is cracked wide open."[36]

Indeed, Köchling realized that there was now a two-kilometer-wide hole in his line at Alsdorf. The first four Royal Tigers from the *506th Schwere Panzer Abteilung* reached the front at Alsdorf and joined the *108th Panzer Brigade*, but three of the gigantic panzers had already fallen victim to American tank destroyers. The menace to the *246th Volksgrenadier Division's* right was so stark that Köchling—having only a day earlier weakened the *246th* to buttress the *49th Infantry Division*—subordinated the latter's *149th Grenadier Regiment* and division artillery to the former.

There was some good news—the *183d Volksgrenadier Division* reported that 2d Armored Division pressure along its front had disappeared. Now Köchling knew that the *Amis* planned to encircle Aachen. He could focus his energies on that threat.[37]

Opposite the 1st Infantry Division on the far side of the city, *Oberst* Engel need not have worried that he would not know when the attack was coming in his sector. There were so many indications that he reported to *LXXXI Corps* that evening that an American assault was imminent.[38]

Dragons in Alsdorf

On October 8, the Germans made a fierce effort to retake Alsdorf and seal the hole in their line. Köchling assembled his reserves—the *Schnelles Regiment von Fritschen*; 2d Battalion, *689th Grenadier Regiment*; a pioneer battalion equipped with flamethrowers; the *108th Panzer Brigade*; and the *506th Schwere Panzer Abteilung*—to execute the attack. *Oberst* Engel, who expected an imminent attack, was alarmed when his division's ten-vehicle StuG IV company was taken away to support the operation, as well.

The German right wing, an hour behind schedule, rolled out of Schaufenberg to Bettendorf through a morning mist, then drove on to Oidtweiler, where the troops ran into a limited-objective attack by Harmon's CCA. Murderous American artillery fire slowed the advance. Nevertheless, the German assault guns and infantry reached the road north of Alsdorf, and some wheeled toward the town. The left wing, meanwhile, maneuvered across the open ground between Alsdorf and Mariadorf. An entire platoon from Company B, 1st Battalion, 117th Infantry Regiment, was cut off and either killed or captured.

At about this time, a platoon of Shermans from the 743d Tank Battalion was supporting an unsuccessful attack on Mariadorf by Lieutenant Colonel S. T. McDowell's 3d Battalion, 117th Infantry. Bereft of infantry support at one point and unable to induce the Germans to surrender, crewmen climbed out to toss grenades into the enemy's foxholes. After the crewmen mounted up again and pulled out, direct fire knocked out three of the vehicles, leaving only tank A-16 in operation. As the unwounded crewman from the other tanks formed up to protect A-16 by fighting as infantry, tank commander Sergeant Donald Mason spotted the German counterattack rolling toward Alsdorf. He radioed his battalion CO, Lieutenant Colonel William Duncan, in his command tank in town.

Shermans from two of Duncan's platoons took the attackers under fire and knocked out three of the German assault guns, and a fourth assault gun broke down. Sergeant Mason also directed artillery fire against the Germans from tank A-16.

McDowell's battalion, which was pushing away from Alsdorf toward Mariadorf, was hit from the rear and found itself in danger of being cut off. The fighting was "at close grips and at bayonet point," reported McDowell, whose OP in a schoolhouse on the southeast edge of Alsdorf was hit from two sides by infantry riding assault guns. It was, he added, "the toughest proposition this battalion has encountered since the beaches." McDowell, liaison officers, engineers, and a wire crew fired from the windows and beat off the Germans. (When asked by one of his company commanders whether the battalion's attack should be halted and the men pulled back, McDowell replied, "Hell, no. You go ahead and secure Mariadorf. I can take care of this situation here." Instead of taking the town, the company lost all but six men in one platoon to a German machine-gun ambush and subsequent counterattack.)

In fact, the German AAR indicates that only two StuG IV assault guns (American reports consistently referred to Mark IV tanks) under the command of *Feldwebel* Klimas and *Oberstleutnant* von Bitter entered Alsdorf, along with a squadron of infantry from *Schnelles Regiment von Fritschen.*

(Klimas was almost a tank ace; the day before, he had destroyed two American tanks and damaged another pair.) The infantry had suffered many casualties from artillery fire on the way in. They nevertheless fought their way to within a hundred yards of the American regimental command group.

Combat in a *Sturmgeschütz* was a grueling experience for the four-man crew. Except in panzer divisions, the crewmen were drawn from the artillery arm. They worked sandwiched into a small fighting compartment that had no system to vent gas from the main gun. The men lacked tanker helmets with earphones, common in other armies, that would have somewhat reduced the noise. In addition to the sound of the cannon, the vehicle had a weak drive train, which forced the driver to run the engine at screechingly high rpms whenever the panzer maneuvered. Instead of an intercom system, the crew used an internal loudspeaker set louder than the sound of battle.

M10 tank destroyers tried to engage the panzers, but by the time they responded to each report on their location, the Germans were gone. Lieutenant Colonel Duncan and Captain Robert Sinclair, a company commander from the 803d Tank Destroyer Battalion, personally set out to find the assault guns but never succeeded in the maze of streets. The Americans began to call Klimas and von Bitter the "Reluctant Dragons."

GIs armed with bazookas came after the assault guns. Klimas spotted one bazooka team just before the Americans could fire and took it out with the machine gun on top of his vehicle. A short while later, however, a bazooka round hit the superstructure, but it did not disable the panzer.

Von Bitter, meanwhile, had been wounded in the leg while outside his assault gun. This may have been courtesy of Lieutenant C. M. Spilman, who claimed that he had shot two panzer crewmen before a round from the main gun blew him down two flights of stairs.

The Germans were down to fifteen *Landsers*.

Shortly after 1600 hours, the German survivors pulled out of Alsdorf and made their way back to friendly lines. Klimas had been wounded three times during the action.[39]

FOLLOWING WITH THE RIGHT

The Old Hickory Division's capture of Alsdorf was the signal for VII Corps to attack.[40] For the next three days, the two arms of the American operation would close, muscles straining, to encircle Aachen.

Huebner had begun maneuvering his troops into position on October 2. The 18th Infantry Regiment slipped out of the line, and the 1106th Engineer Combat Group quietly filled its foxholes.[41] Fortunately, the Germans either did not detect or did not react to the soft spot in Huebner's defenses.

The Big Red One ripped into the Germans in the predawn darkness on October 8. VII Corps' main effort did not, however, hit the *12th Infantry Division*, as Engel had anticipated. The Wild Buffaloes easily fended off what appeared to be mere diversionary attacks at the Donnerberg and Stolberg.[42]

Instead, the 1st Infantry Division struck north through Verlautenheide. The 18th Infantry Regiment had the job of linking up with the 30th Infantry Division to complete the encirclement of Aachen. Its 2d Battalion led off after an hour-long artillery preparation and advanced through the dark between 0400 and 0620 hours to take the fortified village of Verlautenheide. The battalion line served as the line of departure for the 1st Battalion, which had orders to seize the next prominence, Crucifix Hill, supported by the 3d Battalion.

The GIs easily fended off scattered German counterattacks, but thunderous artillery concentrations forced the 1st Battalion to infiltrate through town by squads and delayed its attack until 1500 hours. Many of the men who carried pole or satchel charges, flamethrowers, and bangalore torpedoes toward the pillboxes above them were replacements who had been in the line for only a week or so. Nevertheless, Captain Bobbie Brown, who was wounded three times during the action, led the men of Company C to the crest of the hill, destroying bunkers as they went. The 3d Battalion, meanwhile, quickly captured Hill 192, which lay between Aachen and Crucifix Hill.[43]

The 18th Infantry Regiment was only a mile from the main Aachen-Cologne road. Huebner ordered the regiment to take Hill 231—the Ravelsberg—north of Haaren. The 26th Infantry Regiment would protect the left flank, and the 16th Infantry the right. Huebner told the former—which faced Aachen—to be on its toes, because he was concerned about how the Germans would react the next day.[44]

The *246th Volksgrenadier Division* was now beset by the 30th Infantry Division's attack at the north end of its line and by the Big Red One at the south end. In an effort to ease the burden, Köchling gave Engel responsibility for part of the sector and subordinated the *246th's* two southernmost battalions to the Wild Buffaloes.[45]

As these events were unfolding, Bradley instructed Hodges on October 8, "You should continue your present attack to secure the ground west of Düren, and if the going is easy, you should continue this on toward the Rhine. If the going gets so difficult that you think you have attracted too much in front of you and that you should wait until the British jump off [to clear the west bank of the Meuse] so as to divide the hostile effort, or if you deem it necessary to wait until you can build up more ammunition, we may have to wait. . . . For the time being, the only decision necessary is that you continue your attack to the stream running through Düren."[46]

Bradley had underscored the Roer River as Hodges' objective, even if he could not quite recall the name.

THE GAP NARROWS

Pressure from both jaws on the sole remaining exit route from Aachen built on October 9. In the XIX Corps zone, the 30th Infantry Division came within sight of its boundary with the Big Red One, and plans were readied to mount patrols to establish contact. The 119th Infantry Regiment took Bardenberg from the *49th Infantry Division's 149th Grenadier Regiment*, and one battalion reached the high ground overlooking North Würselen. The 117th Infantry Regiment—working in tandem with the 2d Armored Division—pushed two thousand yards south of Schaufenberg. The 120th Infantry Regiment now had its 1st and 2d battalions in the center of the division line, where they spent much of the day fending off a counterattack mounted out of Euchen.[47]

Counterstroke at Bardenberg . . .

Köchling viewed the loss of Bardenberg with alarm as the hole in his front widened. The tiny corps reserve, consisting of the *108th Panzer Brigade*; a battalion each of panzergrenadiers, infantry, and engineers; and the few running Royal Tigers of the *506th Schwere Panzer Abteilung*, were ordered to retake the town. The *Kampfgruppe* managed to reach the objective during the evening.

Preceded by 20mm gunfire from the *108th Panzer Brigade's* antiaircraft half-tracks, five panzers and three hundred panzergrenadiers rolled out of the twilight and over a roadblock established outside Bardenberg by Company A, 119th Infantry Regiment. Captain Ross Simmons had merged two of his understrength platoons into one to man the position, with his weapons platoon in support. Two companies from the 120th Infantry Regiment were nearby, and he felt "pretty safe."

Simmons did not feel that way long. The panzers drove all three American companies back in disarray. Only nine men from the composite platoon made it back to Simmons' CP in Bardenberg, where the captain established a line using headquarters personnel armed mainly with carbines and pistols. The Germans pressed on, and at 2037 hours Simmons reported that his situation was critical. "We could not hold the position and were forced back to the church on the northwest side of town," Simmons reported. "We built up all around but were forced back in the town about a block."

To escape being surrounded, Simmons led his men out a window. Several men disappeared into the dark, and the captain and five others holed up in a house near the center of town. Expecting capture the next morning, they found instead that Company I had come to the rescue.

The 120th Infantry Regiment also lashed back in support and took Birk, which cut off the German spearhead from supply. In Bardenberg, the 2d Battalion, 119th Infantry, fought to resecure the town. The Germans effectively deployed between ten and twenty half-tracks, some with 20mm guns, and five panzers to support their infantry, which resisted from house to house. During the fighting, Sergeant Neal Bartelsen found himself cut off in a basement from where he could watch the German infantry and tanks. Whispering into his radio, he operated as a forward OP. By nightfall, confronted by unyielding resistance, the 119th Infantry Regiment reluctantly withdrew to the north part of town and pulverized the German-held south with artillery. The men in *2108th Panzergrenadier Battalion* would hold out for two more days.[48]

. . . And Against the Big Red One

Engel, meanwhile, also had orders to counterattack the 1st Infantry Division. Early on October 9 (the day Engel's division was formally converted to a volksgrenadier formation), the Germans saturated Crucifix Hill with artillery and mortar fire. Shortly after dawn, the men of Company C saw three waves of German infantry and combat engineers charging up the hill. The GIs held their fire until the attackers were almost upon them, then unleashed what the 1st Battalion's journal described as a "murderous grazing fire that piled the onrushing Germans in front of their very foxholes." The Germans withdrew, leaving behind more than forty dead and thirty-five prisoners.

Other elements of the 18th Infantry Regiment fought to clear pillboxes that in some cases proved impervious to direct fire from 155mm SP guns. The Germans staged local attacks in up to battalion strength to drive back the GIs, which proved sufficient to bog down the American advance. The regiment reported to division that artillery had stopped the Germans but the fighting near Verlautenheide was so intense that the men had burned out several .50-caliber machine guns. By 1800 hours, the 3d Battalion had cleared Rothe Erde, on the regiment's left, and held high ground offering a clear view of the center of Aachen.[49]

The creative minds in the 1106th Engineer Combat Group, back in the 18th Infantry Regiment's old positions, had also been busy that day. Noting a straight two-mile-long stretch of railroad running directly into Aachen down a grade of 4 percent, the engineers procured an old trolley from Route 13 and loaded it with captured shells and rockets and one case of dynamite. At 1830 hours, they pushed their "V-13," with a six-minute fuse attached, careening toward the city. The vehicle entered German lines and was peppered with small-arms fire until it exploded in a most gratifying fashion.[50]

DESPERATE STRUGGLE FOR THE GAP

The 30th Infantry Division consolidated and mopped up on October 10. Division commanding general Hobbs that day lamented that insufficient forces had been committed to exploit the initial breakthrough of the Siegfried Line achieved by his troops. His men had been in battle for 120 days with no break. He added, "You should not have to drive men as they are being driven now; men should be led, not driven. Such cannot be the case when they are on the go during the day and have to be prepared to fight off the enemy at night." Hobbs' assistant commander, Brigadier General W. H. Harrison, added that the outfit was spread out so thinly that any German counterattack would strike not the 30th Infantry Division but a battalion thereof.[51]

PLANS TO SEIZE THE INITIATIVE

The Germans, meanwhile, had been gathering reserves: the *I SS Panzer Corps*. The corps headquarters had taken charge of the volksgrenadier divisions in line in the Geilenkirchen sector on October 6; only five days later, *XII SS Corps* took command of that area, and *I SS Panzer Corps* was assigned the task of holding open the narrowing corridor to Aachen. It brought some reinforcements to the task, including the *116th Panzer Division* (initially the *60th*

Panzergrenadier Regiment), the *1st SS Panzer Division's 1st SS Battalion*, and two assault gun brigades. As had been so often the case, however, the potentially strong corps was committed piecemeal to the attack.[52]

While *I SS Panzer Corps* gathered, Köchling on October 10 tried again to reach Bardenberg using the *404th Grenadier Regiment* supported by the *108th Panzer Brigade* and the *506th Schwere Panzer Abteilung*. Both armored units had only platoon-size elements available. The Germans attacked in two columns.

The tank-infantry force hit the lines of the 120th Infantry Regiment at 1300 hours. As Lieutenant Leon Neel directed the action under heavy German fire, a single towed 3-inch gun from his 1st Platoon, Company B of the 823d Tank Destroyer Battalion, destroyed three Mark IV tanks and two Panthers over six hours; a second gun knocked out another Mark IV. The battalion's history claims that Corporal Jose Ulibarri personally accounted for four of the tanks with seven rounds in only sixty seconds. Neel's men were also credited with assisting the 230th Field Artillery Battalion in disabling three more German tanks. The tank destroyer platoon suffered no casualties.[53]

A counterattack by the 30th Infantry Division's 119th Infantry Regiment caught the one *Kampfgruppe* in the flank and all but destroyed it. Only 150 men came back.[54]

Capture of the Ravelsberg

During the night of October 9–10 a few miles to the south, two companies of 18th Infantry Regiment doughboys moved out to take the Ravelsberg, the last German-held prominence between the two American corps. The plan was to slip through by stealth and capture the hill without a fight. The column worked its way carefully through the dark, doubling back whenever the GIs encountered Germans, and sneaked by some pillboxes at a distance of only fifty yards. While creeping across a road, the Americans paused to let a German horse-drawn cart pass through their ranks unmolested.

Before dawn, the men reached the hilltop and began to organize a defense. By 0800 hours, they had cleared eight pillboxes and captured the unwary occupants without having to fire a shot. The GIs partook of the hot rations delivered by four more surprised volksgrenadiers during the morning. It was only late in the day that a brief exchange of fire with eight German troops disclosed the fact that the Americans held the Ravelsberg.

Two companies from the 3d Battalion, 18th Infantry, meanwhile, approached Haaren and took control of the northern outskirts and southern section without much trouble.[55]

With encirclement seemingly ensured, Huebner delivered a surrender ultimatum to the Aachen garrison. On a cold gray morning, Lieutenant George Maffey and Lieutenant William Boehme, accompanied by Private First Class Kenneth Kading, who carried a truce flag made from a pillowcase, entered the city in a jeep to deliver the terms. Every effort was made to make sure the Germans knew about the demand. Two public address systems announced the terms to frontline troops, Radio Luxembourg broadcast them, and 210 shells containing leaflets were fired into the city. Drew Middleton, a *New York Times* correspondent, reported, "If the Germans refuse to accept the ultimatum, which appears likely, then the siege of Aachen is likely to be long and bloody."[56]

Fresh Forces for the Counterattack

On October 11, forward units of the 1st Infantry Division reported that enemy troops were streaming in from the direction of Weiden. "Looks as though we can expect a big counterattack," the 18th Infantry Regiment observed. Division requested air support, but VII Corps replied that none was available. The 30th Infantry Division's OPs also spotted ominously heavy road traffic arriving from the northeast.[57]

German counterattacks supported by tanks gained strength over the next two days. The *I SS Panzer Corps* on October 11 took command of the *49th Infantry* and *3d Panzergrenadier divisions*, the latter just heading to the sector from Lorraine. It also received orders to help the *246th Volksgrenadier Division* reestablish a line around Bardenberg.

A *116th Panzer Division Kampfgruppe* (nine Panthers from the *24th Panzer Regiment* and 650 panzergrenadiers), *Obersturmführer* Herbert Rink's *1st SS Battalion*, and eighteen assault guns from the *902d Sturmgeschütz Brigade* reinforced the *404th Grenadier Regiment* to form Attack Group North. The group tried once more to break through to Bardenberg, this time to free the troops encircled there. After stiff house-to-house fighting, the attack reached a company of engineers that had been hunkered down at Würselen's train station since the initial penetration of Bardenberg, but dogged resistance from the 119th Infantry Regiment stopped the advance there. One panzergrenadier battalion commander personally led an attack that resulted in his death and the wounding of two of his company commanders. Only between twenty and thirty troops survived. At this point, Rink—who was supposed to disengage and enter Aachen—decided to attack with his battalion. (American POW interrogations indicated that this self-sufficient battalion had been formed on September 1 from a cadre of SS panzergrenadier training troops filled out with Luftwaffe personnel.[58]) Over the next twenty-four hours, the SS were reduced from 311 officers and men to 172. They managed to destroy two Shermans with panzerfausts.[59]

The Germans also hit the 120th Infantry Regiment's sector again at about 1600 hours but pulled back after losing two more panzers. This time, however, they destroyed one 823d Tank Destroyer Battalion 3-inch gun with direct fire and killed one man and wounded eight more.[60]

Inside Bardenberg, the last resistance by the *2108th Panzergrenadier Battalion* was snuffed out.

Köchling and *I SS Panzer Corps* launched their last big push against the Old Hickory Division on October 12. American fighter-bombers reported German tank concentrations all over the place, and fourteen squadrons working with the artillery pounded them relentlessly. The apparent impact on the coherence of the German operations is reflected in the 30th Infantry Division history's statement, "Where the main effort of the German counterthrust was being made is still obscure."[61]

Evidently having learned little about the futility of driving toward emplaced guns with long fields of fire, the *404th Grenadier Regiment, 108th Panzer Brigade*, and *506th Schwere Panzer Abteilung* attempted a last frontal attack against the 120th Infantry Regiment. The determined assault closed to within four hundred yards of the American positions as tank destroyers claimed three Mark Vs and three Mark VIs. A Sherman commanded by Staff Sergeant Melvin Bieber, Company B of the 743d Tank Battalion, engaged in a wildly uneven simultaneous duel against a Panther and a Tiger. The gunner's sharp work persuaded the Tiger crew to bail out after two hits, and the Panther finally stopped for good after absorbing twelve rounds.[62]

The 119th Infantry Regiment continued to battle the *60th Panzergrenadier Regiment* and *Obersturmführer* Rink's *1st SS Battalion* between Bardenberg and Würselen.[63]

The German pressure was heavy enough that, by noon, Hobbs and Corlett were worried. Hobbs claimed that all of the German divisions that had conducted a fierce counteroffensive against Old Hickory back in August at

Mortain were again present (which was a gross exaggeration). As was so often the case, American artillery and tactical air once more clinched the outcome. After one air strike against a concentration estimated at forty panzers, pilots reported seeing eighteen vehicles ablaze. The 30th Infantry Division's history recorded that by midafternoon, "The enemy legions appeared to be falling back under the terrific pounding inflicted upon them."[64]

Seemingly oblivious to the intervention by fresh German armored reserves, Hodges was becoming fiercely impatient with the slow progress toward the linkup point achieved in the preceding few days by the 30th Infantry Division. Even as the day's fierce counterattacks were winding down, Corlett phoned Hobbs to tell him, "General Hodges tells me we have to close the gap some way." Both Corlett and Hobbs later said that they felt as though they were walking on eggshells. Privately, Hodges told Corlett that he thought Hobbs should be relieved.[65] Instead, Corlett was the one whose days were numbered.

Corlett told Hobbs to make contact with the 1st Infantry Division regardless of boundaries. Hobbs again raised the issue of his shortage of men. Corlett obtained Hodges' permission to attach two battalions from the 29th Infantry Division's 116th Infantry Regiment, then posting the line west of Aachen.[66]

The 1st Infantry Division, meanwhile, faced renewed German pressure on its own front. The *12th Volksgrenadier Division* counterattacked the 18th Infantry Regiment at Crucifix Hill at 1100 hours on October 12. *Oberst* Engel had received the unblooded *1st Sturm Pioniere Regiment*—a motorized infantry unit lacking heavy weapons—to conduct the attack, and he threw a company of his own *27th Fusilier Regiment* into the operation as well. Supported by the concentrated artillery fire of nearly two divisions, his men recaptured the pillboxes atop Crucifix Hill in a dashing assault marked by "bitter courage," according to one American reporter.

By evening, the Americans had reclaimed the position. Dawn revealed a scene of carnage, with bodies lying among wrecked panzers and gun carriages. The *1st Sturm Pioniere Regiment* was no longer combat effective, and its men were dispersed and sent to reinforce other units. The huge wooden crucifix on the hill had been knocked off its base by a shell, which revealed that it was hollow and equipped with a ladder that had turned it into a German OP.[67]

At the left end of Huebner's line, the 26th Infantry Regiment probed the southern edge of Aachen.[68] In response to Huebner's ultimatum, white flags had appeared in all sections of the city. American observation posts noted that German soldiers forced the civilians to remove the flags.[69]

Ordered by Hitler to fight to the last man, the commander of the Aachen "fortress," *Oberstleutnant* Maximilian Leyherr, had refused to surrender by Huebner's deadline on October 11.[70] The Big Red One thereupon launched its promised assault on the city with a bombardment by three hundred fighter-bombers and twelve artillery battalions. XIX Tactical Air Command (TAC) would drop 173 tons of bombs on Aachen from October 11 to 13.[71] Huebner told Collins that he did not want to bomb the city indiscriminately; guns from the 33d Field Artillery Battalion marked specific targets for the aircraft with colored smoke. The air attacks concentrated on targets on the northern and southern edges of the city. Artillery rained down on areas closest to American lines and the center of Aachen. Patrols, however, reported that the bombardment was not greatly impairing the German defenses.[72]

The next day, on orders from Huebner, the 26th Infantry Regiment began to clear an industrial area on the edge of Aachen preparatory to storming the city proper. The fighting raged from building to building, and progress was slow but steady. (The fight for downtown Aachen is addressed in separate detail following.)

Stalemate?

October 13 ushered in three extremely frustrating days for the 30th Infantry Division. Hobbs convinced corps that his regiments were too weak to leave their defensive positions in full knowledge of the strong armored forces to the front, which might counterattack and catch his men in the open. Hobbs decided to attack using his fresh troops on a narrow front at Würselen. Thus the two battalions of the 116th Infantry Regiment—supported by Companies B and G from Harmon's 66th Armored Regiment—pushed off through the lines of the 119th Infantry Regiment. They made quick initial progress to the south edge of Würselen, with their right flank on high ground east of the Würm.

Federalized from the National Guard along with the rest of the 29th Infantry Division, the 116th Infantry Regiment was the direct descendent of the 2d Virginia, the senior regiment in Stonewall Jackson's brigade the day the Confederate general had won his title at Manassas.[73] Perhaps the "Stonewallers," as the men called themselves, were particularly able to appreciate a bold stand.

The entire *116th Panzer Division*, which a day earlier had concentrated at Würselen, stood in their way. The Germans could concentrate artillery fire against the narrow active American front. Tanks and panzergrenadiers used buildings as fortresses. Progress became painfully slow.[74]

Captain James Burt, who commanded the 66th Armored Regiment's Company B, earned the Medal of Honor where the Stonewallers met the Greyhounds, as recorded in his citation:

> In the first day's action, when infantrymen ran into murderous small-arms and mortar fire, Captain Burt dismounted from his tank about two hundred yards to the rear and moved forward on foot beyond the infantry positions, where, as the enemy concentrated a tremendous volume of fire upon him, he calmly motioned his tanks into good firing positions. As our ground attack gained momentum, he climbed aboard his tank and directed the action from the rear deck, exposed to hostile volleys that finally wounded him painfully in the face and neck. He maintained his dangerous post despite point-blank gunfire until friendly artillery knocked out those weapons, and then proceeded to the advanced infantry scout's position to deploy his tanks for the defense of the gains that had been made. The next day, when the enemy counterattacked, he left cover and went seventy-five yards through heavy fire to assist the infantry battalion commander who was seriously wounded. For the next eight days, through rainy, miserable weather, and under constant, heavy shelling, Captain Burt held the combined forces together through the sheer force of his heroic example.
>
> To direct artillery fire, on 15 October, he took his tank three hundred yards into the enemy line, where he dismounted and remained for one hour giving accurate data to friendly gunners. Twice more that day, he went into enemy territory under deadly fire on reconnaissance. . . .

Twice the tank he was riding was knocked out by enemy fire, and each time he climbed aboard another vehicle and continued to fight.

Although the citation mentions the ground attack gaining momentum, in fact the 116th Infantry Regiment did not gain greater momentum on October 14. Hodges personally called Hobbs to express his dissatisfaction.[75]

Relieved by the *116th Panzer Division*, Rink's SS battalion slipped away to join the defenders of central Aachen. Eight assault guns also rolled into the city.[76]

East of Aachen, a patrol from the 18th Infantry Regiment attempted to make contact with the 30th Infantry Division. The men ran into an intense firefight before going a hundred yards, and they pulled back.[77] The two divisions were nonetheless so close that artillery observers from the 18th Infantry Regiment were able to obtain fire support from Old Hickory's divisional artillery.[78]

Reconnaissance elements of the *3d Panzergrenadier Division* arrived in the sector of the *12th Volksgrenadier Division* that day.[79] The VIII Corps had spotted the panzergrenadiers moving north and warned the 1st Infantry Division that it could soon expect more company to its front.[80] The *3d Panzergrenadiers*— Prussians commanded for less than two weeks by veteran panzer soldier *Generalmajor* Walter Denkert—were arriving from Italy (via Lorraine), where they had fought U.S. Fifth Army all the way up the boot to Rome. Prior to that, the division had been destroyed in Stalingrad and reconstituted.

A panzergrenadier division's striking power resided in two three-battalion motorized infantry regiments and a tank battalion (in this case equipped with assault guns), supported by an armored artillery regiment and armored reconnaissance, antitank, and engineer battalions. In the preceding two weeks, the division had absorbed enough replacements to be classified "fighting strength II," or capable of limited offensive operations. Well-camouflaged combat units rolled into concentration areas overnight, while storm troops began probing the American line.[81] The Americans west of the Roer would get to know the Prussian panzergrenadiers well.

On October 14, Model reported that his losses since the Second Battle of Aachen had begun on October 2 amounted to 632 dead and 4,432 wounded or missing. He conceded that, for practical purposes, Aachen was surrounded.[82]

Both Sides Try Again to Break the Logjam

The 30th Infantry Division's G-3 on October 15 concocted a plan born of desperation as the 116th Infantry Regiment continued to battle almost unyielding resistance from the *116th Panzer Division* (progress to date: a thousand yards). The next day, the 119th Infantry Regiment, supported by most of the division's attached tank battalion and the separate 99th Infantry Battalion, was to hook to the right of the 116th Infantry. While the G-3 worked, Corlett called Hobbs again and in the course of a brief conversation uttered the phrase "close the gap" four times. Hopefully, the new plan would break the stalemate.[83]

There was need for a visionary plan. The *116th Panzer Division* had gained the help of the *519th Schwere Panzerjäger Abteilung (Heavy Tank Destroyer Battalion)*, which had one company of the new Jagdpanthers and two of assault guns.[84] The nimble Jagdpanther mounted the dreaded 88mm gun on a Panther chassis in a well-armored superstructure (80mm, or 3-plus inches, up front, sloped at 35 degrees).[85] American tank and tank destroyer guns had little chance of knocking one out unless they got a shot at the side or rear, where the armor was thinner.

To the south, meanwhile, the 1st Infantry Division's 18th Infantry Regiment noted the arrival of the as-yet-unidentified *3d Panzergrenadier Division* and reported at about 1100 hours, "There is no doubt in our mind that there is a big buildup to our front. . . . We expect to fight and are preparing for that." A few minutes later, the 16th Infantry Regiment concurred and expressed concern that the Germans might be strong enough to break through.[86]

A few moments after that, the panzergrenadiers, reinforced by the *506th Schwere Panzer Abteilung's* Royal Tigers, attacked out of the Würselener Wald and through the lines of the *12th Volksgrenadier Division* toward Aachen. *Generalfeldmarschall* Model had ordered that the operation begin later in the day than usual because the tempo of fighting usually declined at that time, and he hoped to achieve tactical surprise. The fact that the division was now directly subordinated to *Seventh Army* command rather than a corps made such high-level meddling easier than usual.[87]

The *8th* and *29th Grenadier regiments* attacked abreast after an artillery preparation, with the Tigers on the right. (The division's motorized grenadier regiments had three battalions each and were relabeled "panzergrenadier reg-iments" on December 1, 1944, with no change in organization.[88]) By 1300 hours, the Germans had overrun two companies from the 16th Infantry Regiment, which reported that the situation was critical.

Massed artillery fire—capped by a dramatic appearance by American fighter-bombers—smashed the attack over the next hour. The *29th Grenadier Regiment* reported, "The enemy artillery fire became stronger than we had ever experienced before, and shells fell almost uninterrupted for hours. Casualties climbed; weapons and equipment were destroyed. Artillery observation planes—as many as four circled constantly over the division—competently directed this massed fire."

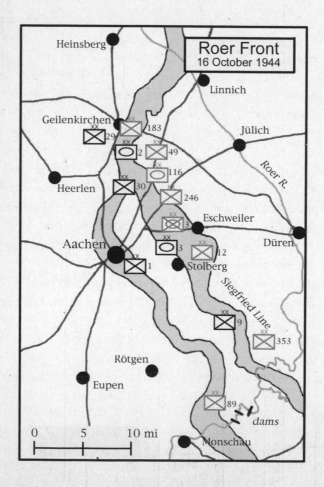

Some of the fighter-bombers had been sent south by the 30th Infantry Division. The American troops reported that the flyboys were strafing the enemy within twenty-five feet of the American line and doing a "beautiful job."

Panzers were burning across the battlefield, and German division commanding general Denkert watched as the intense fire drove his infantry to cover, which left the remaining tanks without support. Denkert pulled back his tanks to good cover. His formation had suffered a pounding; one American company counted 250 dead within and in front of its positions.

The *3d Panzergrenadier Division* risked one more minor sally against the 16th Infantry Regiment after dark, when ten tanks shelled Company G from point-blank range. Americans counterattacking in the dark bypassed the *29th Grenadier Regiment's* spearhead at Verlautenheide, however, which forced the Germans to withdraw.[89]

North of Aachen, the Old Hickory Division implemented its new plan at 0500 hours on October 16. The 119th Infantry Regiment attacked westward across the Würm River, quickly seized Kohlscheid, and established a bridge for tanks by 0530 hours. This flanked the German defenses and opened the way for a simultaneous advance southward along the east bank. Two battalions moved out, and by 0730 hours the 2d Battalion had gained a thousand yards west of Würselen. When German resistance built, the 117th and 120th Infantry regiments fired a diversionary barrage, which suggested that attack was imminent. Virtually all German artillery shifted to deal with this perceived threat, and the 119th got moving again. By 1545 hours, the Big Red One called to say that its OPs had spotted friendly troops south of Würselen.

The Americans had worked their way between the *Windhund Division* and Aachen.

Shortly before 1700 hours, a patrol from Company F, 119th Infantry Regiment, made contact with the 18th Infantry Regiment's Company K. Privates Edward Krauss and Evan Whitis made their way onto the Ravelsberg and stumbled into the 1st Infantry Division lines. Spotting the patrol, the men on the hill called out, "We're from K Company. Come on up!"

"We're from F Company. Come on down!" came the reply. Whitis related, "They out-talked us, and we pushed on up."[90]

The gap was closed.

***

The *3d Panzergrenadier Division* attacked the Big Red One again on October 16 at 0600 hours without an artillery preparation, but the advance burned out, as had the first, in the face of "liberal use of air and artillery fire," as First Army recorded. The German division had suffered heavy losses in men (nearly six hundred) and tanks, to no purpose.[91]

The losses thus far had not been one-sided. In closing the ring around Aachen, XIX Corps had lost 417 men killed and five times that number wounded. The 30th Infantry Division accounted for about two-thousand casualties, or 72 percent, of the total.[92]

Aachen was encircled, but it would be two more days before the 18th Infantry Regiment firmly established a roadblock on the Aachen-Cologne highway, two hundred yards from the nearest 30th Infantry Division strongpoint. American and German riflemen would engage in more bitter close-quarters fighting east of Aachen for days. Pillboxes would change hands time and again. But the main issue had been decided. The ring around Aachen held firm.

INTO THE INFERNO

Battles for dozens of German cities—some of the battles tough ones—lay in the American GIs' future, but Aachen was both the first and the granddaddy of them all.

Lightning Joe Collins left the planning for the assault on the city in the capable hands of Ralph Huebner. Aachen offered little room for finesse. A face-on assault was in order. Nonetheless, Huebner planned a slow, steady escalation of pressure that he hoped would minimize casualties.[93]

Oberst Gerhard Wilck, commander of the *246th Volksgrenadier Division*, had responsibility for the city's defenses. A veteran of the eastern front and a former tactics instructor, he had just taken charge in Aachen from *Oberstleutnant* Leyherr, who was one of his regimental commanders, on October 12. The latter officer had been transferred as the result of a political decision: His father-in-law, former army Chief of Staff *generaloberst* Franz Halder, had been arrested as a suspected participant in the plot to kill Hitler. Wilck, on arriving in the Aachen area on September 25, had told Model that the city should not be defended, an opinion that earned him an angry rebuke. Under specific instructions from *Seventh Army*, *LXXXI Corps* commanding general Köchling required Wilck to swear in his presence to defend Aachen to the last man.[94]

In addition to parts of two of his own badly depleted regiments (the *689th* and *404th Grenadier*), Wilck had available the *1st SS Battalion*, elements of *600th Sturm Pioniere Regiment*, a fortress battalion, a composite battalion, an assault gun brigade, and some of his divisional artillery. American intelligence put the total number of troops at three thousand to four thousand; subsequent prisoner counts indicate that the number was at the high end of that range if not greater. The garrison had enough food for two months but was low on ammunition. Troop morale was high, and the men were willing to fight for every meter of German soil. Köchling would later suggest that Göbbels' promises of wonder weapons just over the horizon genuinely spurred the troops to fight with greater determination. Whether or not Wilck believed the daily radio broadcasts from deep inside the *Vaterland*, they promised help and relief.[95]

Subduing Aachen fell to Colonel John Seitz's 26th Infantry Regiment, which had only two battalions available for the job. The assault force was substantially outnumbered in terms of men, but it enjoyed a huge advantage in armor, artillery, and air support. The regiment attacked from east to west through the city.

Like other German cities once surrounded by protecting walls, the ancient center of Aachen—the *Altstadt*—was encircled by a ring road tracking the route of the old defenses. A web of radial streets cut among often ancient and thick-walled buildings to converge near the great cathedral at the city's center. Northeast of the *Altstadt* was a park in which sat the luxurious Quellenhof Hotel; the natural mineral baths here had attracted the high and mighty for centuries. The German military headquarters occupied the hotel and the neighboring mineral bath house, or *Kurhaus*. A short distance to the west lay three conjoined hills, on the central one of which (Lousberg) sat an observatory after which the Americans named the feature.

Lieutenant Colonel Derrill Daniel's 2d Battalion, 26th Infantry, backed by tank destroyers from Company A, 634th Tank Destroyer Battalion, and tanks from the 745th Tank Battalion, had the dubious honor of clearing the south and center of Aachen. While dug in on the outskirts prior to the assault, Daniel had used the tanks as "snipers" against machine-gun nests and the tank destroyers to blow up buildings suspected of harboring OPs.[96] But now he had to take the buildings—a lot of them.

Daniel's battalion had been conducting limited attacks for days to clear structures along the outskirts before moving into the city itself. Initially, Daniel assigned a mixed force of three or more Shermans and two tank destroyers to support each infantry company. The armor's job was to blast ahead of the infantry, drive the enemy into cellars, and generally scare them. Tanks and tank destroyers had prearranged infantry protection in return, but small-arms fire forced the doughs to move cautiously, dashing from door to door and hole to hole.

Lieutenant Colonel John Corley's 3d Battalion, meanwhile, cleared a factory district on the east side of the city, and Shermans and M10s played backup. When the doughs came under fire, a tank or a tank destroyer returned fire until the riflemen moved in and cleared the building with grenades.

STORMING THE FORTRESS
The two battalions launched their attack on the city proper on October 13. By that day, pilots reported that the city was 85 percent damaged, and a shroud of smoke rose over the rubble to a height of six thousand feet.[97]

An American reporter described 2d Battalion's kickoff: "Only the brisk rattle of machine guns and quick bark of rifles met the doughboys this morning when they climbed out of foxholes and cellars in the outskirts of Aachen, crossed the railroad tracks, and filed down the empty streets between rows of shattered houses. . . . Over the city hung a nauseating smell of death, stagnation and fire. It was slow and difficult fighting. Knots of German infantrymen, holding out in cellars and concrete houses, had to be knocked out at point-blank range. . . ."[98]

Companies F and G from 2d Battalion each had three Shermans and one M10 attached; Company II had three tanks and two tank destroyers. The armor had difficulty negotiating embankments along the main rail line, which cut across 2d Battalion's front. Several successfully slid down a ten-foot bank; others went under the tracks near the Aachen–Rothe Erde train station, only fifteen yards from the main underpass, where the men could see German demolitions installed.[99]

Daniel soon developed a more frugal tactical approach for the urban fighting: A tank or tank destroyer went into action beside each infantry platoon. The armor would keep each successive building under fire until the riflemen moved in to assault it. The crews normally fired high-explosive (HE) rounds on fuse-delay through doors, windows, or thin walls to explode inside. They usually shot with no target visible, just in case a hidden enemy lurked there. Each armored vehicle expended an average of fifty rounds of HE daily.

Only when a building was cleared and the doughs were safe from muzzle blast would the tank or tank destroyer fire on its next target. The process quickly produced tremendous teamwork. Light artillery, meanwhile, crept two or three blocks ahead of the advancing troops; heavy artillery dropped beyond that.[100]

Daniel established checkpoints at intersections and in larger buildings so adjacent units could keep track of one another and stay in line. Each company was assigned an area, and each platoon usually was given a single street to clear. At cross streets, platoons worked about halfway down each block until they made contact with their neighbor. A team of one demolitions man and one flamethrower operator worked with each company; the former used captured "beehive" charges to blow open doors.[101]

George Mucha, a BBC correspondent following Daniel's men, reported:

> The Americans were advancing methodically from street to street. Ahead of us, a few yards ahead, a Sherman tank sprayed the buildings with machine-gun fire.
>
> Suddenly it stopped. There was a German machine-gun nest. We squeezed against the wall until the tank had dealt with this by firing its gun at point-blank range into the house. The street was shaking with the thunder of reports. Above our heads mortar bombs were whining through the air. It was raining. . . . Every ten yards a new house had to be searched from top to bottom for snipers; doors broken in, grenades thrown into suspect rooms.[102]

Almost no reports describe the German use of their own more limited armored assets except during occasional counterattacks. One observer reported that the panzers mirrored the action of the American tanks. They would scoot around a corner and fire on buildings now occupied by GIs.[103]

***

The 3d Battalion also attacked on October 13, with Observatory Hill as its objective. German fire was so heavy in some streets that the GIs climbed from building to building through holes in the walls. Denis Johnston, another BBC correspondent, broadcast a report on the "street fighting" encountered in Aachen—and every following German city defended as a fortress:

> It's a bad misnomer, because the last place you see any sane man is in a street where every yard is usually covered by a well-sited machine gun. It should be called house-to-house fighting, which it literally is. The old hands at the game go through a town keeping inside the houses and using bazookas to knock holes in the dividing walls as they go, and when they come to the end of the block and have to cross the street to the next block, they throw out smoke first and cross over under cover of that. They say it's usually better to clean out a house from the top downwards if you can. Break a hole in the roof and get in by an upper floor if possible. A German in a cellar is considerably less dangerous than a German upstairs.
>
> But of course a lot depends on the type of defense that's being met with; if it mainly consists of sniping, it's best to go slowly and very deliberately, and in small groups. Snipers very often won't fire at a group, when they'll shoot at a single man; they're afraid of giving away their position to the men whom they can't hit with their first shots. But if the defense is heavy, you've got to keep dispersed, move fast, and keep on moving whatever happens.[104]

An unidentified American correspondent with an infantry company reported: "The Germans are fighting here in Aachen with fantastically hopeless savagery. . . . The fierce pattern is always the same. The German lets go with a few rounds from a burpgun. Then American heavy machine guns, emplaced behind walls of debris on either side of the street, tear into the enemy hideout, and an American squad creeps up to it. One infantryman fires in with his rifle, another throws two or three grenades. Then there is no more German [soldier] there. The commander of this outfit, Capt. William H. Fuller of Ludlow, Vt., grins and shouts to his men, 'Good! That's it. When we can't see 'em, we'll scare 'em to death.'"[105]

The 3d Battalion used artillery firing red smoke shells to mark targets for dive-bombers as the doughs worked carefully forward. The Germans countered by crawling through the sewers to already cleared areas and attacked the GIs from behind; the doughs learned quickly to locate every manhole, throw in a few grenades, then block the cover. Regiment noted, "Gains were measured in rooms and houses taken."

Because some structures, including many apartment buildings, were proving impervious to fire from tanks and tank destroyers, the 3d Battalion requested the help of a self-propelled 155mm gun. Division artillery agreed to send one forward.

Company I, working with Company K, took Observatory Hill the next day and deployed just past the top. GIs also entered the park near the Quellenhof Hotel. The first test of the 155mm rifle was most successful—one shot leveled a structure that had fended off tank and tank destroyer rounds. An enthused Colonel Seitz decided to obtain another gun for 2d Battalion.

Wilck Lashes Back

Obersturmführer Rink's *1st SS Battalion* arrived at the Quellenhof on October 15, and not a moment too soon. As Rink and Wilck spoke, an American probe got so close to the CP that the two officers had to join their men in the defense, tossing grenades from an upper-story window. The *Amis* nonetheless took the nearby *Kurhaus*.

Wilck directed the SS and six tanks or SP guns against the uncomfortably close American line at 1530 hours following an intense 120mm mortar barrage. (Sources differ as to what the panzers were; the forward American troops repeatedly identified one as a Tiger, but German records point to assault guns.) The Germans overran Observatory Hill and drove a three-hundred-yard gap between Companies I and K. Even before Rink's attack, Company I, which was dug in on the hill, had bled so thin that it was using its mortar crews as riflemen.[106]

Two panzers and the SS men rolled on to Company K near the *Kurhaus*. One panzer penetrated as far as some woods two hundred yards from the 3d Battalion CP, where two M10s engaged it by firing at its muzzle flash. Corporal Wenzlo Simmons, who was acting as gunner because his commander was absent with a toothache, was credited with killing a Tiger.

Word went up the line. The situation was "sticky."

A desperate effort by Company L managed to retake Observatory Hill, but not the *Kurhaus*, before darkness put a stop to the fighting.[107]

In theory, the German attack was a complementary move to the attempt by the *3d Panzergrenadier Division* to break into the city, but the two operations made so little progress toward each other that this had little meaning in practice. Wilck plaintively signaled *LXXXI Corps*: "Today's counterattack brought high losses. New enemy breakthrough at main train station. MLR as yesterday. Provision of additional forces necessary. What is the status of relief attack from Verlautenheide?"[108]

Wilck's men were badly disappointed when news of the failed *3d Panzergrenadier Division* attack spread. Morale was declining. The men were nervous. Rumors spread that American tanks were breaking through, and now and again outlying units panicked. The infantry and panzer crews blamed each other for disappearing when the fighting got tough.[109]

Rink's SS men nonetheless continued to battle for control of Observatory Hill for the next two days. During one attack, his men infiltrated the Palast Hotel through an underground passage and fought the GIs hand to hand through the halls of the building. Withal, their bravery could not prevent the gradual compression of the German line back through the high ground toward Salvatorberg.[110]

Meanwhile, Outside the Metropolis . . .

While the battle raged in the city's streets, the 18th Infantry Regiment repulsed two tank-infantry attacks on October 18. The *3d Panzergrenadier Division* had regrouped in Würselen after its misadventures at Verlautenheide, and the division's new objective was the Ravelsberg. In view of the experiences in the earlier attacks, *Generalmajor* Denkert echeloned his troops in depth on a narrow front. An attack group from the *8th Grenadier Regiment* led, followed by a second wave of infantry. Antitank guns were ready for deployment on the Ravelsberg once it was captured.[111]

The assault hit the 18th Infantry Regiment's Company K out of the dark from the north at 0630 hours. The wind was blowing, and rain fell in sheets. Two squads in 3d Platoon were quickly overrun, and panzers knocked out the company's machine-gun emplacements.[112]

The spearhead succeeded in taking six pillboxes atop the Ravelsberg against what the Germans considered surprisingly weak resistance. Almost immediately, however, tremendously heavy American artillery fire swept the hilltop and drove the panzergrenadiers into the pillboxes. The fire also interdicted the path to the rear.

The remnants of Company K established a new line along the crest of the hill. By dusk, a platoon from Company B had arrived to reinforce the beleaguered outfit. The GIs immediately set about recapturing pillboxes.

Preceded by an artillery barrage that dumped a hundred rounds per minute on the defenders, the Germans attacked again the next day. Close-quarters fighting raged among the bunkers, but the Americans held. Few of the panzergrenadiers returned from the hilltop.[113]

Near the top of the chain of command, Eisenhower on October 18 decided to shift his main effort to the 12th Army Group, while Monty—for the first time since D-day—played a subordinate roll. This decision set the stage for a major American offensive toward the Roer in November.[114]

That same day, the First Army operations report (reflecting, perhaps, the American view of Monty and the benefits of a broad-front strategy) groused: "Having failed to prevent the encirclement of Aachen, the enemy was now making desperate efforts to break through with reinforcements and supplies to the beleaguered city. Enemy reinforcement of the area continued. This was made possible without undue strain on the slender resources of C-in-C West [von Rundstedt] due to the comparative quiet on the remainder of the Western Front."[115]

Bradley, meanwhile, relieved Corlett from command of XIX Corps without prejudice and recommended that he be returned to the States for rest and medical attention. Bradley appointed Major General Ray McLain, a National Guardsman who had ably commanded the 90th Infantry Division, to replace him.[116] The word in command circles was that General Marshall had hand-picked McLain to silence complaints from National Guard ranks that too few of their number had received senior assignments.[117]

On the German side, *I SS Panzer Corps* was withdrawn on October 19.[118] This signaled the irrevocable abandonment of Wilck to his fate.

On the ground, the fierce fight through the streets of Aachen was unaffected by such high-level considerations.

Coup de Grace

On October 19, Task Forces Hogan and Hughes joined the fight in Aachen. Collins on October 17 had decided to pause and reinforce the 26th Infantry

Regiment with an armored-infantry battalion and a tank battalion (less one company) from the 3d Armored Division, plus the 28th Infantry Division's 2d Battalion, 110th Infantry Regiment. The tankers and armored doughs in Task Force Hogan kicked off at about 0700 hours, and the fresh infantry from Task Force Hughes took over defensive duties. By midday, the 1st Infantry Division judged the eastern portion of Aachen clear and estimated that the fight would be wrapped up in a day or two.[119]

By October 21, *Oberst* Wilck had shifted his CP to a bunker on the slopes of Salvatorberg. The bunker was now full of wounded men; Wilck's units were in tatters, and Wilck had little control over the battle. Corley's troops had reached the German CP and were using a 155mm gun against the outer walls. Wilck surrendered at 1205 hours, commenting, "When the Americans start using 155s as sniper weapons, it is time to give up."[120] (Rink did not give up; he led nineteen of his SS men on a harrowing escape back to German lines, where he was able to provide an eyewitness account of the last bitter fighting to *LXXXI Corps*. Others also escaped—*Oberstleutnant* Erich Stach, a battalion commander in the *246th Volksgrenadier Division*, and one of his lieutenants made it back disguised as Franciscan monks, despite being detained for a while by suspicious *Amis*.)[121]

Officers in the 26th Infantry Regiment considered what they had just gone through "the hardest, toughest, and longest steady fight they had ever had." The two committed battalions had lost 75 men killed and 414 wounded, or the equivalent of more than two rifle companies. The regiment was proud that though the Germans had fought courageously and skillfully, they had been bested by a force half their size. But the division's history concluded, "Aachen, shockingly battered, was ours, and the truth is that, for all its obstinate defense, it was not much save a symbol."[122]

One day in late October, a man wearing the two stars of a major general appeared unheralded at an outpost of the 30th Infantry Division's 119th Infantry Regiment. Clarence Huebner introduced himself to the surprised GIs. "I wish you'd get it around to your people," he said, "that we never could have taken Aachen without your help."[123]

Outside the city, the *3d Panzergrenadier Division* took over the Würselen sector from the *116th Panzer Division*, while remnants of the *246th Volksgrenadier Division* took responsibility for the rest of the panzer division's line. Denkert's panzergrenadier division had suffered so many losses in its hopeless attacks to break the encirclement that it was no longer capable of offensive operations. The *116th Panzer Division* absorbed the *108th Panzer Brigade* to make up for some of its heavy losses.[124]

The VII Corps, meanwhile, ordered the 1st Infantry Division to hold and prepare present positions until ordered to renew its advance eastward.[125] That order would be nearly a month in coming.

TOP OF THE NINTH

On October 18, a Supreme Commander's conference of top Allied officers instructed First Army to drive to the Rhine south of Cologne and seize a bridgehead. The command anticipated that First Army could begin by the first week of November. Montgomery's 21st Army Group was to devote all resources to opening the port of Antwerp. Lieutenant General William Simpson's Ninth Army would support the left flank of First Army until such time as it could wheel northward along the Rhine, when it would be subordinated the the 21st Army Group. By now, the long-range plan anticipated that Ninth Army—back under Bradley's control—would encircle the Ruhr on the north and First Army on the south. The directive took no notice of the Roer River.[126]

Ninth Army arrived in the Roer River sector on October 22 and took up a position between the British and the left flank of First Army. Bradley had initially assigned the army, just arriving from Brittany, responsibility for the Ardennes sector, where its headquarters set up shop on October 2. The change in orders came so swiftly—official if informal word arrived on October 10—that the rear echelon never even reached the Ardennes before diverting to Maastricht, the site of the new headquarters.[127] Bradley later admitted that he shifted Ninth Army because he concluded that Monty would eventually wangle an American army for his command; Bradley preferred to sacrifice Simpson's relatively green organization instead of his own former command, First Army.[128]

Simpson—a quiet, strong-willed Texan with an earthy sense of humor—was a 1909 West Point classmate of Patton. The tall, rawboned cadet had graduated second from the bottom of his class. A born soldier, he had served on the Mexican border and in France, where he reached the rank of lieutenant colonel and earned the Distinguished Service Cross, among other decorations. Bradley had to say of Simpson's command that it was "uncommonly normal."[129] Hell on Wheels' Harmon considered Simpson a great leader and a general's general.[130]

Yet, at the time of its assignment to the Roer area, Ninth Army was in an unusual state. Two infantry divisions from VIII Corps—its sole active corps—were under way to the German border from Brittany, where they had participated in the reduction of the German defenses at Brest. A third division remained in Brittany to contain German troops in the ports of St. Nazaire and Lorient. Ninth Army had three other corps that were still nonoperational in Normandy: III, XIII, and XVI. Of the six infantry and four armored divisions assigned to those corps, none was operational yet; four were grounded because their trucks were being used in provisional units to move supplies, and two were still in the United Kingdom.[131]

The 12th Army Group arranged for a swap of corps between First and Ninth armies, the former picking up VIII Corps, and the later taking control over XIX Corps, on the American left wing. In addition to the 29th and 30th Infantry and 2d Armored divisions (plus the 113th Cavalry Group), the 102d Infantry Division was just arriving from Normandy. Ninth Army decided to use its regiments to relieve outfits on the line, because the division was not yet ready to function as a unit.[132]

Just as Bradley had foreseen, Ninth Army would have a more intimate working relationship with the British than any other American command in the European Theater of Operations (ETO). The first steps occurred shortly after Simpson and his team arrived at the front. In late October, the 104th Infantry Division was attached to the British 21st Army Group for missions in Holland. The American 7th Armored Division, meanwhile, was assigned to Ninth Army but remained in the British area for operations. Ninth Army assumed supply responsibilities for both divisions.[133]

One of the first things that Ninth Army headquarters did—as it looked ahead with remarkable speed and acuity—was seek Bradley's help in dealing with the mine problem. Simpson asked for a special separate tank battalion equipped with mine exploding equipment.[134]

FIFTH *VERSUS NINTH*

The same day (October 22) that Ninth Army took its position on the American left, *Army Group B* inserted *General der Panzertruppen* Hasso-Accardin von Manteuffel's *Fifth Panzer Army* roughly opposite to take charge of the northern end of *Seventh Army's* front and the southern end of *First Fallschirm Army's* front. The new sector ran from roughly Düren in the south to near Maastricht. The area stretching back to the Roer River was the only route leading to the Rhine suitable for mobile warfare. The initial command change was largely a staff exercise; *Fifth Panzer Army* simply took charge of *LXXXI and XII SS corps.*[135]

Model had several reasons for the change. He judged that *Seventh Army's* front—stretching from Geilenkirchen to Trier—was simply too long. Moreover, the battle for Aachen had drawn a growing number of panzer and panzergrenadier formations into the area, and a panzer army staff was better qualified to direct them. Finally, Model hoped that the appearance of the army at the front would mask preparations taking place for the planned offensive in the Ardennes.[136]

The Germans by now assessed that they could stop the American advance toward the Roer River. They harbored no illusions that they could push the Americans back beyond the West Wall around Aachen, however. German intelligence reports indicated that Cologne-Düsseldorf and the Ruhr beyond those cities were the primary American objectives in this sector. The Germans expected the American right flank to try to advance along the axis Monschau-Düren with the goals of capturing Düren and the Roer River dams.[137] Only on the last point did the Germans misjudge American intentions.

The battle around Aachen had fully met von Rundstedt's gloomy expectations for the German part in Eisenhower's attrition drama. As of October 20, the *12th Volksgrenadier Division* was down to fewer than seven thousand men, although all of its battalions remained battleworthy. The *3d Panzergrenadier Division* could count fewer than four thousand men, and all of its grenadier battalions were in bad shape. And the *246th Volksgrenadier Division* (not counting the men about to surrender in Aachen) had merely 1,171 soldiers still on the rolls. The *49th Infantry Division* (now commanded by *Oberst* Peter Körte, who within a week took charge of the *246th* when it absorbed the remnants of his own division) had only one organic rifle battalion to its name and operated only through the means of four battalions attached from other divisions.[138]

CHAPTER 4

THE NOVEMBER OFFENSIVE BEGINS

I anticipate a hell of a big fight.

Lieutenant General William H. Simpson, *AAR, Ninth Army*

Eisenhower opted to keep the pressure on during the winter and ordered the 21st, 12th, and 6th Army groups to mount a broad-front offensive in November.[1] D-day for the 12th Army Group's operation aimed at leaping the Roer River to the Rhine was November 11, weather permitting scheduled air support, and no later than November 16 under any circumstances. First Army, supported by Ninth Army, would make the main effort. Ninth Army, in turn, would get help from the British XXX Corps, which would operate in the northern end of the American zone against the West Wall defenses at Geilenkirchen and take over protection of the Americans' long left flank. The American 84th Infantry Division (less one regimental combat team) was attached to the British for the operation to attack Geilenkirchen from the south.[2]

By now, Bradley—reflecting Eisenhower's repeated guidance—established the main goal of his operation as destruction of the German army west of the Rhine River.[3] First Army's objective was to reach the Rhine, then to bridge it if possible. Ninth Army's objective was to advance to the Rhine in the direction of Essen so it could bring the Ruhr under heavy artillery fire. It would then wheel northward to clear the west bank in cooperation with the British.[4]

Bradley's planners apparently had begun to think somewhat about the danger posed to any Roer River crossing by artificial flooding from the German-held dams in First Army's V Corps sector. On November 11, Hodges and Simpson both instructed their respective corps commanders that troops would not advance beyond the river except on specific orders from the army level, a coincidence that strongly suggests guidance from above.[5] Ninth Army's published history explicitly ascribes this order to the potential threat posed by the dams.[6] The concern did not generate any orders to capture the dams, however, and the establishment of the Rhine as the chief objective for both armies suggests that the 12th Army Group did not view the dams as a deal-breaker. Indeed, Bradley expected that, with luck, he would reach the Rhine in thirty days.[7]

How hard could it be? The desired Roer River crossings were as close as seven miles to American lines. And the ratio of attackers to defenders was almost 5:1.[8]

FIRST ARMY READIES FOR ANOTHER ROUND

Lightning Joe Collins' VII Corps was the only one of the three corps in First Army assigned a role in the November offensive. The corps held a line some twenty miles end to end as the crow flies, but the front bent so that the actual length was closer to thirty miles. The corps' strength was concentrated around Aachen, at the north end of its line.[9]

First Army in late October and early November detected evidence of a German buildup in front of VII Corps and Ninth Army's XIX Corps. It decided to boost VII Corps' punch by adding the 104th ("Timberwolf") Infantry Division, which had just been released from the 21st Army Group. Under Monty's command, the division had been engaged in the fighting to clear the approaches to Antwerp.

Major General Terry de la Mesa Allen—a rugged but personable man—was said to have sworn that he would make his Timberwolf Division the equal of his previous command, the Big Red One. Collins knew that Allen had a reputation for being hard to handle, but he had known Allen at the Infantry School in the 1930s and concluded that he possessed great leadership qualities. Collins put the 104th Infantry Division in the line almost adjacent to Huebner's division with an eye toward stimulating the two commands to greater competitive efforts.[10]

The Timberwolves brought with them the attached 750th Tank and 692d Tank Destroyer (towed) battalions. The 104th relieved the 1st Infantry Division in positions near Aachen the night of November 8–9, and the latter concentrated in what had been the southern end of its sector with a reduced frontage.

The VII Corps also received the 4th Infantry Division from V Corps, with the 70th Tank and 803d Tank Destroyer (SP) battalions attached. These D-day veterans moved into the Hürtgen Forest to replace the battered 9th Infantry Division (less the 47th Infantry Regiment, which remained in place attached to the Big Red One). Finally, First Army allocated to VII Corps a disproportionate share of its 240mm gun and 8-inch howitzer battalions.[11]

Collins called on the 1st Infantry Division to make his corps' main effort. He ordered the Big Red One to attack through the front of the 47th Infantry Regiment in the direction of Langerwehe and to seize Roer River crossings north of Düren.[12] The 3d Armored Division would initially play a supporting role to the infantry division's left.

The town of Gressenich and the Hamich–Nothberg Ridge were the 1st Infantry Division's initial terrain objectives. The division would then pinch out the 104th Infantry Division on the far left, and, when ordered by corps, the 3d Armored Division would seize the Hastenrath-Werth-Köttenich area.[13]

Collins ordered the 104th Infantry Division to focus its efforts north of Eschweiler and to clear the west bank of the Inde River—a small tributary of the Roer—from Inden to Weisweiler. The 4th ("Ivy Leaf") Infantry Division, on the corps' right, had instructions to capture Roer River crossings at Düren and to assist any 1st Infantry Division advance on Cologne.[14] These orders directed the division along a northeastward line of march that bypassed the Roer River dams. But they also incorporated the 4th Division back into the drive toward the objective—a focus that the 9th Infantry Division had lost during its failed push southward into the Hürtgen Forest during October.

The VII Corps was to attack through jungle, man-made and natural. To the north, industrial towns—Eschweiler and Weisweiler—provided the defenders with ample strongpoints. To the south lay the already blood-soaked Hürtgen Forest.

NINTH ARMY: THE NEW TEAM

Ninth Army at the beginning of November held a fourteen-mile front at the eastern end of the Dutch panhandle facing the Cologne plain. The left flank tied into the British Second Army. The right end linked with First Army's VII Corps one mile south of Würselen. The XIX Corps line for much of its length ran parallel to the Siegfried Line and the Roer River, and only at Geilenkirchen did the westernmost West Wall defenses still hold firm.[15]

On November 8, Major General Alvan Gillem Jr.'s XIII Corps became operational and took responsibility for the north end of the Ninth Army line. The corps consisted of two nearly untested outfits, the 102d and 84th Infantry divisions (each less one regimental combat team), and the 7th Armored Division, recently released by the British.[16]

Ninth Army had carefully hoarded its resources during the period of relative inactivity in late October and early November, but it was still short of signal, ordnance, and engineer supplies and some petroleum products. More alarming to commanders was the shortage of 111 medium tanks, roughly 15 percent of authorized strength. And artillery ammunition stocks were so low that Simpson personally approved allocations as far down as artillery brigades, and Ninth Army ordered the use of captured German munitions. Communications Zone (the oft-maligned Com Z) sometimes got the tonnage right but content wrong. In one case, Ninth Army received two railcars full of anvils instead of the engineer supplies requested.

Fortunately, repairs to rail lines through France offered hope of relief in December. And there were bright spots—85 percent of frontline troops, for example, received overshoes during November to protect them against trench foot.[17]

The initial plan had foreseen a simultaneous attack by the neighboring British XXX Corps across the Maastricht in the Nijmegan sector. That attack was scrapped , however, at a conference involving Monty, Bradley, and Simpson on October 31. Instead, the British would conduct minor operations to protect Ninth Army's flank.[18] (It may be that the XXX Corps commanding general, Lieutenant General Brian Horrocks, had exceeded his authority in agreeing to Simpson's informal request that he help out; as Horrocks later put it, his corps had become involved "almost by chance."[19])

The Germans in front of Simpson would not have to worry about much pressure farther north.

Major General Ray McLain's XIX Corps, with the veteran 29th and 30th Infantry and 2d Armored divisions, was Ninth Army's main punch. The 30th Infantry Division—initially strengthened by the 335th RCT from the 84th Infantry Division—had the immediate job of protecting VII Corps' northern flank. Hobbs ordered the division to pivot on its point of contact with VII Corps at Würselen; the division would swing like a giant door south and east to crush any resistance against the 104th Infantry Division.[20] The other two divisions, meanwhile, would drive eastward.

The XIII Corps had orders to work with the British to reduce Geilenkirchen. The 7th Armored Division protected the British right but was ready to exploit any bridgehead across the Roer.[21]

The Ninth Army's operational history of the coming offensive recorded: "High hopes were entertained at this period that the enemy's stronghold could be breached and he be beaten down before the harsh winter of northwestern Europe set in."[22]

Ninth Army's AAR described the terrain in its zone as "flat, open ground stretching forward to the Roer River. Numerous small towns and villages, as well as built-up areas, dotted the land. These were used by the Germans for strong defensive positions; many of the towns were mutually supporting in their defenses. Mining and agriculture shaped the nature of this river valley; huge slag piles, factories, and miners' houses were surrounded by beet and cabbage fields. The road net was good between the larger towns, but the minor roads were poor. Rainy weather reduced trafficability and roads were soon covered with mud. Traction was difficult off the roads."[23]

Buildings that offered good fields of fire had been reinforced. Some had been turned into firing points for tanks. Cellars were often as stoutly built as bunkers. Fire trenches, foxholes, communications trenches, and ditches surrounded the villages. Fields, roads, and direct avenues of approach were liberally sown with mines. The slag piles—which were up to 150 feet high—were fortified and used as observation posts. And aerial photographs revealed that three belts of fortifications—at two, four, and eight kilometers from the Roer—protected Linnich. Two such bands shielded Jülich.[24]

Ninth Army headquarters on November 15 reiterated its request to Bradley that he assign a mine exploder tank battalion to the army. Citing a recent report that a single German battalion had been issued fifty thousand antitank mines, Ninth Army cabled: "It is known that minefields are being placed around many villages and towns and in front of antitank ditches. . . . The action of our armored elements will be severely canalized due to natural terrain obstacles, to enemy-made tank obstacles, and to weather conditions, which are at their worst during the winter months. It is felt that every means conceivable must be fully utilized to assist armored units to overcome these obstacles and retain their all-essential mobility."[25] The 12th Army Group would not attach the 739th Tank Battalion, Special (Mine Exploder), until December 3.

THE OTHER SIDE OF THE HILL

The Germans would call this period the Third Battle of Aachen.

The *Fifth Panzer Army* commanding general, *General der Panzertruppen* Hasso-Eccard von Manteuffel, characterized his layered defenses in front of First and Ninth armies as a "'spiderweb' that caught the advancing or penetrating enemy." Troops always had a fallback line ready. Defensive strongpoints were carefully selected to maximize fields of fire for antitank guns. The antitank guns, moreover, were often colocated with artillery and antiaircraft guns in minefield-ringed "artillery protective positions" to provide mutual support. Adapting tactics used successfully on the Somme and in Flanders a generation earlier, von Manteuffel withdrew three-quarters of his combat troops from the frontline to a "super-MLR" a thousand meters to the rear; this would protect them from preparatory artillery fire before any big attack. The scheme also meant that local commanders had to quickly launch counterattacks once Allied soldiers began to advance.[26]

Fifth Panzer Army expected to face a November offensive, and the stakes were immensely high. The Germans had to hold the Americans west of the Roer River, or the Führer's planned massive counterstroke in the Ardennes would be preempted as the battle overran concentration areas. Indeed, the high command had factored the probability of a November attack by the Allies into its planning for the Ardennes operation. They just had not anticipated an attack on the scale of the one they got.[27]

***

The *XII SS Corps* controlled the *183d Volksgrenadier Division*, which was charged with defending Geilenkirchen. Just to the south, Köchling's *LXXXI Corps* would bear the brunt of the offensive.

Köchling expected the main weight of the American attack to strike at Würselen. Secondary attacks were anticipated south of Geilenkirchen and in the Stolberg-Schevenhütte area. Köchling still had the *12th* and *246th Volksgrenadier* and *3d Panzergrenadier divisions* under command. (The *246th Volksgrenadier* had reconstituted units lost in Aachen and fielded three regiments as usual.) Köchling's reserve consisted mainly of a reinforced battalion from each of the *12th* and *246th Volksgrenadier divisions*, two Tiger battalions (one securely bivouacked in underground garages between Immendorf and Setterich), an assault gun brigade, and a separate assault gun company.[28] The first half of November had provided the men with much-needed rest, and casualties had been low—on average only fifteen men killed or wounded per day in each division.[29]

The Wild Buffaloes of the *12th Volksgrenadier Division* had come through the October fighting in good order, despite sustaining heavy casualties. Late that month, the arrival of two fresh five-hundred-man battalions (one a reserve infantry battalion and the other a Luftwaffe fortress battalion) brought the division back up to fighting strength. Morale was good.

On November 1, Gerhard Engel received word that he had been promoted to *Generalmajor*. Also in early November, the division welcomed the leavening provided by 350 veterans returning from hospitals. Each veteran was worth three raw replacements in battle. On the dawn of the American offensive, the division had only six assault guns and fifteen 75mm antitank guns available for long-range tank defense, but the troops had more than twenty-two hundred panzerfausts, plus some hundred heavier bazookas.

The men could see signs in the first two weeks of November that action was near. These signs included a dramatic increase in flights by *Ami* artillery observation planes (which the men called "oysters"), smoke concentrations fired at German observation positions, shelling of artillery positions (although many remained safely hidden), and the sound of tanks moving into concentration areas. The men busily strengthened their minefields until no gaps remained. By November 14, the Germans were so certain that an offensive was in the offing that Model suggested it was time to pull troops back to the second defense line; antiaircraft units were ordered out of their quarters and into the field.[30]

Köchling assessed that the *3d Panzergrenadier Division*, north of Engel, had also done a good job of preparing for the expected attack. The division was at nearly full strength, and morale was excellent. Many of its panzers (twenty-two *Sturmgeschütz* assault guns and eight *Panzerjäger* IV tank killers, plus several more of each undergoing minor repairs) were safely parked underground, and its battalions were all at average strength or better. The division also had about twenty 75mm antitank guns, a handful of 88s, and nearly thirty-four hundred panzerfausts available. The *741st Panzerjäger Abteilung*, equipped with about ten Hetzers, was attached.

The *246th Volksgrenadier Division* (now commanded by *Oberst* Peter Körte) was less well positioned, but all battalions were nearly at full strength. Most of the replacements had arrived with little infantry training. Still, morale was good. Thirteen Hetzers, eighteen 75mm antitank guns, and three 88mm dual-purpose guns were available for antitank defense. The volksgrenadiers also were well equipped with panzerfausts.[31]

Generalleutnant Max Bork's *47th Volksgrenadier Division* arrived from Denmark to relieve the *12th Volksgrenadier Division* starting November 15. The division had been organized in late September from the remnants of the *47th Infantry Division* (destroyed at Mons) and been so spread out in Denmark that unit training had proved impossible. Half of the troops came from the Luftwaffe and the navy, a third were newly drafted men ages seventeen and eighteen, and the rest were soldiers with experience on the eastern front. All commanders and half of the junior officers had experience on the eastern front. One division veteran later lamented, "Unfortunately, this unit had no tradition and no local ties, i.e., the men came from all parts of the Reich." Moreover, the division's organic Hetzer tank destroyers would not arrive until November 20.[32] Nevertheless, the 1st Infantry Division would soon term these men "the most suicidally stubborn unit this division has encountered in its campaigns on the continent."[33]

Worried that the rotation of the two divisions would weaken his left wing, von Manteuffel on November 14 ordered *Major* Lange, commander of the *506th Schwere Panzer Abteilung* (with thirty-six battle-ready Royal Tigers), to stand prepared to bolster the *47th Volksgrenadier Division's* antitank defenses. Lange had been trying to deflect the assignment, arguing that it was one thing for thirty-ton American Shermans to operate in the hilly terrain south of the Weisweiler-Düren road but another thing entirely for his seventy-ton Royal Tigers to do the same.

A day later, Model intervened to order assault guns from the *3d Panzergrenadier Division* to support the volksgrenadiers rather than the Tigers.[34]

Karl Schacht, a *Landser* in the *115th Grenadier Regiment, 47th Volksgrenadier Division*, later recalled that his company covered the final distance from the railhead to Eschweiler on bicycles.[35] Parts of the division found themselves in deep woods—and they had never practiced woods fighting in nearly treeless Denmark.[36]

Fifth Panzer Army had only the *9th Panzer* and *15th Panzergrenadier divisions*, which constituted *XLVII Panzer Corps*, available in reserve. The corps was deployed in the München-Gladbach area, from where it could support both *XII SS* and *LXXXI corps*. Commanders were aware that additional heavy units were marshaling east of the sector, including the *116th Panzer* and the *2d* and *12th SS Panzer divisions*.[37]

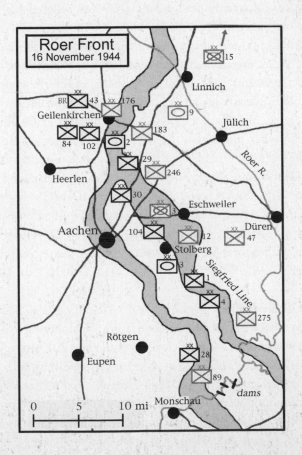

***

Seventh Army's LXXIV Corps manned the sector in front of the 4th Infantry Division with *Generalleutnant* Hans Schmidt's *275th Infantry Division.* Schmidt deployed forward two of his own grenadier regiments—*Oberst* Heinz's *984th* on the right and *Oberstleutnant* Fröster's *985th* (which included the fifty survivors of the fusilier battalion) in the center. On the left was *Regiment von Bottlenberg,* which consisted of a hodgepodge drawn from at least eight grenadier, training, and home defense battalions. Schmidt's third organic grenadier regiment, *Oberst* Feind's *983d,* had largely been parceled out to other division elements and sat in reserve with only some 250 troops. Schmidt reckoned his combat strength at 4,500 men.[38]

The *275th Infantry Division* (as was its neighbor to the south, the *89th Infantry Division*) was fairly newly reorganized and suffered from improvization, gaps in training, and missing equipment. Clothing was inadequate for the harsh conditions; this would cause unusually high numbers of nonbattle casualties in the coming weeks. Officers and NCOs left something to be desired. The artillery regiments were outfitted with an eclectic mix of twenty-five German, Italian, French, and Russian guns and had little ammunition for some of them. Nevertheless, the division had been in battle in the Hürtgen since early October and knew the ropes. Morale was surprisingly good, although the men were tired. The *275th* was well supplied with antitank defenses, including one 88mm and twenty-two 75mm guns and twenty-one assault guns. The *682d Schwere Panzerjäger Abteilung,* with twenty-seven towed 88mm PAK 43 antitank guns, was attached to the division, and some seventy-six nondivisional artillery pieces were on call. As well, an assault gun brigade with between a dozen and fifteen combat-ready panzers was available in reserve.[39]

INTO THE MUD: NOVEMBER 16–22

Bad flying weather delayed the offensive from November 11 to 15. Each day, a code word was passed down the chain of command that indicated a twenty-four-hour delay.[40] Hodges was depressed by the weather, but the IX TAC commanding general, Major General Elwood (Pete) Quesada, told him, "Don't worry about that, General. Our planes will be there when you jump off, even if we have to crash-land every damned one of them on the way back."[41]

November 16 dawned overcast and cloudy, but as the morning wore on, the skies cleared. "Man, look at that ball of fire," Hodges told Bradley. "But don't look too hard; you'll wear it out—or worse yet, maybe chase it away!"[42] At 1105 hours, according to the 104th Infantry Division's unofficial history, men on the ground heard a continuous building roar, "like Niagara Falls."[43] The throaty noise came from thousands of bomber engines. Air strikes commenced at 1145 hours.

Allied air forces conducted a preliminary bombardment, Operation Queen, that represented the largest close-support effort of the war. Different types of air strikes were used in the First and Ninth army zones—carpet-bombing of areas and "patch" bombing of specific targets, respectively. The goal in both cases was to destroy prepared positions, kill enemy personnel, and disrupt communications and supply.

The American Eighth Air Force contributed 1,204 heavy bombers and 485 fighter-bombers to the strike. The Royal Air Force (RAF) supplied 1,188 heavy bombers. Mediums and fighter-bombers from the 9th Bombardment Division of the Ninth Air Force and fighter-bombers of the IX and XXIX Tactical Air commands joined in.

Ninth Army marked its lines with colored panels to prevent accidental bombing of American troops, and it designated targets with colored smoke shells. First Army, which had experienced two accidental bombings of its lines during the opening stages of Operation Cobra—the breakout from Normandy—took far more elaborate precautions. Its antiaircraft guns fired red shells into the air along the line; silver barrage balloons were floated to two thousand feet in altitude at three-hundred-yard intervals four thousand yards to the rear of the line; colored panels were laid; and the air command was induced to place radio beacons near the frontlines. Moreover, bomb bays were opened over the English Channel, and bomb racks were locked while over American lines to prevent any repeat of accidental releases experienced during Cobra.

Ground artillery supported the air strikes by firing at all known flak sites. The 9th Bombardment Division credited the suppressing fire with reducing battle damage to its aircraft from an anticipated 40 percent to 12.5 percent.

On D-day, the RAF dropped 5,640 tons of bombs at Jülich, Düren, and Heinsberg, to which the Eighth Air Force added 3,679 tons dumped on Eschweiler, Weisweiler, Dürwiss, Hehlrath, and Langerwehe. *Major* Fritz Vogelsang, *116th Panzer Division*, wrote in his diary, "An endless stream of heavy bombers is flooding the country. . . . The ground is shaking, and the windows clink without letup. Road crossings, villages, all more or less prominent points are under fierce artillery fire. The front itself is a roaring hell."[44]

Düren, Jülich, and other fortified towns were largely destroyed. In Düren alone, three thousand soldiers and civilians were killed, and the massive destruction created a wave of refugees deeper into Germany.[45] Moreover, the *47th Volksgrenadier Division* was relieving the *12th Volksgrenadier Division* at the precise time of the bombardment, and both units suffered casualties and disorganization.[46] (The exchange was put on hold, and the *47th's 103d Grenadier Regiment* was subordinated to Engel.)[47]

But these were all targets well behind the frontlines.

Reports of the bombing began to pour into *LXXXI Corps*. Soon, *General der Infanterie* Friedrich Köchling felt the ground shaking at his headquarters in Niederzier, just east of the Roer. A flood of thoughts ran through his mind. But all of the orders had already been issued, the attack had long been expected. It was up to the men in the trenches.[48]

Despite the elaborate precautions, a few bombs fell close enough to American positions to spray them with shrapnel. All men had been ordered to take cover, however, and few were hurt.[49]

D-DAY AT GROUND LEVEL: VII CORPS RUMBLES

Launching the 12th Army Group's main effort, VII Corps attacked at 1245 hours against initially light resistance.[50] High explosives destroyed some German artillery OPs, and an unprecedented amount of smoke blinded others. German artillery quickly had to shift to unobserved preplanned fire patterns.[51] The reader will recall that the main German strength was sheltered a kilometer to the rear.

The forward elements of Engel's *12th Volksgrenadier Division* bore the brunt of the VII Corps attack. The *89th Grenadier* and *27th Fusilier regiments* stood in the path of the 3d Armored and 104th Infantry divisions. The *48th Grenadier Regiment* opposed the 1st Infantry Division.[52]

Timberwolves Tackle Stolberg

On the American left, the 104th Infantry Division at first attacked almost due north to clear Stolberg, grab Eschweiler, and cross the Inde River. Closest to Aachen, the 413th Infantry Regiment ran into extensive minefields in the Verlautenheide area and made little headway.

The 414th Infantry Regiment, on the division's right, had perhaps the toughest job: capturing the well-fortified Hill 287—the Donnerberg—which loomed above Stolberg to the east and was held by elements of the *89th Grenadier Regiment*. The German defenses rode out the air and artillery bombardment, and all day long Engel's men threw back rushes by Lieutenant Colonel Leon Rouge's 3d Battalion. Late in the day, 1st Battalion, to Rouge's right, struggled forward a mere four hundred yards before buttoning up at 2300 hours.

The third regiment of the Timberwolf Division had orders to end the stalemate that had existed in Stolberg since September. A battalion from the 415th Infantry Regiment eked out nine hundred yards south of Stolberg, and the 3d Battalion opened three days of house-to-house fighting to evict the *27th Fusilier Regiment* from the town. As the Big Red One had done in Aachen, the GIs worked closely and patiently with tanks, tank destroyers, and SP 155mm guns, which blasted entries into each successive building.[53]

Although the Timberwolves had tasted combat under British command, this was their shakeout action as a full-fledged American infantry division, with the usual attachment of a tank and a tank destroyer battalion. With these attachments, a transportation-rich American infantry division was the rough equivalent of a full-strength German panzergrenadier division.[54]

But infantry divisions since the Normandy invasion had run into coordination problems whenever riflemen and armor unfamiliar with each other had to work together closely on the battlefield. Neither partner had really trained for such coordination before leaving the States, and only the gradual accumulation of understanding and trust under fire led to smooth cooperation and reduced casualties.

Lieutenant Stan Zimmerman led the Shermans of the 2d Platoon, Company B, into the 750th Tank Battalion's first day of combat. The company was attached to Colonel Anthony Touart's 414th Infantry Regiment, which was on the Timberwolf Division's right at the Donnerberg. Zimmerman's platoon was working with the 2d Battalion. He later recalled:

It was midafternoon, and armed with my trusty 1:25,000 map I mounted my tank and started looking for the battalion. While going down this dirt road, I was watching a P-47, which had just finished a bombing mission, but he didn't drop all his bombs. One was dangling from its rack by one hook, and as he approached me, the bomb separated from the aircraft and appeared to be coming directly at me. I learned early the helpless feeling one has in a bombing situation. Fortunately, the thing landed about two hundred yards to my left.

I was told that the infantry was down this road, but I didn't see anyone. I came to a patch of woods, and just beyond the woods were some mounds of dirt maybe eight feet high in an "L" shape. I still had not located the infantry, but I figured they must be in the woods.

Tank commanders had to have their hatch open because it is almost impossible to see anything if you are buttoned up. So I'm looking around, and suddenly from three different locations on the crests of the mounds of dirt popped up three Krauts with panzerfausts. They all fired in consecutive order. The first spittoon traveled down the full length of the right side, missing the tank by about one foot, and the second exploded just behind the tank.

At this point, I told my driver, John Murphy, to back up some. Just as I got that out of my mouth, the third spittoon exploded just in front of the tank. John, in his excitement, let out on the clutch too quickly and killed the engine. One thing that was running through my mind was a little ditty we learned in OCS [officer candidate school]. "Here lie the bones of Lieutenant Jones, the pride of our institution. 'Twas his first night and his first fight, he used the school solution."

Fortunately, we had an M4A3 tank, powered by a 500 HP Ford engine, which restarted easily, and we backed up past the edge of the woods out of panzerfaust range. The infantry was in the woods, and due to their inexperience with tanks, they didn't give me any cover. I learned another dear lesson. You do not get out ahead of your infantry in a close quarter situation.[55]

Despite such miscues, elements of the 414th Infantry Regiment by the end of the day had pushed a thousand yards beyond the Donnerberg's flank.[56]

The Spearhead Hits a Wall

The 3d Armored Division history recorded, "It was doughboy weather, mean and muddy. . . . There wasn't much talk that day: the combat commanders scowled and chewed their lips. The men waited impassively, but they knew very well what the attack would mean. They knew all about the way of a

Sherman in soft ground. The Kraut was a good professional soldier and had plenty of dual-purpose 88s—each of which was capable of holing a medium tank from frontal drive to exhaust. The odds were not especially reassuring. . . . The attack jumped off at 1300 as Division artillery hammered targets to the direct front and rockets cut flaming arcs in the air. The tank tracks spun hard, gripped, and sheets of water flew to the right and left."[57]

The Spearhead Division's CCB initially pushed two columns northeastward; each was made up of a tank battalion and a company of armored infantry. The first, Task Force Lovelady, found a thinly defended route of advance and captured Werth and Köttenich before dark. A panzer on Hill 232 near Hamich, in the 1st Infantry Division's area, accounted for five Shermans before the remainder could knock it out.

The second column, Task Force Mills, hooked westward and almost immediately lost two of the nineteen tanks in its spearhead—one that struck a mine, and a flail tank destroyed by antitank fire. (Belton Cooper, who was an ordnance officer with the division, reports that mines disabled a total of fifteen CCB Shermans that day.) As the tanks swept by Scherpenseel toward Hastenrath, *Hauptmann* Hans Zeplien's Wild Buffalo gunners (*89th Grenadier Regiment*)—some firing from woods in the 104th Infantry Division's zone of advance—claimed thirteen more tanks. The depleted spearhead reached the southern outskirts of Hastenrath, but there were no infantry available to secure the town.

Lieutenant Henry Earl commanded the four tanks that reached a field outside Hastenrath. He later offered a running description of the battle:

> As the tanks came through the minefield, they took up their attacking formation, allowing the maximum frontal fire as well as maximum flanking fire. They flushed out and destroyed a reinforced infantry company that was covering the minefield with small-arms fire. In skirting the left flank of Scherpenseel, it was necessary to go between the town and a fortified building. . . . As the lead tank passed this building, at a distance of about fifty feet, two Germans appeared in a window, one with a rifle, and one with a panzerfaust. They both fired. The tank commander [Earl], who had his head out of the turret hatch, ducked a fraction of a second in time. The panzerfaust struck the tank, rocking it. The penetration was in a non-vital spot. . . . The tank commander hit the

traversing switch, swung the gun around to the window, and fired two high-explosive shells. . . . The entire action took less than ten seconds.

[Earl] slipped in behind the town of Scherpenseel, using the buildings in the background to help cover the movement of his tanks. He spotted a slight movement behind the remains of a shelled-out building, as did the commander of the tank following on his left flank. Both fired. Debris and parts of an antitank gun flew into the air.

[The four remaining tanks reached Hastenrath and deployed to cover roads into town.] As the minutes ticked away, tension mounted and mounted. . . . [Earl] peered from his open hatch, desperately searching for some movement. His gun was trained down the main street. From a pile of debris not more than a hundred yards away came a tremendous blast and at the same time an ear-splitting crack as an armor-piercing shell missed the top of the turret and his head by inches. The gunner had seen the blast at the same time. The gun was slightly lowered and fired. The tank had a round in the breech. The antitank gun had to reload. . . . The gun crew, who were lying down, must have worked the gun into position. . . .

The reports began to come in. [Three] tanks had seven rounds each, the others six rounds [each]. [Earl] called battalion. There was a low whistling at the other end, and then: "We're trying to get in to you, and we'll try some way to get some ammunition down to you."[58]

Earl's tank was soon disabled by antitank fire from long range.

Worried about the 104th Infantry Division's lack of progress—which exposed his left flank—Brigadier General Boudinot deployed infantry, antitank guns, and tank destroyers to cover the hole. He also was somewhat concerned that his advance had outpaced the Big Red One, on his right.

Boudinot concluded that he had gotten a major break that day, as bad as it had been. The lead personnel from the *47th Volksgrenadier Division* had already arrived to organize the relief of Engel's *89th Grenadier Regiment*, and the Germans were off balance.[59]

The Big Red One: Main Effort within the Main Effort
In the center of VII Corps' zone, Lieutenant Colonel Edmond Driscoll's 1st Battalion from the 1st Infantry Division's 16th Infantry Regiment attacked at

noon toward Hamich with two companies abreast. The *48th Grenadier Regiment* resisted fiercely from log- and dirt-covered dugouts, as well as with heavy artillery fire. Progress was plodding.[60]

At 1600 hours, the battalion beat off a counterattack by fifty German infantrymen three hundred yards west of Hamich. Driscoll tried to slip his men into town after dark, but direct and indirect shellfire from heavy guns rained down. "The artillery did not let up for two or three days," commented Driscoll later. Tanks tried to move forward in support but bogged down on the muddy trails through the thick woods.[61]

Colonel George Smythe's 47th Infantry Regiment, meanwhile, advanced toward Gressenich. The men in Lieutenant Colonel James Allgood's 1st Battalion were raring to attack after spending two months in the woods in foxholes that were often filled with rain and snow to within six inches of the top. The men had been under nearly constant artillery fire—a captured German fire control map revealed two company command posts in their exact locations.[62]

Five battalions of artillery joined by mortars pounded Gressenich before the assault. Tanks and tank destroyers fired on identified OPs, such as the church steeple. After rolling easily through the village of Buchhausen, the GIs left the woods and headed down a long, open slope toward the objective. Self-propelled guns and small arms opened up from town, and the advance slowed. Third Armored Division tanks rolling toward Mausbach, west of Gressenich, distracted the German gunners for a while, and doughs from Company C reached the outskirts of town.[63]

In town, the infantry encountered tough house-to-house resistance from about a hundred soldiers of the 1st Battalion, *48th Grenadier Regiment*. Allgood observed, "They were good troops, better than most [we] had met while crossing France." A platoon of Shermans from the 745th Tank Battalion tried to move up in support, but they first encountered antitank guns (eventually dispatched by 4.2-inch mortar fire), then two ran over mines.[64]

By day's end, Engel rated casualties in the *89th Grenadier* and *27th Fusilier regiments* as "appalling." His *48th Grenadier Regiment*, meanwhile, had also suffered considerably and been kicked out of its initial positions. Nonetheless, his men had been able to fall back from their forward defense lines to the prepared main defense line in good order, and those positions were still intact.[65]

Forest Fighting for the 4th

On VII Corps' right flank deep in the Hürtgen Forest, the 4th Infantry Division was beginning perhaps the most brutal segment of the entire offensive. The division recorded in its narrative history: "In many places, visibility did not exceed ten yards. Across the front were stretched belts of mines and barbed wire rigged with booby traps. Dug-in machine guns were set up to cover the entire area with interlocking fire. Artillery, doubly dangerous in the woods because of tree bursts, was accurately laid on every conceivable objective. The weather was extremely unfavorable; constant rain, snow, and near-freezing temperatures were serious impediments."

Sergeant Mack Morriss added a grunt's-eye view in a piece he wrote for *Yank*, the newspaper by and for soldiers: "The bodies of the firs begin close to the ground so that each fir interlocks its body with another. At the height of a man standing there is a solid mass of dark, impenetrable green. But at the height of a man crawling there is room, and it is like a green cave, low-roofed and forbidding."[66]

The division during the week before D-day organized schools for company-grade officers in woods fighting, map reading, and the adjustment of artillery fire. Communications teams, litter bearers, medics, and 81mm mortar platoons received special training for the anticipated difficulties ahead. Patrols probed the German line.

The 12th Infantry Regiment had been committed on the right wing in relief of the exhausted 28th Infantry Division's 109th Infantry Regiment on November 8. The 12th Infantry was in close contact with the enemy well before the offensive began, and by November 15 it had already suffered nearly a thousand casualties from frequent counterattacks and constant shellfire. The regiment nonetheless was able to jump off with the rest of the division on November 16.

Some outfits made minor gains, and others did not. The 8th Infantry Regiment's 2d Battalion almost immediately ran into a band of triple concertina wire covered by small arms and mortars. The two assault companies—E and F—found themselves pinned down on what amounted to a shooting range for the hidden German gunners. Company G advanced in support, only to be pinned down, too. Normandy veterans said they had never experienced such intense shelling. All company commanders and most platoon leaders and NCOs were killed or wounded. Bangalore torpedoes were brought forward but failed to produce a breach, and the battalion was ordered to dig in at the line of departure.

The 12th Infantry Regiment's 3d Battalion also ended the day at its line of departure. Only the 22d Infantry Regiment encountered surprisingly light resistance and moved ahead over the rough terrain for a mile gain.[67]

The men holding up the Ivy Leaf Division were from the *275th Infantry Division's 984th* and *985th Grenadier regiments.* Their commanding general, Hans Schmidt, who had developed a deep professional admiration for the 9th Infantry Division when it fought in this sector, thought the 4th Infantry Division's advance "unsteady and hesitating." Schmidt later commented, "[The enemy] often took a wrong turn and got into our flanking fire."[68]

The Ivy Leaf Division immediately discovered that there was no point in planning more than twenty-four hours ahead. Patrols were never able to advance more than a few hundred yards, and German dispositions usually remained obscure until they exposed themselves by fire. New objectives therefore were assigned each night.[69]

XIX CORPS KICKS OFF WITH LESS THUNDER

The XIX Corps was ready to roll at 1245 hours, per orders. From north to south, the 2d Armored and 29th and 30th Infantry divisions jumped off without the usual artillery preparation in a bid to achieve tactical surprise. Farther north, XIII Corps' 102d Infantry Division also pushed off near Immendorf to cover the 2d Armored Division's left flank.[70]

Fighter-bombers from the XXIX TAC had been isolating and softening up the battlefield since the beginning of November. Aircraft struck fortified villages with incendiary, napalm, and high-explosive bombs whenever reconnaissance indicated activity in them. Marshaling yards, supply depots, and rail chokepoints received continual attention.[71]

As in much of the VII Corps sector, initial resistance was relatively light—at least everywhere except Würselen.[72] But in some cases, "initial" lasted only minutes.

Hell on Wheels Makes Tracks

Major General Ernest Harmon, commanding the 2d Armored Division, was extremely concerned that the downpours that had delayed D-day would create mud so deep that his tanks would bog down. Harmon personally mounted a Sherman in the division's concentration area west of the Würm and drove around the fields. The tank could manage only two to three miles per hour in low gear. Still worried, he turned to the tank commander and asked, "Can we make it, sergeant?"

"Yes, sir."

Harmon was satisfied. If the sergeant and his Sherman could make it, the division could, too. Harmon told Simpson that the mud would not pose an insurmountable problem.[73]

The 2d Armored Division, reinforced by the 102d Infantry Division's 406th RCT; the 2d Battalion, 119th Infantry Regiment; and Squadron B, 2d Fife and Forfar Yeomanry, attacked toward Puffendorf and Gereonsweiler. Because of Hell on Wheels' narrow front, only CCB participated in the first thrust. The division's mission was to sever the Germans' last north-south communications lines west of the Roer, then reassemble to cross the river through a bridgehead to be established by the 29th Infantry Division.

The *183d* and *246th Volksgrenadier divisions* could offer little resistance as Brigadier General Isaac White's CCB overran four towns during the afternoon. By day's end, the combat command had easily taken its initial objectives, including high ground next to Puffendorf. The *246th Volksgrenadiers* reported to Köchling, "The hole can no longer be mended."

Only at Apweiler, where German guns in two minutes knocked out seven Shermans crawling slowly through mud, did the division suffer a significant setback.[74] *Generalleutnant* Lange had taken the risk of rushing his reserve—his fusilier battalion and Hetzer-equipped *Panzerjäger* company—to Apweiler in broad daylight. It was these assault guns that claimed the CCB Shermans after their crews had watched patiently until the Americans were within three hundred yards before opening fire.[75]

Combat Command A waited for the 29th Infantry Division to clear the town of Setterich and capture a crossing there over a major antitank ditch before it entered the fight. Harmon's impatience with the slow speed of this operation would build over the next few days. Queries to Major General Charles Gerhardt, commanding the 29th Infantry Division, on the subject from the corps commander and his deputy suggest that Harmon asked them to intervene, too. Gerhardt, an old cavalryman who relentlessly rode his National Guard division, invariably then applied heat of his own to his regimental commanders.[76]

Blue and Gray Finds Setterich a Tough Nut

The 29th Infantry Division attacked with two regiments abreast deployed in columns of battalions and cut into the *246th Volksgrenadier Division* against initially light and inaccurate small-arms fire. That changed soon enough. Some two hundred yards short of the German outpost line of resistance, south of Setterich, the 115th Infantry Regiment came under withering and interlocking mortar and small-arms fire. The Germans had registered artillery and mortars on the small depressions, which offered some cover. By dark, Company C was pinned down and reduced to three officers and seventeen men.[77]

Lieutenant Joseph Blalock, a platoon leader in Company C, reported, "The crossfire that struck us at the top of the second rise was the most intense and accurate small-arms fire that I have ever encountered. We were within one hundred fifty yards of some of the guns, but we could not locate them." Lieutenant Chester Slaughter, a platoon commander in Company D, added: "After the intense fire struck us, the only way we could move about at all was to follow the beet rows. We tried to assemble the men but were unable to maintain control because we could not rise up to see where we were or what was happening. . . . There was smoke and haze on the ground, and mortar and artillery shells were falling among us constantly. The Germans fired mortars and artillery so that the shells fell at the same time, and the fact that you could hear the artillery shells whistle as they came in but could not hear the mortar shells until they exploded added to the agony of the situation. The men threw away their packs because the Germans saw them above the beet tops and shot at them."[78]

The neighboring 175th Infantry Regiment encountered similar resistance and did not reach its objectives. The GIs ran into bitter resistance at Bettendorf and Siersdorf. "It was 'head on' stuff that was met," recorded the division's AAR.[79]

Old Hickory Finds a Buzz Saw in Würselen

The 30th Infantry Division attacked with its 119th Infantry Regiment in the pivotal position on the right with orders to take Würselen. The regiment CO, Colonel Edwin Sutherland, had only two of his battalions available; the third had been attached to the 2d Armored Division. Whereas the rest of the division had rested before the offensive, the 119th was in constant contact with the enemy in Würselen—the men called the neighborhood "Bloody Triangle"—and the outfit expected a hard fight. Prisoners indicated that the men faced elements of Denkert's tough *3d Panzergrenadier Division*.[80]

Lieutenant Colonel Courtney Brown's 3d Battalion had the job of getting into Würselen. Brown arrayed Companies K, I, and L in order from left to right. The first two faced some five hundred yards of relatively open terrain laced with minefields. Company I fronted on a portion of the town itself that had been shelled into rubble.

The defenders were not surprised. German mortar fire crashed into the ranks as the GIs advanced to their start line.

The doughs moved out at 1245 hours. The two companies attempting to cross the open ground were pinned down by machine-gun fire from pillboxes north of Würselen. Company K managed to crawl forward only 400 yards during the afternoon, and Company I crossed a mere 150 yards.

Captain Leslie Stanford, commanding Company L, attacked with two platoons supported by his third. Sherman tanks from Company C, 743d Tank Battalion, stood ready to assist once the doughs had secured the first road junction. As the two platoons moved out, vicious automatic weapons crossfire from a rubble pile some two hundred yards to the left and a stone structure to the right drove the men to ground. Stanford directed mortar fire onto the emplacements, but the rounds did no harm to the thick overhead cover. Return mortar fire dropped among the riflemen, who were furiously digging for cover.

Company L was also stopped cold. That night, the line of departure served as the MLR. And 3d Battalion's inability to move prevented any action by its running mate, the 1st Battalion. The *3d Panzergrenadiers* had held in Würselen.[81]

The 117th Infantry Regiment, however, achieved its objectives for the day. Mariadorf, which had defied the regiment in October, fell, as did Mariagrube. The 120th Infantry Regiment cut through German defenses at Euchen.[82]

By dark, XIX Corps had registered gains of one-half to two miles along most of its front.[83] But all divisions were heavily engaged. Casualties had been relatively light—30 killed, 241 wounded, and 30 missing—in exchange for more than 800 prisoners taken, plus an unknown number of enemy killed and wounded. But the stiffening resistance suggested that the defenders planned more than a delaying action.[84]

INITIAL GERMAN REACTIONS

About dusk on November 16, von Manteuffel ordered a general withdrawal to the second defense line and placed a *Kampfgruppe* from the *116th Panzer Division* at the disposal of *LXXXI Corps*. That night, *Fifth Panzer Army* shifted its reserve *15th Panzergrenadier Division* into the area south of Erkelenz and the *9th Panzer Division* west of Linnich so they would be available in a timely fashion west of the Roer River. Von Manteuffel detached *Major* Lange's Royal Tigers from *LXXXI Corps* and attached them to the *9th Panzer Division*.[85] Perhaps, in light of the alarming reports from Puffendorf of a 2d Armored Division breakthrough, von Manteuffel already had something in mind.

The *Fifteenth Army* command group had arrived in Königshoven from southern Holland on November 15 to relieve the *Fifth Panzer Army* staff, which was to participate in the Ardennes offensive. (*General der Infanterie* Gustav Adolf von Zangen actually took command for one hour before handing it back to von Manteuffel upon the news that the American offensive had begun.) *Fifteenth Army* was operating under the cover name of "Group von Manteuffel." Because of the American attack, the two staffs overlapped until November 22, giving von Zangen and his team time to familiarize themselves with the situation.[86]

Born on November 7, 1892, in Darmstadt, von Zangen was a World War I veteran who had been called back to the army from a police command in 1935. He had led an infantry regiment during the fighting before Moscow in 1941, where he won the Knight's Cross. The general had served subsequently in France and northern Italy in increasingly important positions. Hitler had selected him to take command of *Fifteenth Army*, effective August 20, 1944. Before moving to the American sector, von Zangen had held the Schelde—Antwerp's opening to the sea—against determined British and Canadian attacks for two months. Von Zangen had personal experience with losses in combat—both of his sons had died, one in France and the other in Russia.[87]

As von Zangen surveyed the front, he realized he faced two dangerous thrusts by the Americans. The first, conducted by Ninth Army, was directed from the Würm River valley toward Linnich and through Aldenhoven toward Jülich. The second axis of attack was that of First Army, which had struck the *LXXXI Corps* in an apparent effort to drive up the Autobahn toward the Roer north of Düren. The German command was mystified—but relieved—that the British were quiescent instead of striking the *XII SS Corps* around Heinsberg. This reduced the need to draw on resources being secretly hoarded for the Ardennes offensive.

VII CORPS STARTS MOVING

The VII Corps renewed the attack at 0800 hours on November 17. The weather had again turned sour and shut down virtually all air support.[88] Each of the corps' divisions was by now embroiled in its own fairly coherent battle.

Timberwolves in the Hills

The 104th Infantry Division again made few gains despite its battle slogan: "Nothing in Hell can stop the Timberwolves!" One battalion crossed into the 3d Armored Division's zone to close a gap in the vicinity of Hastenrath.[89] The rest of the doughs and the 750th Tank Battalion battered themselves against tenacious and fortified defenses, particularly in the streets of Stolberg and on the commanding heights of the Donnerberg, overlooking the industrial town.[90]

Lieutenant Stan Zimmerman's tankers and the infantry had finally hooked up. "The tanks formed a base of fire and gave the infantry covering machine-gun fire to keep the Krauts' heads down until the infantry was ready to pop over the crest. That accomplished, I moved my tank forward to give covering fire for the next objective. I planned to take a position at the left-hand edge of the mound that was perpendicular to my front. That was, I discovered, an ideal place for an antitank mine. The Krauts didn't miss this opportunity, and my tank was disabled. I dismounted my crew, and then moved to my number two tank. The rest of that day, we failed to gain any ground."[91]

In the first three days of helping the infantry roust the enemy from numerous pillboxes and fortified basements, the 750th lost seventeen tanks. (The "seven-five-zero," as the men called their outfit, lost thirty-five tanks in the first seven days of fighting, an astonishing 61 percent of the battalion's total medium tank losses during the European campaign.) The battalion's AAR specifically drew attention to inexperience as a contributing factor in the losses.[92] Stan Zimmerman would later comment, "The infantry that we were supporting had not worked with tanks before, so we were not the only inexperienced personnel on the field. We learned and we learned fast, or we didn't make it."[93]

As far as Collins was concerned, the Timberwolf Division was "slow in showing its mettle" in its first action with VII Corps. Collins told Terry Allen that he expected better results.[94]

The weather turned back in the Americans' favor on November 18, and the IX TAC flew continuous close air support missions for the 104th, 1st, and 4th Infantry divisions. (The *LXXXI Corps* would report that evening, "Strong enemy fighter-bomber forces continuously struck the front and extraordinarily complicated our defense. . . . Promised support from the Luftwaffe did not appear.") A group of fighter-bombers on armed reconnaissance was on call for each division. Ground operations again kicked off at 0800 hours.[95]

The 413th Infantry Regiment finally forced its way past heavy resistance and minefields at Verlautenheide. If nothing got in the way, the regiment had a good chance of bypassing Stolberg to the west and reaching the first key objective, Eschweiler.

The 415th Infantry Regiment, in the division's center, was still stuck in the streets of Stolberg. An impromptu truce broke out when Lieutenant Donowski of Company K put on a Red Cross helmet and advanced with a medic to treat wounded men. A single shot rang out, then all firing ceased on both sides. Germans and Americans laid down their weapons, tied white handkerchiefs on their arms, and for half an hour cooperated giving aid and evacuating the wounded. Then they picked up their weapons and went back to the business of killing.[96]

The 414th Infantry Regiment, on the right, worked through woods near the Donnerberg for twelve hundred yards and came abreast of the 3d Armored Division.[97] More importantly, the regiment managed to clear the strategic heights of Hill 287, as related later by Wes Gaab, a machine-gunner in Company M:

> The hill was dominated by a huge bunker, which some say was three stories deep and surrounded by numerous pillboxes and connecting trenches. . . .

The attack resumed early in the morning. . . . Through heavy fire, countless mines, and booby-traps, a small group of GIs somehow made it to the top of the hill. We found refuge under a knocked out Tiger tank, which the Germans had used as a pillbox. There were two dead Germans still inside the tank. We were less than one hundred yards to the left of the bunker. The dirt under the tank had been excavated and provided just enough room for the five of us. It was about midday when we finally got to the top. Then something strange occurred. We suddenly realized that it was all quiet. The shooting on both sides had stopped. We assumed 2d Battalion had successfully taken Hill 287. We even cracked out the K-rations to celebrate. But if 2d Battalion had taken the hill, why were there only five of us here—where were the others? We learned later that they had pulled back to a row of battered houses at the foot of the hill.

I was at the end of our under-tank fortress, so I was elected to go out and take a look around. I borrowed an M-1 from someone since my sidearm was a .45 and we didn't even have the machine gun set up. I crawled over to what looked like a low coop that could have housed chickens or rabbits. I rested the M-1 on the top and looked around. There was no one to be seen until a head slowly appeared above the top of the bunker. He was a German soldier using binoculars. He wasn't looking at us to his right, but down the hill in the direction from which we had come. I shot him. Within minutes, I saw Germans pouring out of the rear of the bunker. They were in a trench with only their heads and shoulders showing above ground. I fired on them with the M-1, and the heads would disappear only to reappear in a matter of seconds. They were in a big hurry to get out of here. [The *12th Volksgrenadier Division* reported the bunker cut off but assured higher command that an effort would be made to recapture it.[98]]

When the last had left the bunker, I returned to the tank and told the other four what had happened. We were sure it was all over for us. We waited for the Germans to surround us, but they never came. What did come was even more frightening. The clanking, rumbling sound of a tank coming up behind us. He put two rounds into our tank at point blank range. Miraculously we weren't even scratched. He didn't do the two dead Germans in the tank any good. We then heard him back down the hill and all was quiet again.

We remained under the tank for the rest of the day with infrequent trips out to see if we could locate any of our buddies, but there were none to be seen. We didn't realize it at the time, but we five GIs had taken and held Stolberg Hill 287.[99]

The good weather persisted through the morning of November 19. It was enough to allow the IX TAC to fly another 450 ground-support missions but not enough to improve the mud underfoot.[100]

The 104th Infantry Division nonetheless gained traction and made more substantial progress along its line. The 413th Infantry Regiment pushed twenty-five hundred yards and by midday had patrols on the outskirts of Eschweiler. One battalion had almost reached Rohe by evening. The 414th Infantry Regiment fought forward a thousand yards through woods.

For Engel, the day was one of serious problems on his right wing. With the Donnerberg lost to the Timberwolf Division, and the neighboring *3d Panzergrenadier Division* falling back, his defenses at Stolberg were taking on the characteristics of a worrisome salient. Engel decided to withdraw his MLR in Stolberg to prepared positions on the northern fringe.[101] As a consequence, the 415th Infantry Regiment advanced a thousand yards to the northern edge of town in continuing house-to-house fighting.[102]

A Near Thing at Hastenrath

As of November 17, the 3d Armored Division's Task Force Mills had a major scrap on its hands with the *89th Grenadier Regiment* at Hastenrath and Scherpenseel. The rest of the task force had worked its way forward to the tiny armored spearhead. The Americans held part of both towns, and bitter street fighting surged back and forth. Brigadier General Boudinot ordered CCB's reserve forward to help Task Force Mills, but the troops quickly became entangled with bypassed Germans. Once the troops shook loose, they were pinned down by artillery fire. Mills' tank battalion by evening was reduced to eight medium and seven light tanks and was fighting for its life as the Germans tried to close with and destroy the surviving vehicles.

Boudinot urged Lieutenant Colonel Mills to hold at all costs and ordered additional tanks forward to help the combat command's reserves get through. Mills was operating in a fishbowl, however. Combat Command B was still well ahead of the infantry divisions on both flanks, and Mills' men were taking fire from commanding ground in three directions. The fighting continued until 2130 hours.[103]

The *LXXXI Corps* commander, *General der Infanterie* Friedrich Köchling, rushed the *47th Volksgrenadier Division's 103d Grenadier Regiment* to Scherpenseel during the evening to strengthen the *89th Grenadier Regiment's* line. (The *47th Division* commander, *Generalleutnant* Max Bork, suffered a leg wound during the morning but was still in charge of his division.) The *89th Grenadiers* were given a reduced front covering Hastenrath and the slopes to the west, which allowed Engel to begin assembling a reserve near Eschweiler—which was under growing threat from the Timberwolf Division.[104]

On November 18 in Hastenrath, the 3d Armored Division's Lt. Col. Herbert Mills fell victim to a shell fragment at 0600 hours during street fighting. Combat Command B's reserves finally reached the exhausted men from Mills' task force (temporarily commanded directly by the regimental CO, Colonel John Welborn) at about 0900 hours. The task force pushed the *103d Grenadier Regiment* out of Scherpenseel and the *89th Grenadier Regiment* out of Hastenrath, and by 1130 hours the Americans were mopping up and wondering whether they had enough surviving infantry to hold if the Germans were to counterattack.[105]

The Germans had their own problems. The *103d Grenadier Regiment* regrouped on high ground northeast of the villages, including Hill 187—right in the path of the oncoming 47th Infantry Regiment. The 3d Armored Division settled in under mortar and artillery fire while waiting for the 104th Infantry Division to come abreast on the left. The Americans repulsed several small counterattacks between Hastenrath and Scherpenseel.[106]

By the next day, gains on both 3d Armored Division flanks by the 104th and 1st Infantry divisions were pinching CCB out of the line. The armored division went into reserve and licked its wounds.

Epic Struggle for Hamich

In the 1st Infantry Division's zone, Driscoll's 1st Battalion, 16th Infantry, on November 17 tried again to crack the *48th Grenadier Regiment's* defenses in

Hamich. Nearby, the 47th Infantry Regiment cleared Gressenich by 1030 hours, thereby opening Driscoll's road link to the rear.[107]

Driscoll's troops could see that trenches linked the buildings and fortified basements in Hamich, so they knew that a tough fight lay ahead. At about 1300 hours, a platoon of tanks finally arrived to support an attempt to enter town, but an artillery barrage and grazing machine-gun fire from the buildings stopped the assault cold. Casualties were heavy—as much as 70 percent of them coming from the continual artillery fire. By the next day, the rifle companies would be reduced by an average of half. A Sherman from Company A, 745th Tank Battalion, knocked out an assault gun, but a panzer in turn knocked out a heavily armored M4A3E2 Jumbo assault Sherman from only sixty yards away.[108]

The Germans pushed back. Three panzers reached the foxhole line of Company B, on 1st Battalion's right flank. With retreat the only alternative, the battalion instead called in artillery fire on its own forward positions, which drove off the Germans.[109]

While these actions were unfolding, the fresh *104th Grenadier Regiment* of the *47th Volksgrenadier Division* moved onto Hill 232, north of Hamich,[110] which for some time had given German artillery observers excellent coverage of the Big Red One's activities (except in the deep woods at the right end of its line). Indeed, German artillery fire struck American concentrations with unerring accuracy. Back near Schevenhütte, German interdictory fire directed at the few roads proved distressingly effective.[111] Direct fire from assault guns on the ridge, meanwhile, interfered with some operations by the 3d Armored Division's 33d Armored Regiment near Köttenich.[112]

A concerned Engel, meanwhile, requested tank support and was given a *Kampfgruppe* commanded by *Oberst* Hans Bayer, CO of the *116th Panzer Division's 16th Panzer Regiment*. It consisted of 1st Battalion, *24th Panzer Regiment* (nineteen Panthers); the 1st Battalion, *60th Panzergrenadier Regiment*; the *116th Panzeraufklärungs Abteilung* (Armored Reconnaissance Battalion); a company of engineers; one artillery battery; and one flak battery that was to be used against ground targets. Engel also had available at Hamich seven *Panzerjäger* IV tank killers from the *3d Panzerjäger Abteilung*; these were probably the panzers that had caused so much trouble for Driscoll's men that day.[113]

***

Driscoll's 1st Battalion on November 18 managed with the help of tanks and tank destroyers to penetrate Hamich, where the GIs and the *48th Grenadier Regiment* clawed at each other in the streets and buildings. Three M10s from 3d Platoon, Company C, 634th Tank Destroyer Battalion, actually reached the edge of town five minutes before the infantry. During the advance, they had engaged four "Tigers" that were threatening to overrun the doughs. The tank destroyers claimed one probable and two sure kills for the loss of one M10. (*Oberst* Bayer's *Kampfgruppe* had arrived in town. German records indicate that he had no Tigers in his command. Unless an unreported unit was in the area—there was some talk in the German command of sending King Tigers but no recorded decision to do so—some of the references to Tigers here and following are cases of misidentification by American troops.)

As Driscoll's 1st Battalion reached the edge of Hamich, a bazooka fired from a basement hit one M10 and killed the driver. An artillery shell struck the turret of a second tank, wounded two men, and ruined the traverse mechanism.[114]

During the morning, five panzers counterattacked from Hill 232. P-47s and artillery drove the panzers and supporting infantry back to cover.[115]

By noon, 1st Battalion GIs had fought their way to the intersection in the center of town. About this time, a counterattack by two hundred to three hundred infantry supported by fifteen tanks hit the American line. Lieutenant Colonel Charles Horner Jr.'s 3d Battalion was just advancing to assist Driscoll's men. To the riflemen, it seemed that the assault came "from every direction." A Tiger in hull defilade methodically fired into the trees over the GIs' heads, showering them with shrapnel.[116]

Sergeant Roland Urbohm, commanding the M10 with the damaged traverse mechanism, had also reached the intersection in Hamich. He sighted his 3-inch gun by jiggling the left and right tracks, and disabled two panzers. His CO, Lieutenant Colonel Henry Davisson, called this the most remarkable piece of tank destroyer marksmanship he ever witnessed.[117]

Technical Sergeant Jake Lindsey manned a position with 1st Battalion's Company C. Fighting during the day had killed three and wounded thirty-one of his buddies, and his platoon—still commanded by Lieutenant James Wood—was down to six men. The other two platoons amounted to only eleven more. A company of grenadiers and five tanks charged toward the tattered command. The GIs drove back the panzers with rifle grenades from a range of fifty yards and chased off grenadiers trying to set up a machine gun. Following six German failed assaults—strengthened by fresh troops—Lindsey reportedly fixed his bayonet and charged a group of eight grenadiers, despite the pain from a shell fragment in his knee. Lindsey killed two men and captured three men, two machine guns, and five burp guns.[118] The Germans left behind one hundred dead and twenty-five seriously wounded. Lindsey was credited with personally dispatching twenty of them and was awarded the Medal of Honor.

By the end of the day, the Americans had pushed slightly east of Hamich.[119] Engel reported that the *48th Grenadier Regiment* had been reduced to a combat strength of 150 men and a half dozen or so each of mortars and field pieces.[120]

The 16th Infantry Regiment's 2d Battalion, meanwhile, captured Hill 232, north of Hamich, after a devastating fifteen-battalion artillery barrage. There is some confusion as to who was on the hill at this point. The *47th Volksgrenadier Division's* commanding general, *Generalleutnant* Max Bork, reported that his *104th Grenadier Regiment* lost the position after having suffered 250 casualties. The 1st Infantry Division identified the defenders as Engel's *12th Fusilier Battalion*, which agrees with a document written by Engel.[121] The fact that the *104th Grenadier Regiment* would soon launch a counterattack suggests that both stories may be correct. Moreover, the 16th Infantry Regiment's G-3 journal indicates that, shortly after the hill fell, prisoners were reported from both German units. In any event, the 2d Battalion, 16th Infantry Regiment, dug in to defend the knoll. Mines and muddy tracks prevented three tanks that had supported the assault from joining the doughs.[122]

Bork's grenadiers, who were to be joined by some fifteen tanks and two hundred reconnaissance men from *Oberst* Bayer's *Kampfgruppe*, counterattacked that night, but the attempt to retake the heights failed miserably. The operation came apart after a replacement lieutenant (captured to tell his tale) got lost and eventually led Bayer's panzers straight into Hamich.

The panzers, commanded by *Rittmeister* August Böke, fired flares to coordinate with the panzergrenadiers as they burst into town. Soon, a Sherman and an M10 were burning, adding an eerie light to the scene. The unplanned attack rolled over parts of two American infantry companies and reached the center of town.

The situation was fluid, and odd things happened in the dark. One panzer and an SP gun tipped into shell holes. A Panther pulled up within eight yards of a Sherman, whose gunner fired a round through the turret side that blew the German commander out of his hatch. Private First Class Carmen Tucharelli knocked out another tank—sitting just outside Company K's CP—by firing a bazooka down into the turret from a second-story window.

The trend looked so grim that the Americans called down artillery fire on the center of town. The GIs were largely protected in buildings and cellars; the Germans were out in the open. Three panzers, including Böke's command tank, and several other vehicles in town were hit and destroyed. Although the *Rittmeister's* driver and radio operator were killed, he escaped unharmed. A battalion of panzergrenadiers advancing to support Böke's tanks and reconnaissance troops was shattered by the barrage.

By the wee hours of the morning, the defenders reported that the panzergrenadiers and most of the panzers had been driven off. The Germans reported six tanks and two assault guns lost; three M4s and two tank destroyers were knocked out in exchange. The American tankers of Company A viewed this night as the hardest fighting they experienced in the Hürtgen Forest. Although the riflemen were screaming for more bazooka ammunition, the situation had stabilized.[123]

The 1st Battalion of the *104th Grenadier Regiment* attacked Hill 232 just before dawn without its misdirected tank support and was cut to pieces. In one company, only the commander survived, and he had eight bullet holes in his coat and one in his handkerchief.[124]

The *47th Volksgrenadier Division* requested permission to withdraw its troops from Hamich and establish a new line to the east, but *LXXXI Corps* refused.[125] Indeed, *Generalfeldmarschall* Model that day decided to commit the entire *47th Volksgrenadier Division* to take responsibility for the southern end of Engel's line opposite the Big Red One. Model was also concerned that the Americans would drop paratroopers east of the Roer and ordered increased readiness in that area.[126]

Other elements of the Big Red One pushed northeast along the Wehe and into the Grosswald Forest east of Schevenhütte.[127] The 26th Infantry Regiment, on the right, attacked in the woods at 1300 hours but made little progress.[128]

***

Major William Sylvan was a staff officer in Collins' headquarters and, with the corps commander's permission, kept a diary. He recorded that 1st Infantry Division commanding general, Huebner, on November 19 told Collins that he was holding the enemy in check. "Hold the enemy in check!" snapped Collins. "I don't need you to do that, I want you to advance. This is an offensive."[129] But the Germans were not cooperating.

About dawn, Engel's *48th Grenadier Regiment*, supported by *Kampfgruppe* Bayer, struck the 16th Infantry Regiment again at Hamich and the hill north of town. Bayer's command by now had available only two battle-ready Panthers. The Germans once more reached the village, but their attempt to push on toward Gressenich was broken up by artillery fire.[130]

While the drama in Hamich was unfolding, the 47th Infantry Regiment passed through the Hamich area (briefly tangling with the Germans on the edge of town) and attacked to the north.[131] The 1st Battalion opened a bloody three-day effort to capture Hill 187, which was fiercely defended by the *47th Volksgrenadier Division's 103d Grenadier Regiment* (just pushed there by the 3d Armored Division). The defenders mistakenly believed that they were once again under assault by the 3d Armored Division.[132] The vicious close-quarters fighting earned the 1st Battalion, 47th Infantry, a distinguished unit citation.

The 26th Infantry Regiment, meanwhile, drove a salient deep into the woods along a stream that ran toward Jüngersdorf.[133] The *47th Volksgrenadier Division's 115th Grenadier Regiment* was just arriving in the sector and immediately launched a battalion-size counterattack backed by artillery. The Germans swung around the 2d Battalion's flank to take it from the rear, but Private First Class Roland Littleton—manning an outpost for Company G—spotted the first wave of infantry. Littleton opened up with his BAR and continued firing even after taking a round in the stomach. When the GIs had beaten off the assault, eighty bodies lay in front of Company G's positions, twenty of them around Littleton's foxhole. The defenders lost some fourteen men.[134]

Private First Class Francis McGraw manned a heavy machine gun in Company H nearby. McGraw's Congressional Medal of Honor citation described the action: "Braving an intense hour-long preparatory barrage, he maintained his stand and poured deadly accurate fire into the advancing foot troops until they faltered and came to a halt. The hostile forces brought up a machine gun in an effort to dislodge him but were frustrated when he lifted his gun to an exposed but advantageous position atop a log, courageously stood up in his foxhole and knocked out the enemy weapon. A rocket blasted his gun from position, but he retrieved it and continued firing. He silenced a second machine gun and then made repeated trips over fire-swept terrain to replenish his ammunition supply. Wounded painfully in this dangerous task, he disregarded his injury and hurried back to his post, where his weapon was showered with mud when another rocket barely missed him. In the midst of the battle, with enemy troops taking advantage of his predicament to press forward, he calmly cleaned his gun, put it back into action and drove off the attackers. He continued to fire until his ammunition was expended, when, with a fierce desire to close with the enemy, he picked up a carbine, killed one enemy soldier, wounded another, and engaged in a desperate firefight with a third until he was mortally wounded by a burst from a machine pistol."

Under pressure from Hodges and Collins to show more progress, Huebner committed his reserve. The 18th Infantry Regiment attacked between the 16th and 26th regiments along the Wehe and reached the town of Wenau.[135] The remnants of one battalion from the *104th Grenadier Regiment* ran into the Americans as they tried to withdraw and were annihilated. The other battalion of the regiment survived because it was holding part of the defensive line near Heistern and Wenau.

The *47th Volksgrenadier Division's* problems did not end there. It assessed that a 3d Armored Division (actually the 47th Infantry Regiment) break-through in the *103d Grenadier Regiment's* sector was only a matter of days away. It had to commit its final reserve, probably its field replacement battalion, to battle at Hücheln. Supporting panzers were withdrawn, and the division had to bring forward the twelve guns from the 1st Battalion of its *147th Artillery Regiment* to provide antitank defense. With that move, the division's artillery declined to eighteen light and nine heavy guns.[136]

Horror in the Hürtgen

The 4th Infantry Division on November 17 faced more dense forest, barbed wire, mines, booby traps, and heavy mortar and artillery fire. The 8th Infantry Regiment attempted to advance in a column of battalions. The 2d Battalion blew a path through the barbed wire that had stymied it the previous day but was so badly weakened by casualties that it could not advance beyond the concertina.

Lieutenant Bernard Ray received a posthumous Medal of Honor for an act of self-sacrifice that created the hole in the German wire, as recorded in his citation:

> The American forces attacked in wet, bitterly cold weather over rough, wooded terrain, meeting brutal resistance from positions spaced throughout the forest behind minefields and wire obstacles. Small-arms, machine-gun, mortar, and artillery fire caused heavy casualties in the ranks when Company F was halted by a concertina type wire barrier. Under heavy fire, 1st Lieutenant Ray reorganized his men and prepared to blow a path through the entanglement, a task which appeared impossible of accomplishment and from which others tried to dissuade him. With implacable determination to clear the way, he placed explosive caps in his pockets, obtained several bangalore torpedoes, and then wrapped a length of highly explosive primer cord about his body. He dashed forward under direct fire, reached the barbed wire and prepared his demolition charge as mortar shells, which were being aimed at him alone, came steadily nearer his completely exposed position. He had placed a torpedo under the wire and was connecting it to a charge he carried when he was severely wounded by a bursting mortar shell. Apparently realizing that he would fail in his self-imposed mission unless he completed it in a few moments, he made a supremely gallant decision. With the primer cord still wound about his body and the explosive caps in his pocket, he completed a hasty wiring system and unhesitatingly thrust down on the handle of the charger, destroying himself with the wire barricade in the resulting blast.

A planned attack through the 2d Battalion line by 1st Battalion never came off, because a German counterattack struck at an opportune moment to disrupt the operation. The 12th Infantry Regiment, meanwhile, was stymied by mines.

Colonel Charles (Buck) Lanham's 22d Infantry Regiment again advanced through woods to its objective against light resistance. Artillery, however, claimed a heavy price for the gains: By this, the second day of the offensive, two battalion commanders had been killed and the third wounded. The 2d Battalion's S-3, who moved up to take command, also died, and Company F lost every officer but two lieutenants.[137]

***

The greatest anxiety in the mind of the *275th Infantry Division* commanding general, *Generalleutnant* Hans Schmidt, involved his far right wing, where his division intruded slightly into the Big Red One's zone and lost contact with the *47th Volksgrenadier Division*. Indeed, only the position of the American corps boundary appears to have saved Schmidt from watching his right battalion be flanked and rolled up. The situation in the center was dicey, too, and only massed artillery fire and the commitment of the weak *983d Grenadier Regiment* prevented an American breakthrough.[138]

Seventh Army and *LXXIV Corps* commanders visited Schmidt at his CP, and the three generals concluded that the *275th* would not hold much longer on its own.[139] *Seventh Army* reluctantly added more muscle to Schmidt's sector. During the day, the *116th Panzer Division* deployed a second *Kampfgruppe*, this one to buttress the *275th Infantry Division's* defenses against the 4th Infantry Division's push. The *Kampfgruppe* consisted of the remnants of the division's two panzergrenadier regiments, amounting to about a battalion in strength, supported by antitank elements. *Seventh Army* had no other reserves and concluded that it would have to begin stretching the front held by the *272d* and *277th Volksgrenadier divisions* on *LXXIV Corps'* left to free up elements of the *89th Infantry Division* to reinforce the right wing. Army headquarters also began to comb its other two corps for even individual battalions that it could move north to the threatened sector.[140]

The 4th Infantry Division crawled a thousand yards toward Grosshau on November 18.[141] Already, the division was experiencing serious resupply and evacuation problems because of the general absence of roads. Whenever tanks from the 70th Tank Battalion could move forward, they fired at bunkers and at the machine-gun nests that controlled every firebreak. The tanks advanced ahead of the infantry to crush concertina wire and detonate antipersonnel mines. The doughs advanced in the grooves cleared by the tracks.[142]

The informal history of the 70th Tank Battalion offers this description of the frustrating conditions in the forest from the tanker's perspective:

No soldier who was there will ever forget Hürtgen Forest—it was simply hell. The 70th moved into the Hürtgen in mid-November. The air was damp and bitter cold, especially inside of a moving tank. Snow covered most of the ground but underneath was soft, slippery mud that hampered a tank's every move. There was danger everywhere: Danger of bogging down, danger of ambush in the dense woods, and danger of moving along the mined roads. Enemy artillery and mortar fire was almost incessant. Great tall trees were stripped and chewed to shreds by the continuous pounding of artillery from both sides. Every time a shell burst among the trees the explosion sent a deafening roar echoing throughout the forest. Tanks entering the thick woods were road-bound and extremely vulnerable to mines and bazooka fire. Oftentimes infantrymen were not available to lead them through, so tankers had to advance alone, sweating it out every inch of the way.

The 70th fought twenty-four separate engagements with the enemy in the Hürtgen death trap from 16 November to 12 December 1944. The tanks were used both offensively and defensively, depending on the situation, which at the time was most unpredictable. The Jerries counterattacked every night in an attempt to regain the ground they had lost during the day. . . . The entire Hürtgen fighting cost the 70th a total of ninety battle casualties and twenty-four tanks (twelve of which were later repaired).[143]

The crews in the 803d Tank Destroyer Battalion were also trapped in this hell. Their M10s had open-topped turrets, so the men were more vulnerable to airbursts than were the tank crews and even the infantry, who could often dig foxholes and drag logs across the tops for protection.

The defending *275th Infantry Division* executed a slow withdrawal from one prepared position to another, a tactic that would characterize its operations almost daily for the remainder of its engagement against the 4th Infantry Division. In each case, a heavy artillery barrage covered the *Landsers* while they broke contact and moved to the rear. Small-scale counterattacks were frequent. Sergeant Mack Morriss recorded, "The infantry welcomed [the counterattacks] because then and only then the German came out of his hole and was a visible target, and the maddened infantry killed with grim satisfaction."[144]

Prisoners indicated that the *116th Panzer Division's Kampfgruppe* had entered the fray and the *89th Infantry Division's 1055th Grenadier Regiment* was now active in the sector, too. The reinforcements from the *89th Infantry Division* were moving right into the center of the hard-pressed *275th Infantry Division's* line. Moreover, *Seventh Army* remained so concerned that it promised more help. Brandenberger had managed to extract the battle-weakened *344th Infantry Division* from *LXVI Corps* during the shuffle of units in preparation for the Ardennes offensive. Commanders doubted the division was up to the rigors of forest fighting, but no other reserves were available.[145] By evening, the commander of the *1058th Grenadier Regiment* appeared at Schmidt's CP to arrange for the arrival of his men by truck the next day.[146] Berlin, meanwhile, authorized von Rundstedt to commit the *402d* and *403d Volksartillery corps* to the Roer sector to prevent a breakthrough.[147]

The 4th Infantry Division made virtually no progress in the Hürtgen on November 19.[148] Reflecting the confused nature of forest fighting, a bypassed German unit attacked the 22d Infantry's regimental headquarters during the afternoon. Some forward companies could not be resupplied at all, which stopped their planned operations. Engineers went to work around the clock to open supply routes, clear mines, and repair bridges.[149]

The Germans were under tremendous stress, too. A German medic, captured by the Ivy Leaf Division, carried a diary in which he wrote on this day:

> My God, today is Sunday. With dawn, the edge of our forest received a barrage. The earth trembles. The concussion takes our breath. Two wounded are brought to my hole, one with both hands shot off. I am considering whether to cut off the rest of the arm. I'll leave it on. How brave these two are. I hope to God that all this is not in vain. To our left, machine guns begin to chatter—and there comes *Ami*.
>
> In broad waves you can see him across the field. Tanks all around him are firing wildly. Now the American artillery ceases and the tank guns are firing like mad. I can't stick my head out of the hole—finally here are three German assault guns. With a few shots we can see several tanks burning once again. Long smoke columns are rising

toward heaven. The infantry takes cover, and the attack slows down— it's stopped. It's unbelievable that with this handful of men we hold out against such attacks.

And now we go forward to counterattack. The captain is leading it himself. We can't go far though. Our people are dropping like tired flies. We have got to go back and leave the whole number of our dead and wounded. Slowly the artillery begins its monotonous song again. . . .[150]

COULD IT BE?

On the evening of November 19, *LXXXI Corps* commanding general Köchling cabled *Fifteenth Army* command, "If the enemy attacks continue, we must reckon with a breakthrough to Jülich and Düren."[151] Only desperate efforts could hold the high ground overlooking the Roer Valley.[152]

The weather was lousy again on November 20, dumping rain on the men engaged in bitter house-to-house fighting in places such as Hehlrath, Rohe, Wenau, and Heistern, and on others slogging through the Hürtgen woods.[153] Yet, as Köchling's alarming analysis suggested, there were signs that the cumulative pressure across VII Corps' front might be approaching the point of accomplishing a breakthrough somewhere along the line.

The 104th Infantry Division attacked with two regiments at 0800 hours. The infantry cleared Rohe and reached Helrath, where more street fighting ensued. The 415th Infantry Regiment pushed down the Inde River valley through the wooded area southwest of Eschweiler.[154]

The 414th Infantry Regiment joined the attack at 1100 hours. One battalion reached Bergrath; another established contact with the 1st Infantry Division, on the right.[155] The Timberwolves were proud that they had kept up with a certain veteran division.[156] Because the linkup between the infantry divisions pinched the 3d Armored Division out of the line, the armor assembled in corps reserve.[157]

Lieutenant Stan Zimmerman's tankers from 2d Platoon, Company B, 750th Tank Battalion, enabled the infantry to enter Volkenrath, just down the road from Hastenrath, which was defended by 1st Battalion, *89th Grenadier Regiment.*[158] Zimmerman recalled:

The captain combined the two remaining tanks of 3d Platoon and my four tanks and instructed me to attack the town of Volkenrath but to stop out of panzerfaust range and punch holes in the houses for the infantry. . . . I told [my tank commanders] we would exit the woods in a column. Immediately upon clearing the woods, they were to fan out so they could bring their fire to bear on the houses and get good separation between tanks to reduce the size of the target for the enemy. "Turn on your stabilizers before you start and give 'em hell." And let me tell you, all hell broke loose. There was a whole lot of incoming, going out of the woods one tank behind the other, crossing about a thousand yards of open, muddy ground. I'll never know how we did it without getting a tank hit. Well, anyway, we got within three hundred yards of the town and sat there expending our ammo. It seemed like a century before the infantry finally passed through our line and entered the town with little resistance. As they were passing through, one dough climbed up on my tank, slapped me on the shoulder, and said, "Boy! That was a real Hollywood charge." I was in no mood, and I said, "Get the hell off my tank." Four of the tanks were bogged down in the mud, and as a result only two tanks were able to continue on into town with the infantry.[159]

The grenadiers battled back, however. The American tanks and infantry were virtually cut off for two days, and fierce fighting claimed six Shermans and two assault guns.[160]

The Big Red One's 18th Infantry Regiment, just to the south, jumped off thirty minutes after the Timberwolves. The GIs cleared Wenau and bypassed Heistern, leaving the mopping up to the reserve battalion. The regiment then pushed across open ground toward Schönthal.[161]

Heistern offered a good view of the terrain all the way to Langerwehe, and the three assault guns and the one engineer and two infantry companies left to the *104th Grenadier Regiment* fought to hold the ground. The regimental CO, *Oberst* Josef Kimbacher, led his last battalion in a poorly conceived counterattack at 0330 hours. After suffering 250 casualties and Kimbacher's capture, the defense collapsed early on November 21.[162]

The 26th Infantry Regiment battled through heavily wooded terrain on the division right. The *47th Volksgrenadier Division's 115th Grenadier Regiment* launched another battalion-size counterattack at Laufenburg.[163]

The *LXXXI Corps,* meanwhile, ordered Bork to turn over the *103d Grenadier Regiment* to Engel. Leaving the forest fighting to Bork's *104th Grenadier Regiment,* Engel withdrew the remnants of his *48th Grenadier Regiment* during the evening as a reserve.[164]

The 4th Infantry Division gained a few yards here and lost some there. Two days of fighting had netted a mere thousand yards of ground.[165]

Major George Mabry Jr., who had taken command of the ill-starred 2d Battalion, 8th Infantry, only days before, was awarded a Medal of Honor for his actions that day. (He had already received a Distinguished Service Cross for bravery at Normandy on D-day.) After a brief respite out of the line to absorb two hundred replacements, the dispirited battalion—still 40 percent understrength—advanced again into withering machine-gun fire and mine-fields. When the scouts sought cover and refused to budge, Mabry advanced to the point of his column.[166]

Mabry's citation offered a vignette of the action:

> During the early phases of the assault, the leading elements of his battalion were halted by a minefield and immobilized by heavy hos-tile fire. Advancing alone into the mined area, . . . Mabry established a safe route of passage. He then moved ahead of the foremost scouts, personally leading the attack, until confronted by a booby-trapped double concertina obstacle. With the assistance of the scouts, he dis-connected the explosives and cut a path through the wire. Upon moving through the opening, he observed three enemy in foxholes whom he captured at bayonet point. Driving steadily forward he paced the assault against three log bunkers which housed mutually supported automatic weapons. Racing up a slope ahead of his men, he found the initial bunker deserted, then pushed on to the second where he was suddenly confronted by nine onrushing enemy. Using the butt of his rifle, he felled one adversary and bayoneted a second, before his scouts came to his aid and assisted him in overcoming the

others in hand-to-hand combat. Accompanied by the riflemen, he charged the third bunker under point-blank small-arms fire and led the way into the fortification from which he prodded six enemy at bayonet point. Following the consolidation of this area, he led his battalion across three hundred yards of fire-swept terrain to seize elevated ground upon which he established a defensive position which menaced the enemy on both flanks, and provided his regiment a firm foothold on the approach to the Cologne plain.

Division intelligence identified the arrival of the *1058th Grenadier Regiment*, part of the *344th Infantry Division*.[167] (The *344th* was the recently reorganized *91st Luftlande [Airmobile Infantry] Division* and in some accounts is still referred to by its old designation.) The arrival of the first two companies near Grosshau had brought joy to Schmidt's CP in the *275th Infantry Division*, but the delight faded when American fire routed the men, who could not be reorganized until the next day. Nonetheless, by evening most of two battalions had buttressed the most threatened points in the line. An advance party from the division headquarters also arrived with word that the *275th* would soon be relieved.[168]

Meanwhile, on direct orders from Model, the corps and division operations officers from the adjacent army sectors personally surveyed the battlefield along the boundary to firmly establish their responsibilities for maintaining contact.[169]

Effective midnight November 20, First Army temporarily shifted the boundary between VII and V corps northward to give V Corps full responsibility for clearing Hürtgen and Kleinhau.[170] This decision offers another indication that First Army at that time viewed most of the Hürtgen Forest operations as distinct from those aimed at the Roer River, because V Corps was not considered part of the latter. (First Army's letter of instructions, issued on October 26, had specified that V Corps was to be prepared to advance on Bonn upon army order *after* VII Corps had penetrated the enemy's main position.[171])

The 104th Infantry Division's 413th Infantry Regiment started the day on November 21 at 0800 hours by mopping up Helrath and Rohe. At midday, the regiment jumped off and rolled a mile toward Dürwiss.[172] A mile spurt in this offensive was so unusual as to be notable. With that push, the Timberwolf Division's axis of advance swung to the right and now paralleled those of the other divisions along the front.

The 415th Infantry Regiment advanced up both sides of the Inde River and fought its way into Eschweiler.[173] The *27th Fusiliers* managed to hang on in the western part of town and was relieved that the American efforts to work their way through the streets appeared to be halfhearted.[174]

The 414th Infantry Regiment advanced toward Nothberg. It, too, encountered house-to-house fighting in Bergrath and Bohl. The *89th Grenadier Regiment* was so hard-pressed that two batteries from the *12th Artillery Regiment* that could not be extricated were thrown into the frontline defenses.[175]

The German defenders fighting the Timberwolves bought the precious commodity of time that day. Undetected by the Americans, the *12th Volksgrenadier Division* was readying the next fallback line east of Eschweiler.[176]

On November 21, the 1st Infantry Division finally broke the logjam in the 47th Infantry Regiment's sector. The *103d Grenadier Regiment*, which had already suffered at least two hundred casualties, lost Hill 187 for good.[177] The 47th Infantry delivered the coup de grace in the form of metal on target. Collins ordered VII Corps to concentrate all available artillery— twenty battalions, mostly 155mm or larger—in a three-minute barrage on the prominence; Collins believed this to have been the heaviest concentration on a single target in the war. Those who survived were more than ready to surrender.[178] Late on November 21, the 47th Infantry Regiment established contact on its left with the Timberwolf Division. It now held a two-mile front facing Nothberg and Hücheln.[179]

The fight was by no means one-sided. The 3d Battalion, 47th Infantry, was being ground up as it struggled through dense forest toward Bovenberg. Some three hundred yards short of the objective, the GIs were pinned down by interlocking fire from both flanks and the front, whence they came under extremely accurate mortar fire. Tree bursts and bullets blocked all routes of escape. The battalion lost more men on November 21 than the entire regiment had lost in a single day to that time.[180]

The 16th and 18th Infantry regiments gained a half mile across open ground north of Heistern and through the valley and woods of the Wehe Heistern. The 26th Infantry Regiment made some progress through the forest toward Merode.[181]

The *47th Volksgrenadier Division* realized that it now faced a critical battle to defend the Kammerbusch, the last defensible high ground in its sector. Led by the regimental adjutant, the tattered remnants of the *104th Grenadier Regiment*, reinforced by the division's combat engineer battalion, hunkered down and laid its last mines. The neighboring *103d Grenadier Regiment* was down to two officers and 228 men, but at least the division's Hetzer tank destroyers had finally arrived at the front and were deployed to help fend off the inevitable attack. The *115th Grenadier Regiment* was still in reasonably decent shape in the Lucherberg-Gey-Merode area. That evening, Köchling passed to Bork Model's praise for his excellent leadership of his division to date.[182]

The 4th Infantry Division alone in VII Corps remained stuck that day.[183] The division took a pause to reconnoiter and supply forward units with ammunition, rations, and repaired weapons. Casualties actually climbed, however, because of heavy shellfire.[184]

Tanks and assault guns stiffened the German defenses, almost always from camouflaged, dug-in positions. The Ivy Leaf Division's reports would make daily reference to the Germans' effective use of these limited armored resources for the rest of the month.[185]

With the shift of the corps-division boundary, the 121st Infantry Regiment, 8th Infantry Division, assembled behind the 12th Infantry Regiment and attacked through the line. All Ivy Leaf battalions in this sector were disengaged by evening.[186]

The *275th Infantry Division* also disengaged during the day, and at 2000 hours turned over responsibility for the sector to the *344th Infantry Division*.[187] But the promised relief for the troops proved a chimera when the weak *344th* absorbed the remnants of the *275th*. The combined command was about the size of a full-strength infantry division. A cadre of officers and NCOs from the *275th* was sent to the Schleswig-Holstein to begin rebuilding the unit.[188]

***

As usual, most of VII Corps was to attack at 0800 hours on November 22.[189] The Timberwolf Division's 415th Infantry Regiment, however, sent its 1st Battalion forward in a sneak attack at 0300 hours. Two companies supported by engineers advanced through Eschweiler's dark streets and reached the city center at about 0600 hours. The regiment reported few casualties during this bold operation, and there was good reason. The *27th Fusilier* and *89th Grenadier regiments* had already slipped away eastward to man the next defensive line.[190]

The 104th Infantry Division rolled ahead into a seeming vacuum. Most of the outfit advanced a quick two miles—the greatest one-day gain in the corps since November 16—from Dürwiss toward Pützlohn. Then two regiments turned east and added another two thousand yards into the Inde Valley.[191]

The 1st Infantry Division, however, made little progress against fierce resistance from Bork's volksgrenadiers. The Germans perceived a grave threat in the Big Red One's approach toward Langerwehe and employed heavy artillery and mortar fire to support the hard-pressed defenders. The 18th Infantry Regiment had to defend ground taken against two tank-backed counterattacks.[192]

In the grim Hürtgen Forest, the plight of the 4th Infantry Division was reflected in the news that two of its regiments that day had finally eked out gains of "up to six hundred yards."[193] During the night, the *1057th Grenadier Regiment* replaced the last panzergrenadiers in the line opposite the Ivy Leaf Division.[194]

A week of some of the heaviest fighting to occur on the western front had certainly produced plenty of attrition on both sides, but VII Corps had pushed back the German line only a bit rather than cracking it. The onslaught had to continue, with no end in sight.

XIX CORPS MATCHES THE PACE

On the second day of the November offensive, the 29th Infantry Division assaulted a chain of fortified towns: Bettendorf, Schleiden, Siersdorf, and Setterich. None would fall that November 17.

The 1st Battalion, 116th Infantry Regiment, for example, encountered heavy machine-gun fire from zigzag trenches girdling Setterich 150 yards from the outermost buildings. As *Hauptmann* Kuppinger's 1st Battalion from the *246th Volksgrenadier Division's 352d Grenadier Regiment* crouched in those positions, Company C got a few men into the trench line, but not enough to overwhelm the defenders. The riflemen battled one another from corner to corner through the zigs and zags. One American would fire, a second would throw a grenade, then the two would rush the next corner. A few Company B men also gained the trench line. Darkness found the doughboys huddling in shoulder-deep, narrow, and waterlogged accommodations while mortar and artillery shells burst around them. The Germans reported that their MLR changed hands three times that day.[195]

By evening, the 29th Division commanding general, Major General Charles Gerhardt, had concluded that his boys were not going to get the job in Setterich done by themselves. (Indeed, his opposite number at about the same time reported that morale among his tired troops was excellent because of their success thus far in beating off attacks by a better-equipped and more numerous foe.)[196] Gerhardt phoned Major General Ernest Harmon at the Hell on Wheels CP and invited the armored division to lend a hand. Gerhardt also asked if his infantry could work in the 2d Armored's zone, to which Harmon readily agreed. Next, Gerhardt contacted the commander of the 116th Infantry Regiment and told him to use whatever troops necessary to capture Setterich. Another call to Hell on Wheels produced an offer of seventy-five tanks. "Now we're talking business," said Gerhardt.[197]

And so, reinforced by the 2d Battalion, the 1st Battalion, 116th Infantry, entered Setterich the next day, supported by tanks from both the 747th Tank Battalion and 2d Armored Division. This time, the Shermans rolled up to the trenches and blasted any resistance. Soon, the doughs were moving from house to house, rooting out defenders. Another day of stiff fighting was necessary to finish the job.[198]

The *3d Panzergrenadier Division* evacuated Würselen the night of November 16–17 once it realized the danger posed by the 104th Infantry Division's advance to the south and evidence that the 30th Infantry Division would apply an opposing jaw to the north. With Würselen off the agenda, the 30th Infantry Division busied itself with the capture of Hoengen and Linden.

Captain George Sibbald's Company E, 117th Infantry, faced vicious resistance offered by the *404th Grenadier Regiment* (temporarily subordinated to the *3d Panzergrenadier Division*) from a barracks outside Hoengen. Sibbald arranged for a combined five-minute barrage by an artillery battalion and mortar company at noon, after which two Shermans from the 743d Tank Battalion pulled forward and fired on the first structures. Doughboys rushed the buildings after they had been softened up. The team inched forward, building by building, until the Americans reached a railroad spur north of Mariadorf. Moving quickly now, the company advanced into Hoengen and secured it before dark.

The 120th Infantry Regiment, meanwhile, at 0700 hours dashed into Linden, where it surprised the 1st and 3d battalions of the *3d Panzergrenadier Division's 8th Grenadier Regiment*. The Germans had just completed their night march out of Würselen and did not have time to set up their defenses. The GIs took almost all of 1st Battalion prisoner and bagged a total of 326 prisoners of war (POWs).

The American advance left a hole between the volksgrenadiers and the *8th Grenadier Regiment*. Only a weakened battalion of the *246th Volksgrenadier Division's* artillery regiment—American air strikes had destroyed a battery and killed many officers—covered the gap with direct fire. The division unsuccessfully tried to organize an attack by an alarm (reserve/rapid reaction) company and half its available Hetzers to restore the situation. It also ordered its *Feld Ersatz Bataillon* (Field Replacement Battalion) and an attached fortress antitank company equipped with captured Soviet guns to the west side of the Roer.[199]

Panzers at Puffendorf

While the 29th and 30th Infantry divisions inched forward against fierce resistance on November 17, the 2d Armored Division battled both mud and a full-blown German counterattack at Puffendorf. The Germans viewed the penetration by Hell on Wheels as the most pressing threat in the sector. Von Rundstedt authorized the use of the reserve *9th Panzer* and *15th Panzergrenadier divisions* to contain the menace. German radio, anticipating victory, called the counterattack the "largest and most decisive tank action on the Western Front." Jack Bell, a war correspondent for the *Chicago Daily News Service*, called it "a battle virtually lost in the shuffle of world-shaking events. It was a battle which shook the earth of this sector."[200]

The Panthers from the *9th Panzer Division*—now commanded by *Generalmajor* Harald Freiherr von Elverfeldt—accompanied by the *506th Schwere Panzer Abteilung's* Royal Tigers, struck early in the morning.[201] The Mark VI Royal Tiger was a 70-ton monster with 150mm (6 inches) of sloped front armor and an 88mm gun that had an even higher muzzle velocity than that found on the feared Tiger I.[202]

Colonel Paul Disney's Task Force 1 (CCB) was just forming up for the day's attack when twenty to thirty panzers, supported by infantry and artillery, burst through heavy morning mist into its positions. Artillery and small-arms fire had already been striking the assembly area since the early hours. Shortly after dawn, high-velocity armor-piercing (AP) shells began to plow furrows in the earth among the tanks of 1st Battalion, 67th Armored Regiment, just as the 2d Battalion was arriving for the attack. Some of the fire was long-range gunnery by Royal Tigers, several of which *Fifth Panzer Army* commanding general von Manteuffel had ordered dug in on high ground because they were suffering high numbers of breakdowns.[203]

A tank battle ensued, which the Germans won decisively. The American tanks were drawn up on line and lacked the depth to support their own advance by fire. The high-velocity German guns knocked out Shermans from ranges starting at three thousand yards. Shells from 75mm and 76mm Sherman guns mostly bounced harmlessly off the panzers' front armor. Only a shot from the side or rear—or a lucky hit on a track or on the underside of the Panther's gun mantlet (the round would ricochet through the thin roof armor)—could stop the German tanks. The panzers also had wider tracks than the Shermans and were better able to maneuver in the deep mud.

One report captured the essence of the action: "Sergeant Julian Czekanski, a Company D . . . tank commander, sighted a German tank and fired on it without apparent effect. The tanks on the right flank were now taking direct hits. One of them, Lieutenant Karl's, flared up like burning celluloid, but all five crew members escaped. There were too many tanks in the draw, too little room for maneuver. Two enemy Mark VI and four Mark V tanks were observed scuttling from the woods on the western fringe of Gereonsweiler through the mist that clung persistently to the high ground. A fall of bluish smoke sifted down into the draw. Two more mediums on the right went up in flames. Then in the space of a few minutes, four of the light tanks were burning."[204]

With some companies reduced to less than platoons, and with ammunition running out, the 1st and 2d battalions at 1600 hours disengaged and withdrew to the outskirts of Puffendorf. During the withdrawal, Sergeant Czekanski's tank suffered a direct hit that wounded him and set the vehicle on fire. The task force hunkered down to defend the town against recapture.

Czekanski's platoon leader, Lieutenant Pendleton, sat in a lane on the edge of town. His tank had one round of AP, two of smoke, and six of HE remaining. Pendleton spotted a Panther moving across his front but concluded that he was in no position to seek out battle. The Mark V crew had spotted him, though, and the Panther fired as it advanced. Pendleton's gunner fired two rounds of smoke, and the panzer retreated. Soon, it approached again. Pendleton fired four rounds of HE, one of which struck the driver's hatch and convinced the panzer crew to draw off again.

The company commander, Lieutenant Robert E. Lee, arrived just as Pendleton was dismounting from his tank. "For God's sake, Lee, get me some help!" Pendleton shouted.

"What do you think that little gadget behind me is?"

Lee was guiding into position Lieutenant Cecil Hunnicutt's platoon from the 702d Tank Destroyer Battalion. Just then, the Panther reappeared and fired an AP round down the lane, barely missing the first M36.

"That was direct fire, wasn't it?" asked Hunnicutt.

"You're goddamned right it was!" replied Pendleton.

Hunnicutt pulled his tank destroyer into position and fired two rounds after the Panther, which ended the dispute for the moment. Artillery fire also discouraged the Germans; three Royal Tigers were set ablaze in a single barrage.

Soon, T2 tank recovery vehicles and half-tracks carrying ammo for the tank guns began to arrive. Nevertheless, had the Germans pressed the attack during the night, supplies probably would not have been adequate to defend Puffendorf.[205]

Ninth Panzer Division attacks struck other CCB task forces during the morning. The M36s (and a few remaining M10s) from the attached 702d Tank Destroyer Battalion engaged the attackers and knocked out six panzers during the day. The newly deployed M36, which carried a 90mm gun, was undergoing its first large-scale battle test. The 90mm could kill the Panther and Tiger at ordinary combat ranges, but the Royal Tiger demanded the simultaneous attention of two or more M36s, and generally a side shot even then. That said, one M36 crew knocked out a Royal Tiger north of Friealdenhoven on November 19 at twelve hundred yards; the 90mm round holed the turret side, passed entirely through the breach ring of the 88mm gun, and nearly penetrated the far turret wall.

***

The day's fighting cost the 2d Armored Division eighteen medium and seven light tanks destroyed and about the same number damaged and out of action. Fifty-six men were killed and 281 wounded, and 26 went missing in action (which for tankers often meant burned to unrecognizable cinders in their Shermans). The Americans claimed seventeen panzers destroyed.[206]

The Germans and Americans generally took a defensive posture the next day, but with the fall of Setterich the 2d Armored Division had enough room to commit CCA. On November 20, the *9th Panzer Division* lashed back again with sixty to eighty Tigers and Panthers. Lieutenant Colonel John Beall, CO of the 702d Tank Destroyer Battalion, threw a German trick from North Africa back at the enemy. A few American tanks approached the Germans, then fled, which lured the Germans within range of his 90mm guns.[207]

The Jerries had their own tricks, however. The 702d's AAR recorded: "The enemy used the heavy armor of his Mark VI tanks to full advantage. In several instances, the enemy maneuvered his heavily armored tanks into position between three thousand and thirty-five hundred yards from our [tank destroyers] and tanks and opened fire. At this distance, our [tank destroyers] could not penetrate the front of the Mark VI, and the enemy evidently knew this for he [kept] only his heavily armored front exposed. At this distance, our 90mm gun would ricochet off the Mark VI, and usually the high-velocity gun of the Mark VI would penetrate and knock out our vehicles."

The German counterattack also struck the positions of the 102d Infantry Division's 405th and 406th Infantry regiments on November 19 and 20, and the crews from the attached 771st Tank Destroyer Battalion experienced a major tank battle as their first real action. By now, the *15th Panzergrenadier Division* had joined the *9th Panzer Division*. Shortly after dawn on the first day, the German thrust penetrated the American lines. Company C's Lieutenant George Killmer ran from vehicle to vehicle in the confusion and brought his guns to bear against four Mark IVs and four Panthers. When wounded crewmen evacuated one M10, Sergeant Walter Nedza recruited two riflemen to help him serve the gun, climbed into the turret under fire, and dispatched a Mark V. The rest of the company eliminated the remaining seven panzers and lost only one M10 in the firefight. A few hours later, the company's gunners knocked out three more Panthers.

Battle on November 20 cost Company C more dearly. The tank destroyers in the course of three engagements accounted for two Royal Tigers, but the massive panzers knocked out six M10s. Several times, the crews watched in frustration as their 3-inch rounds bounced off the Tigers' thick hides. Company A, meanwhile, fired on Royal Tigers about noon and stopped two of them. The battle against the panzers cost the battalion five men killed and twenty-two wounded.[208]

By November 21, the 2d Armored Division was again making slow forward progress, although German tanks, often dug in, remained a major problem. That day, the 2d Armored Division pushed onto the high ground around Gereonsweiler and captured that town. Ninth Army commander Simpson had identified the spot as the key terrain feature west of the Roer River.[209]

One tank officer summed up the battle in these terms: "We won because of sheer numbers. Our men had too much will-to-win for Jerry to stomach. We knew we were licked tank-for-tank, but the boys went in [to] a free-for-all, ganging [up] on the Tiger until they knocked him out."

Sergeant Louis Weir, a Sherman tank commander, added, "I want a tank with a 90mm gun."[210]

The Outer Shell Cracks

The two American infantry divisions had also faced growing resistance while the tank battles raged around Puffendorf.

The 29th Infantry Division fought its way through a series of small road centers. Ninth Army characterized the resistance as "bitter, fanatical." To make matters worse, the Luftwaffe stepped up its activities against American ground targets.[211]

The 29th Infantry Division had been working with its attached tank battalion—the 747th—since Normandy and was a showcase for the painful learning process that still afflicted tank-infantry cooperation. The team members had the advantage of familiarity. In early November, moreover, SCR-300s compatible with infantry portable radios had been installed in seven tanks per company.[212] But during operations on November 18, the infantry had decided to experiment with putting its platoon leader in the bow gunner's position in the supporting command tank. Lieutenant Homer Wilkes, a cowboy turned tanker, described the results during an attack on Beggendorf:

> With a section on either side of the road, the [tank] platoon advanced to just out of bazooka range of the enemy trenches and shelled the foe as the infantry advanced.
>
> The area was heavily mined to the extent one could hear antipersonnel mines exploding as the tank tracks broke trip wires. And yet there were no casualties among the infantry as far as any tanker could tell.
>
> Then both second section tanks were disabled by mines.
>
> Next the infantry attack faltered and their platoon leader, in the command tank, could not get them to move. Here was an impasse not thought of by the planners of this novel tank-infantry team action. Something had to be done and quick, or the soldiers would dig in.
>
> The infantry officer said, "I can't control the men from in here. I'm leaving."
>
> [I] said, "Alright. If I place tanks on the right flank firing in from that direction, can you get into town?"
>
> "Yes," he replied. And he opened the hatch, scurrying forward with bullets kicking up dust at his feet.
>
> The order was given. . . . As the tanks turned to face town, a German stood up at the trench and fired a bazooka. Sergeant [Herman] Deaver's gunner shot him center of mass with a high explosive, fuse quick. The enemy round fell short.
>
> The tanks then sprayed the town until the infantry platoon entered. All action ceased by 5:15 P.M.[213]

The 29th Infantry Division began to roll on November 20; it gained two miles. Near Schleiden, Wilkes' platoon encountered a Tiger I tank, which had 100mm (4 inches) of frontal armor—impervious to rounds from a Sherman's gun at any range. The 75mm cannon, carried by nearly all the infantry-support tanks, had been selected in part because it fired a highly effective HE round. Prewar doctrine said that tank destroyers, not tanks, were supposed to fight panzers, a philosophy that did tank crews little good when they had no choice. Wilkes described the action:

At this time a Mark VI engaged three Company A tanks in a gun battle at the range of 2,000 yards, the Tiger having an 88mm, high muzzle velocity gun. One Company A tank was commanded by Sergeant Herman Deaver.

Deaver first fired a high explosive, fuse quick, hitting and breaking one track. He then turned to armor piercing, which failed to damage the Tiger. The foe was slowly traversing for the purpose of engaging the three Americans, therefore the Company A men used their only recourse. They commenced pounding his turret with high explosives, which jarred the tank and gave the crew concussion.

The German knocked out two of the tanks and shot the vane sight off Deaver's turret, located in front of the commander's head, without hitting Deaver. Eventually, the Mark VI ceased firing. Then Deaver set him aflame using white phosphorus.

Later, Deaver inspected this tank to find all the turret crew dead. It was not an affair to inspire confidence in American tanks. Our main gun was useless firing armor piercing, and Deaver used thirty rounds of high explosive plus the rounds expended by the other tanks prior to their destruction.[214]

The 29th Infantry Division chalked up another two miles on November 21.[215] In the face of this threat, *LXXXI Corps* commanding general Köchling asked von Manteuffel's permission to withdraw the center of his corps to the well-fortified strongpoints along the line Aldenhoven-Eberich-Lohn-Pützlohn-Weisweiler. Köchling was pleasantly surprised when von Manteuffel approved (presumably with von Zangen's agreement). Köchling later said that this was his most worrisome moment during the fighting between Aachen and the Rhine.[216]

The Luftwaffe put in another major appearance on November 21, which underscored how seriously the German command viewed the situation. Forty-five aircraft bombed and strafed targets throughout the XIX Corps sector night and day.[217]

The 30th Infantry Division, meanwhile, had faced discernibly tougher going on November 18. Colonel Robert Frankland's 1st Battalion, 117th

Infantry Regiment, was ordered to attack from Hoengen and take Warden. Two attacks during the early hours failed because the captain commanding Company A, 743d Tank Battalion, refused to advance in support. The doughs encountered fierce fire from automatic weapons and assault guns and were thrown back each time. The infantry finally approached Lieutenant Colonel William Duncan, commanding the tank battalion, and asked that he deal with his recalcitrant officer. Duncan relieved the captain following a brief investigation. A third assault, supported by the Shermans carrying four doughs each and raking German positions with machine-gun fire, carried the town. Frankland was amazed at the amount of ammunition found stored in the houses and commented, "Jerry intended to hold that burg."[218]

The 3d Panzergrenadier Division reported that, with the loss of Warden, its MLR had collapsed.[219] The Old Hickory Division widened the breach on November 19 and spurted forward two miles.

Major Wayne Culp, commanding the 3d Battalion of the 117th Infantry, had the village of St. Jöris as his objective. A hastily pulled together conglomeration of troops, including the 2d Battalion, *29th Grenadier Regiment*, and elements of the *246th Volksgrenadier Division*, held the town.

Culp committed two companies, one to attack up each side of the main road into town. He placed four riflemen on the decks of each of six Shermans from the 743d Tank Battalion. One of each foursome carried a BAR. At 0800 hours, an artillery barrage struck St. Jöris, and the 120th Infantry Regiment laid down covering fire from the flank. Culp's 3d Battalion, 117th Infantry, surged forward across the distance to the buildings so quickly that the barrage had to be lifted four minutes early. In St. Jöris, the GIs found German gunners cowering in their shelters from the artillery concentration, and the GIs quickly took more than a hundred prisoners. It was 0900 hours. Nearby Kinzweiler fell just as quickly to 2d Battalion.[220]

The 119th Infantry Regiment seized Weiden and established firm contact with the 104th Infantry Division, on its right. With that, the Old Hickory Division's swinging door maneuver came to a successful conclusion. At a cost of 60 killed and 474 wounded, the division had mauled the *3d Panzergrenadier Division* and *404th Grenadier Regiment*. (The panzergrenadier division was down to seven battle-ready assault guns, although another eighteen were undergoing only minor repairs.) The XIX Corps headquarters on November 20 instructed the 29th Infantry Division to turn over two thousand yards of its front so that Old Hickory could continue to drive toward the Roer.[221]

The 30th Infantry Division reached Fronhoven on November 21. It had managed to advance a bit more than three miles since the beginning of the offensive.

With higher command now worried that the *LXXXI Corps* front might be torn open, Köchling had been able to obtain two fresh resources for his next battle line around Barmen, Koslar, Bourheim, and Kirchberg. The first was the *340th Volksgrenadier Division*. By order of the Führer, the division had received an extra month of training to make it an attack unit when it reorganized from an infantry division beginning in September following its destruction on the eastern front. Only 350 men survived from the old division; the rest were the usual mix of convalescents, raw recruits, and Luftwaffe and naval personnel. The second acquisition, as several unhappy Sherman crews had discovered, was the *301st Schwere Panzer Abteilung* (*Tiger/Fkl*), a battalion equipped with twenty-nine Tiger Is and numerous small radio-controlled (*Funklenk* or *Fkl*) explosive-bearing armored vehicles. (Sixteen of the Tigers, however, were out of battle for major repairs.) The battalion was subordinated to the *3d Panzergrenadier Division*. Model, meanwhile, informed von Manteuffel that elements of the *10th SS Panzer Division* would be moved forward from Erkelenz to Linnich.[222]

Yet there was a note of incipient optimism despite the American gains. *Oberst* Körte, commanding the ragged *246th Volksgrenadier Division*, reported to Köchling, "The MLR between Linnich and Jülich is well constructed and strongly manned; the defense will be iron-strong."[223]

Slamming on the Brakes

Hell on Wheels' CCB spent November 22 trying to get into Merzenhausen, which was held by *Hauptmann* Kuppinger's 1st Battalion, *352d Grenadier Regiment* (which had fought so stubbornly for Setterich), and several Tigers from the *301st Schwere Panzer Abteilung*. At first, American prospects looked good. Flame-throwing Crocodiles from Squadron B, 1st Fife and Forfar Yeomanry, hosed down German positions, which had an electric effect on the German infantry. White flags began to wave all over the place. Just before 1000 hours, however, the Crocodiles were all destroyed by direct fire, and the white flags disappeared.

Company G of the attached 2d Battalion, 119th Infantry, was ordered to conduct a bayonet charge, but that never got off the ground because the men were subjected to heavy fire as soon as they left their positions. Company F, 66th Armored Regiment, finally charged into town, at the cost of four tanks. Infantry followed, but the doughs had battled only a third of the way into town when a Tiger tank counterattacked. The Tiger knocked out a Sherman and drove the infantry to shelter. The Germans knew that the Americans were stuck in the western part of town and rained artillery fire on them. The men outside buildings found that as soon as they dug a foxhole, it filled with rainwater.

Combat Command B would spend the next day holding on, beating off counterattacks, and regrouping.[224]

The 29th Infantry Division's forward roll halted abruptly on November 22 when the outfit reached Koslar and Bourheim, two miles outside Jülich. The division had reached the city's inner ring of defenses, an interlocking line of fortifications running through Koslar, Bourheim, and Kirchberg. The GIs fought all day against the fresh *340th Volksgrenadier Division*, for no gain. Major General Gerhardt had another conversation with Major General Harmon: "Your boy [liaison officer] Mansfield wants to know when we're going to move. It won't be soon. We have a war on again. They didn't pull out, and so we're up against it."[225]

The 3d Battalion, 116th Infantry, assaulted Koslar, backed by Shermans from the 747th Tank Battalion. The doughs advanced in skirmish formation.[226] The tanks advanced some three hundred yards to their rear by sections; two or three tanks were always firing, and the rest were grinding slowly ahead. Three tanks fell victim to antitank fire, and a platoon commander was killed.

Machine-gun and small-arms fire erupted from concertina-protected trenches 150 yards west of Koslar while mortar rounds exploded among the attackers. As dusk deepened, Companies I and L managed to get a few men into the forward trenches, and rifle and grenade duels raged along the position. The tanks ran into a minefield, and four were quickly disabled.

The GIs held on overnight under heavy artillery fire. The mud had so caked their M1s that they had to kick back the operating handle to chamber another round. The 2d Battalion, committed on the left, was in a similar fix.

But so were the Germans. Mud clogged firearms so generally that only grenades were much use in the close-quarters combat. Fighting in the mud, moreover, was particularly exhausting. Nonetheless, the Germans in Koslar would hold out for six more days.

At Bourheim, a direct attack by Companies E and F, 2d Battalion, 175th Infantry Regiment, across sugar beet fields produced little for the 29th Infantry Division but heavy casualties to small-arms, mortar, and artillery fire. Wilkes' company, which supported the attack, by now was down to two tanks of the seventeen with which it had started the offensive. The doughs reached the edge of town, but a German counterattack threw them back out. The battalion retired to reorganize.[227]

For reasons not entirely clear (perhaps new-unit jitters, having also suffered heavy losses), the defending unit—2d Battalion, *696th Grenadier Regiment*—also withdrew. The *340th Volksgrenadier Division* commander, *Oberst* Theodor Tolsdorf, realized that the loss of Bourheim could unhinge his entire MLR; he ordered 2d Battalion, *694th Grenadier Regiment,* to secure the town.[228]

As darkness fell, Captain Robert Gray, commanding Company F, organized the twenty survivors from his own outfit and Company E into two squads. At 1800 hours, the tiny command entered Bourheim unopposed. Patrols cautiously worked through the streets. They were alone. Gray gathered his troops on the edge of town and set up defensive positions. The captain reported his good fortune back to the battalion CO, Lieutenant Colonel Claude Melancon, who immediately ordered the rest of his outfit forward.

Unfortunately the volksgrenadier battalion was advancing in the opposite direction from Kirchberg. The Germans took up residence in zigzag trenches protected by barbed wire and opened fire on the advancing Americans, who were silhouetted by a burning haystack. Gray's men were too close for the American battalion to risk mortar fire on the trenches. Indeed, Gray was now cut off.

Just after midnight, Melancon ordered his men to pull back to Aldenhoven. Gray later reported, "When the battalion withdrew, all hell broke loose in the vicinity of Companies E and F in Bourheim. A German unit started to come into town from the west end and, failing to stop or answer when ordered to do so by our sentries, was fired upon. Almost immediately, the enemy was on all sides firing burp guns and rifles and throwing grenades. One grenade was thrown into the CP, destroying the radio and killing the operator. A perimeter defense was futile, and I decided to try to break through to our lines."

The fierce house-to-house fighting restored the German MLR, but at a high cost. The volksgrenadier battalion's rifle companies lost on average a third of their men.[229]

Gray led fifteen soldiers out, then sneaked back to see whether he could find any of his missing men. He could not. The Germans in Bourheim would hold out until November 26, when a severe local ammunition shortage caused by transport problems would do them in.[230]

On November 22, the 30th Infantry Division, too, encountered much tougher resistance. Rain and mud forced supporting armor to stick to roads. Panzers appeared and contested the 120th Infantry Regiment's attempt to take Lohn in conjunction with a planned 104th Infantry Division assault on neighboring Pützlohn. Three of the tanks were Tigers from the *301st Schwere Panzer Abteilung*, which took up positions on high ground. One shot from a Mark VI destroyed a Sherman and killed the entire crew and four doughs on the back deck. M10s engaged the clearly visible panzers, but their 3-inch rounds bounced harmlessly off their thick armor. Eventually, the panzers lost interest or ran low on ammo, and they withdrew to the east. (The Americans did knock out two of the *301st*'s radio-controlled vehicles loaded with explosives, which the Americans dubbed "doodlebugs.")[231]

Old Hickory also had its second run-in with Jagdpanthers from the *519th Schwere Panzerjäger Abteilung*, which operated against its flanks around Lohn and "caused considerable trouble," according to the division's history.[232]

By day's end, Old Hickory had a tenuous toehold in Lohn. Its attack closer to Pützlohn had failed.

By this point, Ninth Army noted that the pattern of battle was firmly established. The defenses in depth prevented much maneuver by the attackers. "The enemy, knowing how the attack must come, had only to block it head-on and inflict the maximum casualties and delay."[233]

BRITISH XXX CORPS PRESSURES GEILENKIRCHEN

When Lieutenant General Brian Horrocks' British XXX Corps attacked the Siegfried Line defenses on November 18, the attached American 84th Infantry

Division made the main effort. The subordination of the American division to Horrocks had come about as informally as the British involvement in the offensive itself. Simpson had invited Horrocks to dinner to meet Ike, who was visiting Ninth Army in early November. "Well 'Jorrocks,'" Ike asked, "are you going to take on Geilenkirchen for us?" Horrocks replied that he had only one division free. "Give him one of ours," Ike told Simpson.[234]

The British corps and its 43d Infantry Division had concentrated on November 9 in the rear area of XIII Corps. Three days later, Horrocks had taken operational control over the 84th Infantry Division and responsibility for the XIII Corps' line from Teveren, on the new interarmy group boundary, northwest to Maeseyck and east to the western edge of Immendorf. The British 43d was ready to attack from the west and the U.S. 84th from the south through positions of the 102d Infantry Division.[235]

The 84th Infantry Division, like the rest of Ninth Army eventually, would become familiar with British nomenclature and terms. When "the AGRA [Army Group of Royal Artillery] was going to sweeten it up a bit," the Americans learned, the AGRA would reinforce a barrage. Indeed, artillery terminology was important at the moment because, unlike Ninth Army, 30 Corps was rich in artillery ammunition. The 84th Infantry Division's artillery was able to fire twice the volume of shells as that expended by the divisions in XIX Corps. And British divisional artillery expended twice that volume again.[236]

Horrocks offered his British perspective on the green Americans: "The more I saw of the 84th, the more impressed I became with the system of training that had been evolved during the war in the U.S.A. It worked on the sausage-machine principle. The different ingredients in the form of men, officers, and material were poured in at one end, and a complete division trained for war came out at the other."[237]

The presence of the Würm River, which flowed through Geilenkirchen, was the only terrain feature to distinguish the area from the flat, open terrain studded with hamlets, mines, and slag piles in the XIX Corps' zone. The Germans had evacuated civilians from the rail and road center, but before they left they had dug additional positions to complement the steel and concrete defenses of the Siegfried Line. The town itself was not built into the defenses, and no pillboxes would be encountered inside the community. Several nearby villages—including

Süggerath, Würm, and Beeck—did contain bunkers. Pillboxes dominated key terrain features, trenches connected the bunkers, prepared positions were ready on reverse slopes, and antitank ditches blocked approach routes.

Generalleutnant Wolfgang Lange's *183d Volksgrenadier Division*, the main defending unit, fielded perhaps thirty-two hundred men at the end of October. Lange had just inspected the frontline between Geilenkirchen and Immendorf early that morning. He, for one, did not expect an offensive that day.[238]

Colonel John Roosma's 334th Infantry Regiment attacked toward the high ground between Geilenkirchen and Prummern at 0700 hours on November 18. The morning was clear and cold, but the ground was a soggy mess. American tank destroyers and tanks from the British Sherwood Rangers Yeomanry Regiment (Horrocks had sent his most seasoned unit) were assigned for close support, but many of the fields were impassable even to tracked vehicles. Initial progress by the infantry was rapid, but the armor lagged behind.

Lieutenant Colonel Lloyd Gomes, commanding 1st Battalion, 334th Infantry, personally moved from platoon to platoon when the advance slowed under mortar fire as the green riflemen approached the defensive line. He got each outfit moving, and the doughs rushed the trenches running between the bunkers. The German infantry retreated into the fortifications. Gomes later said, "Once you drive the Germans into pillboxes they give up like rats in a trap because they can only fire through apertures, and it is not too difficult to get on their blind side. TNT and grenades are excellent persuaders." By dark, his men held Prummern.

The 333d Infantry Regiment, commanded by Colonel Timothy Pedley Jr., attacked on November 19 with orders to seize Würm and Geilenkirchen. The GIs found resistance to be surprisingly light. In Geilenkirchen itself, they encountered occasional sniper fire but had reached the town center by 0900 hours.

The 84th Infantry Division pushed on until it encountered the first real resistance south of Süggerath, just northeast of Geilenkirchen, in midafternoon. Higher command had deemed that Allied units were too close to one another to permit supporting artillery fire. British tanks arrived; some supported the advance by fire and others moved into the village, with riflemen from Lieutenant Colonel Thomas Woodyard's 1st Battalion, 333d Infantry, following behind them. Orders were to keep moving to the high ground beyond town.

VII Corps commander Maj. Gen. J. Lawton (Lightning Joe) Collins (left) and Field Marshal Bernard L. Montgomery confer during the Battle of the Bulge. Collins executed the main effort to reach the Roer River; Montgomery was Bradley's rival in matters of strategy. *National Archives, Signal Corps photo*

(Left to right) Supreme Allied Commander Europe Gen. Dwight D. Eisenhower, 12th Army Group commander Lt. Gen. Omar N. Bradley, and 1st Army commander Lt. Gen. Courtney Hodges directed the American advance toward the Roer River. *National Archives, Signal Corps photo*

Generalfeldmarschall Gerd von Rundstedt was reinstated as Commander in Chief West as the Allies thundered toward the German border in early September 1944. *National Archives, German newsreel*

Generalfeldmarschall Walter Model, commanding *Army Group B* after September 4, 1944, accomplished the "miracle in the West" that staved off an immediate Allied advance deep into Germany. *National Archives, German newsreel*

A 3d Armored Division Sherman tank moves through the first line of dragon's teeth in the Siegfried Line on September 15, 1944. *National Archives, Signal Corps photo*

A "Jumbo" assault Sherman fires its 75mm gun at a target in Aachen during the preattack bombardment of the city in early October 1944. The Jumbo carried much thicker armor than a standard Sherman and could withstand more punishment. *National Archives, Signal Corps film*

Riflemen from Company M, 26th Infantry Regiment, work with tanks to clear a street in Aachen on October 15, 1944. The 1st Infantry Division developed tactics for patiently securing each building as the troops advanced through the city. *National Archives, Signal Corps photo*

The Germans, who were now fighting for their homeland, defended every city, town, and village from Aachen to the Roer River as if each was a fortress. *National Archives, German newsreel*

This slag heap near Mariagrube was attacked by the 30th Infantry Division on November 16, 1944. These man-made hills were common in the mining country facing Ninth Army, and German troops often fortified them. *U.S. Army photo*

Royal Tigers from the *506th Schwere Panzer Abteilung* (left) and *9th Panzer Division* Panthers prepare for the damaging counterattack against the 2d Armored Division near Puffendorf beginning November 17, 1944. The Tigers carried the dreaded 88mm gun, and their thick armor could deflect most shots from American tanks. *German newsreel, courtesy of International Historic Films*

Tankers from the 743d Tank Battalion knocked out this *Sturmgeschütz* III in Warden on November 18, 1944. This was the most common of several types of turretless armored vehicles lumped together as "assault guns"; a battalion or more of these typically supported a German infantry or panzergrenadier division. The 75mm gun could easily handle the Sherman tank, which had relatively thin armor. *U.S. Army photo*

A machine-gunner with the 104th Infantry Division fires at fortified houses in Stolberg as the offensive begins. The white beam is a tracer round captured in this frame of film footage. *National Archives, Signal Corps film*

A wounded 4th Infantry Division rifleman receives attention from the medics after being hit during the advance toward Grosshau in the Hürtgen Forest on November 18, 1944. *National Archives, Signal Corps photo*

These 1st Infantry Division riflemen walk through Hamich, the scene of bitter fighting at the start of the November Roer offensive. One of at least three *Panzerjäger* IV tank killers destroyed during fierce counterattacks here sits in the middle of the street. *National Archives, Signal Corps film*

Exhausted panzergrenadiers (probably from the hard-fighting *3d Panzergrenadier Division*) roll toward yet one more counterattack against the advancing Americans. *National Archives, German newsreel*

The appearance at Merzenhausen of these British Crocodiles, with the 2d Armored Division, on November 22, 1944, had an electric effect on the German defenders. *National Archives, Signal Corps photo*

German prisoners taken at Jüngersdorf about November 27, 1944, display the exhaustion felt by riflemen on both sides. *National Archives, Signal Corps photo*

The 335th Infantry Regiment, 84th Infantry Division, supported by 7th Armored Division tanks, attacks near Beeck on November 29, 1944. *National Archives, Signal Corps photo*

Shermans from the 771st Tank Battalion form up before the next attack toward Linnich in November 29, 1944. The tanks carry logs to put under the tracks for traction should a tank bog down in the mud. *National Archives, Signal Corps photo*

This view from a spotter plane shows an artillery barrage blasting German defenses at Barmen on December 1, 1944. *National Archives, Signal Corps photo*

GIs enter Lucherberg, the scene of fierce fighting beginning on December 3, 1944, because it occupied strategic high ground west of the Roer. *National Archives, Signal Corps photo*

These German panzergrenadiers are in one of the zigzag trenches that were widely used on the Roer plain. *National Archives, German newsreel*

A German soldier fires a panzerfaust somewhere west of the Roer River. The rocket could easily knock out a Sherman tank. Because of the weapon's short range, this was often as dangerous for the gunner as for the target. *German newsreel, courtesy of International Historic Films*

M4A3s from the 774th Tank Battalion pass a knocked-out *Sturmgeschütz* III near Gürzenich, Germany, on December 17, 1944. *National Archives, Signal Corps photo*

Riflemen from the 83d Infantry Division fight from house to house in the outskirts of Düren, only yards from the Roer River. *National Archives, Signal Corps photo*

A 9th Infantry Division observer overlooks the Roer River northeast of Schmidt. *National Archives, Signal Corps photo*

By mid-December 1944, the Germans were looking at the west bank of the Roer from positions on the eastern side, such as this one. *German newsreel, courtesy of International Historic Films*

GIs haul extra ammunition on sleds as they ready to attack Eicherscheid on January 30, 1945, during the 78th Infantry Division's drive toward the Roer River dams. *National Archives, Signal Corps photo*

This aerial view of the Schwammenauel Dam was issued to the 78th Infantry Division. Cratering from bombing raids is visible on the dam's face. *National Archives, Signal Corps photo*

This view of Urfttalsperre Dam was taken from a 9th Infantry Division observation post on February 5, 1945. Craters from aerial bombing are visible below the dam, and water spills over a portion of the top damaged in an air raid. *National Archives, Signal Corps photo*

These 84th Infantry Division riflemen prepare to cross the Roer River near Linnich on February 23, 1945, as mortar rounds drop nearby. *National Archives, Signal Corps photo*

The doughs paddle across the Roer in their assault boats. *National Archives, Signal Corps photo*

Doughs from the 102d Infantry Division pass through what is left of Linnich in February 1945. *National Archives, Signal Corps photo*

The advance did not quite reach the objective by dark, and casualties began to mount from fire originating from bypassed German infantry in Süggerath.[239]

Woodyard decided that he had to take the high ground or his command would be hit by a major counterattack. He personally led a small team of men from Company C forward along a railroad embankment. He later reported:

> We reached a point about six hundred yards northeast of Süggerath and were just getting ready to go up the high ground to our right. We were ambushed. That's what it was. Those guys jumped us. There were six or seven Jerries on both sides of us. There was a machine gun ahead of us. I couldn't use the radio.
>
> We got all tied up in some telephone wires and couldn't swing free. The Germans had cut all the telephone and telegraph lines from each section of poles, and they were lying along the railroad track and beside it in a low ravine.
>
> One Jerry stood right up on the tracks with a machine pistol. He [had probably been] lying between the tracks. He just stood up and let go. He hit the man right behind me in the throat. Some of our boys fired and got a couple of them.
>
> This quieted them down. We thought maybe they were pulling back. A group from Company C was following about seventy-five yards back, but they were pretty slow.
>
> I got my compress and began to take care of the wounded man. . . . Then some Jerry threw a grenade and I was hit in the left arm. I don't know why I wasn't killed. Blood was spurting from my arm. I rolled over, still tangled up in the wire. I couldn't see a thing, and I didn't know whether the man I was holding died or not. . . . It was 1830.[240]

The 102d Infantry Division's 405th Infantry Regiment was attached to the 84th Infantry Division on November 19 and joined its operations. The 84th Division commanding general, Brigadier General Alexander Bolling, decided to employ the 2d Battalion, 405th Infantry, to cover his flank west of Immendorf.[241] The battalion attacked toward Beeck behind British tanks through pouring rain and artillery fire. After the loss of several tanks, the GIs dug in for a miserable night.[242]

***

On November 21 and 22, elements of the *15th Panzergrenadier* and *10th SS Panzer divisions* reinforced the faltering *183d Volksgrenadier Division*, and the latter was subordinated to *XLVII Panzer Corps*. Ninth Army noted, "The new formations defended their ground with far more vigor. . . ."[243] A regiment from the *15th Panzergrenadier Division* failed in an attempt to retake Geilenkirchen, but the Germans now had enough force available to stabilize the line.[244]

THE GERMAN VIEW: GAINING TIME FOR THE COUNTERBLOW

By November 22, the Germans had lost, on average, six kilometers (four miles) along the front since the beginning of the 12th Army Group's offensive on November 16. Von Zangen assessed that several factors were controlling the course of battle. First, the Americans had attacked before the German defenses were fully developed, but on the bright side they were advancing systematically from village to village rather than pursuing daring operations deep into German territory. His own line was thinly held, and only the timely intervention of the *XLVII Panzer Corps* had prevented the collapse of the *183d Volksgrenadier Division* near Linnich. The American air force was causing considerable trouble. But the weather and mud were so bad that the Americans at times could not even use their tanks.

The grudging withdrawal of Engel's *12th Volksgrenadier Division* around Eschweiler offered von Zangen encouragement. His artillery—blessed with ample ammunition and excellent observation—was playing a key role, particularly around Linnich-Geilenkirchen and before Düren. Mobile and deeply echeloned tank defenses had combined to take a heavy toll on the attackers.

Von Zangen needed to hold a bridgehead on the west bank of the Roer to protect the buildup for the coming Ardennes offensive. Moreover, the more damage he could inflict on the attackers, the less able they would be to deploy south once Hitler's counterblow had begun. In the best case, he could pin some of the American divisions in place. It troubled von Zangen that because of extreme secrecy he could not explain to his corps and division commanders why they had to fight so desperately west of the river to guard preparations for the offensive instead of withdrawing behind its protecting waters.

Von Zangen concluded that defending the high ground along the Linnich-Lindern road would be particularly important in the next phase of the battle, because it offered good observation of much of the Roer Valley. He needed to buy time for his own defenses, too. Engineers were only beginning to strengthen fortified positions on the east bank of the Roer.[245]

CHAPTER 5

GERMAN RESISTANCE HARDENS FURTHER

At the end of November, the enemy's overall situation on the Western front, particularly in the zone of advance of the First U.S. Army, showed a marked improvement despite our attack.

FIRST UNITED STATES ARMY, REPORT OF OPERATIONS,
1 AUGUST 1944–22 FEBRUARY 1945

Bradley had cracked the outer layer of the German defenses before the Roer in First and Ninth armies' sectors and covered roughly half the distance to the goal in a week. German commanders were determined to slow that pace dramatically.

FIRST ARMY BULLS AHEAD

On November 22, Collins modified the VII Corps operations plan, effective at midnight. The 104th Infantry Division was directed to capture the Weisweiler-Frenz-Inden area; the idea of pinching out the division was thus dropped. The Timberwolves' focus changed, however, from supporting the 1st Infantry Division, on their right, to operating in concert with XIX Corps, on their left.

The Big Red One, meanwhile, was sent toward the high ground above the Roer in the Langerwehe-Merode-Schlich area and along the main Eschweiler-Düren road. The 4th Infantry Division was directed to take the high ground in the Grosshau area. Both divisions were to establish bridgeheads across the river once they had reached their objectives.[1]

Waterloo at Pützlohn

The 104th Infantry Division again set the pace on November 23. By now, Collins enthusiastically credited Terry Allen with "making hay"—and making good on his boast about how good the Timberwolves would be.[2]

The 414th Infantry Regiment made substantial progress along the Inde River, and after darkness fell it advanced up the left bank of the stream to the outskirts of Weisweiler. The 415th Infantry Regiment, meanwhile, spent the day mopping up Eschweiler.[3]

In contrast to the previous day, however, the Germans offered unyielding resistance from high ground near Pützlohn, courtesy of some Tiger tanks and the *3d Panzergrenadier Division*—particularly *Hauptmann* Weise's 3d Battalion, *29th Grenadier Regiment*, which fought for control of the village itself. Paul Chronister was a lieutenant in Company K, 413th Infantry Regiment. He later wrote, "As I remember Pützlohn, with the taking of the town and Hills 272 and 303, it was more or less the Waterloo for the 3d Battalion of 413th Infantry." He described the action:

> We went to the right side of Pützlohn and to the backside under the cover of darkness. The 1st Platoon went first and went through town and set up defense on our left side of town. The 2d Platoon started clearing out the houses as they went and ran into sniper fire, and the lieutenant and platoon sergeant were killed, along with several other men from the 2d Platoon.
>
> The 3d Platoon took over a farmhouse with a rock wall enclosed farmyard and set up defense facing the east. This was the headquarters of the unit in charge of the defense of Pützlohn, which 3d Platoon captured.
>
> The machine gun section that I was with followed 3d Platoon. The mortar section was attached to Captain Brown's headquarters, and they were to follow the machine guns, but they waited too long and it got too light and they were unable to get into town.
>
> The machine gun section started to go through town and confronted a German soldier who was walking in front of a German tank. We couldn't see the tank as it was around the corner, but we sure could hear it. He saw us and put up his hands and took two or three more steps toward us. An expression went across his face as plain as

day. It said, "Why should I be surrendering to you when I have a German tank behind me?" He made a *fatal* mistake when he turned and ran, getting only another couple steps. Needless to say, we moved to another section of town. . . .

I stepped into a room, saw a German in a room across the street which was only about twenty-five feet away. He saw me at the same time I saw him. He started to raise his gun as I started to raise mine, and it looked like a draw to me. I was not interested in a draw, so I just stepped back.

Then I found out the company commander and mortar section had not made it into the town. I functioned as company commander since I was the only officer around. At that time we didn't know where 1st Platoon was. The 1st Platoon and company commander had no SCR-300 [backpack] radios. Therefore 2d Platoon and 3d Platoon and machine gun sections had no means of communication. Later we learned the radio with 1st Platoon got knocked out early in the morning.

When 3d Platoon sent prisoners back, they sent Sergeant Ladner and Sergeant Slover [forward], each with an SCR-300 radio. Sergeant Slover made it, and Sergeant Ladner didn't.

This gave us some means of communication. Sergeant Gropp and I were trying to get some artillery fire on about five tanks setting out in the open. And he said to me, "Thanksgiving Day, what do we have to be thankful for?" I looked at him and said, "You are alive, are you not?"

Coming back to the artillery fire we were trying to get, about an hour later we got it right where we wanted, but the tanks were long gone. The whole front was screaming for artillery fire.

About mid-afternoon, they launched a counterattack with three tanks and about twelve infantrymen behind each tank. The 3d Platoon had their men dug in outside the courtyard, and by the time the tanks got into town, there were no infantrymen left [behind them].

The 3d Platoon didn't have any bazooka men, and I sent my runner, John Dresch, to the 2d Platoon to get their bazooka man. I took one look at him and saw he was a new man in the company and probably didn't have any extra training in firing the bazooka, so I asked him if he had fired the bazooka before, and he said yes, once in training. I said that was as often as I had fired, so go ahead. He hit a tank, but the bazooka didn't go off. I think he forgot to pull the safety pin.

The last [German] infantryman who almost made it into town was in clear view of where we were. With me were Sergeant Akin, Dresch, and the bazooka man. Akin said, "He is moving, shall I shoot him?" I said I didn't care. In a little bit he shot him with a tracer. Akin said, "I sure didn't know that a tracer was in my gun and wouldn't have shot him if he hadn't reached for his gun."

While this was taking place, the three tanks had stopped about fifty yards away and all turned their guns toward us. I figured they would knock the stone wall down that we were behind into pieces. I thought we had all bought it. We all crawled under a little something. I crawled under an old hand-turned grinding stone, which offered no protection. For some reason, they didn't fire. Maybe it was our mothers' prayers or ours or the fact that we were in their defense headquarters or maybe they were as nervous in the service as we were, especially when they turned around and found no infantrymen around. After a period of time they withdrew to another part of town.

Some time toward evening, we got instructions on the radio that a company from the 1st Battalion was coming in to relieve us. . . .

So ends Thanksgiving Day of 1944. Our company will remember it, as I will, and all of us who walked out that night have something to be thankful for. You are thankful for every firefight that you walk away from.[4]

The 750th Tank Battalion, which was supporting the 413th Infantry Regiment's attack, lost seven tanks in the course of the day.[5] The *301st Schwere Panzer Abteilung* reported two Tigers lost at Pützlohn. *Hauptmann* Weise's battalion was reduced to thirty men during the fight for the village.[6]

The 1st Infantry Division spent another frustrating day on November 23, beating against stubborn resistance with little gain to show for it.[7] The 4th Infantry Division's 8th Infantry Regiment scraped out a gain of seven hundred yards along the Schevenhütte-Düren road, and the 12th Infantry Regiment crawled another five hundred yards toward Grosshau through minefields and artillery fire.[8]

The VII Corps made only tactical gains along most of its front on November 24. The 3d Armored Division rejoined the fight when Major General Maurice Rose issued oral instructions to CCA to secure the high ground between Langerwehe and Frenz. A task force commanded by Lieutenant Colonel Walter Richardson, CO of the 3d Battalion, 32d Armored Regiment, was formed for the job. In addition to his own outfit, Richardson commanded a battalion from the 47th Infantry Regiment and a platoon each of tank destroyers and combat engineers.

Luck smiled on the Germans. The Americans failed to detect a gap outside Hücheln that Group Engel had no way to plug. Instead, they attacked right into the positions in town held by the 1st Battalion, *27th Fusilier Regiment*, and an antitank platoon.

The task force pushed toward the northeast between two railroads and immediately encountered strong opposition. By dark, the combat command had captured Hücheln, but the defenders had avoided a potential disaster.[9]

Tanks in the Woods

The best news for VII Corps on November 24 came from perhaps the least expected quarter. The 4th Infantry Division gained almost half a mile along the Schevenhütte-Düren road, and advances through the woods brought the outfit almost to the eastern edge of the Hürtgen Forest. The 12th Infantry Regiment overran the German line in its sector and found the enemy confused and disorganized; one battalion CP was captured before the occupants even realized they were under attack. American troops now held the high ground overlooking Grosshau, but artillery and mortar fire from the far side of the clearing checked further progress.[10]

The next day, rain turned the few available roads and trails to seas of mud, and tanks and tank destroyers found it virtually impossible to support infantry operations. Prepositioned German assault guns, however, were able to keep up a deadly fire near Grosshau.[11]

The 12th Infantry Regiment's 2d Battalion nevertheless made a crucial gain after pushing off against light small-arms fire at 0800 hours. The battalion captured terrain overlooking the town of Hürtgen, namesake of the whole cursed forest, and was able to support by fire an attack on the village by the 5th Armored Division's CCR. The 5th Armored Division's history describes that assault:

At 2400 Company B of the 10th [Tank Battalion] left Rötgen and moved toward its designated area on the road. When the infantry company arrived, the men jumped from their halftracks and sought cover in the basements, for heavy artillery was already falling around them.

Marching in a column of twos, the infantry company moved out at 0530 toward the front line between Germeter and Hürtgen. Rain and snow slanted through the pine trees, turning the muddy roads into quagmires, making their march a step-by-step struggle. The company was led by an 8th Infantry Division guide, one of the twenty-two men left of his company, and was to follow a path marked with white engineer tape. The heavy artillery and stormy weather had long since removed this marker, and the company walked in the heavily mined forest without a marked passage. The Germans had sewn the area heavily with wooden-box *Schü* and other antipersonnel mines, and almost immediately explosions and cries for "medics!" filled the forest. At dawn, the Germans began to pour in more and more artillery. Small-arms fire increased.

Casualties skyrocketed, and when the tanks arrived at the jump-off point at their scheduled time, 0730, the infantry company was badly battered.

On the road between Germeter and Hürtgen, an 8th Infantry Division light tank had struck a mine, blocking the road. A tank retriever went forward to remove it, but the retriever, too, hit a mine and was disabled. An effort was made to dynamite the light tank off the road, but this caused a large crater which made as formidable an obstacle as the disabled tank.

Despite the cratered road and the heavy casualties already suffered by the infantry company, the attack started at 0730. The tanks lurched toward Hürtgen, with Lt. Jack McAuley leading. McAuley's tank neared the crater, and he called back on the radio, "I'm going to try to jump the damned thing." His tank gathered speed, roared up the soupy road, his tracks throwing a brown spray of mud to the rear. At the crater's edge, the driver put on one final burst of speed, but the crater was too wide. The tank slammed into the crater's side, rolled to the left and lay half on its side, but it was in perfect defilade. McAuley could fire his 75 only by using his elevating mechanism to traverse and his traversing mechanism to elevate. From this position, the officer and his gunner, Cpl. William S. Hibler, fired round after round into enemy positions. The 95th [Armored Field] Artillery and Lt. James M. McFadden's 47th Assault Gun Platoon continued pounding the Germans in Hürtgen. Company B of the 10th had already lost three tank commanders to snipers, who were firing from the woods on the left.

Engineers were called up to bridge the crater so the column could slip around McAuley's tank and push on to Hürtgen. Captain Charles Perlman, commander of Company C, 22d Engineers, came up to assist the engineers, was wounded, and was evacuated. Heavy artillery and mortar fire rained down on the engineers as they worked. Captain Frank M. Pool, Company B, [was] hit by a German burpgun while standing in his turret directing the bridging operations but refused to be evacuated. He climbed out of his tank to help the engineers and while on the ground was wounded again, this time by mortar fire. He again refused to be evacuated but was soon so weak from loss of blood that evacuation was necessary. Lieutenant Lewis R. Rollins took over the company.

By 1030, working under heavy fire, the engineers had bridged the crater. Lieutenant McAuley ordered Sgt. William Hurley to move his tank over the span so he could fire on the right flank and protect the column, but Hurley's tank hit a mine, again blocking the road. While carrying out these orders, Sergeant Hurley was wounded by sniper fire and was evacuated.

Then S/Sgt. Lawrence Summerfield, who was later given a battlefield commission, managed to snake his tank around the other two disabled Shermans and almost to the bend in the road that led into Hürtgen. Just as his tank pulled up to the corner, a German antitank gun, which had been zeroed [in] on the corner, fired at him and missed. As the shots zoomed by Summerfield's tank, his gunner, Cpl. Benny R. Majka, knocked out the German gun with one round from his 75. Just then, another German gun opened fire on Summerfield's tank, knocking it out. . . .

At this time, Capt. Richard Lewis's Company B, 47th [Armored Infantry Regiment], had only eighty men left out of two hundred twenty-five. . . . It was a hopeless job to continue the attack.[12]

***

The 22d Infantry Regiment, meanwhile, sent its 2d and 3d battalions to envelop Grosshau, skipping the usual artillery preparation in order to achieve surprise. Difficulty in bringing armor forward delayed the 2d Battalion's attack, but both outfits fought through fierce resistance and reached their objectives during the morning.

At 1145 hours, the 3d Battalion tried to cross open terrain into Grosshau from the north. The Germans reacted immediately, and fire from assault guns, mortars, and small arms halted the assault. Supporting tanks and tank destroyers burst into flames. Sergeant Mack Morriss briefly described the 70th Tank Battalion's charge: "[The tanks] lunged forward, and some of them still dragged the foliage of the forest on their hulls when they were knocked out. One crew abandoned their tank, leaving behind all their equipment in the urgency of the escape. But they took with them the mascot rooster they had picked up at St. Lô."[13]

Cecil Nash, a tank platoon commander in Company C, remembered the attack:

> I could see the Germans walking around in a patch of woods beyond the forest about 2,000 yards ahead and to our right. It had all the earmarks of a trap, of them trying to draw us out. In hindsight, we could have plastered that patch with phosphorus and smoked them out, but we didn't. We had been told not to use it, as Germans claimed it was gaseous and hence in violation of the Geneva Convention.
>
> [The platoon moved out, and the first tank was hit immediately]. Al Orner, my driver, stopped, but I told him to go around it. We did, and got about a hundred yards into open country when they got us. There was a blinding flash, and my legs folded under me. Ralph Planck, my gunner, was hit in his rear end, and the loader, Al Kieltyka, in the back.... Orner and the assistant driver were not wounded and helped us get to the ground and away from the burning tank before it exploded.... As it happened, the rest of our platoon was also knocked out and needed help, and the same with the [tank destroyers] who were with us.[14]

Nash counted fourteen vehicles burning.

After another fruitless charge, the weakened battalion dug in along the wood line above town.[15]

Model Stiffens the Line

Generalfeldmarschall Model was juggling his forces to ensure the integrity of his front. On November 25, *XLVII Panzer Corps*, now consisting of the *9th* and *116th Panzer, 10th SS Panzer,* and *15th Panzergrenadier divisions*, took charge of the defensive line roughly between Lindern and Merzenhausen. These divisions had constituted *Army Group B's* reserves.[16]

The *LXXXI Corps*, meanwhile, began to extract what remained of the *246th Volksgrenadier Division* from the line for several days to reorganize. The artillery crews limbered their guns and headed to the rear, followed that night by the antitank units. The infantry battalions would follow early the next morning. The first dozen assault guns from the *667th Sturmgeschütz Brigade* arrived to buttress Bork's *47th Volksgrenadier Division*, and nineteen more were on the way.[17] So was the *3d Fallschirmjäger Division*.

The 104th Infantry Division on November 25 finally threw the Germans off the high ground east of Pützlohn. It also finished mopping up Eschweiler. Combined with the progress at Weisweiler, the division had established control over the length of the Inde River west of Weisweiler.[18]

Hauptmann Hans Zeplien's 14th (*Panzerjäger*) Company of the *89th Grenadier Regiment* was supporting the defenders of Weisweiler and had a busy day against the 414th Infantry Regiment. *Feldwebel* (Sergeant) Peters' 1st Antitank Platoon was deployed with *Hauptmann* Ripcke's 1st Battalion at Am Oberen Schildchen. The two NCOs and twenty men were armed with a mix of one-man panzerfausts and crew-served bazookas.

During the morning, the defenders managed to cut off two American infantry companies. A detachment from the 750th Tank Battalion and a platoon of division reconnaissance troops battled their way toward the surrounded doughs.[19]

The antitank men waited while the *Ami* tanks got close enough for them to use their rocket launchers. Peters and *Unteroffizier* (Corporal) Möller hit three M5 Stuarts between them, two of which burned. Möller and his assistant were wounded, however, a common fate for the gunners. *Landsers* Bauer and Miller were consumed by flames when they shot a Stuart from too close a range and were caught in the explosion. (The 750th Tank Battalion reported the destruction of only two M5s in the encounter, with one entire crew and another officer killed.)

Zeplien would later credit his crazily brave eastern front veterans for setting the example for his replacements for how to play this deadly game. The company suffered badly under the heavy American attack: Twelve men were wounded and eighteen went missing in action.[20]

Clearing weather in the afternoon of November 25 brought American close-support air strikes around Weisweiler, Frenz, Lammersdorf, Inden, and a couple of towns in the 1st Infantry Division zone. But it was another day of halting gains through mud and artillery fire.[21]

Heinz Schnelle was a seventeen-year-old member of the assault platoon, 3d Battalion, *5th Fallschirmjäger Regiment,* one of the first elements of *Generalmajor* Wandehn's just arriving *3d Fallschirmjäger Division* to work its way into the line in front of the Big Red One near Langerwehe. Schnelle's unit had been reorganized in October and November in Holland, primarily from Luftwaffe personnel. Few German airborne troops were trained to jump at this stage in the war; such divisions were notable mainly because they were extremely strong infantry formations (sixteen thousand men) fielding three battalions per rifle regiment instead of two. Before heading to the Roer sector, some veteran *Fallschirmjäger* filled out the unit. The *LXXXI Corps* assessed, "The division is made up of the best human material, although mainly briefly trained and led by inexperienced officers." In Schnelle's platoon, all riflemen carried submachine guns or assault rifles. There were also MG42s, crew-served bazookas, and grenade launchers.[22]

Schnelle spent his first night at the front in the basement of a needle factory under heavy American artillery fire. The veterans tried to calm the green soldiers. Otto Pape, a machine-gunner, called out, "Stop, or I'll tell my dad!" every time a shell exploded close overhead. Schnelle read a prayer book he had picked up on the way to the front.

Schnelle recalled his first action, "At noon the order came: 'Assault platoon march!' The *Amis* attacked. . . . We ran back and forth between the needle factory and the tunnel under the tracks on Schönthal Road, through gardens, backyards, stables, kitchens, living rooms, bedrooms, along the Wehebach [creek], always under fire."[23]

Somewhat farther north, the 3d Armored Division's task force, under Lieutenant Colonel Walter Richardson, moved out at 0830 hours toward its next objective between Langerwehe and Frenz. Twelve of the thirteen attached tanks bogged down in mud, and Richardson watched in agony as accurate antitank fire set several of his immobile Shermans ablaze. Needless to say, progress was slow. One engineer team alone removed more than a thousand antitank mines from the route of advance. Nevertheless, Richardson would slog his way onto the objective by the next day.[24]

American aircraft returned on November 26 to drop a hundred tons of bombs on German targets in front of the 1st and 104th Infantry divisions. *Generalmajor* Engel complained to *LXXXI Corps*, "Some Luftwaffe missions are urgently needed because the *Jabos* [*Jagd-Bombers*, or fighter-bombers] are fiercely attacking not only our infantry but our artillery. The lack of intelligence [on the enemy's positions], moreover, is taking our artillery out of the battle." Köchling, after contacting von Zangen, told Engel he could expect the Luftwaffe to reappear that afternoon.[25]

On the left, the 104th Infantry Division took Frenz and mopped up Weisweiler.[26] *Hauptmann* Ripcke would be awarded the Knight's Cross for his tenacious defense at Weisweiler. *Hauptmann* Zeplien's company lost another five men killed, two wounded, and one missing as the defenders retreated through town. Another two of his soldiers died in the blast as they destroyed an American tank from close range.[27] The *89th Grenadier Regiment* nonetheless held out at the Frenzerburg Castle, which provided an anchor to Engel's suddenly endangered right flank.[28]

Castle Keep

The eighty men of Company K, 2d Battalion, 47th Infantry Regiment, on November 26 walked carefully along a railroad line running through a sugar beet field. The company had an easy job. All it had to do was guard the regimental left flank while the other guys did the heavy lifting for the day.[29]

A short distance ahead, *Hauptmann* Ripcke had deployed *Oberleutnant* Willi Schriewer's 1st Company at Frenzerburg Castle, a medieval fortress that struck one observer as looking more Victorian than Gothic. The castle was laid out in two squares with a courtyard in the center of each, offering the appearance of a figure eight from above. The main section included a mansion protected by crenelated walls and a water-filled moat. A gatehouse with a stout wooden gate faced the outer section, but the drawbridge was down. Stables and barns formed the outer square.

In front of Company K, the top of Frenzerburg Castle was visible above trees on the far side of the field. Suddenly, all hell broke loose when mortar and machine-gun fire lashed the GIs. Lieutenant Chester Jordan, a platoon commander, later recalled trying to get his men moving forward out of the fire. "I felt sympathy, because running on [sugar] beets is like running on loosely packed bowling balls."

The doughboys reached the woods, where they surprised several German soldiers just setting up a machine gun. The Germans surrendered. The castle, the Americans realized, lay on the far side of yet another sugar beet field. Company K's commanding officer was hit by shellfire, and Lieutenant William McWaters took charge.

With incoming fire still whipping around the company, McWaters decided to rush the complex with his remaining sixty men. Company K charged forward and overran a foxhole line manned by some forty poorly trained service troops, who surrendered after a couple of them had been shot. The fifty remaining Americans took shelter in the outer buildings and secured their prisoners in a basement.

Jordan told his bazooka man, Private First Class Carl Sheridan, to knock the hinges off the massive gate. Sheridan destroyed one of the hinges before he was gunned down. The private was awarded the Medal of Honor for his efforts.

Only 150 yards separated the combatants. As darkness fell, *Oberleutnant* Schriewer assembled a group of eleven men, who crept toward the American-held buildings. They encountered a squad of tired dogfaces asleep in one basement. As *Landser* Böhm later recalled, "At first they did not want to surrender and come out. But after we fired a shot with the panzerfaust into the adjacent cellar room, fifty [*sic*] Americans did come up, one after the other, hands up in the air. [The American accounts make clear that fewer men than that were involved.] We could also liberate thirty German soldiers, mostly wounded." The Germans left the American wounded behind in the basement when they pulled back.

During the German raid, Jordan was in a pigsty talking to an artillery forward observer who had just arrived. A burp gun poked through the door beside his head and hosed down the interior. Nobody was hit, but Jordan was left with ringing ears.

Three Sherman tanks and some extra infantry from Companies F and G, meanwhile, had arrived to help Company K. After firing at the castle walls for a while, the tanks ground forward through the twilight. One of the tanks bogged down, and a second tipped into the moat. The third approached the main gate.

Oberleutnant Ludwig Havighorst and eighty combat engineers from the *3d Fallschirmjäger Division* were just arriving to relieve the grenadiers when the Shermans attacked. The men made up 15th Company, 3d Battalion, *5th Fallschirmjäger Regiment*. Five of Havighorst's young soldiers (most of the division's troops were between sixteen and nineteen years old and lacked combat experience) had been wounded by artillery on the way in.

While the Sherman fired energetically in all directions, Havighorst ran into the castle with three men and an "antitank gun"—presumably some sort of rocket launcher. The *Fallschirmjäger* set up the weapon on a table in one of the halls and sighted on the Sherman. Just at that moment, the tank fired its main gun through the window, and the explosion showered the men with stone.

"To the other hall!" Havighorst ordered. The men ran and set up the weapon again. They had an even better view. Their first shot struck the tank, and flames rose from the rear. The crew bailed out and dashed to safety.

The next morning at 0400 hours, elements of *Gruppe Engel's 89th Grenadier Regiment* (some ninety men, backed by two companies of *Fallschirmjäger*) and fifteen assault guns counterattacked to help the *Fallschirmjäger* in the castle. The Americans brought heavy fire to bear just as the assault was starting, and there were many German casualties.[30] The attackers reached the road beside the outbuildings but got no farther. Artillery hit two of the assault guns, but one worked its way into the outer courtyard and caused some consternation until a few GIs threw enough grenades at it to scare off the crew. There was a good bit of shooting back and forth the rest of the day.

At about 1500 hours, while the grenadiers in the castle were sneaking out the back exit, German-born American captain William Ewald approached the building in response to a request by Havighorst for a cease-fire to evacuate the seriously wounded. Ewald offered the Germans some cigarettes and encouraged them to surrender, because their plight was hopeless. Havighorst shared some corn schnapps and politely disagreed. After the two negotiated a two-hour cease-fire, the American told Havighorst that if his company were to depart between 2300 and 0100 hours that night, they would not be fired upon. Failing that, the Americans would shell the castle into rubble. The *Fallschirmjäger* escorted Ewald back to American territory.

Shortly before 0100 hours, Havighorst received orders to withdraw. He led his men to fallback positions a thousand meters to the rear.

Unaware that the Germans had gone, three tank destroyers pounded the castle gate with 90mm shells for several hours early the next day. When the infantry charged in, they found only the bodies of sixty German soldiers and some civilians deep in the cellars. The Americans had lost thirty-five killed and two hundred wounded.

The Big Red One on November 26 established firm control over the Weisweiler-Langerwehe road and fought up a hill overlooking Langerwehe.[31] The artillery preparations for the attacks by the 16th and 18th Infantry regiments hit the German lines just as reinforcements from the *3d Fallschirmjäger Division* were arriving, and the terrified green troops surrendered in large numbers. (Perhaps having foreseen such problems, Model that day had instructed that the *Fallschirmjäger* should be used only for defensive missions.)[32]

The 4th Infantry Division consolidated and slightly expanded its gains. The division staff prepared for operations against Kleinhau in conjunction with V Corps' 8th Infantry Division and CCR, 5th Armored Division. One patrol wormed its way into Grosshau after dark and reported hearing the sounds of tracked vehicles.[33]

Almost Out of the Woods

On November 27, VII Corps reached the forward edge of the modified immediate objectives that Collins had established on November 22. The 1st Infantry Division cleared the hill above Langerwehe, and lead elements of the 18th Infantry Regiment entered the town. To the south, a battalion of the 26th Infantry Regiment stormed Jüngersdorf. The regiment had finally worked its way partially free of the Hürtgen Forest.[34]

The 4th Infantry Division emerged from its corner of the forest, as well, and advanced a half mile around Grosshau in coordination with the 8th Infantry

Division.[35] The Germans defended the town with dug-in tanks supported by assault guns and emplaced machine guns.[36]

Mexican-born private Marcario Garcia was an acting squad leader in Company B, 22d Infantry Regiment, during the assault on Grosshau. His Medal of Honor citation described his part in the fighting: "Attacking prepared positions on a wooded hill, which could be approached only through meager cover, his company was pinned down by intense machine-gun fire and subjected to a concentrated artillery and mortar barrage. Although painfully wounded, he refused to be evacuated and on his own initiative crawled forward alone until he reached a position near an enemy emplacement. Hurling grenades, he boldly assaulted the position, destroyed the gun, and with his rifle killed three of the enemy who attempted to escape. When he rejoined his company, a second machine gun opened fire, and again the intrepid soldier went forward, utterly disregarding his own safety. He stormed the position and destroyed the gun, killed three more Germans, and captured four prisoners. He fought on with his unit until the objective was taken and only then did he permit himself to be removed for medical care."

Only repeated attempts enabled two companies from the 22d Infantry Regiment to reach the edge of town by evening. Tanks, tank destroyers, and antitank guns were rushed forward to strengthen the position at about 1800 hours.[37]

Grim reports arrived at *LXXXI Corps* beginning early in the day. The *47th Volksgrenadier Division's* defense of the Kammerbusch was collapsing. Just to the south, the Americans were threatening Merode. *Generalmajor* Engel told Köchling, "The men are exhausted and incapable of further resistance. There are many reports that they can no longer lift their machine guns." The entire right wing opposite XIX Corps was also under intense pressure (see following). Köchling concluded that he would have to throw a regiment of the *246th Volksgrenadier Division* back into the line.

Köchling could see one ray of hope. The Roer was at flood levels in many stretches, and Köchling had little worry that the Americans could cross the river unless they captured a bridge intact.[38]

***

On November 28, the *Fallschirmjäger* in Heinz Schnelle's *5th Regiment* were ordered to recapture Jüngersdorf. Schnelle recalled:

> The first part of the assault went smoothly, just like on the training ground. The group leaders gave their orders and we started charging. But when the groups to our right had just reached the outskirts of the village, gunfire set in. Right away I could hear the men screaming: "Sergeant Mürkens down! Stomach wound!" To our right the battle raged in full steam, and we approached . . . our target, despite being under heavy fire ourselves. . . . The other groups stormed the village, shouting "Hooray" and all. I only thought how many of them didn't even have a grown-man's voice yet!
>
> We were about twenty meters away from the house but we were stuck there. Constantly under *Ami* fire and we couldn't even see them! Whenever we thought we had silenced them with our [machine gun] or submachine guns, they answered with the loud, rattling sound of their heavy [machine guns].[39]

The GIs eventually threw back the *Fallschirmjäger* assault after inflicting heavy losses.

The Battle for Inden

While the 1st Infantry Division battled through the streets of Langerwehe and Jüngersdorf on November 28, the 104th Infantry Division's 413th Infantry Regiment pushed into Inden and Lamersdorf, just to the south, against the grenadiers and assault guns of Denkert's *3d Panzergrenadier Division*. The German defenders for two days had held onto strongpoints located on a series of hills west of Altdorf, Inden, and Lamersdorf. To their rear ran the Inde River. The eastern bank was higher than the western and provided good observation of the battlefield. The high ground east of the river at Lucherberg also was a key observation point for directing artillery.[40] That same high ground overlooked the Roer River from Schophoven to Düren, which lent the town of Inden—the gateway to Lucherberg—far more importance than its modest size suggested.

An anonymous panzergrenadier described the situation this way: "The Inde, right behind us, is a river that the enemy will have to cross in order to get to the Roer. It is about eight meters [twenty-five feet] wide, cold, the current is wild, it is very difficult to wade through it; tanks cannot drive through the riverbed. The river crossings in Altdorf, Inden, and Lamersdorf are prepared to be blown up."[41]

Inden stretched along the west bank of the river; only its northern half was more than one street wide. An extension of the settlement along the east-west Highway 56, which traversed a bridge in the center of town, occupied the far bank.

The Americans, who attacked before dawn without an artillery preparation to ensure surprise, surrounded several of the strongpoints. The GIs needed to eject elements of the *29th Grenadier Regiment* (supplemented by *Kampfgruppe Nohse*, some fifty men from the *Fifth Panzer Army Alarm-Bataillon*) from Inden and Lamersdorf. The *8th Grenadier Regiment* held Altdorf. Direct air support assisted the advance by striking Pier and Lucherberg a short distance to the German rear. (The 30th Infantry Division would seize Altdorf that day and throw the panzergrenadiers there across the Inde River—see following.)[42]

Expecting little resistance, the Americans entered Inden by 0530 hours, when the 1st Battalion's Company C, led by Captain Ralph Gleason, sneaked into town unobserved, then advanced toward the river. Malfunctioning radios immediately isolated the platoons from one another, but the GIs moved eastward toward the river without encountering any opposition. Second Lieutenant Jerry Page, leading the 2d Platoon, reached the northernmost of two vehicular-foot bridges in Inden, where he discovered demolition wires. After he cut the wires and deployed one squad to cover his rear, Page led his men across the river and dug in, covered by a 60mm mortar section on the west bank. Only a few buildings were scattered along the east bank at this point. A road stretched away toward a railroad track some fifteen hundred yards distant.

The Germans caught on at about 0830 hours. Bullets began to zing by, and a German mortar opened fire on Page's mortar section. Page decided to move into a nearby building that offered a better position from which to cover the road and, just as important, currently sheltered German soldiers who were firing at his men. The 2d Platoon cleared the building, but by 1130 hours heavy stuff was falling on it from the east. Having established no contact with the rest of the company, Page pulled back across the bridge. The other two platoons in Gleason's company, meanwhile, had become hotly engaged against infantry and armor as they worked their way toward the river. Gleason finally reached Page shortly after noon and set up his CP in a factory overlooking the bridge.

It came as some surprise to Denkert that the bridges in Inden still stood. So certain had he been that American bombers or artillery would have destroyed the spans that he had bridging equipment standing by so he could move his vehicles to the eastern bank when retreat became necessary. He realized that he had to destroy or take firm control of the bridge commanded by Page's fire to keep the Americans on the west side.

The initial counterattack by the panzergrenadiers was perhaps only an attempt to make up for the cut demolition wires. From the American perspective, the first sign of trouble was the appearance at about 1230 hours of a "Tiger" that pounded the 2d Platoon and Gleason's CP with its main gun. (American participants and German prisoners of war insisted that there were four Tigers in Inden, but the *3d Panzergrenadier Division* on November 28 reported that it had only four *Sturmgeschütz* assault guns and four *Panzerjäger* IVs in town.) The first infantry charge hit the Americans in midafternoon but was driven off. The panzergrenadiers carried pole charges, which led Gleason to believe that their mission was to destroy the bridge.

Before dark, Gleason ordered the 2d Platoon back across the river, and Page had to clear the same building again. Meanwhile, a platoon from Company A arrived to reinforce Gleason at his CP, and the remainder of that company deployed on his flank.

At about 2115 hours, Denkert's men launched a serious attack. *Leutnant* Herford's 3d Battalion, *29th Grenadier Regiment*, supported by the alarm battalion's *Kampfgruppe* and the eight assault guns, hit Gleason's position. Herford's battalion was weak, but it was the only one in the regiment not already reduced to "exhausted" status. A panzer knocked out the machine gun that Company C had sited outside the factory to cover the bridge. Page's platoon was cut off.

After a panzer had fired roughly twenty-five rounds into the factory, the panzergrenadiers stormed it using grenades and burp guns. Gleason and an unknown number of men retreated to the second floor, where they held out in defiance of calls to surrender. About fifteen Americans slipped out the back. Private John Taylor reached Company A's CP, only to be evicted when the panzergrenadiers overran that, too, at about 0100 hours. Shortly before dawn, Gleason surrendered, and the *3d Panzergrenadier Division* reported taking eighty-four prisoners. Company C's 3d Platoon became isolated, and the men hunkered down in a schoolhouse for two days while Denkert's men swept by back and forth outside the windows.

The Germans reached the western exit from town, where the road runs toward Pattern. Company I, attached to 1st Battalion, had just taken up positions in houses to the west of the main north-south road in the northwestern section of Inden. The Americans stopped the panzergrenadiers there, with the decisive fight occurring at the church a block north of Highway 56. The anonymous panzergrenadier recorded, "Every house is contested. A counterattack advances all the way back to the church as soon as the enemy pressure decreases." The panzergrenadiers dug in.[43]

The Germans in Lamersdorf, which lies a short distance south of Inden on the river's west bank, repulsed three attacks during the day. After darkness fell, Captain Sanford Bush's 2d Battalion, 413th Infantry Regiment, managed to infiltrate the southern part of the village. *Leutnant* Wilde and *Leutnant* Schramm led a counterattack accompanied by two assault guns and three tank destroyers. They threw one American company out of town entirely, overran a platoon from a second one, and brought back eighteen prisoners.[44]

The next day, the Americans and Germans fought back and forth through the streets of Inden. Lieutenant Page led his isolated platoon northward along the east bank of the river. About four hundred yards north of the bridge, the men cut lengths of wire from a fence and spliced them together. A private swam to the far bank and tied the wire there. The rest of the platoon then crossed, holding onto the wire to avoid being swept downstream—or drowning, for those who did not swim.

At 1500 hours, the 413th Infantry Regiment and the 750th Tank Battalion launched a concerted attack to get a grip on the town. Artillery laid down a thick smoke screen. Company B Shermans charged from the southwest, and Company A's tanks rolled in from the northwest. Company D's light tanks carried two platoons of infantry into Inden from the west. Once the assault force reached the buildings, two more companies of infantry were to advance along the main road. The panzergrenadiers knocked out several tanks, however, and only three Shermans made it into town. The others bogged down or withdrew under direct antitank fire.

Nonetheless, the doughboys of Companies K and L reached Inden. Lieutenant Colonel William Summers, CO of the 3d Battalion, 413th Infantry, took charge over all forces in town, attached his three Shermans to Company L, and ordered a second concerted push. The attack kicked off at 2040 hours against tenacious resistance from every building. Nonetheless, by 2300 hours, all American units had established contact with one another.[45]

In Lamersdorf, meanwhile, Captain Sanford Bush's 2d Battalion attacked at dawn backed by four tanks and again clawed its way into the southern part of town. Grenadiers destroyed three Shermans, and German observers on Lucherberg called down heavy artillery on the attackers, which brought them to a stop. The Americans came on again from the west under cover of smoke in the early afternoon, when five Company B Shermans peeled off from the assault at Inden to strike Lamersdorf. Two Shermans made it into town to help Bush's men, but the other three got stuck in mud.

The Americans fought their way through town by 2130 hours. German assault and antitank guns claimed five American tanks, and the infantry knocked out another, but all the German antitank guns were destroyed in turn. Denkert had issued a withdrawal order at noon. The troops were so closely engaged, however, that they could not comply until after dark. The exhausted panzergrenadiers slipped across the river and blew up the bridge.[46]

Köchling ordered Denkert to retake Lamersdorf with all available forces. At this point, Denkert snapped. "This order will destroy the rest of the division!" He claimed that the *Amis* had two dozen tanks in Lamersdorf, whereas his worn-out infantry had no antitank defenses. Denkert suggested that corps engage the enemy with artillery. Incredibly, over the course of the evening the disagreement over whether to launch the attack went up to army, then army group. Finally, word came back down. There would be no assault.[47]

That night, the *246th Volksgrenadier Division* took over the northern end of Denkert's sector, and the *3d Fallschirmjäger Division* relieved him in the south.[48] Denkert's division had lost three-quarters of its infantry. It had only seven assault guns and eight tank destroyers left in action. Its artillery regiment was left with a single howitzer east of the Inde River. On the other side of the ledger, the panzergrenadiers claimed to have destroyed forty-two American tanks in two weeks and inflicted heavy casualties.[49] The division would now rebuild to play a role in the Ardennes.

The GIs in the rubble of little Inden did not even notice the changes on the other side. Someone was still fighting back hard. It would take the Americans two more days to cross the Inde River and another day to finish clearing the town. The two battalions committed at Inden and Lamersdorf by then had lost the manpower equivalent of two companies killed, wounded, or captured—about the same blood price paid for the metropolis of Aachen.[50]

A Debacle at Merode

The 1st and 2d battalions of the *5th Fallschirmjäger Regiment*, under the command of *Oberstleutnant* Becker, marched into Merode on November 26 to relieve the *115th Grenadier Regiment. Hauptmann* Siegfried Platz, commanding the 2d Battalion, established his headquarters in the basement of Merode Castle.[51]

Merode was a fortified village blocking one eastern exit from the Hürtgen Forest to the Roer River. Defenders had an unobstructed view to the forest's edge. A single rutted road led from the trees to the village.[52]

The first patrol from the 1st Infantry Division's 26th Infantry Regiment appeared at the tree line above Merode on November 28. The GIs established an observation post in a forest ranger's house,[53] while two Shermans from the 745th Tank Battalion worked their way through the woods to the tree line. Heavy artillery fire convinced the tank crews to withdraw. A shell hit the track of the lead tank, however, and it slid onto its side in a ditch.[54]

On November 29, the 26th Infantry Regiment's 2d Battalion—Lieutenant Colonel Derrill Daniel's Aachen veterans—attacked toward the village with Company F on the left and Company E on the right. Five tanks from Company C, 745th Tank Battalion, and two M10s from the 634th Tank Destroyer Battalion supported the assault wave. As soon as the men emerged from the woods, artillery and mortar fire rained down on them.

Hauptmann Otto Krannich was an artillery observer with the *47th Volksgrenadier Division* who had stayed until the *Fallschirmjäger* observers were fully established. He recounted, "Around 11 A.M. about ten Sherman tanks came down Monschauer Weg, turned right at the edge of the forest in order to join forces with the infantry advancing out of the woods. They formed a wide line of about three to four hundred meters. The tanks had already fired, and some of the buildings were burning. I immediately ordered my battery to start firing at the edge of the forest, and we were relatively successful in finding targets. Immediately afterwards I fired another two sets of rounds, that is ninety-six shells, aiming at the edge of the forest and about two hundred meters in front of that. I could observe that the enemy suffered heavy losses, two tanks had to stop for a while, and the complete attack had slowed down, even bogged down."[55]

Private First Class Alvin Bulau was a loader in one of the Shermans under Krannich's barrage. He recorded in his memoirs: "The Germans have heard all the noise, and now they are throwing more stuff than I have ever seen. I can see a squad of men moving across behind JB's tank. Good Lord! A heavy shell just hit in the middle of them. All I can see is black smoke and bits of dirt falling. The smoke's clearing. All I can see are two men. One is dead for sure. . . . There is a loud crash. I see fire going every way. I am on the floor, and the lieutenant is on top of me. We just had a hit on the front end."[56]

A hundred yards ahead of the GIs, a chain of bunkers blocked the way. The GIs set about clearing the pillboxes with the usual slow, methodical methods. Suddenly, resistance appeared to collapse—or the German troops were pulled back. The two American companies entered Merode at about 1500 hours.[57]

Both companies had been weakened. Lieutenant Sidney Miller's 2d Platoon, Company F, for example, had orders to take control of Merode Castle, but only four of his men survived to reach the edge of town. One by one, the remaining Shermans and M10s fell victim to artillery fire or panzerfausts. The GIs established defensive positions in houses and waited for reinforcements, but none came because of the heavy shellfire falling between Merode and American lines.[58]

The *5th Fallschirmjäger Regiment* ordered the 1st Battalion and part of the 2d to reestablish the defensive line west of town. Backed by the heavy guns of the *5th* and *8th regiments* and a single tank, *Oberstleutnant* Becker late on November 29 personally led his men in an attack that cut off the American companies. The *Fallschirmjäger* fired panzerfausts into the basements, while the panzer took care of the upper stories.[59]

Alarm had spread to the headquarters of the 26th Infantry Regiment by the wee hours of November 30. Panzers could be heard firing in town. There was no radio contact with anyone who could direct artillery fire to support the isolated companies, and all efforts had failed to remove a disabled tank blocking the only route for more armor to move forward. Daniel, in his CP near the edge of the woods above Merode, was discouraged.[60]

The last radio message to reach Daniel reported, "There's a Tiger tank coming down the street now, firing his gun into every house. He's three houses away now, and still firing into every house. . . . Here he comes. . . ." With that, all contact with the two companies ceased. Under cover of darkness, Technical Sergeant John Parker, of Company E, led fifteen men back to American lines. Back at battalion, the fate of the others remained unknown. Only continued German mortar fire on parts of the town indicated that some GIs still held out.[61]

The Germans knew, however. More than 120 Americans had fallen, and another 165 surrendered, including 10 officers. The young and green *Fallschirmjäger* had also suffered heavy casualties. Americans in a few cellar strongpoints would hold out until December 3.[62]

The *Fallschirmjäger* continued their attack on November 30 and drove the depleted 26th Infantry Regiment five hundred yards back into the forest. Both sides were pretty well exhausted.[63] The 26th made several attempts to break back into Merode, but to no avail.

Meanwhile, Deeper in the Hürtgen Forest . . .

The 4th Infantry Division had been tied up for days struggling to clear Grosshau. The Germans defended every building and still held high ground east of town, from which assault guns and antitank guns poured in supporting fire. The Ivy Leaf Division did not deem the town secure until November 29.[64]

Working in coordination with an infantry battalion attacking eastward out of Grosshau, the 46th Armored Infantry from CCA of the 5th Armored Division on November 30 advanced along the new intercorps boundary and secured the high ground east of town to the far edge of the clearing. The armored infantry had a tough time, in part because they encountered heavy fire from a hill supposedly cleared the day before by CCR.[65]

The remainder of the 4th Infantry Division, meanwhile, made modest gains during its last hours in this sector.[66] Soon, the battered outfit would be moving to a quiet piece of ground in the Ardennes to rehabilitate itself.

The division's G-1 offered this perspective on the fighting endured during the month:

The fighting in the Hürtgen Forest was so intense that daily requisitions [of replacements] were necessary. Even then, it became impossible to maintain the units at anything near [authorized] strength. . . . As many as six hundred fifty men a day were processed. . . .

As in all tough fighting, the highest percentage of casualties was among the leaders. A good soldier might start an attack as a rifleman and by the time the objective was taken find himself acting squad leader. In order to control and employ his squad, he must move about among his men. The result was that he became a casualty himself in a short time.[67]

NINTH ARMY DRIVES TO THE ROER

The Ninth Army's General Simpson lost the luxury of relying on British XXX Corps to run the battle at Geilenkirchen on November 23, when the 84th Infantry Division was attached to XIII Corps. The British 43d Infantry Division had made its last contribution—an unsuccessful attack on Hoven and Kraudorf—the day before. After three days of constant rain, the men from the 84th Infantry Division fought in water literally up to their waist in their foxholes on the road to Mullendorf. Tanks and tank destroyers could not get through the mud to support the doughs.

The XIII Corps spent the period of November 24–28 shifting units around in preparation for jumping into the broader offensive on November 29. The 113th Cavalry Group took over the extreme left, where it would maintain contact with the British. The 84th Infantry Division held the center, and the 102d Infantry Division relieved the leftmost elements of XIX Corps' 2d Armored Division.

At a staff meeting on November 24, the corps commander, Major General Alvan Gillem, told his division commanders that they would cross the Roer once they were firmly anchored along the west bank.[68]

The Germans desperately needed this break in the action. The *XLVII Panzer Corps* had suffered heavy losses fighting the American left wing. As of November 25, the *15th Panzergrenadier Division* had been reduced to ten battle-ready Mark IV tanks in its *115th Panzer Battalion*, wheras the *104th* and *115th Panzergrenadier regiments* numbered between one hundred and two hundred men in each battalion. The *9th Panzer Division* was so weak that its infantry elements were combined into two *Kampfgruppen* of between one hundred and two hundred men and subordinated to the *15th Panzergrenadier* and *10th SS Panzer divisions*. The *9th Panzer's* five or so remaining Mark IVs and Panthers were attached to the *Kampfgruppen.*

The German corps commander, *General der Panzertruppe* Heinrich Freiherr von Lüttwitz, offered this comment on the condition of his men, not very different from the American side: "The continuous rain, the impossibility of feeding the troops regularly during the pitch-dark nights, the long service in the positions without prospect of being relieved preyed on the strength of the panzer-grenadiers and the infantrymen. Pale and hollow-eyed, sick and drenched through, unshaved and unwashed for days, facing an enemy who had abundant supplies, these men fulfilled their duty to the utmost." Constant replacement of men and squad, platoon, and company commanders had so reduced cohesion that his troops were rarely capable of much more than defensive action.[69]

On the plus side, one of the elite *10th SS Panzer Division's* panzergrenadier regiments, plus an additional battalion, had arrived from Holland. The six or eight running Royal Tigers from the *506th Schwere Panzer Abteilung* were attached to the SS. And the corps also still fielded some 150 artillery pieces.[70]

XIX CORPS STRUGGLES

McLain's XIX Corps completed the transfer of the 2d Armored Division's CCB sector to the 102d Infantry Division at 1800 hours on November 23. Combat Command A was still mired in Merzenhausen, where it managed to push only another hundred yards into town against fierce house-to-house resistance. The destruction of another Sherman brought that attack to a stop. The crew reported that they had been nailed by a panzer hidden in a large building with a sliding door. The Germans opened the door, the panzer fired, and the door closed again.

Armored doughs formed a bazooka-and-Molotov-cocktail team to set the building on fire. They succeeded in starting a blaze but were driven back by heavy fire before they could see whether the plan had worked.

Hauptmann Kuppinger tried to throw the Americans out of the south-western part of town, but the Germans could make no more headway than their enemies had, despite bitter fighting. That evening, the 2d Battalion of the *340th Volksgrenadier Division's* 695th Grenadier Regiment arrived in

Merzenhausen to relieve Kuppinger's tired men. The GIs would face fresh troops the next morning.[71]

The 29th Infantry Division was still bogged down at Koslar, but the 3d Battalion, 175th Infantry, managed to reenter Bourheim. The 747th Tank Battalion's Company A—now up to four Shermans—and two Company B tanks supported the operation by fire. Lieutenant Homer Wilkes recorded, "The weather was murky. The position—on the Roer uplands. A man at five hundred yards was practically invisible, although the area was open, so-called tank country."

At about 1000 hours, the Shermans came under fire from a high-velocity gun on the eastern bank of the Roer. Wilkes could see only the muzzle blast and white tracers as shells rocketed by. He led his tanks into a draw and called for artillery support, which was denied with the explanation that American troops held the target area. (They would actually take that ground only after three more months of fighting.) "If those are your troops," Wilkes responded, "why are they firing a German gun at our tanks?" He never did get fire support.

Concerned about panzers reported nearby at Linnich and Kirchberg, all of the 3d Battalion's and the regiment's antitank guns, plus four 3-inch guns from the 821st Tank Destroyer Battalion, were rushed into Bourheim and set up to cover the approaches from the north and northwest.

The vicious street fighting had cost the *340th Volksgrenadier Division* dearly; the 1st Battalion of the *694th Grenadier Regiment* was reduced to sixteen men. Ten assault guns and five Tigers had been lost around Bourheim and Koslar, and only eight of the former and three of the latter remained in action. Attempts to deploy the radio-controlled armored vehicles had failed utterly because of American artillery fire, antitank guns, and smoke shells that blinded the controllers. The division commander, *Oberst* Theodor Tolsdorf, reported to Köchling that he lacked the strength to hold at Bourheim, and unless he could withdraw to a shortened MLR, the line would collapse.[72]

In the 30th Infantry Division sector, the 120th Infantry Regiment took another crack at Lohn in coordination with the 104th Infantry Division's attack at Pützlohn. The 2d Battalion had the honors. For the first time in the offensive, the Germans perfectly anticipated the assault and caught the GIs with a crushing artillery barrage, in which some seventy men fell wounded. The survivors plunged ahead and took the objective.[73]

The doughboys in the 119th Infantry Regiment's 3d Battalion ate turkey for Thanksgiving at dawn, then conducted a lightning advance into Pattern that caught the defenders completely off guard. The town fell in forty minutes without the loss of a single GI.[74] During the advance, tankers of the 743d encountered Jagdpanther tank killers. The battalion AAR recorded:

[Company A] tanks were in assault position at Aldenhoven, Germany. Here orders for the attack on Pattern, Germany, were awaited. At 1245 hours, orders came. Eleven batteries of artillery fired twenty minutes on the objective from H-hour. Infantry jumped off at H-hour and Company A tanks moved out in support at II + 20. For us, this meant a dash down the Aldenhoven-Pattern road with the tanks driven wide open. The terrain was level and open, but it was impossible to maneuver the mediums on the soft ground. As the leading tank led this racing column at twenty-five miles an hour, it sighted a minefield across the road about five hundred yards out of Pattern. There was nothing to do but stop. The entire column then "sweated it out" for fifteen minutes as direct enemy fire came to our left, until a pioneer platoon, which had been sweeping the road to our rear, caught up and cleared a path of safety through the mines.

Elements of Company B were in position on a hilltop commanding Pattern to the west and southwest. From this location direct fire was put on the enemy—a diversion which developed into a mousetrap, two of the new *Panzerjäger* Panther [Jagdpanther] enemy tanks being the mice. For as Capt. David W. Korrison . . . led Company A tanks into the town, the sights of his 75mm gun were crossed by two of these newest type of enemy armor, attracted by Company B's fire. Captain Korrison celebrated Thanksgiving by knocking out both tanks at a range of less than fifty yards. . . . A third *Panzerjäger* Panther was claimed after we first blasted holes in a building in order to reach the vehicle at less than a hundred yards. It was knocked out by laying our fire through this aerated building.

Dense German flak positions around Jülich forced fighter-bombers to loiter so high that the pilots could not spot panzers in the rain and mist at ground level. The GIs and air liaison worked out a system under which ground troops would mark a panzer with a colored smoke shell. The pilots would dive at the smoke, and usually they could spot the target in time to release a bomb. A near miss was often good enough, because it would turn over the panzer or break a track.[75]

A Lull in the Storm

A lull in XIX Corps attacks followed; it lasted until November 27. The divisions needed time to regroup. Moreover, the neighboring VII Corps advance had been somewhat slower, and Major General McLain decided to hold up while Collins' men cleared Weisweiler, Langerwehe, and Jüngersdorf.[76]

Ninth Army recorded the atmosphere in its operations report:

> The battlefield was a dreary spectacle. The sun was seldom seen. A grayish mist predominated. The cabbage and beet fields, not a pleasant landscape under the best conditions, were sodden from the constant rain and gashed and ripped by shell bursts, bomb craters, and the treads of tracked vehicles.
>
> The villages, mostly rows of miners' houses, were drab enough at the start of the battle. Now they were desolate, with shreds of curtains trailing from broken windows and walls toppled into rubble in the streets, exposing the remnants of smashed furniture.
>
> The American shelling and bombing had been intense, but after our troops occupied the towns, the enemy tried to smother them with his artillery. The result was utter ruin.[77]

Ninth Army noted that fresh German forces were appearing on its front. The *10th SS Panzer Division*, commanded by *Oberführer* Friedrich Boch, appeared in the Lindern-Linnich area. Boch issued an order entitled "Behavior of SS Troops in Germany," which reminded his men that they were now fighting in the Reich and would have to abandon habits of burning and pillaging that they had acquired in occupied territories.[78]

But Not at Bourheim

The lull did not affect the men in Bourheim on November 24 and 25. The GIs, with critical help from fighter-bombers and artillery, fended off repeated attacks by a handful of *301st Schwere Panzer Abteilung* Tigers and the 1st Company, *695th Grenadier Regiment* (the first assault led personally by division commander Tolsdorf).[79] Even with vehicles returned after repairs, there were only nine operational Shermans left in the 747th Tank Battalion.[80]

On the second day, at 0800 hours, six Tigers backed by the 1st Battalion, *694th Grenadier Regiment*, came out of the rain again. This time, they managed to get into town. German artillery fire had driven the tank destroyer crewmen guarding the Pattern road into their foxholes, and they could not get back to their 3-inch gun before the Germans overran the defensive line. Other guns were out of ammunition.

First Sergeant Joseph Staley, of Company I, reported: "One [panzer] stopped outside the house where the command post was located and fired its gun into the basement. The projectile went through the outer wall of the house, through the basement roof, which was made out of concrete reinforced with steel rails, passed into a passageway behind the basement, and exploded, blowing out the back of the house. We went out the hole. . . ."

Technical Sergeant John Erman added:

First Sergeant Staley called me over a telephone and said, "Send a bazooka team to the command post and blow up this damned tank." We had no more bazooka ammunition. . . . The tank continued shooting into houses and went to the middle of the town and tried to turn around. The brick wall of a house fell down on the tank as it had its rear against the house. The sides and rear of the tank were covered with rubble, and the tank could not pull itself out of the trap.

Two bazooka teams began trying to get into position but failed because of the rubble. When they fired at the front of the tank, the rocket glanced off. The crew saw the bazooka team and drove them away with machine-gun fire.

Second Lieutenant Robert L. Graeber, leader of the 1st Platoon, Company M, ran up with an eighteen-pound satchel charge of TNT, crawled through the building, and threw the charge under the tank.

It failed to explode. He got another charge, but this time the crew saw him and drove him away with machine-gun fire. Another German tank backed up to the crippled tank. A man got out and hooked the tanks together, and they started moving out of town. As they left, our planes came in and strafed them on the Jülich road.[81]

Similar fighting continued in Koslar, where German counterattacks cut off three companies from the 116th Infantry Regiment for nearly three days.[82]

The Roer River had finally taken its place in the attention of SHAEF. On November 28, the G-3 plans section discussed options revolving around the assumption that the First and Ninth armies would be stopped at the Roer, "an eventuality," it judged, "which is not unlikely." The planners judged that reinforcing the two armies' effort was an unattractive but possibly unavoidable option. The only alternatives they saw were the possibility of turning the line by attacking out of Luxembourg and the hope that gains in the south might draw German resources away from the Roer front. In short, they were out of ideas. Little did they know that fighting in Luxembourg would, indeed, soon have a major impact on the Roer situation.[83]

Commenting on operations during the preceding few days, the Ninth Army G-2 noted on November 30, "Progress had not been as great as anticipated." The principle reason, Ninth Army conceded, was "the vigorous reaction of the enemy, who seemed to fight with increasing ferocity as the Allies approached ever closer to his great defense line of the Rhine River."[84]

XIX CORPS REACHES THE ROER

The 2d Armored Division's CCA finally cleared Merzenhausen on November 27 in conjunction with attacks to take the high ground just outside the town and overlooking the nearby village of Barmen. The fighting was as ferocious as it had been every preceding day, if not worse. *Oberst* Tolsdorf reported that his troops lost four Tigers in only ten minutes.

Staff Sergeant Guy Bates' squad of Company F, 119th Infantry, conducted the assault on one of the last houses in town. When the GIs reached the top of the cellar steps, the impeccably dressed German battalion commander ascended and presented his pistol to Bates; the Germans recorded 229 men assumed taken prisoner in Merzenhausen. All buildings were cleared by 1700 hours.[85]

Not yet knowing the fate of his isolated 1st Battalion, the *695th Grenadier Regiment* commander, *Major* Meissner, persuaded the extremely reluctant commanders of three Tigers to support a counterattack into Merzenhausen by his antitank company. At dusk, the task force penetrated the town and reached the area of the battalion CP, where the bodies of several staff officers were found. Heavy American fire prevented the recovery of the bodies, and the task force commander was wounded. Under the cover of fire from six more Tigers that had arrived north of town near the railroad station, the command withdrew.

The battle for Merzenhausen was over, and the *695th Grenadier Regiment* hardly existed any longer. Tolsdorf concluded that his division would soon be annihilated. He requested permission to withdraw to the east bank of the Roer, a request that was granted with the stipulation that bridgeheads be retained at Jülich and Hasenfeld Gut.[86] With the volksgrenadiers pulling back, Barmen, the last town before the Roer River in Hell on Wheels' sector, would fall quickly the next day.

The 29th Infantry Division reached the Roer River near Kirchberg on November 28.[87] Thanks to the withdrawal of the volksgrenadiers, Kirchberg also turned out to be fairly easy pickings for the men of 2d Battalion, 175th Infantry Regiment, who attacked out of ruined Bourheim. Major General Gerhardt received word that his division's first patrol had reached the river's bank by 1138 hours.[88]

The Old Hickory Division, meanwhile, renewed its attack when it tried to take Altdorf on November 28 in conjunction with the 104th Infantry Division's attack on Inden. The men had to advance over a bald piece of high ground and were quickly pinned down. The 120th Infantry Regiment decided that only a night attack had any chance of success. The 1st Battalion kicked off at 0430 hours in the dark. The division's history recorded:

> B and C, the two assault companies, were formed into eight platoon files after the battalion moved on a compass course to the line of departure and jumped off on time, preceded by four squads spread out in a skirmish line, with a grenade launcher on every man's rifle. To achieve surprise, only the normal artillery harassing fires on enemy rear areas

were fired. The "natural" route of advance was avoided on the correct assumption that it would be well covered with defensive fires at the slightest hint of an attack; this route was constantly under fire as the attack developed.

Air bursts of artillery supporting the attack on Inden to the south illuminated the area enough to give the enemy warning, after the men had moved forward one hundred yards from the line of departure, and the machine guns outside Altdorf opened up. They were quickly disposed of by rifle grenades fired at the flashes by the entire line of skirmishers, after the latter advanced under fire to within effective range. During the delay, Company A, in reserve, moved up beside the assault units and they all advanced swiftly into town.

For two hours, an animated battle raged in the darkness of the town. In addition to the Germans firing small-arms weapons at the men moving in the dark to the buildings they were to seize, seven enemy tanks roamed the main street of the town trying to escape. A platoon of the reserve company had moved into Altdorf laden with as many mines as it could hand-carry, with the mission of placing hasty mine-fields at both ends of the settlement to keep tanks out. The minefields trapped the tanks, and the bridge leading over the river to the east was also taken before the tanks could escape.

Their consequent attempts to get out and those of the infantrymen stalking them made a strange battle. Two enemy tank commanders exposed themselves trying to peer through the darkness and were picked off by riflemen. One tank blundered into a building and was trapped after its lights had been shot out. It was set ablaze with a white phosphorus grenade. The attackers hit every tank at least three times and as often as fifteen times with bazookas, rifle grenades, and every other weapon at hand, but the heavy armor repelled even bazooka rounds in all except one case. Technical Sergeant Vincent Bernier knocked out a halftrack personnel carrier with a rifle grenade and then accounted for a Mark V with a bazooka round at close range. Six of the tanks [eventually] were able to escape over the bridge, which was later destroyed by an enemy artillery round. Seventy-four prisoners were taken.[89]

***

From the German perspective, the situation appeared to border on breakdown. The attack at Kirchberg had broken contact between the *340th Volksgrenadier* and *3d Panzergrenadier divisions*. The *LXXXI Corps* ordered Denkert to throw all available resources (which turned out to be only three assault guns and a few riflemen) into restoring the situation at Kirchberg. Köchling scraped up two Tigers to help the *340th Volksgrenadiers* defend an endangered railroad bridge across the Roer. The Tigers were east of the river and had to cross the bridge to reach the volksgrenadiers. (American artillery fire damaged the bridge in any event, and the Germans decided to blow it for good late in the day.) Köchling also assigned the *246th Volksgrenadier Division's 404th Grenadier Regiment* to Tolsdorf and ordered the formation to Flossdorf.

Model, meanwhile, lectured von Zangen about not allowing his divisions to burn out, which he said was nearly the case for the *340th Volksgrenadiers*. (Indeed, *LXXXI Corps* that day judged that it might have to write off one of the division's regiments and considered a second combat ineffective.) Model did not, however, offer any fresh troops.[90]

XIII CORPS KICKS OFF ANEW

During the waning days of November, the 84th Infantry Division had readied itself to seize the high ground northeast of Beeck and the villages of Lindern, Leiffarth, and Würm. The division had been given the 7th Armored Division's 40th Tank Battalion as armored support. The 102d Infantry Division was to conduct a limited-objective attack between Lindern and Linnich to protect the 84th's right flank. The British 43d Infantry Division would protect its left.[91]

Elements of the *9th Panzer*, *10th SS Panzer*, and *340th Volksgrenadier divisions* defended the bunkers near Beeck, Lindern, and Linnich. The SS had not arrived in time to complete the planned relief of the exhausted *9th Panzer Division's Kampfgruppe* in the area. The battered panzer division had orders to shift to Heinsberg to receive replacements and twenty-four new Mark IV tanks. Three Tigers from the *506th Schwere Panzer Abteilung* were with the SS at Lindern, however, and another five were available at Linnich. A lack of engineers had prevented planned mine laying on the outskirts of Linnich.[92]

On November 29, XXIX TAC flew nearly three hundred sorties against German troop concentrations. Fighter-bombers dropped eighty-five tons of bombs and nearly five thousand gallons of napalm.[93]

The ground attack did not begin well. The 3d Battalion, 335th Infantry, jumped off in the direction of Lindern at 0630 hours. Major Robert Wallace, battalion CO, reported that he quickly lost contact with Company K but could hear that they had run into automatic weapons fire. At 1030 hours, the commander of Company I radioed back to say he was down to twenty men and surrounded by Germans. Wallace heard nothing more from him.

In fact, Company K had been hardly bothered by the machine-gun fire and had entered Lindern. One surviving platoon from Company I made it as well. The men quickly dealt with a few snipers, all the resistance that the weak *9th Panzer Division's Kampfgruppe* could offer. The GIs dug in, expecting the worst. All radios had been damaged or were defective.[94]

The American barrage had badly disrupted German communications, and commanders received vague word that the Americans had reached Lindern. Both the *15th Panzergrenadier* and *10th SS Panzer division* elements in the vicinity were ordered to send reconnaissance patrols to the town.[95]

At about 0800 hours, the Americans in Lindern spotted three tanks approaching from the flank and thought they were friendly. The first panzer was only some forty yards away before they realized their mistake. A bazooka round bounced off the first panzer, but the Germans may not have even realized that they had encountered Americans, because they drove off.

The crews in three Royal Tigers that approached a few minutes later from a row of pillboxes in the direction of Randerath knew the scene. The panzers fired a few rounds without doing too much harm and withdrew after a sergeant shot one commander with his M1.

Lieutenant Leonard Carpenter, commanding Company K, later related: "The tanks could have rolled up the line of foxholes and wiped us out. Some of the men talked about pulling back. . . . We had a strength of two and one-half platoons then. We had Germans to our front, to our rear, and all around us. We had no antitank platoon, no communications, no ammunition except small-arms ammunition, some bazooka and mortar rounds, and were running short of that." Carpenter could count six panzers within eight hundred yards of his position.

Several men who volunteered to go back for help were never seen again. At about 1400 hours, American ingenuity kicked in when a GI used telephone wire and tape to get a radio working. Carpenter reached an American tank commander, who could relay word to battalion. "When we got word out, our morale shot up about 600 percent. . . . It was about 1430 when we saw six General Shermans. Boy! We figured the whole German Army couldn't drive us out of there." A short while later, Company L arrived to reinforce the American hold on Lindern.

The *9th Panzer Division* counterattacked to retake the key lost ground around Lindern and Linnich. The *Kampfgruppe* during the day had received a battalion of replacements and seven Mark IV tanks. The weak, poorly oriented command was capable of little more than a poke at the enemy.[96]

The main effect as far as the Americans in Lindern were concerned was a surge for two days in penetrations by tank killer teams that accounted for several Shermans from the 40th Tank Battalion. Men with panzerfausts worked close to the tanks while burp-gunners kept the crewman pinned inside. A few long-range duels took place with panzers.[97]

The 333d Infantry Regiment, meanwhile, reached the outskirts of Beeck.

On the right flank, Brigadier General Frank Keating had all of the 102d Infantry Division's regiments under his control for the first time and had the 771st Tank Battalion attached for support. His main objective was Linnich, on the Roer River.

The 405th Infantry Regiment rolled forward a thousand to fifteen hundred yards before stopping in the face of intense fire.[98] High-velocity rounds slammed into Sherman after Sherman, despite a smoke screen that partially shielded the advancing troops. That night, after the riflemen had dug in, they could see nine friendly tanks burning brightly.[99]

The 405th Infantry made no progress on November 30. On the division's right, the 407th Infantry Regiment slowly cleared Germans from dug-in emplacements around Welz. Six of eight tanks committed to support the GIs trying to reach Flossdorf fell victim to antitank fire.

The 102d Infantry Division was stymied. Losses in infantry had been low, but the 771st Tank Battalion had suffered badly. Brigadier General Keating requested additional tank support and received the 7th Armored Division's 17th Tank Battalion to use only if absolutely necessary.[100]

THE GERMAN PERSPECTIVE

Despite the heroic efforts of the fighting men, developments looked somewhat bleak as November drew to a close, no matter where one stood. The

American XIX Corps was on the Roer. The *XLVII Panzer Corps*, on the north wing, had committed its last reserves and was barely maintaining a line, and the corps commanding general, von Lüttwitz, worried that an American breakthrough to the Roer was imminent there, too.[101]

Von Zangen had lamented the success of the 104th Infantry and 2d Armored divisions in reaching the Inde River on November 28, despite a tenacious defense by the *3d Panzergrenadier Division* well supported by artillery and assault guns. American tactical air strikes against artillery positions and villages just to the rear of his line were causing problems. The next day, the Americans held the entire ridgeline overlooking Düren. *Fifteenth Army* lacked the troops to do anything about that.[102]

Fallschirmjäger Heinz Schnelle offered a foxhole-level perspective: "We had been driven back into the flat land. The enemy held the heights that overlooked the terrain, foothills of the Eifel. His situation was ideal. He could observe us at all times and he dictated the course of events with his crushing superiority in numbers."[103]

The rest of the *3d Fallschirmjäger Division*, fresh from Holland, moved into the line on November 29 and 30 in the Langerwehe-Inden area to bolster the battered defenses. The *5th* and *8th Fallschirmjäger regiments* finished relief of the *47th Volksgrenadier Division* around Jüngersdorf and Merode. Holding this terrain was crucial, for in clear weather an observer could see Cologne from Langerwehe or Merode.[104]

The *47th Volksgrenadier Division* had been reduced to a shadow of itself in only two weeks. All six rifle battalions were rated *abgekämpft*, or fought out. One hundred four officers and 4,260 men had fallen.[105] Karl Schacht's company in the *115th Grenadier Regiment*, for example, was down to eight men.[106]

Fallschirmjäger units would also relieve the first tired elements of the *12th Volksgrenadier Division* over the next few days. The division had orders to pull back for refitting in preparation for the Ardennes offensive. Engel's proud Wild Buffaloes had also taken a pounding. The total strength of each infantry regiment, including the heavy guns, was two hundred to three hundred men, and all rifle battalions were reported at "weak" status. The division's casualties since November 16 amounted to roughly twenty-five hundred men.[107]

The *363d Volksgrenadier* and the *10th SS Panzer divisions*, meanwhile, replaced the exhausted *340th Volksgrenadier Division*. In nine days of combat, the latter division had lost forty-eight officers and nearly two thousand men. The *340th* needed to rebuild for an assigned role in the Ardennes offensive, too.[108]

CHAPTER 6

A DEFENSIVE VICTORY

With his back to the Rhine, [the German] fought for each grubby crossroads village as if it were the Brandenburg Gate in Berlin.

Omar N. Bradley, *A Soldier's Story*

Another round of wrangling over strategy between Montgomery and Eisenhower took place as November gave way to December, but Ike was by now firmly committed to his course of action. The two commanders met on November 28 and again the next morning. Monty argued that the Allies had failed to achieve their aims since October and suggested that there had been a "strategic reverse," points he reiterated in a written summary of the talks that he sent to Eisenhower. Ike disagreed and replied that, although the Ruhr was an important objective, "never let us forget for one second that our primary objective is to defeat the German forces that are barring our way into Germany."[1] He also forwarded a message from the 12th Army Group summarizing the number of prisoners alone taken along its front. Eisenhower told Monty that the operations seemed worthwhile, regardless of territorial gains, because German losses exceeded those of the Allies.[2] This was a bald statement of Ike's war of attrition.

Eisenhower, Montgomery, Bradley, Simpson, Hodges, and Tedder met in Maastricht at Ninth Army HQ on December 7. Monty was again pugnacious, but this time he suggested that one of the main objectives should be wearing down German strength at a faster pace than Allied strength. Ike probed Montgomery, and for the first time the two grappled directly with the Supreme Commander's central idea of grinding up Germany's armed forces. Montgomery scuttled the tentative emergence of common ground by again insisting on a single northern thrust to the Ruhr, a notion that Ike again rejected in favor of a two-thrust approach.[3]

Meanwhile, with Ninth Army at the Roer, no force on Earth was going to stop Bradley before he reached that river's banks along the length of his front. Little did he know that the "other fellow," as he was wont to say, was willing to let him do that as long as he did not actually cross the river before December 16.

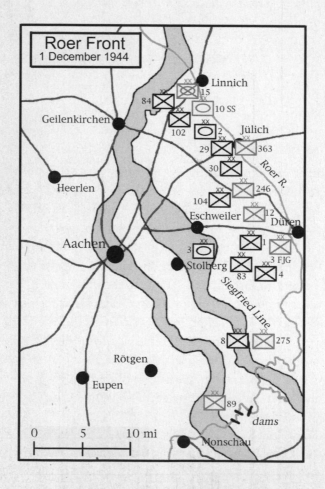

FIRST ARMY CALLS IN FRESH PLAYERS

First Army undertook a substantial realignment of divisions during the first week of December, a step it deemed necessary to permit the renewal of its offensive. On November 28, Hodges had apparently decided that VII Corps needed an infusion of fresh strength. He ordered that the VIII Corps' 83d Infantry Division swap sectors with the exhausted 4th Infantry Division beginning December 1. The exchange of command responsibility for the respective sectors took place at 1600 hours on December 7, and the final troop movements were completed four days later. The 5th Armored Division, less Combat Command Reserve (CCR), was shifted from V Corps to VII Corps. And V Corps, having played a small role in the offensive around Hürtgen, received orders to clear more of the Hürtgen Forest and to reconnoiter in force toward Hasenfeld, west of the Roer River.[4]

The rested 9th Infantry Division, meanwhile, reentered the line to replace the battered Big Red One. Huebner on December 1 had told Collins that he was giving up on the two companies in Merode as lost.[5] Collins noted that the division had been in near constant action since D-day and concluded, "I could ask no more of it."[6] The relief commenced on December 5 and finished at 2400 hours on December 7.

The 3d and 5th Armored divisions moved into new assembly areas while the exchange of infantry divisions was under way. Oddly, Hodges removed from VII Corps the heavy artillery battalions he had provided to support the offensive. Minor adjustments were made to the intercorps boundary around Grosshau.[7]

Collins suspended most offensive operations during the realignment in VII Corps through December 9, but that did not stop the fighting.[8]

On the first day of December 1944, VII Corps' 104th Infantry Division was embroiled in a third day of fighting in Inden. To the south, the 1st Infantry Division's 26th Infantry Regiment could find no way to relieve two companies cut off in Merode. The 4th Infantry Division was still engaged in heavy fighting in the Hürtgen Forest near Grosshau, with little to show for it.[9]

The *246th Volksgrenadier Division* had taken responsibility for the defenses in Inden on December 1. The volksgrenadiers moved three Hetzers to the west bank and deployed three assault guns and two Jagdpanthers on the eastern side.[10] Köchling, however, ordered the division to abandon all positions on the west bank of the river. The volksgrenadiers blew the bridges after withdrawing their equipment except for two Hetzers that were marooned on the west bank. Given a few riflemen in support, the crews were ordered to inflict as many casualties as possible, then destroy the vehicles.

Undaunted, the Timberwolves had already planned a night attack, which late on December 2 successfully established a bridgehead across the Inde River. Assault troops waded across the river with their guns empty, their bayonets fixed, and grenades at the ready. They had been ordered to take the eastern bank without shooting in order to maintain surprise, and the plan went like clockwork. Three companies from the 414th Infantry Regiment that crossed in the center of Inden captured fifty young German soldiers, who were reported to be very frightened. Company I, 415th Infantry, crossed the partially destroyed railroad bridge between Inden and Lamersdorf. Shells fell around the company, but no men were lost, and the first inaccurate small-arms fire did not pester them until they were well established on the far bank. Within twenty-four hours, the division eliminated the rest of the resistance in town and began constructing a new bridge.

Linchpin at Lucherberg

The momentum carried the division southeast into Lucherberg, which the 415th Infantry Regiment assaulted on December 3. The village, home to five hundred souls in better times, was made up of stout brick buildings and overlooked the Inde to the west and the Roer to the east. The town played a major role in the German defense scheme west of the Roer, and the *9th Fallschirmjäger Regiment, 3d Fallschirmjäger Division*, had received orders the day before to establish a tank defense strongpoint in the village. The same morning that the 415th Infantry Regiment entered Lucherberg, the *Fallschirmjäger* regiment's 3d Battalion arrived from the opposite direction. The battalion had only two officers left, but it still fielded 419 troopers.

As Company I took machine-gun fire just outside the village before dawn, the company's commanding officer, Lieutenant John Olsen, yelled to his men, "I'm making a rush to the town. Come if you like, or stay and be wiped out by artillery fire in the morning!" To a man, two nearby platoons rose, dashed across uneven ground as bullets whizzed by them, and clambered up a steep clifflike hill into town. A German tank fired at near point-blank range, and men dove into holes for cover. Fortunately, the German gunner could probably see little or nothing in the dark. A few bazooka rounds convinced the panzer commander to pull back. The remaining fifty men of Company I cleared four buildings and took fifteen prisoners. Lieutenant Olsen was mortally wounded during the fighting.

Still before dawn, the Americans spotted a column of infantry approaching the village. Unsure of their identity, the Americans held their fire until the figures came close enough to show themselves to be Germans. GIs in two houses opened up, and figures dropped to the ground. A confused situation developed, with the American-held houses divided from one another by German troops or German fire.

At about 0400 hours near the village church, a German medical lieutenant colonel approached Lieutenant Edwin Verelli, who had taken command of the company, and through sign language arranged a truce to recover the wounded. About forty German and twenty-five American soldiers set aside their weapons and began administering aid. While this was going on, however, both sides were sending more men into the strategic village. An American platoon arrived and dug in. Thirty fresh *Fallschirmjäger* appeared and began shooting at the Americans. The medical officer stopped the firing, but by now an entire company or so of *Fallschirmjäger* had arrived and started to gather up the American weapons.

Staff Sergeant Leon Marokus, who spoke German and was backed up by the German medical officer, argued with the *Fallschirmjäger* officer in command (probably *Hauptmann* Strehler, 10th Company) that he was violating a truce. The angry *Hauptmann* finally agreed to give the Americans their weapons and fifteen minutes to get out of town. It appears, however, that he kept several prisoners, including Lieutenant Verelli. (Marokus later reported that Verelli had fired at some Germans during the truce, which could explain his detention.) While another lieutenant and the German medical officer served as hostages, the sides disengaged. Lieutenant John Shipley, a mortar forward observer, took charge and concentrated the forty-five men he could round up in a double house, where he decided to make a stand. Within fifteen minutes, the hostages were released, and firing broke out.

Shipley had some critical assets: Lieutenant Arthur Umer, who was an artillery forward observer, and two SCR-300 radios. During the day, the *Fallschirmjäger* tried repeatedly to overrun the tiny command. Shipley directed 81mm mortar fire as close to the house as fifteen yards, while Umer called down artillery strikes on other targets in town. More than two thousand rounds crashed into the Germans during the day.

The *Fallschirmjäger* directed machine-gun fire into the building from three directions. One German trooper fired a bazooka into a door; it jarred but did not break the invaluable radios. Another worked his way up to a window and threw in several grenades before an American grenade killed him. At one point, Shipley radioed that he was having difficulty seeing out of his basement CP because of bodies outside the window. American ammunition began to run low by afternoon.

At 1500 hours, the cavalry arrived in the form of Company L. Now both sides had a firm hold on part of town.[11]

The *404th Grenadier Regiment, 246th Volksgrenadier Division*, supported by the *3d Fallschirmjäger Division's 8th Regiment* attacking at Lamersdorf, launched an unsuccessful bid to seal off the Timberwolves' breakthrough. Seven of the Jagdpanther tank killers from the *519th Schwere Panzerjäger Abteilung* supported the main thrust.

The volksgrenadiers reported that they experienced "colossal confusion" because of American air strikes and shelling throughout their sector. The men lay in water and mud, and two Tigers from the *301st Schwere Panzer Abteilung* that were working with the *Fallschirmjäger* were hit and towed out by assault guns. Coordination between the infantry and the assault guns—which had not been subordinated to the *404th's* command—broke down, and heavy casualties were the result.[12]

Emil Weiss, who was a grenadier in Company 6 of the *404th*, recorded: "Combat was very tough, especially the hand-to-hand fighting. The Americans attacked with tanks over and over again. They mostly shelled the area around the train station, our center of gravity. In our final attack, the *404th [Grenadier] Regiment* was wiped out except for forty-four men. Most of the casualties were due to artillery fire."[13]

More American rifle companies entered Lucherberg. By evening on December 4, the GIs held nearly all of the buildings, and the first Shermans and towed tank destroyers had arrived to establish an antitank defense. With

Lucherberg in American hands, the German artillery east and southeast of town was endangered. It was successfully moved to the eastern bank of the Roer with only minor losses.[14]

The Timberwolf Division settled down to consolidate its gains. Model, during one of his frequent visits to *LXXXI Corps* HQ, told Köchling on December 4 to try again to retake Lucherberg. There was enough artillery ammunition available to support only one more big attack by the *246th Volksgrenadiers*.

On December 5, American tanks, tank destroyers, doughs, and artillery fought off a final fierce counterattack on Lucherberg supported by 180 artillery tubes and 14 Tigers, Panthers, and assault guns. The Germans reached Lucherberg but could not take it. The infantry traded shots, grenades, and bazooka rockets during another round of furious house-to-house fighting.

Two panzers worked their way into Company F's positions and knocked out an antitank gun and a Sherman. One stopped next to the 1st Platoon CP, and the second beside the 3d Platoon CP. One fired at the company CP, killed the artillery forward observer, and seriously wounded the company commander and several men. Sergeant George Burns of the 2d Platoon obtained a bazooka from a tank destroyer located in the town square, worked his way down the street, and fired at one tank from the 1st Platoon CP. The explosion killed several infantrymen standing beside the panzer, which began to withdraw.

Burns returned to his platoon for more ammo. Advancing again, he ran into the panzer near the 3d Platoon CP and fired hurriedly from the hip. Again, several German infantrymen fell, and the panzer limped away at half speed. As the panzers left town toward Echtz, the tank destroyer knocked out the damaged tank.

Eleven of the panzers of various types involved in the attack were incapacitated, although only two were total losses. Casualties were extremely high among German infantry officers.[15]

Grenadier Emil Weiss related the attack, which was to follow a planned two-thousand-round artillery barrage, from his perspective:

> The 404th and 689th [regiments], 246th [Volksgrenadier] Division, *Major* Ritter [commanding], carried the assault to about 150 meters short of Lucherberg. We took up positions 200 meters outside Lucherberg. From here the infiltration should be initiated by tanks

after a brief artillery assault. We waited for the artillery barrage, but it only comprised about 600–800 rounds, much less than planned. As soon as it stopped we rose and charged at Lucherberg. The Americans must have noticed the attack early because there was no artillery activity, only single shots, while on the other days there had always been barrages on our dugouts.

The attack bogged down under the sudden outburst of the American artillery, which formed a ring around Lucherberg. Even American positions were hit by that wild barrage. We suffered heavy casualties. . . . Lucherberg had been attacked in a semi-circle, along 800 meters of front-line. But the enemy did not capitalize on this moment of weakness, instead he just remained where he was.[16]

By midafternoon, the 415th Infantry Regiment deemed the town secured. Company I by this time had lost six men killed, fourteen wounded, and twenty-two missing. All company officers were among the killed or captured.[17]

The *LXXXI Corps* commander, Köchling, later wrote that the failure to retake Lucherberg "sealed the fate" of German forces west of the Roer between Schophoven and Düren.[18]

Lightning Joe Collins wrote to Terry Allen: "I regard the operation which involved the seizure of Lamersdorf-Inden-Lucherberg as one of the finest single pieces of work accomplished by any unit of the VII Corps since D-day. . . . We regard the Timberwolf Division as one of the finest assault divisions we have ever had in this corps."[19]

Beginning on December 6, the 104th Infantry Division launched a series of limited-objective attacks against stubborn resistance in the direction of Pier. It established outposts in front of Lucherberg on December 9. The division had reached the end of its first phase of operations.[20]

The SHAEF G-2, in its intelligence summary for the week ending December 3, pointed to the Germans' "grim, skilful, and hitherto successful defense of the Roer." The G-2 speculated that the Germans had been propping up the front by trimming the fat from the Ardennes sector and Holland.

NINTH ARMY MOPS UP

Having reached the Roer River, Ninth Army's XIX Corps began to rotate units for rest and training. The 30th Infantry Division on November 30 began exercises in woods fighting for the anticipated battles in the forests on the far side of the Roer. The 2d Armored Division also underwent training and rehabilitation. Both divisions would take an unexpected detour via the Ardennes later in December.

The unfortunate exception was the 29th Infantry Division, which sat across the Roer River from Jülich. *Generalleutnant* August Dettling's *363d Volksgrenadier Division* now manned three small bridgeheads on the western bank at the Jülich Sportplatz, Hasenfeld Gut, and a patch of woods near the bridge on the Aldenhoven road.[21]

Incredibly, the defenders of the small German pockets held off determined attacks by the 116th Infantry Regiment for a week—and dealt out heavy casualties. Minefields protected the German firing positions. A tunnel complex at the Sportplatz allowed the defenders to move about in safety, and machine-gun nests had superb fields of fire across the eight hundred yards of open ground outside the facility. The swimming pool alone had a machine gun in each corner, supported by an assault gun. OPs on the higher eastern bank allowed German artillery observers to provide extremely effective artillery support. On December 7, the task passed to the 115th Infantry Regiment.[22]

Late on December 8, the *363d Volksgrenadier Division* reported that it could no longer hold the bridgeheads and requested permission to withdraw its five remaining companies (two at the Sportplatz and three at Hasenfeld Gut). Köchling refused.[23]

The GIs needed all day on December 8, and the help of Shermans from the 747th Tank Battalion, to clear out the rearguard at the Jülich Sportplatz. Twenty-four Germans surrendered there, surrounded by the bodies of forty-two of their comrades. Köchling appealed to von Zangen over the senseless waste of the companies and requested permission to withdraw them. By the time approval came down, it was nearly too late; all contact had been lost. Ten men exfiltrated on inflatable bladders or by swimming from Hasenfeld Gut, and fifty-five (most wounded) from the Sportplatz.

By nightfall, the 29th Infantry Division controlled the entire west bank in its sector. To get there, the division had lost more than five hundred men killed and some eighteen hundred wounded. [24]

***

The XIII Corps, on Ninth Army's left, also still had business at hand in early December.

The 102d Infantry Division threw two regiments toward Linnich early on December 1, but neither gained any appreciable ground in the face of steady German fire. Brigadier General Keating decided to commit his third regiment—the 406th—that afternoon. Keating laid on his heaviest artillery barrage in three days while the 92d Chemical Battalion's 4.2-inch mortars fired thousands of smoke shells to block the view from the far side of the Roer.

The infantry from the 2d Battalion, 406th Infantry, accompanied by Shermans from the 17th Tank Battalion, pushed off at 1400 hours across tableland toward the slope rising to Linnich. The men followed fifty yards behind their rolling barrage, and German artillery burst behind them. Advancing in this strange zone of calm, the regiment lost only three men. The infantry disposed of the few antitank guns that challenged the advance, and although two tanks were lost, the men entered Linnich at 1615 hours. A German force of some 150 men, backed by two damaged panzers, held the village. The *10th SS Panzer Division* reported that it had no reserves and could not restore the situation; isolated units fought on here and there, generally out of communication with higher authority.

The next day, when the doughs cleared the town, the commanders of the two forces were surprised to discover that their CPs had been right across the street from each other all night. A feckless counterattack toward Linnich by SS staff and supply troops produced nothing but more casualties.[25]

The XIII Corps was anchored on the Roer River.

Von Zangen wrote off Lindern for lost the evening of December 1 and Linnich the next day.[26] The *10th SS Panzer Division* troops in the sector were withdrawn beginning December 1, leaving the defense to the volksgrenadiers. Some of the latter felt left in the lurch, and surrenders shot up.[27]

Von Zangen later suggested that his forces were so badly mauled that a hard push would have broken through and crossed the Roer River. Von Lüttwitz shared that view.

German artillery finally experienced ammunition shortages during the first days of December (it had expended so much that *Army Group B* had

had to forward ammunition earmarked for the Ardennes offensive). But on December 3, the *9th Panzer Division* was able to withdraw into reserve, joined a day later by the *116th Panzer Division*. German morale generally remained high.

The *XII SS Corps* reported abating battle for the period of December 5–15. Its one remaining hold on the west bank of the Roer at Heinsberg was no longer under serious pressure. The *15th Panzergrenadier Division* was able to withdraw for rehabilitation. Troops were digging more field fortifications along the east bank.[28]

Ninth Army noted the Germans' energetic work as "evidence of a grim determination to defend the area between the Roer and the Rhine Rivers." This could not have filled a single man with joy. Between November 16 and December 8, Ninth Army had suffered 1,779 men killed, 7,640 wounded, and 1,169 missing or captured.[29]

FIRST ARMY'S FINAL PUSH

Among the high and mighty, Monty had again opened the issue of who would make the main effort. On December 7, Ike, Montgomery, Bradley, and their chiefs of staff met in Maastricht for another round of wrangling. Eisenhower decided that the main effort would shift back to the north. As Bradley had earlier feared, Monty would be given control over Ninth Army. But Eisenhower again refused to stop all other offensive operations to permit Montgomery to launch a single full-blooded attack along the northern route.[30]

Analysts from SHAEF judged that the pressure along the entire front was costing Germany nine thousand permanent or long-term casualties per day, or the equivalent of five divisions per week. It appeared that Ike's war of annihilation was, indeed, gradually destroying the German army in the West.[31]

Bradley was aware from Ultra intercepts that the Germans had built up a substantial armor reserve near Cologne, but his G-2 expected that the panzers would be used to counterattack once the Americans reached the good tank country beyond the Roer. Nobody seriously considered the Ardennes.[32]

The VII Corps renewed the offensive at 0630 hours on December 10. This time, it would not stop until it, too, reached the banks of the Roer River.[33]

Corps artillery fired a forty-minute counterbattery preparation against fifty German artillery positions, with excellent effect. The IX TAC bombed the towns of Schophoven, Echtz, and Schlich, as well as other targets.[34]

Major General Robert Macon's 83d ("Thunderbolt") Infantry Division, on the corps' right, supported by the 774th Tank Battalion, moved out through falling snow with two regiments and by day's end had taken Strass and most of Gey. Capture of those two towns would permit the employment of 5th Armored Division elements on Macon's right.

Resistance at Strass was fierce. The 330th Infantry Regiment's 3d Battalion—which lost two commanding officers in the course of the day—gained the town only after a vicious assault by tanks and infantry in the face of heavy mortar and artillery fire. Almost immediately, German infantry and panzers counterattacked, and Companies L and K were cut off in the center of town for some time. Artillery fire overnight was so heavy that resupply proved impossible. The division's history commented, "If Jerry was beaten, he either didn't know it or was too stubborn to admit it."[35]

The 104th Infantry Division kicked off at 0745 hours on the corps' left. The Timberwolves gained up to two thousand yards and by the end of the day had pushed past the crest of a ridgeline southeast of Inde, reached the outskirts of Pier, and gained a half mile beyond Lucherberg. Panzers bolstered the tenacious defenses at Pier and Schophoven.[36]

The refreshed 9th Infantry Division, supported by the newly established CCR of the 3d Armored Division in the corps' center, surged forward along its entire front between Luchem and Jüngersdorf for gains of a mile or more. Four supporting tanks mired in a ditch, but they were so placed that they could provide direct fire support against the individual buildings around Jüngersdorf, Merode, and Schlich.

After a discouraging start that cost Task Force Hogan eleven tanks in one hour, the Americans entered Obergeich. It was here that a 3d Armored Division legend was born, as recorded in its history *Spearhead in the West*: "In the mud-bound terrain, tanks and armored cars proceeded slowly, bogging down frequently and receiving heavy antitank, artillery, and small-arms fire. Leading the armor were two small figures. The first was a GI carrying a BAR and a seemingly inexhaustible supply of grenades. The second was a lieutenant, strolling along with no weapon at all except his cane. With it, the officer pointed out machine-gun nests and other strongpoints for the following tankers to attack. Neither of these doughboys attempted to duck the constant rain of heavy German mortar and shellfire. They walked upright, the dough spraying every position with his BAR and tossing grenades to right and left. About him, terrified Jerries rose from their slit trenches and walked forward to surrender. . . . Together, the two small figures led the armored column into the town of Obergeich, which was subsequently captured by the tanks, and there they disappeared."

In the center of the sector, CCR's Task Force Kane and the 60th Infantry Regiment entered the town of Echtz. Fighting continued all night.[37] Observed by Lightning Joe Collins, the 39th Infantry Regiment overcame fierce resistance to capture Merode, where the regimental commander, Colonel Van Bond, established his command post in the castle.[38] The lost companies of the Big Red One were avenged.

Fallschirmjäger Heinz Schnelle was still dug in with his battalion near Jüngersdorf. For days, they had heard the sounds of tracked vehicles to their front, and they knew that an attack was coming. Schnelle recalled: "All day long, detonations and explosions, that was all we heard. Artillery, grenade launchers, tanks, fighter-bombers with bombs and on-board guns, they all made our lives a living hell. . . . Tanks stood on fire, and they burned like smoking barrels of tar—we could see them through the artificial clouds. The shrieking, rumbling tanks of the enemy closed in."

The battalion CO ordered his men to stand fast. They knew what that meant and burned their pay books. The American advance swept by, and Schnelle and his surviving comrades had no choice but to surrender.[39]

Despite this intense pressure, on December 10 von Zangen's *Fifteenth Army* was given responsibility for the *LXXIV Corps* area in the Hürtgen Forest to relieve *Seventh Army* for the Ardennes offensive.[40]

American GIs enjoyed close air support again on December 11. Fighter-bombers pounded the Germans in Hoven, Schophoven, and Mariaweiler.

The presence of the *301st Schwere Panzer Abteilung's* Tigers and a brigade of assault guns shored up German defenses in the area. Von Rundstedt instructed that every fight west of the Roer had to be so fierce that the Americans would not dare to risk a river crossing. As a precaution, von

Zangen ordered the Jagdpanthers from the *519th Schwere Panzerjäger Abteilung* to the east bank of the Roer to intercept and destroy any American armored push across the river.[41]

The 104th Infantry Division finally captured Pier. An attack by one battalion launched at 0400 hours swarmed forward two thousand yards on the division's right, taking the town of Merken.[42] The defenders in Schophoven, however, held on with bitter determination.

East of Echtz, direct fire from self-propelled and antitank guns slowed the 9th Infantry Division advance. Doughboys and tankers nonetheless managed to move three-quarters of a mile along the Weisweiler-Düren road and clear Schlich and D'horn.[43]

Desperate German counterattacks hit the 83d Infantry Division and pushed back the line in several places. Fighting swirled around Strass, Schafberg, and Gey. The battalion in Strass was cut off entirely. An armored-infantry battalion from the 5th Armored Division's CCB attempted to pass through the Thunderbolt Division near Bogheim, but it was shot up so badly that Collins the next day had to attach a battalion from the 330th Infantry Regiment to CCB to make up for the losses.[44]

While the Timberwolves mopped up Pier and Merken, 9th Infantry and 3d Armored division troops on December 12 clawed their way into Hoven and Mariaweiler. The *3d Fallschirmjäger Division* reported that the seven Tigers working with its men in Hoven destroyed eleven American tanks. The leading battalions from *Generalleutnant* Bork's hastily replenished *47th Volksgrenadier Division* reentered the line late on December 11 to relieve the *3d Fallschirmjäger Division*. (As of December 9, Bork reported that rifle companies had, on average, some fifty men each and most were commanded by senior NCOs.) The Tigers working with the *Fallschirmjäger* were ordered to the east bank of the Roer, from where they could support by fire. The *104th Grenadier Regiment* almost immediately lost Hoven, but its 2d Battalion held on grimly in Mariaweiler despite suffering 30 to 40 percent casualties. The Germans began to blow the last key bridges across the river.[45]

The 83d Infantry Division managed to reestablish tenuous contact with its men in Strass. Food had to be dropped to the men by artillery liaison planes.

Bork's volksgrenadiers, well supported by Hetzers and artillery on both banks of the river, frustrated Macon's efforts to open the door for the 5th Armored Division.[46] Nevertheless, by day's end, VII Corps controlled nearly all of the defended towns on the west bank of the Roer River north of Düren, which itself lay only half a mile from American lines.

The VII Corps' Collins abandoned any idea of crossing the Roer River. On December 13 he instructed: "*All divisions* upon reaching the Roer River will take positive measures to secure the west bank within their zones of action from enemy raids, mine-laying patrols, and infiltration. The minimum number of troops consistent with this mission will be maintained in forward areas."[47] Von Zangen could express only relief that the Americans halted as they came abreast of the Roer's waters.[48]

Also on December 13, the 104th Infantry Division cleared Schophoven. Francis Felix, a rifleman with Company F, 414th Infantry Regiment, experienced the battle as his first attack after joining the outfit as a replacement. He later recalled:

> I was in front at the crossroads and a farmhouse. We got in a small orchard and all hell broke loose, and the next thing I knew I was all alone out there. I crawled in a horseshoe shape across the roads and up to a lean-to on the house, and my sergeant told me to go into the main house. Later on, everybody in the lean-to was captured, my sergeant and lieutenant and all the men with them.
>
> As I went in the house, I heard a squeaking noise and looked down the road. I saw three tanks and armored personnel carriers. I could see the men in the open part and could probably have shot them, but I was scared to death. The three tanks went in the orchard and fired into the lean-to and one of our men went out with a bazooka and knocked out the middle tank and at the same time he fired, someone in an out-building shot him in the knee.
>
> Then the tanks left with all the men from the lean-to walking between the tanks, so we couldn't fire at them.
>
> A little later, I was standing in the middle of the kitchen putting my canteen bottle away and there was an explosion at the back door

and the room filled with plaster dust and I felt something hit my left foot—it felt about the size of a half-dollar. I felt my foot and it seemed OK, but later on I felt blood in my boot. I had two fragments in my foot.

Another man screamed his legs were blown off, and when the dust cleared his legs were full of [shrapnel]. Another man was laying [sic] on the floor, and his whole back from his head to his heels was full of it. I wouldn't go down to the basement to the aid man because I felt whoever threw the grenade was still out there.

I went across the hall to a little room like a pantry, and in a few minutes here came a mean looking guy with a burpgun trying to see in the window. I knew if I yelled at him he could spray the window and he couldn't miss. I raised my rifle real slow and aimed at his heart. He fell on his right side with the gun still under his arm and his hand still on the trigger. His mouth was still twitching, so I shot him again in the head.[49]

That same day, the Timberwolf Division noted that some 15 percent of its casualties had been cases of combat fatigue. The cases were concentrated in badly chewed-up units where leaders were killed and the men had no idea what was supposed to be going on. Major General Allen instructed that, henceforth, warning orders would be issued with sufficient time that all troops could be oriented on the mission.[50]

The 83d Infantry Division, meanwhile, pushed three thousand yards into Gürzenich, just across the Roer from Düren, and the tip of the Wenau Forest, southwest of town. The 2d Battalion, 329th Infantry, crossed fifteen hundred yards of open ground on the final spurt into Gürzenich. The men worked their way close to the center of town against determined resistance from the volksgrenadiers. The Thunderbolt Division now held a salient deep into the German defenses.[51]

Landser Karl Schacht's *115th Grenadier Regiment, 47th Volksgrenadier Division*, held the trench line at Gürzenich. The American assault overran his company's position, and Schacht was the only member of his squad to avoid capture and make it back to the company's new line at Mariaweiler. In the face of renewed American attacks in the afternoon, the local commander on December 14 blew up the railroad bridge across the Roer River. The remaining German troops picked their way across the bridge fragments to safety on the far side. Sent back across with an assault unit a few days later, Schacht would be captured after falling asleep in a basement, so exhausted after three days without sleep that the Americans were marching past before he even knew they were attacking.[52]

The VII Corps spent December 14 mopping up areas southeast of Schophoven, southwest of Mariaweiler, and along the edges of the Wenau Forest. Only the 5th Armored Division, finally able to attack through a temporary zone at Gey, took much new ground. The next day, the 104th and 9th Infantry divisions consolidated their positions and patrolled the west bank of the Roer River.[53]

The 83d Infantry Division renewed its attack; it advanced seven hundred yards to the edge of Berzbuir and captured Kufferath. Supported by infantry and cavalry, the 5th Armored Division gained a thousand yards to reach the edge of the woods at the Roer opposite Kreuzau.[54] The Germans would hold out for only another week in a handful of small and shrinking bridgeheads in the American sector. For practical purposes, the fight west of the Roer was over. And with that, the Americans had almost achieved the crossing of the Roer River first ordered by Lightning Joe Collins three months earlier. Almost.

Köchling's staff issued flood warnings to its divisions along the east bank of the Roer. The general instructed, "The MLR in the Roer sector is the Roer itself."[55]

RECKONINGS

The official U.S. Army history conceded: "When the offensive had opened on 16 November, the First Army had been looking beyond the Roer to the Rhine. A month later the troops and their commanders must have been gratified to gain the Roer, which originally had been an intermediate objective."[56] First Army's VII Corps had suffered 15,908 battle casualties since November 16 to get there. Of those, 2,448 men died. Tank losses probably amounted to about 200.[57]

Ninth Army likewise lamented: "The operation that had aimed at the capture of Cologne and the closing up to the Rhine was now stalled along the muddy western banks of the flood-threatened Roer."[58] Ninth Army's human casualties amounted to just over 10,000, including 1,133 killed and 6,864 wounded.[59] Ninth Army had lost fifty-three medium tanks from November 16 to 30 and about thirty more in the first two weeks of December. The army's AAR for November noted: "The superiority of German Mark V and VI tanks over our medium tanks of the M4 series in armor, armament, and gun power [had become] more apparent." By early December, Ninth Army's armored section would report a shortage of trained tank crews due to high battle loss rates.[60]

Ninth Army also had more broad problems with manpower. It requisitioned replacements based on estimated losses over the next forty-eight hours until November 22, when it suspended that system because of critical shortages in the theater's ground forces replacement system. The 6th Army Group had gained priority in the supply of replacements of combat personnel. At the end of November, Ninth Army's flow was slashed dramatically, and Simpson was told to expect alleviation of the problem no earlier than January 1945. Simpson had already taken measures to reduce nonbattle casualties, including the adoption of

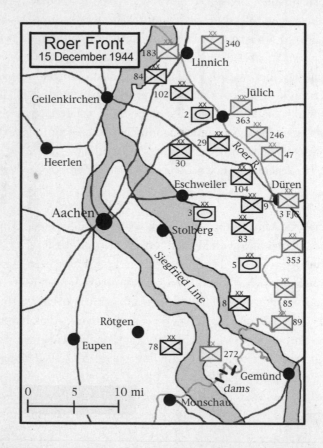

a policy of immediate relief and rotation of units once they had taken an objective and gone over to the defensive.[61]

Bradley, for his part, was cheered by estimates indicating that the Germans had been suffering casualties at a rate roughly double his own. Eisenhower during the fall had ordered exhaustive daily assessments of enemy losses, because he wanted to fight only where the other side's losses were twice his own unless a vital objective mandated otherwise.[62] Bradley had achieved Ike's target. Nonetheless, Bradley termed the overall results of the November offensive a "disappointment."[63]

Von Zangen offered this evaluation of the situation: "The [American] offensive was concluded before the first attack objective was fully reached! The Roer crossings were not captured, although they were, without a doubt, the important prerequisite for the continuation of enemy operations." Von Zangen quotes the OKW diary as saying: "The defense of the Roer was the most difficult part of the Ardennes offensive! The *Fifteenth Army* commander justifiably rated the German effort a defensive victory."[64]

CHAPTER 7

THE DAMS OF PERDITION

The winch machinery to lower the gate had been destroyed, and the gate itself had been blown. This eliminated any possibility of closing the tunnel spilling the water from the lake into the river below.

REPORT TO THE COMMANDING GENERAL, 78TH INFANTRY
DIVISION, ON THE INSPECTION OF THE SCHWAMMENAUEL
DAM BY ENGINEERS, FEBRUARY 9, 1945

All of the efforts and sacrifice during the drive to the Roer River meant nothing in terms of reaching the main objective—the Rhine—as long as the Germans held the Roer dams. As the 30th Infantry Division's history put it, "Ninth Army, in dragging itself to the Roer, had only attained a new and serious water barrier."[1] The Allies dared not risk crossing the river, because artificial flooding could cut off any units on the east bank and leave them vulnerable to annihilation by known and growing panzer reserves.

WHAT THEY KNEW, AND WHEN THEY KNEW IT

There is ample evidence that commanders and planners considered the issue. Ninth Army planners, for example, in October drafted an estimate of the situation and possible lines of action for the anticipated advance to the Rhine

River. The engineer headquarters provided a terrain analysis to inform the effort. The report noted:

> Artificial flooding, to an extent sufficient to render the river unfordable below Linnich, is possible by manipulation of controls at dams and reservoirs further upstream. There are three large dams upstream from Düren. Their destruction would inundate the valley in the area under study, endangering any units operating therein and making any crossing of the valley impracticable. . . .
>
> A recently published report of interrogation of a prisoner of war indicates that the lower dam was constructed entirely as a defensive measure and that it is mined. According to the report, the inhabitants of Düren have been required to carry out practice alerts for evacuation in the event of flooding. . . .
>
> Routes of communication east of the Roer River will be in danger of temporary severance by artificial flooding until after the demolition of the Roer River dams or their seizure by First Army.[2]

Ninth Army also asserted in its history that as of late October, "these dams counted for much in the calculations of the American commanders and the employment of their strength."[3]

First Army, in its post hoc operations report, explained an intercorps boundary shift in late October in the following terms: "The purpose of this boundary was to place the 28th [Infantry] Division under the operational control of V Corps so that it could participate in an offensive to be launched by V Corps to seize certain dams on the Roer River."[4]

Yet the dams at that time were not specified as an objective for V Corps or the 28th Infantry Division. Indeed, the official U.S. Army history provides an exhaustive examination of the record that shows that, through November 1944, commanders from the 12th Army Group down through the divisions fighting in the Hürtgen Forest did not consider the Roer River dams to be an objective.[5] Several possible reasons suggest themselves.

Commanders may have assumed that the problem would take care of itself in the course of First Army's anticipated advances along its front. They may also have reasoned that V Corps could speedily grab the dams when operations along the lower Roer so demanded. (Ninth Army's operations report covering the November offensive offers ambiguously: "During the planning of the advance to the Rhine, it was assumed that the dams would be overrun by the First Army and that the chances of the enemy destroying them were not great."[6]) In either case, U.S. commanders underestimated the German determination and ability to defend the dams.

Or the senior generals may have bungled the problem. Their conspicuous lack of enthusiasm for the entire subject of the Hürtgen Forest in postwar writings hints that they may have perceived some vulnerability on the matter.

And well they might. Between October 6 and 16, the VII Corps' 9th Infantry Division had fought to capture Schmidt, a town close to the Roer dams, but with the aim of seizing the road net—not the dams. The division's two attacking regiments had gained a mere three thousand yards at a cost of forty-five hundred casualties.[7]

Even heavier were V Corps' sacrifices to clear the heart of the forest. The 28th Infantry Division launched First Army's second attack on Schmidt on November 2. Although the 112th Infantry Regiment reached Schmidt one day later, a German counterattack threw back the regiment and battered the division for more than a week. The "Bloody Bucket" division, as the men renamed their red keystone shoulder patches, suffered more than six thousand casualties and lost many supporting tanks and tank destroyers.[8]

The German *Seventh Army* Chief of Staff, *Generalmajor* Rudolf von Gersdorf, later commented, "The German command could not understand the reason for the strong American attacks in the Hürtgen Forest after the effectiveness of the German resistance had been ascertained. . . . The fighting caused the American troops heavy losses without bringing them any tactical or strategic success of decisive importance at that time. The advantage of tying down strong German forces and preventing the reconditioning of the divisions for other tasks was cancelled out by the fact that even for American divisions, the Hürtgen Forest had become a 'death mill.'"[9]

The realization that the dams simply had to be taken settled into the upper ranks by early December. Ninth Army recorded in its operations report that someone in the ground forces—the actor is not clear—floated a plan for the air forces to destroy the dams. Major General Elwood Quesada, at the IX TAC, dismissed the scheme, but Brigadier General Richard Nugent, commanding the XXIX TAC, thought it was worth a try. The 12th Army Group apparently convinced SHAEF to support the proposal, and on December 3 nearly two hundred heavy bombers from the RAF Bomber Command flew over Urfttalsperre Dam. For some reason, however, they did not bomb. Two hundred aircraft returned the next night, but only twenty-five Lancasters and three Mosquitoes dropped ordnance, which did not materially damage the structure.

At a conference at SHAEF on December 5, Eisenhower insisted on another try, over the objections of RAF Air Chief marshal Sir Arthur (Bomber) Harris. On December 8, a total of 205 aircraft dropped nearly eight hundred tons of bombs on the Urfttalsperre, Schwammenauel, and Paulushof dams. Two bombs hit the Urfttalsperre and eighteen the Schwammenauel, to no effect. More than a thousand tons of bombs were dumped on the Urfttalsperre Dam three days later. Slight damage to the top at one end released an insignificant amount of water. The 12th Army Group abandoned the air option.[10]

Ninth Army's planning for a crossing of the Roer River, meanwhile, took full cognizance of any operation's vulnerability to flooding that would result from the destruction of the Roer dams.[11] And First Army on December 6 issued its first letter of instruction to mention the dams as an objective. Hodges instructed V Corps, reinforced by the 2d and 78th Infantry divisions, to seize the Schwammenauel and Urfttalsperre. The corps was to attack on army order no earlier than December 13.[12]

The Germans suffered no confusion over the strategic importance of the dams. When asked after the war why the Germans had defended the Hürtgen Forest so bitterly, *Seventh Army* chief of staff von Gersdorf answered succinctly, "We fought to protect the Roer River dams." He also noted that as long as there were large numbers of German troops west of the Roer River, German commanders worried that Allied air strikes might damage the dams and cause a flood that would cut off their units.[13]

This observation suggests that had the Americans seized the dams early on, there might have been no bloody battle to reach the Roer, because the Germans would have *had* to withdraw or be fatally weakened for the same reason the Americans later dared not cross the river. By German reckoning, this would have prevented the launch of the Ardennes offensive. Nevertheless, Ike's determination to crush the German army and Hitler's demonstrated ability to gather reserves would have combined to produce a bloody struggle somewhere else in this might-have-been world.

In early November, the Germans had installed antiaircraft batteries at the dams to prevent their destruction by air and prepared the dams and electrical turbines for demolition in case it became necessary to flood the river.[14] Model reserved to himself any decision to loose the waters from the dams.[15]

By the beginning of December, German commanders considered the continued defense in the area of the dams to be of such great importance that *Seventh Army*, with Model's concurrence, reluctantly decided to commit the *272d Volksgrenadier Division*. The division was flagged to participate in the Ardennes offensive, and German planners understood that the volks-grenadiers were likely to sustain heavy casualties that would undermine the division's later effectiveness. Nonetheless, an American breakthrough could imperil the Ardennes attack itself.[16]

When von Zangen and *Fifteenth Army* took control from *Seventh Army* over the *LXXIV Corps* sector in the Hürtgen Forest on December 10, von Zangen very much viewed the battle as part of his overall defense of the Roer River line. A losing fight at Bergstein was just winding down, and von Zangen worried that the position gave the Americans an ideal vantage point overlooking the west bank of the Roer.[17]

The *272d Volksgrenadier Division*, brought up from the Simmerath area, had launched a final attack to retake Bergstein with the support of the artillery from several divisions and the attachment of two or three *Panzerjäger* companies. But after some initial success, the assault had withered with heavy losses.[18]

Von Zangen worried that trends were dire. Units in areas not involved in the Ardennes offensive were stretched so thinly that "rehabilitation" was often a joke even when theoretically possible. Replacements were being fed into the line with inadequate orientation and training. The relationship between combat missions and capabilities was increasingly out of balance, because the high command paid more attention to their situation maps than assessments of the actual capabilities of divisions. Growing fuel scarcities limited mobility.[19]

FIRST TRY FOR THE DAMS

For the Americans, capturing the dams posed a daunting challenge. All roads to them approached from the east. To the west lay what one army-level report described with breathtaking understatement as "rugged terrain."[20]

The V Corps offensive to reach the dams kicked off on December 13 as ordered by First Army. From north to south, the 78th, 2d, and 99th Infantry divisions advanced between twelve hundred and three thousand yards on the first day. The 8th Infantry Division supported them with demonstration attacks along the Kall River. By December 14, German resistance had become fierce, and the advance ground to a halt throughout the V Corps sector. The next day was no better.[21]

The Germans had good reason to fight so tenaciously. On the morning of November 16, Hitler's great Ardennes counteroffensive ripped into First Army. The V Corps' operation ended before it had really begun.

The Roer River front settled down after Hitler launched his last gamble, Operation *Wacht am Rhein*. Three armies struck the thinly held VIII Corps line in the Ardennes, intent on splitting the Allied front and driving on to Antwerp.

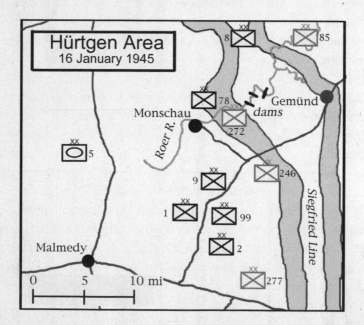

Many German divisions from the Roer sector, including the stalwart *10th SS Panzer*, *3d Panzergrenadier*, and *3d Fallschirmjäger divisions*, were committed to the attack. A planned supporting offensive by von Zangen's *Fifteenth Army* out of the Heinsberg salient, on the west bank of the Roer, was canceled on December 20. Several units that were to have participated, including the *9th Panzer*, *15th Panzergrenadier*, and *340th Volksgrenadier divisions*, were instead sent south to the main battle area. *Fifteenth Army* also lost three volksartillery corps to the offensive. Local attacks aimed at pinning American units in place—conducted by the *183d Volksgrenadier Division*, west of the Würm, and the *47th Volksgrenadier Division*, near Düren—resulted in heavy losses. The Americans hardly noticed them.[22]

Hodges mirrored the German deployments and thinned the Roer front to free divisions to send south to contain the growing Bulge, as the German penetration in the Ardennes quickly became known in Allied ranks; Ninth Army also sent many of its divisions south to the main fight. By early January, Ninth Army controlled a defensive screen of only five infantry divisions. (The 5th Armored and British 43d Infantry divisions were also in Ninth Army's zone but were under operational control of the U.S. First and British Second armies, respectively.) Artillery units went on a starvation diet of ammunition, which contributed to the relative calm.

On December 20, much to Bradley's dismay, Eisenhower transferred First and Ninth armies to the operational control of the 21st Army Group. On December 22, the boundary between Ninth and First armies was shifted south, and XIX Corps took over responsibility for what had been the VII Corps line. Ninth Army trucks provided logistical support to First Army as well—and Simpson soon had to assign personnel to make certain that the vehicles were not "unlawfully detained."[23]

On December 27, *Fifteenth Army's* left wing was extended as far as Elsenborn—the northern shoulder of the Bulge.[24] Thin screens of Americans and Germans eyed each other warily across the Roer River.

Hitler held the initiative for eleven days. Then the Allies struck back. On January 16, First and Third armies met at Houffalize, Belgium, just about the center point of the Bulge at its maximum extent. The next day, First Army reverted to Bradley's command, but Ninth Army remained under Monty's control.

FALL OF THE DAMS

By late January, Bradley wanted to continue attacking eastward without pause to reach the Rhine River at Bonn. He later admitted one reason: "This route through the Eifel would carry us south of the Roer dams and thus enable us to reach the Rhine without becoming entangled in another dam campaign." Montgomery, however, insisted that First Army reclaim its pre-Bulge sector and responsibility for capturing the dams; Ike agreed with him. Bradley would have to go after "those dam sites," as he later punned.[25]

The G-3 of the 12th Army Group acknowledged the task on January 20. Bradley assigned the job to the 8th and 78th Infantry divisions but conceded that more divisions could prove necessary to the purpose.[26]

A SHAKY DEFENSE

German forces in the Hürtgen could no longer count on the Reich to provide many more resources. On January 12, the Soviets launched their greatest offensive of the war. Over the next week, 180 divisions shattered the German line in East Prussia and Poland. By January 27, Soviet troops were within a hundred miles of Berlin and had overrun the strategic Silesian industrial basin. After pondering the loss of the coal mines there, Hitler's armaments wizard Albert Speer wrote the Führer a memo that began, "The war is lost." Violent arguments over strategy wracked the German high command, and army chief of staff Heinz Guderian secretly begged Foreign Minister Joachim von Ribbentrop to try to arrange an immediate armistice in the West. Hitler shifted the *6th SS Panzer Army* from the western front, and by February nearly every new or repaired panzer to leave a German factory was shipped eastward.[27]

Despite all the setbacks, the German armed forces retained a remarkable will to fight. One corps commander in the Roer sector later commented, "We front soldiers did not know that there was no longer any sense in carrying on the war." Yet a certain unease regarding the war of attrition—without the apparent prospect of another offensive—was creeping in. The corps commander caustically observed, "Letting oneself be shot in the main line of resistance (tenacious defense) in order to seek decisions in another place might be reasonable, but one can only let oneself be shot once." There was sufficient dissent on this issue that several courts-martial were ordered in *Fifteenth Army* and *Army Group B* in early 1945.[28]

With the failure of the Ardennes offensive now evident to all, von Zangen concluded that holding the dams was more critical than ever to his Roer front. Promises of reinforcements for defenses along the Roer River itself proved to be empty. Worse yet, even in *LXXIV Corps'* critical sector west of the dams, troops were being pulled out to fill holes elsewhere and replaced by units of inferior quality.[29] North to south, the German line looked as follows.

General der Infanterie Karl Püchler now commanded *LXXIV Corps*, which he had taken over from Straube in mid-December. In late January, the corps received reinforcement in the form of a volksartillery corps with Russian-made 10.2cm and 15.2cm guns. Three huge 42cm mortars with ample ammunition also deployed at Einruhr but could not fire without permission from OKW.[30]

The *272d Volksgrenadier Division* held the Siegfried Line defenses from south of Simmerath northeastward to Kesternich. The division, badly chewed up in the Bulge, was shifted to *LXXIV Corps'* sector on January 27 to reorganize. The division's six thousand men were well dug in.[31]

In mid-January, the *346th Volksgrenadier Division* was withdrawn from the area near Monschau and shifted south to *LXVII Corps*. *Oberst* Kittel's battle-weary *62d Volksgrenadier Division*, pulled from the Ardennes, arrived to replace it. Snow and icy roads delayed the division's deployment until January 25. The division's history claims that morale was surprisingly good.

After an emotional exchange over the division's weak condition with Kittel and one of his regimental commanders, Püchler was so worried that he requested permission to keep the division out of the line for reorganization. Model flatly rejected the proposal. Scheduled for rehabilitation, the *62d Volksgrenadier Division* received eight hundred replacements (many barely trained) and drew on *Führerreserve* in its *Feld Ersatz Bataillon*. Still, available weapons went wanting for crews. Kittel judged his *164th* and *190th Grenadier regiments* "improvisations," and he held back the *183d Grenadier Regiment* at Gemünd, because it was only a skeleton. American shells harassed the men as they shuffled to the front. The next day the artillery buried the division operations officer under the rubble of a house and tore up the phone lines.

Concerned about possible envelopment of his right, Kittel established the *Schwerpunkt* (main point) of resistance at Simmerath-Konzen, where he placed *Oberst* Arthur Jüttner's *164th Grenadier Regiment* backed by his heavy and two of his light artillery battalions. The volksgrenadiers were only tenuously tied in on their left and held an overextended front. To make matters worse, Kittel was reassigned on January 27, leaving one *Oberst* Martin in charge.[32]

To the south of the *62d* and separated by a five-kilometer gap, the northern-most unit in *LXVII Corps* (*General der Infanterie* Otto Hitzfeld commanding), *Generalmajor* Wilhelm Viebig's *277th Volksgrenadier Division*, had been involved on the far northern shoulder of the Bulge and held positions dating from the end of offensive operations. Because the division had been whipped into shape under frontline conditions after its formation in November 1944, and because it had participated with high hopes in the December offensive, its disappointment with the failure was all the more acute within the ranks. Morale was bad.

The offensive had cost the *277th* two-thirds of its experienced personnel. One of its three regiments was down to battalion size and would soon be dissolved. Two battalions were out of the line helping the overwhelmed *Feld Ersatz Bataillon* train the thousand replacements received during January. That left four battalions in the line to hold a fifteen-kilometer front. Gaps of up to a thousand meters separated units. The division had nine antitank guns and an assault gun company.

To the left of the *277th*, the *89th Infantry Division* was in bad shape and falling back under American pressure. The division, which had recently arrived from the *LXXIV Corps'* sector, was rated "just still fit for defensive war-fare." As of January 29, the *277th* no longer knew where its neighbor's right flank was located.[33]

On January 28 and 29, *Oberst* Arthur Jüttner and his men observed obvious *Ami* preparations for an offensive from the freezing defensive positions of the *62d Volksgrenadier Division*.[34] The troopers in the *277th Volksgrenadier Division* likewise had watched American troops brazenly mass to their front in late January, but they lacked the artillery ammunition to do anything about it. Division officers assessed that the forbidding terrain and absence of east-west roads in its sector made an American attack there unlikely.[35]

The Americans struck on January 30.

BETTER LATE THAN NEVER
The timing for V Corps' renewed bid to capture the dams hinged on the XVIII Airborne Corps' seizure of Büllingen, at the far left of its counteroffensive to erase the Bulge. Major General Clarence Huebner now commanded V Corps.

His former command, the Big Red One, now led by Brigadier General Clift Andrus, took Büllingen from the *89th Infantry Division* on January 29 and opened the door for him.

The V Corps operation unfolded in the midst of massive shifts in areas of responsibility for American armies and corps. The big picture was this: First Army had received orders to take over Ninth Army's sector along the Roer River as far north as Merken. Ninth Army would concentrate to take part in a joint offensive with the 21st Army Group; it would finally cross the Roer. First Army was to clear up the "dam situation" as soon as possible, then push a corps forward to the Erft River to protect Ninth Army's right flank. Hodges on February 4 issued instructions that rejiggered his corps' zones to accommodate his new responsibilities. Lines moved, and many divisions were resubordinated.[36]

On January 30, the 9th Infantry Division attacked toward the dams through the Monschau Forest in an easterly direction. The division operated at night for the first time, a practice that became immensely popular with the infantry because they suffered lower casualties.[37] The Old Reliable Division rolled three thousand yards over elements of the *62d* and *277th Volksgrenadier divisions* and terrain once taken, lost, and now regained. Alzen fell early, and soon the doughs were in the open country south of the Roer River.[38]

Just to the north, XIX Corps' 78th Infantry Division, which held a salient into the first line of West Wall pillboxes in the Monschau corridor, struck south from the Lammersdorf area in support. Major General Edwin Parker Jr.'s Lightning Division was barely a shade past green, inexperienced and previously unbloodied.

Enter the 78th, Stage Left

Fittingly, given the intertwined dramas of the men on the Roer plain and deep in the Hürtgen Forest, fate decreed that a Ninth Army division under First Army control would finally seize the earthen water barrier that had so bedeviled all and sundry. Indeed, the Lightning Division's regiments would do so under the direct orders of another division's commander, one who had first breached the Siegfried Line near Aachen back in mid-September.

The XIX Corps assigned a tremendous amount of support to the 78th Infantry Division operation. Corps engineers, corps artillery, and the XXIX TAC lent their help. Tank attachments amounted to the punch of an armored division: CCA, 5th Armored Division; the 736th Tank Battalion, Mine Exploding (less one company); Company A of the 739th Tank Battalion;

Squadron B of the Fife and Forfar Yeomanry (flame-throwing Crocodile tanks); and the 893d Tank Destroyer Battalion (self-propelled). (The 774th Tank Battalion would be attached on February 3.)

At 0530 hours, a preparation fired by one heavy, three medium, and six light artillery battalions—augmented by a company of 4.2-inch mortars and the tank destroyer battalion—crashed into the pillboxes and trenches held by the *272d Volksgrenadier Division* near Kesternich and Simmerath. To the north, the 8th Infantry Division fired a massive barrage as well and launched a feint to distract the Germans. Fog hovered over the freezing battlefield until the afternoon hours.

At 0535 hours, the 310th and 311th Infantry regiments attacked abreast; two hours later, CCA drove southward between them toward Eicherscheid. The artillery preparation had lasted only five minutes because of ammunition shortages, which gave the Lightning Division an unanticipated advantage in that the Germans stayed in their shelters until almost too late, waiting expectantly for the rest of the barrage to fall.

Initial progress was fairly rapid along most of the line, but Lieutenant Colonel Richard Keyes' 2d Battalion, 311th Infantry, ran into furious resistance when it struck toward Kesternich, at the left end of the division's front. Each company of infantry had a section of tank destroyers attached for close support; a full platoon of Shermans worked with the assault echelon of Company F. In theory, the doughs and tankers could communicate by radio, and squad leaders could talk to individual tank commanders via the field telephones mounted under the rear decks of the Shermans.

The battalion quickly drove back the German outpost line but ran into barbed wire and minefields at the MLR. The defenders, men of the *981st Grenadier Regiment*, hammered the attackers with small-arms fire from their bunkers and trenches and directed mortar and artillery fire on the GIs, who were bunched up in the paths cleared of antipersonnel mines by the tank tracks. Suddenly, a 75mm gun opened up on the Shermans. Knowing that a hit almost certainly spelled a kill, the tank commanders maneuvered to find cover, and the attack bogged down.

After sizing up the situation, Lieutenant Nufer, who commanded the assault platoon of Company F, leaped aboard a Sherman and directed it forward; he waved for his men to follow. As small-arms fire intensified, the tank hit a mine and stopped. Nufer tumbled from the deck but jumped to his feet and grabbed two sections of bangalore torpedo carried on the Sherman's deck. He blew a gap through the mines and wire and beckoned the next Sherman forward. Then he jumped aboard and rode the Sherman through the first German line, followed by his men.

The volksgrenadiers were deployed in depth, however, and as the other two companies and more tanks exploited the breakthrough, they encountered heavy mortar, artillery, and small-arms fire every way they turned. Battalion CO Keyes related, "The situation became confusing. The battle had lost its coordination and the fighting had become piecemeal." Keyes criss-crossed the battlefield to find his company commanders and rallied his men for a renewed drive to clear Kesternich at 1500 hours. Although he had succeeded in reunifying his battalion's efforts, the all-too-frequent problems arose of doughs and tankers unfamiliar with one another. Keyes lamented, "The tank-infantry coordination was not favorable. The tanks seemed to expect the infantry to lead them, and the infantry was prone to wait for the tanks. The telephones on the rear of the tanks were out in every instance, and the radio net was an on-and-off proposition." At dark, the Germans still held some buildings in town.

Even where progress was more rapid, the battle was no walkover. Lieutenant Colonel Andy Lipscom, whose 3d Battalion, 311th Infantry, captured Huppenbroich, just to the south of Kesternich, reported:

> We were fighting the elements. The men were tired when they moved up the hill. The snow was very deep. The wind was very high, sweeping the snow into their eyes so that they could barely see or hear. They were so very numb and tired that they couldn't hit the ground when the artillery and mortar fire fell beside them. They were too tired to rush the target in following up a friendly artillery concentration on the enemy, so that the artillery was not very effective since the enemy had an opportunity to recover before they were closed upon.
>
> Huppenbroich was stubbornly held by the enemy with well placed machine-gun and small-arms fire. Every house contained enemy, and every house was fought for. The company commanders with the artillery forward observers were up with the forward elements directing heavy artillery concentrations within seventy-five yards of our troops.

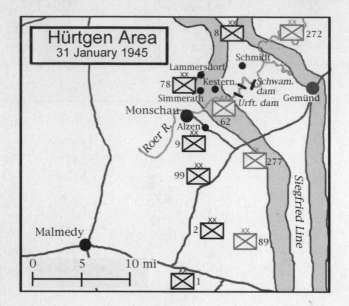

That night, Lipscom occupied the CP of the *981st Grenadier Regiment*, where food was still warm on the stove. But the volksgrenadiers still held the southern edge of town.

Konzen fell quickly to the 310th Infantry Regiment, helped out by mine-clearing American Shermans and British flame-throwing Crocodiles.

Combat Command A, working with the 1st Battalion, 311th Infantry, rolled through a gap in minefields opened by flail tanks and engineers. Fresh and accumulated snow complicated operations in this sector, too. A company of tanks, its three platoons arrayed in a wedge formation, churned through snow toward the Eicherscheid, firing as it went. Some tanks bellied up on unseen stumps, and others wallowed in snow banks. On the other hand, snow whipped up by the wind screened the Shermans and made German antitank fire inaccurate.

Oberst Arthur Jüttner's *164th Grenadier Regiment, 62d Volksgrenadier Division*, had major problems when its right flank was exposed by the penetration of the *272d Volksgrenadier Division's* line. Jüttner's 2d Battalion fell back before the onslaught toward Eicherscheid. Moreover, Jüttner and his men that very morning had learned that the Soviets had entered their home region in Upper Silesia, and worry for their families gnawed at their guts.

The American tanks, which had left the freezing infantry behind to struggle through the snow, charged into Eicherscheid after a time-on-target barrage by twenty-one corps artillery battalions plastered the defenders. Debris was still falling when the Shermans reached the first buildings. By 1600 hours, the doughs had caught up, and the tank-infantry team moved methodically from house to house. Eicherscheid was cleared by 1800 hours.[39]

By evening, the attackers had reached Imgenbroich, Eicherscheid, Huppenbroich, and Kesternich—the line previously reached in abortive operations in the area. The Americans had passed the last prepared defensive positions all along the line. They had suffered light casualties and taken 450 prisoners.[40]

The next day, January 31, the 9th Infantry Division took Widdau and established contact with the 78th Infantry Division, on its left. Resistance was fairly strong—including a spirited counterattack by *Fifteenth Army's* alarm battalion—but deep snow and mines proved to be the biggest obstacle. *Oberst* Jüttner's *164th Grenadier Regiment* was ordered eastward and took up positions outside Widdau; that papered over the breach for the moment.

The 78th Infantry Division's 311th Infantry Regiment finished clearing Kesternich in a dog-eat-dog fight. Tanks, tank destroyers, and infantry still had trouble working together. Communications were again a mess as long hours wore out radio batteries and artillery shrapnel disabled the phones mounted on the tanks. Riflemen often had to cover the buttoned-up tankers' periscopes to get their attention. Nonetheless, the armor concentrated fire on strongpoints and bashed holes in the walls of houses with their cannons, through which the riflemen threw grenades, then charged forward.

The Germans, meanwhile, retreated out of their last toehold in Huppenbroich. The 310th Infantry Regiment mopped up resistance around Konzen and Imgenbroich. The 78th Infantry Division had secured all objectives outlined in its attack order from XIX Corps. Combat Command A also had all but completed its assigned mission and secured the high ground around Eicherscheid; it was detached from the 78th Infantry Division the next day.[41]

Under the Microscope

On the first day of February, the 9th Infantry Division tied on its right into the 2d Infantry Division, on its right. The two units would now push northeastward in team, running over anything in the way. The 78th Infantry Division held its ground, and the 102d Cavalry Group screened the remaining gap along the Roer River east of Widdau.[42]

The next day, the 2d Infantry Division charged nearly four miles toward the northeast. The 9th Infantry Division drove out of the Monschau Forest and rolled two miles ahead toward Dreiborn. The division's thrust reached Herhan, where the Americans severed the main supply route for the *272d Volksgrenadier Division* and overran artillery positions of both the *272d* and *62d Volksgrenadier divisions.*[43]

The V Corps took operational control over the 78th Infantry Division at 1800 hours on February 1, and the division received a new objective: Schwammenauel Dam. Huebner told division commanding general Parker that this was the "most vital job on the Western Front at this time." With the mission came intense pressure. Bradley, Hodges, and SHAEF stayed in close contact, and Huebner dropped in frequently at the division CP. As Lieutenant Colonel Robert McKinney and his operations staff drew up their plans, they were sure of one thing: The 78th would not be yet one more division to make its main effort in the form of a frontal assault along the almost hopeless direct approach across the Kall River toward Schmidt. Instead, the division would take Rurberg and attack Schmidt from the southwest; only then would it turn southeastward toward the Schwammenauel Dam.[44]

The *272d* and *62d Volksgrenadier divisions* were decimated by February 3— all regiments in contact having been reduced below battalion strength—and the *89th Infantry* and *277th Volksgrenadier divisions* were faltering. Confusion was such in the *277th*, which had retreated to the Siegfried Line bunkers, that it at times relied on intercepts of American radio communications to know which of its pillboxes were still fighting.

Model turned again to the crack troops who had stopped the Americans at the Roer. Battle groups from the *12th Volksgrenadier Division*, plus two regiments of the *3d Panzergrenadier Division*, rushed to plug the emerging hole in the *62d Volksgrenadier Division's* sector, but they could barely contain the breakthrough from reaching Euskirchen. *Generalmajor* Denkert took command of the remnants of the *62d* and deployed them on the *3d Panzergrenadiers'* right wing near Gemünd, braced by some of his heavy weapons. *Oberst* Jüttner and the survivors from his regiment reached the new defensive position by clambering across the damaged top of the Urfttalsperre Dam.

The near collapse of the *62d Volksgrenadier Division* also forced the battered *272d* to bend its left flank back to the east. It was able to establish a new line anchored along the Kall River north of Schmidt that ran west of that town and tied into the Roer River south of Rurberg.[45]

But V Corps continued to gain ground. Dreiborn fell to the 9th Infantry Division after stiff house-to-house fighting, including a last stand in the town's castle. The 60th Infantry Regiment had swooped into the town at night, having left the noisy armor to the rear to maintain surprise; the German defenders were shocked to find two white-clad American battalions in their midst at 0430 hours. When the fighting inside the castle ended at about 1700 hours, observed the division's semiofficial history, "the hungry, worn-out victors looked as haggard as did the vanquished."

The 78th Infantry Division resumed its push eastward with the CCR, 7th Armored Division, and the 774th Tank Battalion attached. The division recrossed the Roer River at Dedenborn, where the doughs swam across the freezing torrent while hanging onto a cable, under fire all the while.[46]

The next day, the Lightning Division gained another two miles and captured Rurberg—defended mainly by clerks, cooks, and mechanics—and the nearby high ground that dominated the terrain west of the small Paulushof Dam. The division G-2 commented, "The 78th Division's attack was in the nature of a steamroller, taking everything the enemy had to offer."

The 9th Infantry Division gained thirty-five hundred yards to the shore of the lake created by the Urfttalsperre Dam. Company A of the 47th Infantry Regiment reached the dam itself. Plans for one *Leutnant* Adam of the *62d Volksgrenadier Division* to blow the dam were thwarted when ethnic Polish troops under his command declined to signal the approach of American riflemen and surrendered instead. The Germans launched a counterattack supported by tanks against division elements approaching Schleiden, but the assault was driven off.[47]

The V Corps pushed forward more slowly on February 5 as the reorganization of the front began and the heretofore simple choreography was scrapped. The independent 517th Parachute Infantry Regiment was attached from XVIII Airborne Corps and received orders to enter the line between the 78th and 9th Infantry divisions. The 9th Infantry Division gained a thousand yards toward Gemünd.[48]

The 78th Infantry Division now pushed northeastward toward Schmidt. At this point, Huebner intervened and ordered Parker to change his plan of attack. Division G-3 McKinney explained later: "Corps asked Division what it was doing. The division indicated that it was sending the 310th [Infantry Regiment] through the 309th to take Schmidt. Corps didn't like that and said for the division to send the 309th, which was fresher, into Schmidt. At the time the change was made, the enemy was confused. In attempting to change the plan, Division found that its units were scattered about and that the maneuver of making the change in regiments caused great confusion. The 310th sat on the side of the road. By the time the 309th was brought up, the enemy was back on its feet. Late in the afternoon, Division told Corps that it was impossible to change the plan and get Schmidt. Corps didn't like it, so Division told them to get somebody else. Corps then said to go ahead with the original plan, so Division ordered the 310th to go after its original objectives."

The 310th Infantry Regiment and the 517th Parachute Infantry Regiment jointly cleared pillboxes between Strauch and Schmidt. But the Germans were, indeed, back on their feet: Denkert's *8th Panzergrenadier Regiment* had shifted into the area and been subordinated to the *272d Volksgrenadier Division* with orders to seal the breach. The hurriedly rescheduled American attack—the battalions advanced without proper briefings—resulted in heavy casualties and left the 310th in bad shape. McKinney judged that Huebner's fiddling delayed capture of Schmidt by two days.[49]

The 9th Infantry Division, meanwhile, made some progress toward Gemünd.[50]

On February 6, von Zangen transferred control over what was left of *LXXIV Corps* to *Fifth Panzer Army*.[51] Men from the *3d Fallschirmjäger Division's 6th Fallschirmjäger Regiment* reinforced positions west of the dams, but they were too little too late. Badly weakened in the Bulge, the division was simultaneously attempting to reconstitute by absorbing remnants of the *5th Fallschirmjäger Division*.[52]

The 78th Infantry Division was back on its original plan. There had been more wrangling with V Corps; it wanted to launch a night attack, which

Parker opposed. Corps prevailed this time. Parker's troops struck at 0300 hours but ran into stiff resistance and made little headway. Confusion caused by fighting in thick forest in the dark contributed to the problems.

In the course of the day, Major General James Gavin, commander of the 82d Airborne Division, visited V Corps headquarters. He encountered Huebner and Parker bent over a map. The corps commanding general was drawing quarter-inch lines in blue to represent individual battalions as he told Parker how he should approach the Schwammenauel Dam. Gavin was dismayed at the degree to which Huebner was trying to run the battlefield from his map room.[53]

Despite the less-than-lightning-speed advance by Parker's troops, the trend must have been clear at *Army Group B* headquarters. On Model's orders, engineers sabotaged the valves in the Schwammenauel Dam. The Roer River flood was on, although the advancing GIs did not know it.[54]

Take the Dam!

Because of his division's slow progress, Parker decided to strike the next morning with all three regiments abreast. The plan worked, in part because the Germans had pulled back their MLR to Kommerscheidt and Schmidt. The GIs entered both villages, then advanced as far as Harscheidt. American troops on the Schmidt ridge now looked over the Schwammenauel Dam near Hasenfeld.[55]

Huebner nevertheless was frustrated with the pace of advance, as was Hodges, who called him shortly before noon on February 8 to make that clear. Huebner asked Craig, who coincidentally had just walked into the corps headquarters, if his 9th Infantry Division could help reach the dam. Whether Parker's disagreements with corps in the preceding days had anything to do with Huebner's decision is not clear. Craig replied that he could act immediately, and he had elements of Colonel John Van Houton's 60th Infantry Regiment moving toward Hasenfeld by 1700 hours. Craig took charge of the 78th Infantry Division sector and two of its regiments.[56]

Van Houton's 2d Battalion, 60th Infantry, at daybreak on February 9 attacked through the 310th Infantry Regiment with little knowledge of what might be in front. The Germans still held houses on the outskirts of Schmidt, and the battalion became engaged at once. Van Houton committed his 3d Battalion, and the two battalions were able to advance abreast with supporting tanks driving up the road. The advance bogged down when mines were encountered on the road and two or three panzers opened fire from high ground on Hill 418.

Van Houton commandeered a mine flail to clear the road. Artillery and Cannon Company smoked Hill 418, and the tanks rolled forward to engage the panzers. The Germans withdrew toward Hasenfeld, and the Shermans followed, careful to keep to the German tread marks to avoid mines. Company G, supported by tanks and Companies I and L, entered Hasenfeld. Despite a tenacious defense by a sizable infantry force and three panzers, the town was cleared after dark. The door to the dam was open.[57]

Finally, at 2100 hours, Lieutenant Colonel Robert Schellman's 1st Battalion, 309th Infantry, and attached engineers reached the Schwammenauel Dam. Company A cleared the upper portion, while Company B fought its way down to the base of the dam, where engineers inspected the valve house. The bridge across the top of the dam had been blown, and the Germans still fired across the Schwammenauel from a pillbox at the south end. Nevertheless, they were effectively deprived of control.[58]

The damage was already done, however.

The Roer rose more than five feet in front of Ninth Army between February 9 and 11 and overflowed its banks in the entire sector. The river attained an average width of four hundred yards, and as much as two thousand yards in some places. Engineers estimated that the deluge would last at least six days.[59]

The news was bleak, but this problem could arise only once. The Germans had but a brief respite to look to their manifold problems.

Hitler demanded to know why Ordensburg Vogelsang, a training center for future Nazi leaders on the south bank of the Urfttalsperre Dam's lake, had not been defended. Field commanders, who had bigger problems and had never even considered fighting for the useless facility, were stupefied.[60]

CHAPTER 8

ACROSS THE ROER

If we were to force the Rhine by late spring, we could dawdle
no longer on the Roer.

OMAR N. BRADLEY, *A SOLDIER'S STORY*

There were still a few German troops west of the Roer River in early 1945.
That situation did not last long.

OPERATION BLACKCOCK

On January 16, British XII Corps attacked the Heinsberg salient. The corps
deployed three divisions and a commando brigade, supported on the right by
the U.S. 102d Infantry Division. The XII Corps gave "the Jocks" from the 52d
Lowland Division, in the center, the main task of taking Heinsberg. Monty's
famous "Desert Rats" of the 7th Armored Division carried the ball on the left,
and the 43d (Wessex) Infantry Division did so on the right.

Monty provided tremendous artillery support: eight field regiments, six
medium regiments, and some heavy and super-heavy guns. Standing ready
were the 1st Canadian Rocket Battery, which could fire a salvo of 350 rockets
that were equivalent to 5.5-inch shells. Also standing ready were the huge
spotlights that created "Monty's moonlight" by bouncing their beams off
clouds to provide just enough illumination for advancing troops at night.
The "funnies" of the 79th Armored Division (such as flamethrower and
mine-clearing flail tanks) completed the ensemble.

The troops were well prepared to fight across the snow-covered ground. Riflemen had snowsuits, and tanks wore a coat of whitewash.[61] The weather was bitterly cold, and the blizzards and sleet storms were fierce.

The defending *176th Volksgrenadier Division*, responsible for most of the line, had limited armor support and held a thirty-kilometer front.[62] The *183d Volksgrenadier Division*, on the German left, had been thinned out—first by supplying a specified number of officers and soldiers, then one platoon from every rifle company—to provide reinforcements for divisions exhausted in the now clearly failed Ardennes offensive. Morale had sunk.[63]

Nevertheless, the defenders had enjoyed ample time to ready their positions. Three prepared lines ran roughly parallel to the Roer River. The first was a continuous series of trenches and weapon pits protected by barbed wire and mines, these backed by reserve positions a half mile to the rear. The second complex of improved positions was two miles behind the first. The third extended from the West Wall proper through Heinsberg. More than 150 artillery pieces and 18 assault guns backed up the infantry.[64] There was also a Tiger tank battalion in the sector.

The 7th Armored Division, 8th Armored Brigade, and the 155th Brigade from the 52d Lowland Division launched the first blow, an operation intended to punch a hole in the German lines at Susteren, on the Dutch border. The spearhead would, if the plan worked out, execute a sweeping drive toward Roermond, then cut south behind the German defenses. The Jocks climbed aboard Canadian "Kangaroos"—turretless Sherman tanks converted to armored personnel carriers—for the attack, although they had never worked with armor before.[65]

The 7th Armored Division quickly ran into vigorous resistance and a blown bridge. Engineers built a new one, at the cost of heavy casualties, only to watch German fire destroy it. They built it again, and this time the division pushed into Susteren. The sweeping drive had slowed to a crawl. The British spent days fighting to clear villages east of Susteren, a task made all the harder by the appearance of Tigers in support of the German infantry trying desperately to hold each town.[66]

The *Fifteenth Army* commanding general, von Zangen, would later critically attribute to the British an offensive plan that merely pushed his defenses rather than create a breakthrough that would cut off his troops.[67] In fact, XII Corps tried exactly that, but the tenacious defense offered by the *176th Volksgrenadier Division* foiled the plan.

Finally, on January 19, the 8th Armored Brigade and the 52d Lowland Division were able to launch their drive eastward through Susteren toward Heinsberg. Tanks slipped and slid on the treacherous roads. Almost immediately, SP guns knocked out four Shermans from Squadron A, 13/18th Hussars. Squadron B had worse luck; it ran into a determined German counterattack backed by Tigers at Waldfeucht on January 21. By midday, the Germans had retaken most of the town from the 5th King's Own Scottish Borderers (KOSB), and panzers and panzerfausts had set Shermans burning all over the place. In one day, the Hussars lost twenty tanks.[68]

On the right, the 43d Infantry attacked on January 20 backed by Churchill tanks. Resistance in this sector was less determined than elsewhere, and by January 24 the division held the ground overlooking the Roer River.[69] The XII Corps had worked its way up to the last German line of defense.

Lieutenant Peter White commanded a platoon of the tough, hard-scrapping men in the 4th KOSB, with which the 7th/9th Royal Scots had drawn the assignment of taking Heinsberg itself. White recalled, "Heinsberg was a largish place lying on the edge of the valley of the rivers Würm and Roer, and right under the heavy guns of the Siegfried Line, a fact that we grew to appreciate fully before the action was over."[70]

The 52d Lowland Division Jocks pushed off after midnight on January 24 to the accompaniment of Sherman tank engines. German artillery pounded the attackers while they trudged forward past a burning Churchill Crocodile and Shermans spinning their tracks in the snow. Monty's moonlight created a ghostly landscape. The infantry columns followed lines of pink Bofors tracer rounds fired over their heads as guides toward their objectives. The men reached a rise before Heinsberg and could see the town erupting with the explosions of British artillery fire.

By 0230 hours, the Jocks reached the edge of Heinsberg. Lieutenant White's platoon was, per orders, digging in when artillery fire swept the position. White recalled, "Just then, when we were only partly dug in, a sudden fiendish volley of shells shrieked into eruption right among us. . . . The whole position was blanketed with a haze of flashes, the most appalling noise, blast, and smoke. It was our own 25-pounders. . . ."

Jocks tried to merge with the freezing slush at the bottom of their unfinished holes. The company CP was unable to contact the artillery to move the barrage forward. The fire lifted after what seemed an eternity but was only a half hour.

With the coming of dawn, the Germans could see the Jocks well enough to rake the freezing men with artillery, mortar, and machine-gun fire. As the seemingly endless day wore on, White was summoned back to the company CP. Making his way through the murderous fire, he found most of the men there casualties; he was in command. Lance Corporal Alexander Leitch, the company signaler, had reached the artillery by radio and was calmly calling in covering fire. One of Leitch's legs had been almost severed, and the other was badly wounded. White put a tourniquet on Leitch's leg, but the lance corporal refused to be evacuated. White, a former artilleryman, adjusted the fire through Leitch for forty-five minutes. Leitch began to lose coherence and was finally evacuated; he had earned a Distinguished Conduct Medal.[71]

Heinsberg fell that day, and by January 26 the last German forces were ejected from the salient. The victory had cost the Jocks 100 men killed and 750 wounded.[72] The surviving Germans were able to withdraw across the Roer in good order, but they had suffered heavy casualties as well.[73]

THE GOAL LONG SOUGHT: OPERATION GRENADE

Ninth Army planners in early February turned again to the challenge of crossing the Roer and reaching the Rhine. In mid-January, Simpson had proposed to Field Marshal Montgomery that Ninth Army attack northeastward toward the Rhine. The route avoided the troublesome forests and exploited four areas of Allied superiority: armor, air support, abundant transport, and access to gasoline. Simpson pointed out that any difficulties in moving divisions north from the Bulge to participate would be compounded on the German side.

Montgomery saw that such an attack would mesh perfectly with his plans for an offensive by the Canadian First Army southward between the Meuse (Maas) and Rhine rivers. On January 21, Montgomery issued his orders. The Canadian pincer would be called Operation Veritable, and that of Ninth Army Operation Grenade. The aim, Monty explained in his instructions, was to seize intermediate objectives en route to the Ruhr, "wear down the enemy's strength at a greater rate than our own," and destroy all German forces between Nijmegan and the line Jülich-Düsseldorf.

Montgomery had finally joined the war of annihilation. Ike, naturally, approved. Indeed, Monty's operation was only one piece of Eisenhower's plan to eliminate all substantial German elements remaining west of the Rhine, which would free up the resources for a sixty-division offensive into the heart of Germany. The British (though not Montgomery, this time) again posed objections to the broad-front approach, and Ike again stood firm.

The Canadians struck on February 8 through miserable weather and across flooded ground. The advance was painfully slow, but an advance it was.[74]

Simpson's initial target date for starting Operation Grenade was February 15, per Monty's orders. But the date was soon advanced by five days to take advantage of the Canadian pressure on German forces. Forecasts based on the November-December offensive anticipated losses of a thousand battle casualties and five hundred nonbattle casualties per day over a ten-day period. For once, those estimates would prove high.

Ninth Army confronted substantial logistic problems in concentrating a large number of divisions in its area. An early thaw and heavy rains compounded problems of space as roads crumbled and rivers rose enough to force the closure of some bridges.

Prisoners provided Ninth Army's G-2 with an accurate picture of the forces disposed by the enemy in its sector on the far side of the river. Intelligence assessed that some eighteen thousand men held the German MLR. Elements of the *8th Fallschirmjäger Division*—only a thousand men—were located near Roermond. Three volksgrenadier divisions occupied most of the front (from north to south the *176th*, *183d*, and *363d*) with sixty-five hundred men total. The *59th Infantry Division* held the area north of Jülich between the *183d* and *363d Volksgrenadier divisions* with five thousand men. Miscellaneous units accounted for another thousand soldiers. German reserves amounted to nineteen thousand men, including a panzergrenadier (the *15th*) and two panzer (the *116th* and *Panzer Lehr*) divisions, although it appeared as D-day approached that all of these had already been committed against the Canadians. Intelligence suspected that either or both the *9th* and *11th Panzer divisions* were near Cologne. At worst, the attackers would outnumber the defenders by a 5:1 margin.

German morale along the front was bad after the failure of the Ardennes offensive and the nonappearance of the "miracle weapons" promised by Nazi propaganda chief Göbbels. Beginning in mid-January, desertions began to become a problem for the first time, a fact kept out of official reports until much later.[75]

Simpson intended to hurl XIII and XIX corps against the German defenses. The former still had the 102d and 84th Infantry divisions deployed along the river, backed by the 5th Armored Division. The latter's 29th and 30th Infantry divisions faced the Germans, and the 83d Infantry and 2d Armored divisions constituted the corps reserve. Simpson also had the 95th Infantry Division in army reserve.

On February 6, Ninth Army had taken responsibility for British 12 Corps' sector as far north as Roermond. Major General John Anderson's XVI Corps, consisting of the 35th and 79th Infantry and 8th Armored divisions, took charge of the sector. The entire west bank of the Roer River now belonged to the Americans, and XVI Corps, too, became part of Operation Grenade.

The operations staff developed two plans; the selection would hinge on ground conditions. The first step for both was to establish firm bridgeheads around Linnich and Jülich, executed by XIII and XIX corps, respectively; XVI Corps would initially stage a demonstration and cross the river later. Plan I then outlined a rapid push with maximum employment of armor across dry or frozen ground. Plan II called for a methodical advance across the familiar wet ground. In either case, Ninth Army would exploit aggressively any breakdown in opposing forces.

After all the bother about the Roer dams, Ninth Army's letter of instructions explicitly anticipated crossing with the dams in enemy hands. There would be a buildup rapid enough to ride out five or six days of flooding.[76] Planners no longer had to worry about powerful panzer reserves that might destroy American units isolated for a few days east of the Roer.

The boundary between Ninth and First armies had been adjusted repeatedly to accommodate Hodges' needs in taking the Roer dams. A final tweak set the line somewhat south of Jülich for Operation Grenade and gave each army half of Aachen and its respective road net.

First Army now readied itself to cross the river and cover Simpson's right flank until he was safely anchored on the Rhine. Only then did Hodges have a green light to resume his attack toward Cologne. Hodges had VII, III, and V corps lined up north to south. They would attack successively in echelon in that order, beginning with an assault by Collins' VII Corps in concert with Ninth Army. Each division in the other two corps would cross the Roer by sideslipping northward to use the bridgehead already established by the neighboring division, then turn back south to resume operations in its own sector.[77]

The VII Corps' old nemesis, the *12th Volksgrenadier Division* (temporarily commanded by *Generalmajor* Rudolf Langhauser while Engel recovered from wounds suffered in the Ardennes), held the east bank in the Düren sector under the control of *LVIII Panzer Corps*. The Wild Buffaloes had been withdrawn from the Ardennes on January 17 and shifted northeast of Münstereifel for accelerated reconstitution. Reflecting the division's remarkable priority for manpower, it was back up to a fighting strength of about three thousand riflemen by January 25. Its three regiments were now organized with three four-hundred-man battalions each, although piecemeal commitment of the *89th Grenadier Regiment* would reduce it to two battalions by the day the Americans crossed the Roer. Only the assault gun company, which had six of its fourteen guns stranded on the road from the Ardennes by lack of fuel, was badly below par. Attachment of a brigade of twenty-four panzer assault guns on about February 15 offset the problem, however.[78]

The flooding of the Roer forced indefinite postponement of Operation Grenade. The Ninth Army's chief engineer now forecast that prohibitively high and rapid water would last between two weeks and seventeen days.[79]

While they waited, American units trained, scouted, and scoured aerial photographs that were updated whenever weather permitted. Ninth Army added the 75th Infantry Division, transferred to its ranks from the 6th Army Group, far to the south. The 12th Army Group supplied extra service troops to handle the buildup of ammunition and other supplies. Five hundred C-47 transport aircraft were readied to bring in enough materiel to support an entire division for one day if needed. At the same time, however, Simpson had to turn over the 75th and 95th Infantry divisions to British Second Army to cover for forces that had been sent to reinforce the casualty-claiming Canadian drive.[80]

The Ninth Army's senior engineer on February 21 determined that it would be possible to cross and bridge the swollen Roer River as of February 23. Simpson set D-day for 0330 hours on that date.[81]

At 0245 hours on the appointed day, all artillery units along a twenty-five-mile front—plus antiaircraft batteries—unleashed a stunning barrage, the largest ever fired on the western front. Ninth Army had the 34th Field Artillery Brigade, with three 240mm howitzer battalions and one 8-inch gun battalion, deployed astride the boundary between XIII and XIX corps, from where it could

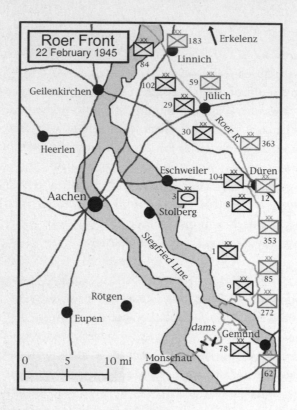

support both. The night was clear, and the moon bright. The Germans had not believed the river to be passable yet and were caught completely by surprise.[82]

XIII CORPS: THE LINNICH BRIDGEHEAD

The 102d Infantry Division, on the right adjacent to XIX Corps, staged the main assault in the northernmost zone. Just before D-day, the division commander, Brigadier General Keating, told his staff that the plan for the crossing "violates all the accepted principles of an attack across a river." Instead of crossing on a broad front, he was expected to attack through bottlenecks at Linnich and Rurdorf. He hoped that a diversionary smoke screen at Flossdorf would convince the Germans that he was attacking on a broader front than he was.

The Germans responded to the opening artillery barrage with mortar fire along the riverbanks. The first raiding party crossed the river at 0300 hours and wiped out several machine-gun nests. At 0330 hours, the 407th Infantry Regiment attacked south of Linnich with 1st Battalion on the left and 2d on the right. The

405th Infantry Regiment crossed at Rurdorf in a column of battalions led by the 1st. Only weak small-arms and mortar fire challenged the assault; although a few boats lost control and drifted away, there was not a single known case of drowning. By dawn, both regiments had already closed on their initial objectives. Only at Boslar, where artillery broke up a series of tank-infantry counterattacks by the *363d Volksgrenadier Division*, did the GIs face much of a fight.[83]

The 84th Infantry Division was limited to a single crossing site, but it was determined to make the best of the situation. Leading with a single battalion, the 334th Infantry Regiment launched thirty-five assault boats bearing Companies A and C toward the far shore at 0330 hours. The second wave, with Company B and headquarters, followed fifteen minutes later. By 0405 hours, the 1st Battalion was across without the loss of a single boat. By 0610 hours, the battalion had seized Korrenzig, its first objective, which the *59th Infantry Division* had abandoned but for some sick and wounded.

The division built up rapidly and attacked to the northeast into the left flank of the *183d Volksgrenadier Division*. The GIs quickly surged four miles up the highway toward München-Gladbach and seized the communications center of Baal—the most spectacular advance in Ninth Army that day. The volksgrenadiers staged several ineffective counterattacks at Baal, one of the few places along the front where the Germans struck back all day.[84]

XIX CORPS: THE JÜLICH BRIDGEHEAD

The 30th Infantry Division, on XIX Corps' right, was assigned the most challenging stretch of river—between Jülich and Düren. During November planning, the area had been deemed unsuitable for any crossing. But the need to protect the flanks of the assaults on those two cities resulted in orders to get across the Roer there, anyway.[85]

GIs began crossing the river before the artillery barrage. Fighting the strong current, small groups of riflemen entered assault boats and paddled across in the dark to provide cover for engineers, who installed guide ropes and footbridges. In the 119th Infantry Regiment's sector, the Roer was already bridged by 0310 hours, and doughboys began to walk across twenty minutes later. A scattering of light artillery fire was the only reaction from the *363d Volksgrenadier Division*. By 0430 hours, Selgersdorf, the first objective, had been cleared; most of the shell-shocked German company in residence had to be dragged from cellars.

Planned bridging and ferry operations proved impossible in the 120th Infantry Regiment's sector because of the strong current and shellfire. Plan B worked: Alligator amphibious armored vehicles earmarked for the Rhine River crossing were available and ferried nearly two companies across. Other doughs used the bridge built by the 119th Infantry. Before dawn, the 120th, too, had taken its first towns against light resistance.

The division's engineers constructed a vehicular bridge in less than twenty-two hours. Tanks and tank destroyers roared across to join the doughs. Major Clayborn Wayne, an infantry battalion executive officer, summed up the day's work: "On the whole, it was a beautiful crossing."[86]

The assault in the 29th Infantry Division's zone north of Jülich came off in a similar fashion. The 115th Infantry Regiment crossed entirely in Alligators and boats. After an SP gun knocked out several freshly built bridges in the 175th Infantry Regiment's sector, the engineers moved them farther upstream.

The defending *59th Infantry Division* had expended most of its artillery ammunition by noon. With the Americans already behind its fighting positions along the Roer, the division feverishly shifted its regiments in an attempt to maintain a cohesive line. Despite some lively German fire, by dark the 29th Infantry Division had reached most of its objectives and was almost to the rest of them.[87]

VII CORPS: THE DÜREN BRIDGEHEAD

Lightning Joe Collins finally had Düren square in his sights. The town had defied his efforts to reach it for five months. The VII Corps now consisted of the 104th Infantry Division, Brigadier General Bryant Moore's 8th Infantry Division, and the 3d Armored Division.

The Wild Buffaloes of the *12th Volksgrenadier Division*, who had time and again held VII Corps in check since the early days at Aachen, occupied Düren. They would, in the words of the official U.S. Army history, offer the "hardest fight of all" during the Roer crossing.

The *12th Volksgrenadier Division* held its line with the *27th Fusilier Regiment* on the right and the *48th Grenadier Regiment* on the left; each was reinforced by a platoon of assault guns. The *89th Grenadier Regiment* and *12th Fusilier Battalion* held the third reserve line of defenses. The antitank company's 75mm guns were deployed in depth behind the MLR. Two 88mm antiaircraft battalions were available for tank defense in the sector but were not subordinated to

Generalmajor Langhauser. Several villages were designated localities to be defended to the last man. To the division's left, the *353d Volksgrenadier Division* defended the southern part of the planned 8th Infantry Division attack zone.

The opening barrage caused considerable casualties among the Wild Buffaloes but did not break their fighting spirit.[88] The American infantry divisions crossed the Roer beginning at 0330 hours.

The 8th Infantry Division, on the corps' right, struggled against a strong current and heavy artillery fire. The 28th Infantry Regiment's 3d Battalion, which pushed off during the artillery preparation, completely surprised the defenders, yet some 40 percent of the attacking force was swept downstream in their assault boats. That was the best news of the day. Only five of twenty boats from the 1st Battalion's assault companies made it across. One hundred forty men from the reserve battalion who braved the current reached the far shore, but so many boats swamped that they had but thirty rifles among them and had to hide in abandoned German trenches.

The 13th Infantry Regiment had a worse day. Only thirty-six men from the 2d Battalion reached the eastern bank, to be joined later in the day by two more platoons. A dozen 3d Battalion men made it over, of whom six survived to tell the tale. Darkness enabled the regiment to push four companies across, but they managed to eke out a mere four hundred yards from the water's edge.

Neither the *12th* nor *353d Volksgrenadier divisions* counterattacked to wipe out this pathetically weak toehold. Perhaps it was due to *Generalmajor* Engel's absence, or perhaps, after months of bleeding, the Wild Buffaloes were no longer what they had once been.[89]

Both of the Timberwolf Division's attacking regiments—the 415th on the left and the 413th on the fringes of Düren—quickly discovered that they were making a combat assault. The 415th had a relatively easy time, but Joseph Capone, a rifleman with Company E, later recalled how hot the action was in his battalion's sector at Stammel:

> "Let's go" came the captain's determined voice as he led the way. During the march, I became confident of the successful accomplishment of our mission. We of Company E and of the battalion had been fully oriented in every minute detail. We could not fail.

We reached Merken about 0130 hours. Under the cover of buildings we smoked a last cigarette and said a final prayer. At 0230 hours we proceeded through to the eastern end of the town where the assault boats were hidden and then carried them through hip-deep floodwaters to a point as close to the actual river as possible. We came back one hundred fifty yards and "sweated it out."

At 0300 hours our artillery began hitting the eastern bank of the Roer. This was said to be the greatest barrage ever mustered on the Western Front. . . .

At 0330 hours the jump-off order was given. This was it! We, of 2d Squad, 3d Platoon, went to our boats, struggled to the river, and immediately shoved off. A powerful enemy counterfire was proving effective upon the first two boats. This caused the men in our boat to become excited and to lose control as the fast current threw us downstream and grounded us. I jumped into the water from my position at the rear of the boat and gave it a shove. At that moment the current caught the boat and, in making a desperate leap to catch it, I lost my helmet, which sank quickly to the river's bottom. A feeling of nakedness crept over me as the constant enemy fire grew fiercer. A look back showed confusion and turmoil on our western bank.

What was happening to the company was in the minds of all of us as we reached the enemy bank safely, but frightened, in an assault crossing through an intense enemy fire that landed us far downstream and below our mark. The boat was quickly secured by the two front engineers as we in the squad went up the bank. As we spread out and hit the ground, I, along with my squad leader, took cover in a shell hole, for Jerry was still throwing plenty of firepower. We had a twelve-man squad, plus three men from Company H [weapons] with a .30-caliber [machine gun], and a few men from the other boats who did make it to shore. At this point, things looked very bad. My squad leader decided to have the men spread out on each side of the .30-caliber and dig in. He was mortally wounded in getting up from his position to pass on his plans to the men. Upon my call, the assistant squad leader crawled to my position where I relayed to him the situation. All hell was breaking loose and still the company had not come ashore. A short time later an incoming shell hit between the BAR man and his assistant, with mortal effect.

The platoon medic got ashore and immediately set about his work of first aid. "Doc," as we called him, was admired by all the men of the company because of his superb work under fire. While he was rendering aid, we fired scattered, harassing shots to our front not knowing their effect. In the course of the next ten minutes, our squad suffered two riflemen killed, and the assistant squad leader and two riflemen wounded. In our squad, that left two riflemen, Eddie and me, and about nine others. After an endless wait for help I grew desperate and decided to take Eddie and go upstream to look for elements of the company. I informed the assistant squad leader of the 1st Squad, and off we went back over the bank. How we made it I'll never know, for our silhouettes were obvious to the enemy.[90]

Captain Hayden Bower commanded Company K, 413th Infantry, which formed part of the assault wave on the division's right, close to Düren. The company suffered swamped boats and eight or nine men lost in the swift waters of the Roer, and smoke from the artillery preparation made it difficult to see. Bower nonetheless pushed on by the light of burning buildings and took the company's first objective, a paper factory just east of the river. His battalion CO, Lieutenant Colonel William Summers, then ordered him to seize the next objective, as he later recalled:

The Asylum, a former mental institute, was a two-story brick building with a tower on the front, on the top of the hill that controlled Düren by observation because of its height and was the VII Corps's main objective. Colonel Summers assured me that our own 385th Field Artillery Battalion would coordinate a rolling barrage of all the supporting fires right up the hill in front of our attack. This sounded good to me because we had great confidence in the ability of the 385th to support us with accurate fire, no short rounds.

We reorganized the company and tried to resupply everyone with their correct equipment and ammunition that had been brought over by later boats. Leading up the hill on the right side of our sector was a row of houses alongside a road. To our left was a bare field and a line of trees that could give some cover from enemy observation. I decided to attack in a column of platoons up the line of houses as fast as we could follow the artillery barrage—just fifty yards behind it. We were that confident in our gunners!

The plan was for Lieutenant Crook and 1st Platoon to lead. I would follow with my command group and the artillery forward observers, then 2d Platoon, and Weapons Platoon. I had Lieutenant Skinner, my second in command, take Lieutenant Coffin, 3d Platoon's new leader, and the platoon up our left flank through the trees. Then they were to cut over across the top of the hill towards the Asylum to support our attack, while maintaining visual contact with the 415th on their left. Lieutenant General Collins wanted to [capture] the Asylum by 3:00 P.M. that day. Through powerful twin artillery telescopes, from the three-story creamery building on our side of the river, generals Collins and [division commanding general] Terry Allen would keep constant watch on our every move.

The artillery preparation began at 2:15 in the afternoon, for I had estimated that we would need at least forty-five minutes to make it up to the top of the hill. I moved out right after Crook's 1st Platoon, with the balance of the company following me up the row of houses. Company K men were well trained in how to follow an artillery rolling barrage, but we reminded them again just how important it was to hug the advancing fire as close as possible in our attack. The line of our artillery fire was perpendicular to our advance, and the sight of the shell rounds landing and bursting in front of us was very unnerving! We could see the shells land and explode, their shrapnel screaming up and out from each burst. One's natural desire was to hold back for fear of being hit by its shrapnel, but we had to hug the line of fire in our advance for the protection it gave us from enemy resistance and counterfire. Lieutenant Jones, my 385th Field Artillery forward observer, was at my side, constantly on his radio, making the adjustments needed as he moved the barrage up fifty yards at a time. We still had about three hundred yards to run up the hill. Little did we realize at the time that our day's work would result in our 3d Battalion, 413th Infantry, being awarded the Presidential Distinguished Unit Citation for successfully crossing the Roer River and taking the main objective of the VII Corps.

The 385th Field Artillery did a magnificent job of moving the barrage ahead of us. We were running as fast as we could behind their fire. I anxiously anticipated that the flying shrapnel would fall short and hit some of our men, and they would drop to the ground, dead or in agony, but this did not seem to be happening, and I thanked God for our luck, so far. Later Sergeant MacBride, of Texas, said, "We didn't have time to clear out the houses along the way or we'd have fallen behind our artillery barrage, so we just ran by and riddled them with our fire as we went. . . ."

My command group continued to lag behind. I then remembered that I had once heard that anger can sometimes make a man give the extra effort needed to accomplish a task. So I said, "Come on you S.O.B.'s, if I can keep up so can you!" I knew they were angry with me and I really had a high regard for both of them. What was important right then was that they had to keep trying and making that last effort even though our legs seemed like lead and our lungs were on fire and taking another breath or stopping was almost impossible. We finally made it! We reached the Asylum successfully. We stumbled onto the back porch steps and almost collapsed. I had to quickly consolidate Company K's possessions and clear the Asylum.

The 1st and 2d platoons moved in to clear out any resistance and they eventually held off three successive German counterattacks. . . . The 3d Platoon, coming from the left, were firing their weapons as they advanced on the Asylum, to support our assault, when they caught some Germans trying to escape out the rear and took them prisoners. I quickly moved the 3d Platoon into position to help us defend the Asylum. . . .

As soon as we had secured the Asylum, I immediately called Colonel Summers on my SCR-300 radio and asked what time he had on his watch. He said "2:57 P.M." and I said, "Fine, the Asylum is ours. On to Cologne!"[91]

Only two minutes earlier, Collins had entered the 413th Infantry Regiment's CP and demanded to know when Summers was going to take the Asylum. Summers radioed in as if on cue, "We are on the objective."[92]

Still, neither the 8th nor the 104th Infantry division was able to construct a bridge—and get armor across—until after dark because of deadly German fire.[93]

INTERMEDIATE OBJECTIVE TAKEN

Ninth Army and VII Corps were firmly across the Roer River. Ninth Army had lost only 92 men killed, 913 wounded, and another 61 missing. The VII Corps had sacrificed 66 men killed, 280 wounded, and 35 missing.[94]

The Third Reich had almost exactly ten weeks left to live—considerably less time than it had taken Collins and his men to cover the handful of miles from the dragon's teeth to the east bank of this modest river in western Germany. In ten short weeks, American and British soldiers would have raced to the North Sea coast, the Elbe River, and Czechoslovakia.

This day, attacking divisions pushed ahead one to four miles along the entire length of the Roer River front.[95]

Generalfeldmarschall Walter Model had no more miracles in his pocket. *Alles war kaput.*

Fifteenth Army on February 23 ordered desperate efforts to regroup troops and reestablish communications with *LXXXI Corps*, which was cut off from all communication near Lövenich. The *XII SS Corps*, which attempted to take control over forces in the area, reported that there were not enough resources available to establish a new defensive line, as ordered. The Roer River line, the corps reported, had collapsed.[96]

Von Zangen fed what few troops he could get into the battle. The *338th Infantry Division* arrived from Alsace on February 24 and entered the line before Erkelenz two days later. The division had only two regiments, each with two battalions of about two hundred men apiece, and a two-hundred-strong fusilier battalion, but it lacked antitank defenses and most of its artillery. The lead elements of the *11th Panzer Division* began to arrive that night; they retook Gevenich but had to retreat when adjoining units on both flanks failed to arrive. By then, most of the divisions already in the line were fighting from what had been their artillery positions.[97]

Von Zangen's opposite numbers at Ninth Army noted that "the inability on the part of the enemy to withstand our pressure became more clear as the momentum of the attack was accelerated." Ninth Army viewed the appearance of the *338th Infantry Division* as symptomatic—"a futile attempt to stem the rapid advance."[98]

Opposite VII Corps, the *12th Volksgrenadier Division* held on in the streets of Düren until February 25. The *10th Panzergrenadier Regiment* from the *9th Panzer Division* was attached to the hard-pressed volksgrenadiers on February 24. Nonetheless, unable to rotate battalions and regiments as the Americans could, the fighting men were quickly exhausted. The *LVIII Panzer Corps* committed the *3d Panzergrenadier Division* on the Wild Buffaloes' right, but disaster struck: A surprise tank attack captured the regimental staffs of the *29th Panzergrenadier* and *27th Fusilier regiments* as they were meeting to transfer the sector.[99]

The 5th Armored Division crossed the Roer on February 26 and unleashed a slashing drive to the north and northeast. The Germans, who had anticipated an attack eastward, were caught by surprise. Supported by the 84th and 102d Infantry divisions, the armor rolled over the *338th Infantry Division* and took Erkelenz.[100]

McLain's XIX Corps swung north and made progress similar to that being racked up by XIII Corps. Hell on Wheels' CCB crossed at Jülich on February 26 and plunged into battle beside the 30th Infantry Division. Anderson's XVI Corps had begun crossing the Roer the night before and now turned to roll up remaining Siegfried Line fortifications from the flank. Ninth Army had all its corps engaged and was moving full steam ahead.[101]

In First Army's sector, Collins moved Rose's 3d Armored Division across the river the night of February 25 and unleashed it the next day. Collins settled on a standard procedure. He attached an infantry regiment to Rose's division, which allowed Rose to form six task forces, each consisting of a tank and an infantry battalion. Each task force typically also received supporting tank destroyers, artillery, and engineers. The division reconnaissance battalion, when reinforced, could operate as a seventh task force. Rose normally attacked in four columns, and he flexibly maneuvered his task forces so that two usually attacked each defended town. The infantry divisions protected the flanks, mopped up, and took over the lead when an obstacle such as another river required breaching.[102]

The 3d Armored Division overran a battery of the *12th Volksgrenadier Division's* artillery on February 27, a sure sign that the Wild Buffaloes were caving under the overwhelming pressure. The volksgrenadiers by now were down to between five hundred and six hundred riflemen. Still, befitting its record, the division would absorb replacements and fall back stubbornly, surviving to fight again east of the Rhine River.[103]

***

On February 28, with most of the remaining German armor on the western front concentrated in the Roer sector, von Zangen swapped sectors with the neighboring *Fifth Panzer Army*. His summary for that day was: "The *Fifteenth Army* had been thrown back from the Roer to the Erft. The right wing had been smashed. Contact to the *First Fallschirm Army* was disrupted. The units of the army were not able to hold out any longer, nor did they have the strength to protect particularly the flank. . . ." But Hitler refused to authorize any withdrawal across the Rhine River.[104]

Ninth Army considered that the last day of February was "breakthrough" day, when the back of German resistance along the approaches to the Ruhr was broken. By then, Ninth Army had erected four vehicle and seven treadway bridges across the Roer River. The road to the Rhine was wide open.[105]

EPILOGUE

Ninth Army's AAR recorded in March: "The outstanding success of the Roer River crossing and the crushing sweep to the Rhine with low casualties had brought our army troops' morale to a new high. They were ready to rush on and finish off the German Army."[106] The first XIX Corps troops reached the waters of the Rhine on March 2.

On March 7, VII Corps captured Cologne, on the Rhine River. The corps had traveled more than six hundred miles from Utah Beach. As one measure of its activities, it had captured 140,000 prisoners, more than half of First Army's total and more than all of Third Army's to date.[107]

On Collins' right, III Corps' 9th Armored Division that same day captured intact the Ludendorff railroad bridge, across the Rhine at Remagen. Hodges quickly established a firm bridgehead on the eastern side. Once across the Roer, American forces required less than two weeks to breach the Reich's most formidable geographic barrier.

Just as the Germans had viewed the Roer battle as the key first round in the Ardennes offensive, the battle to cross the Rhine along Eisenhower's main axis of advance had, to a great extent, played out along the Roer River. The Allies would leap the Rhine at many points before the end of March. After that, just as Ike had planned, there was little left to stop the Allied rush eastward.

In the years since the longest battle ended, few have cared to look back and dwell on a time when more than thirty thousand young Americans, and an even greater number of Germans, fell dead or wounded in the rain and mud west of the Roer River. Although the deeds of fighting men elsewhere during the war capture imaginations to this day, the tale of the hard-fighting outfits that clawed their way to the Roer—who recalls the 102d Infantry Division?—is, sadly, all but forgotten.

Both sides won something in the bitter struggle. At the level of the generals, the prize was deemed to have been worth the price. The Americans won in the sense that they nearly always drove forward, and they did finally cross the Roer

River. Yet one can hardly term a bloody twenty-mile advance over the course of five months—to gain what was, after all, an intermediate objective—a great American victory, no matter how valiant the struggle. Still, Eisenhower had sought this battle of attrition, and it contributed to the triumph he anticipated for his broad-front strategy.

If the defense of the Roer sector was simultaneously a defensive victory for the Germans, it was a pyrrhic one. The bloodletting drained Germany of manpower that she could no longer replace, and the offensive that the desperate struggle secured—Hitler's failed gamble in the Ardennes—broke the back of the Wehrmacht in the West.

APPENDIX A

APPENDIX A

DIVISIONAL ORDER OF BATTLE, KEY UNITS

AMERICAN

1st Infantry Division (Big Red One)

    16th Infantry Regiment
    18th Infantry Regiment
    26th Infantry Regiment
    1st Reconnaissance Troop (mechanized)
    1st Engineer Combat Battalion
    1st Medical Battalion
    Divisional artillery (3 x 105mm, 1 x 155mm battalions)
    Special troops (Quartermaster, signal, et cetera)
    Armored attachments: 745th Tank Battalion, 634th Tank Destroyer Battalion

2d Armored Division (Hell on Wheels)

    Headquarters Company
    Service Company
    Combat Command A
    Combat Command B
    41st Armored Infantry Regiment
    66th Armored Regiment
    67th Armored Regiment
    17th Armored Engineer Battalion
    82d Armored Reconnaissance Battalion
    142d Armored Signal Company
    Divisional artillery (3 x armored field artillery battalions)
    Divisional trains (including ordnance, supply, et cetera)
    Armored attachment : 702d Tank Destroyer Battalion

3d Armored Division (Spearhead)

    Headquarters Company
    Service Company
    Combat Command A
    Combat Command B
    36th Armored Infantry Regiment
    32d Armored Regiment
    33d Armored Regiment
    23d Armored Engineer Battalion
    83d Armored Reconnaissance Battalion
    143d Armored Signal Company
    Divisional artillery (3 x armored field artillery battalions)
    Divisional trains (including ordnance, supply, et cetera)
    Armored attachment : 703d Tank Destroyer Battalion

4th Infantry Division (Ivy Leaf)

> 8th Infantry Regiment
> 12th Infantry Regiment
> 22d Infantry Regiment
> 4th Reconnaissance Troop (mechanized)
> 4th Engineer Combat Battalion
> 4th Medical Battalion
> Divisional artillery (3 x 105mm, 1 x 155mm battalions)
> Special troops (Quartermaster, signal, et cetera)
> Armored attachments: 70th Tank Battalion, 803d Tank Destroyer Battalion

9th Infantry Division (Old Reliable)

> 39th Infantry Regiment
> 47th Infantry Regiment
> 60th Infantry Regiment
> 9th Reconnaissance Troop (mechanized)
> 15th Engineer Combat Battalion
> 9th Medical Battalion
> Divisional artillery (3 x 105mm, 1 x 155mm battalions)
> Special troops (Quartermaster, signal, et cetera)
> Armored attachment : 746th Tank Battalion

29th Infantry Division (Blue and Gray)

> 115th Infantry Regiment
> 116th Infantry Regiment
> 175th Infantry Regiment
> 29th Reconnaissance Troop (mechanized)
> 121st Engineer Combat Battalion
> 104th Medical Battalion
> Divisional artillery (3 x 105mm, 1 x 155mm battalions)
> Special troops (Quartermaster, signal, et cetera)
> Armored attachment : 747th Tank Battalion

30th Infantry Division (Old Hickory)

> 117th Infantry Regiment
> 119th Infantry Regiment
> 120th Infantry Regiment
> 30th Reconnaissance Troop (mechanized)
> 105th Engineer Combat Battalion
> 105th Medical Battalion
> Divisional artillery (3 x 105mm, 1 x 155mm battalions)
> Special troops (Quartermaster, signal, et cetera)
> Armored attachment : 743d Tank Battalion, 823d Tank Destroyer Battalion

104th Infantry Division (Timberwolf)

413th Infantry Regiment
414th Infantry Regiment
415th Infantry Regiment
104th Reconnaissance Troop (mechanized)
329th Engineer Combat Battalion
329th Medical Battalion
Divisional artillery (3 x 105mm, 1 x 155mm battalions)
Special troops (Quartermaster, signal, et cetera)
Armored attachments: 750th Tank Battalion, 692d Tank Destroyer Battalion

GERMAN

3d Panzergrenadier Division

103d Panzer Battalion
8th Grenadier/Panzergrenadier Regiment
29th Grenadier/Panzergrenadier Regiment
3d Artillery Regiment (mot) [motorized]
103d Panzeraufklärungs Abteilung (Armored Reconnaissance Battalion)
3d Panzerjäger Abteilung (mot) (Tank Destroyer Battalion)
3d Pionier Abteilung (Engineer Battalion)
3d Nachrichten Abteilung (Signals Battalion)
Divisional support units

9th Panzer Division

33d Panzer Regiment
10th Panzergrenadier Regiment
11th Panzergrenadier Regiment
102d Artillery Regiment
9th Panzeraufklärungs Abteilung (Armored Reconnaissance Battalion)
287th Army Flak Battalion
50th Panzerjäger Abteilung (Tank Destroyer Battalion)
86th Panzerpionier Bataillon (Armored Engineer Battalion)
85th Panzernachrichten Abteilung (Armored Signals Battalion)
Divisional support units

116th Panzer Division (Windhund, or Greyhound)

16th Panzer Regiment
60th Panzergrenadier Regiment
156th Panzergrenadier Regiment
146th Panzer Artillery Regiment
116th Panzeraufklärungs Abteilung (Armored Reconnaissance Battalion)
281st Army Flak Battalion
226th Panzerjäger Abteilung (Tank Destroyer Battalion)
675th Panzerpionier Bataillon (Armored Engineer Battalion)
228th Panzernachrichten Abteilung (Armored Signals Battalion)
Divisional support units

12th Infantry/Volksgrenadier Division (Wild Buffaloes)

    27th Fusilier Regiment
    48th Grenadier Regiment
    89th Grenadier Regiment
    12th Fusilier Battalion
    12th Artillery Regiment
    148th Artillery Regiment
    Divisional support units

47th Volksgrenadier Division

    103d Grenadier Regiment
    104th Grenadier Regiment
    115th Grenadier Regiment
    147th Artillery Regiment
    Divisional support units

49th Infantry Division

    148th Grenadier Regiment
    149th Grenadier Regiment
    150th Grenadier Regiment
    149th Fusilier Battalion
    149th Artillery Regiment
    Divisional support units

89th Infantry Division

    1055th Grenadier Regiment
    1056th Grenadier Regiment
    1063d Grenadier Regiment
    189th Fusilier Battalion
    189th Artillery Regiment
    Divisional support units

183d Volksgrenadier Division

    330th Grenadier Regiment
    343d Grenadier Regiment
    351st Grenadier Regiment
    219th Artillery Regiment
    Divisional support units

246th Volksgrenadier Division

    352d Grenadier Regiment
    404th Grenadier Regiment
    689th Grenadier Regiment
    246th Artillery Regiment
    Divisional support units

275th Infantry Division

>983d Grenadier Regiment
>984th Grenadier Regiment
>985th Grenadier Regiment
>275th Fusilier Battalion
>275th Artillery Regiment
>Divisional support units

340th Volksgrenadier Division

>694th Grenadier Regiment
>695th Grenadier Regiment
>696th Grenadier Regiment
>340th Artillery Regiment
>Divisional support units

344th Infantry Division

>1057th Grenadier Regiment
>1058th Grenadier Regiment
>832d Grenadier Regiment
>344th Artillery Regiment
>Divisional support units

363d Volksgrenadier Division

>957th Grenadier Regiment
>958th Grenadier Regiment
>959th Grenadier Regiment
>363d Fusilier Battalion
>363d Artillery Regiment
>Divisional support units

Sources: American: U.S. Army Center of Military History, www.army.mil/cmh-pg. German: Lexicon der Wehrmacht, www.lexicon-der-wehrmacht.de.

APPENDIX B

TABLE OF EQUIVALENT RANKS

U.S. ARMY	GERMAN ARMY AND AIR FORCE	GERMAN WAFFEN-SS
None	Reichsmarschall	None
General of the Army	Generalfeldmarschall	Reichsführer-SS
General	Generaloberst	Oberstgruppenführer
Lieutenant General	General der	Obergruppenführer
	Infanterie	
	Artillerie	
	Gebirgstruppen	
	Kavallerie	
	Nachrichtentruppen	
	Panzertruppen	
	Pioniere	
	Luftwaffe	
	Flieger	
	Fallschirmtruppen	
	Flakartillerie	
	Luftnachrichtentruppen	
Major General	Generalleutnant	Gruppenführer
Brigadier General	Generalmajor	Brigadeführer
None	None	Oberführer
Colonel	Oberst	Standartenführer
Lieutenant Colonel	Oberstleutnant	Obersturmbannführer
Major	Major	Sturmbannführer
Captain	Hauptmann	Hauptsturmführer
Captain (Cavalry)	Rittmeister	None
First Lieutenant	Oberleutnant	Obersturmführer
Second Lieutenant	Leutnant	Untersturmführer

Source: Hugh M. Cole, *United States Army in World War II, The European Theater of Operations, The Lorraine Campaign.* Washington, DC: Historical Division, Department of the Army, 1950.

GLOSSARY

AAR: After-action report
Ami: German slang for American
AP: Armor piercing
CO: Commanding officer
CP: Command post
Dough/doughboy: American infantryman
ETO: European Theater of Operations
Fallschirmjäger: Paratrooper/parachute
G-1: Personnel staff or officer
G-2: Intelligence staff or officer
G-3: Operations staff or officer
GI: American infantryman
Grenadier: Honorific for the German infantry
HE: High explosive
KIA: Killed in action
Landser: German slang for rifleman
MIA: Missing in action
MLR: Main line of resistance
OP: Observation post
Panzergrenadier: German armored infantry
Panzerjäger: Loosely, tank destroyer, but a *Panzerjäger* company
                might consist mainly of bazookas
RCT: Regimental combat team
S-2: Intelligence staff or officer
S-3: Operations staff or officer
Schwere Panzer Abteilung: Heavy tank battalion
Schwere Panzerjäger Abteilung: Heavy tank destroyer battalion
SHAEF: Supreme Headquarters Allied Expeditionary Force
SP: Self-propelled
Sturmgeschütz: Assault gun
WIA: Wounded in action

NOTES

CHAPTER 1: AN INTERMEDIATE OBJECTIVE

1. First United States Army, Report of Operations, 1 August 1944–22 February 1945, 41. Memorandum: "3rd Armored Division, Penetration of the Siegfried Line, 12–25 September 1944," 2d Information and Historical Service, VII Corps Team, 14 May 1945.

2. *Lage-Bericht*, 12 September 1944, records of the *LXXXI Armee Korps*.

3. *Spearhead in the West* (Frankfurt, Germany: 3d Armored Division, 1945), 95. Hereafter *Spearhead in the West*.

4. First United States Army, Report of Operations, 1 August 1944–22 February 1945, 41.

5. H. R. Knickerbocker, et al., *Danger Forward, The Story of the First Division in World War II* (Washington, DC: Society of the First Division, 1947), 277. Hereafter Knickerbocker, et al.

6. Opns Memo 91, Headquarters VII Corps, 12 September 1944.

7. J. Lawton Collins, *Lightning Joe, An Autobiography* (Baton Rouge, LA: Louisiana State University Press, 1979), 247. Hereafter Collins.

8. Ibid., 267.

9. Ibid., 269. Charles B. MacDonald, *The Siegfried Line Campaign: United States Army in World War II, The European Theater of Operations* (Washington, DC: Office of the Chief of Military History, Department of the Army, 1993), 67–68. Hereafter MacDonald, *The Siegfried Line Campaign*. Charles Whiting, *Bloody Aachen* (New York, NY: Stein and Day, 1976), 33. Hereafter Whiting, *Bloody Aachen*.

10. MacDonald, *The Siegfried Line Campaign*, 67–68.

11. First United States Army, Report of Operations, 1 August 1944–22 February 1945, 45. *Fernspruch*, 116th Panzer Division to *LXXXI Armee Korps*, 9 September 1944.

12. Omar N. Bradley and Clay Blair, *A General's Life* (New York, NY: Simon and Schuster, 1983), 337. Hereafter Bradley and Blair.

13. First United States Army, Report of Operations, 1 August 1944–22 February 1945, 45, 47.

14. MacDonald, *The Siegfried Line Campaign*, 67–68.

15. Collins, passim.

16. Omar N. Bradley, *A Soldier's Story* (New York, NY: The Modern Library, 1999), 154. Hereafter Bradley.

17. Charles Whiting, *Siegfried, The Nazis' Last Stand* (London: Pan Books, 2003), 95. Hereafter Whiting, *Siegfried*.

18. Ibid.

19. Collins, 269.

20. *Generalleutnant* Gerhard Graf von Schwerin, commanding general, 116th Panzer Division. "116th Panzer Division from the Seine to Aachen." ETHINT 18, October–November 1945. National Archives), 37ff. Hereafter von Schwerin. CSDIC/200/MU/15/M36, interrogation report of von Schwerin's personal secretary, Sgt. Maj. Gerhard Lademann, 2 May 1945.

21. *Fernspruch*, 116th Panzer Division to *LXXXI Armee Korps*, 14 September 1944.

22. Willam L. Shirer, *The Rise and Fall of the Third Reich* (New York, NY: Fawcett Crest, 1983), 1411–413.

23. *Generalmajor* Rudolf Christoph Freiherr von Gersdorf, Chief of Staff, Seventh Army, "Seventh Army; Siegfried Line—Defense of the Siegfried Line," ETHINT 53, 24 November 1945, National Archives, 2." Hereafter von Gersdorf, "Seventh Army; Siegfried Line—Defense of the Siegfried Line." CSDIC/200/MU/15/M36, interrogation report of von Schwerin's personal secretary, Sgt. Maj. Gerhard Lademann, 2 May 1945.

24. "Penetration of the Siegfried Line by the 16th Inf. Regt." Combat Interviews, 1st Infantry Division, National Archives.

25. AAR, 26th Infantry Regiment, 1st Infantry Division.

26. Knickerbocker, et al. 277.

NOTES

27. George Forty, *US Army Handbook 1939–1945* (Phoenix Mill, UK: Sutton Publishing Ltd., 1998), 76ff. Hereafter Forty, *US Army Handbook 1939–1945*. Collins, 247.

28. MacDonald, *The Siegfried Line Campaign*, 70.

29. *Fernspruch*, 9th Panzer Division to *LXXXI Armee Korps*, 10 September 1944.

30. "Immediate Report No. 61 (Combat Observations)," Headquarters 12th Army Group, 22 September 1944.

31. *Spearhead in the West*, 95–96. *Fernspruch*, 116th Panzer Division to *LXXXI Armee Korps*, 10 September 1944. Independent *Sturmgeschütz* Units of the Wehrmacht, http://members.tripod.com/~Sturmvogel/stug.html.

32. Combat Interviews, 9th Infantry Division, Lt. Col. Lee W. Chatfield and Capt. John W. ManIndoe, National Archives.

33. MacDonald, *The Siegfried Line Campaign*, 4.

34. Capt. Harry C. Butcher, *My Three Years with Eisenhower* (New York, NY: Simon and Schuster, Inc, 1946), 637–39. Hereafter Butcher.

35. War Diary, Office of the Secretary, General Staff, SHAEF.

36. Dwight D. Eisenhower, *Crusade in Europe* (Garden City, NY: Doubleday and Company, Inc., 1948), 280. Hereafter Dwight Eisenhower. David Eisenhower, *Eisenhower at War 1943–1945* (New York, NY: Random House, 1986), 407. Hereafter David Eisenhower.

37. MacDonald, *The Siegfried Line Campaign*, 6.

38. Bradley, 396–98, 420.

39. SHAEF/17100/18/Ops(A), "Advance to Breach the Siegfried Line, Appreciation," 1 September 1944.

40. Chester Wilmot, *The Struggle for Europe* (Ware, England: Wordsworth Editions Limited, 1997), 468. Hereafter Wilmot. MacDonald, *The Siegfried Line Campaign*, 8.

41. MacDonald, *The Siegfried Line Campaign*, 9.

42. B. H. Liddell Hart, *History of the Second World War* (New York, NY: G. Putnam's Sons, 1970), 560. Hereafter Liddell Hart. *Fernschreiben*, Model to Rundstedt, 8 September 1944, *Heeresgruppe B, Ia, Lagebeurteilungen, Wochenmeldungen*, National Archives.

43. Bradley, 400.

44. Bernard Law Montgomery, *The Memoirs of Field-Marshal the Viscount Montgomery of Alamein, K.G.* (New York, NY: The World Publishing Company, 1958), 242. Hereafter Montgomery.

45. FWD-13765, "Eisenhower to All Army Commanders: Present condition of the enemy and future missions," 4 September 1944.

46. *Northern France*, CMH Pub 72-30 (Washington, DC: U.S. Army Center of Military History, not dated), 25. Hereafter *Northern France*.

47. Liddell Hart, 559. Wilmot, 479.

48. Wilmot, 347.

49. First United States Army, Report of Operations, 1 August 1944–22 February 1945, 51.

50. Dwight Eisenhower, 302. *Major* Percy Ernst Schramm, "OKW War Diary (1 Apr–18 Dec 1944)," MS # B-034, not dated, National Archives, 151. Hereafter Schramm.

51. Liddell Hart, 559.

52. Wilmot, 435ff.

53. Schramm, 159–60.

54. Wilmot, 478–79. MacDonald, *The Siegfried Line Campaign*, 31ff. Thomas E. Griess, ed., *The West Point Military History Series, The Second World War, Europe and the Mediterranean* (Wayne, NJ: Avery Publishing Group Inc., 1984), 355. Hereafter Griess. Heinz Günther Guderian, *From Normandy to the Ruhr, With the 116th Panzer Division in World War II* (Bedford, PA: The Aberjona Press, 2001), 127. Hereafter Guderian.

55. MacDonald, *The Siegfried Line Campaign*, 34–35.

56. Wilmot, 489.

57. Headquarters, 12th Army Group, "Letter of Instructions Number Eight," 10 September 1944.

58. Bradley, 419.

59. FWD-14764, "To Army Commanders: Discussion of plan to push into Germany, and enlarging his current directive," 13 September 1944.
60. Dwight Eisenhower, 307.
61. T 370-31/Plans, SHAEF, 2 September 1944.
62. Liddell Hart, 561.
63. See Wilmot, 531.
64. Dwight Eisenhower, 126, 225–26, 228.
65. Butcher, 636.
66. David Eisenhower, 408.
67. FWD-13765, "Eisenhower to All Army Commanders: Present condition of the enemy and future missions," 4 September 1944.
68. Dwight Eisenhower, 126.
69. Bradley, 435.
70. Montgomery, 243, 268.
71. Ibid., 272–73.
72. MacDonald, The Siegfried Line Campaign, 20.
73. First United States Army, Report of Operations, 1 August 1944–22 February 1945, Annex 5, Appendix I, 63.
74. AAR, 749th Tank Battalion.
75. Combat Interviews, 3d Armored Division, Lt. Col. E. C. Orth, National Archives.
76. MacDonald, The Siegfried Line Campaign, 20, 386.
77. Bradley, 226.
78. MacDonald, The Siegfried Line Campaign, 20–21.
79. First United States Army, Report of Operations, 1 August 1944–22 February 1945, 45–46, 62–63.
80. Wilmot, 471.
81. *Generalmajor* Rudolf Christoph Freiherr von Gersdorf, Chief of Staff, Seventh Army, "Questions for Consideration and Reply," MS # A-892, not dated, National Archives. Hereafter von Gersdorf, "Questions for Consideration and Reply."
82. Von Gersdorf, "Seventh Army; Siegfried Line—Defense of the Siegfried Line," 1.
83. Von Gersdorf, "Questions for Consideration and Reply."
84. Von Gersdorf, "Seventh Army; Siegfried Line—Defense of the Siegfried Line," 1–2.
85. Ibid., 1. Memorandum from *Korpsnachrichtenführer* to *Abteilung Ia, LXXXI Armee Korps*, 20 September 1944.
86. Von Gersdorf, "Seventh Army; Siegfried Line—Defense of the Siegfried Line," 1–2, 5. Von Gersdorf, "Questions for Consideration and Reply." Guderian, 179.
87. MacDonald, *The Siegfried Line Campaign*, 69. *General der Infanterie* Friedrich Köchling, commanding general, LXXXI Corps, "The Battle of the Aachen Sector," MS # A-989 to MS # A-998, series begins 16 December 1945, National Archives. Hereafter Köchling. Von Gersdorf, "Seventh Army; Siegfried Line—Defense of the Siegfried Line," 3. Von Gersdorf, "Questions for Consideration and Reply."
88. *Ia, Wochenmeldungen, LXXXI Armee Korps. Generalleutnant* Hans Schmidt, "*3. Teil. Kämpfe in Nordfrankreich*," MS # B-372, not dated, National Archives. Hereafter Schmidt, "*3. Teil. Kämpfe in Nordfrankreich*." *Generalleutnant* Siegfried Macholz, "*Die Kämpfe der 49. I.D. von der Maas bis an den Westwall Nördlich Aachen und um den Westwall (2.9.–10.10.44)*," MS # B-792, 26 February 1948, National Archives. Hereafter Macholz.
89. Von Gersdorf, "Seventh Army; Siegfried Line—Defense of the Siegfried Line," 3. *General der Infanterie* Erich Straube, "*Einsatz des Generalkommandos LXXIV. Armeekorps (Sept. bis Dez. 1944)*," MS # C-016, not dated, National Archives. Hereafter Straube.
90. Von Gersdorf, "Questions for Consideration and Reply."
91. "Military Geography Study No. 8," Engineer Headquarters, Ninth Army, 25 October 1944.

CHAPTER 2: TRAPPED IN THE SIEGFRIED LINE

1. "Penetration of the Siegfried Line by the 16th Inf. Regt." Combat Interviews, 1st Infantry Division, National Archives.

NOTES

2. First United States Army, Report of Operations, 1 August 1944–22 February 1945, 48–49.

3. "Penetration of the Siegfried Line by the 16th Inf. Regt." Combat Interviews, 1st Infantry Division, National Archives.

4. Collins, 270.

5. *Tagesmeldungen, Ia, H.Gr.B*, National Archives.

6. Memorandum: "3rd Armored Division, Penetration of the Siegfried Line, 12–25 September 1944," 2d Information and Historical Service, VII Corps Team, 14 May 1945.

7. Combat Interviews, 3d Armored Division, Maj. H. M. Mills, CCB, National Archives.

8. First United States Army, Report of Operations, 1 August 1944–22 February 1945, 49. Memorandum: "3rd Armored Division, Penetration of the Siegfried Line, 12–25 September 1944," 2d Information and Historical Service, VII Corps Team, 14 May 1945.

9. First United States Army, Report of Operations, 1 August 1944–22 February 1945, 49.

10. *Handbook on German Military Forces* (Baton Rouge: Louisiana State University Press, 1990), 66. Hereafter *Handbook on German Military Forces*.

11. Von Schwerin, 43ff. Guderian, 135.

12. Ibid.

13. Capt. Joseph B. Mittelman, *Eight Stars to Victory, A History of the Veteran Ninth U.S. Infantry Division* (Washington, DC: The Ninth Infantry Division Association, 1948), 240. Hereafter Mittelman.

14. Ibid., 242–45.

15. Combat Interviews, 9th Infantry Division, Lt. Col. Lee W. Chatfield and Capt. John W. ManIndoe, National Archives. *Oberst* Hasso Neitzel, "89th Infantry Division (13 Sep–1 Oct 1944)," MS # B-793, not dated, National Archives, 9–10. Hereafter Neitzel.

16. Mittelman, 244.

17. *Generalleutnant* Paul Mahlmann, "353d Infantry Division (9–18 Sep 1944)," MS # B-232, not dated, National Archives, 2. Hereafter Mahlmann. Straube. MacDonald, *The Siegfried Line Campaign*, 87.

18. First United States Army, Report of Operations, 1 August 1944–22 February 1945, 53.

19. *Generalmajor* Rudolf Christoph Freiherr von Gersdorf, Chief of Staff, Seventh Army. "The Battle of the Hürtgen Forest, Nov–Early Dec 1944," MS # A-891, 12 December 1945, National Archives, 9. Hereafter von Gersdorf, "The Battle of the Hürtgen Forest, Nov–Early Dec 1944."

20. Neitzel, *passim*.

21. "Immediate Report No. 70 (Combat Observations)," Headquarters 12th Army Group, 29. September 1944.

22. Combat Interviews, 9th Infantry Division, Maj. Thomas A. E. Mosely Jr., National Archives

23. Opns Memo 93, Headquarters VII Corps, 16 September 1944.

24. First United States Army, Report of Operations, 1 August 1944–22 February 1945, 45–46, 62–63.

25. Collins, 270.

26. First United States Army, Report of Operations, 1 August 1944–22 February 1945, 50.

27. Von Gersdorf, "Seventh Army; Siegfried Line—Defense of the Siegfried Line," 3.

28. Feldgrau, www.feldgrau.com. *Organisatorische Gesamtübersicht über Zusammenlegung, Aufteilung, Auflöung, Bildung von Div. Verbänden und Bildung von Korpsabteilungen im Jahre 1944,* OKW/2201, 7-77, Roll 786, Frames 5514261–5514262, National Archives. T78-352, "*Anlage zu OKH/Chef H. Rüst. U. BdE/AHA (Ic),*" files of Wehrkreis II, Bundesarchiv. Guderian, 222. Tommy Maurice Löwenzahn-Nilsson, letter to author, August 2003.

29. *Fernschreiben*, Model to Rundstedt, 8 September 1944, *Heeresgruppe B, Ia, Lagebeurteilungen, Wochenmeldungen*, National Archives. *Op.-Befehle, Band 3*, Army Group B, National Archives.

30. *Generalmajor* Gerhard Engel, "The First Battle Near Aachen, 16 September to 22 September 1944," MS # A-971, 27 March 1946, National Archives. Hereafter Engel, "The First Battle Near Aachen, 16 September to 22 September 1944." Lexicon der Wehrmacht, www.lexiconderwehrmacht.de. *Handbook on German Military Forces*, 161. Whiting, *Siegfried*, 33–34.

31. Engel, "The First Battle Near Aachen, 16 September to 22 September 1944."

32. "Penetration of the Siegfried Line by the 16th Inf. Regt." Combat Interviews, 1st Infantry Division, National Archives.

33. Engel, "The First Battle Near Aachen, 16 September to 22 September 1944."
34. Memorandum: "3rd Armored Division, Penetration of the Siegfried Line, 12–25 September 1944," 2d Information and Historical Service, VII Corps Team, 14 May 1945.
35. Engel, "The First Battle Near Aachen, 16 September to 22 September 1944." MacDonald, *The Siegfried Line Campaign*, 87.
36. First United States Army, Report of Operations, 1 August 1944–22 February 1945, 49.
37. Combat Interviews, 3d Armored Division, Lt. Col. William R. Orr, National Archives.
38. Combat Interviews, 3d Armored Division, Maj. H. M. Mills, National Archives.
39. "3rd Armored Division, Penetration of the Siegfried Line, 12–25 September 1944."
40. Engel, "The First Battle Near Aachen, 16 September to 22 September 1944."
41. Combat Interviews, 3d Armored Division, Maj. O. H. Carter, CO 2d Battalion, 47th Infantry Regiment, National Archives.
42. Engel, "The First Battle Near Aachen, 16 September to 22 September 1944."
43. Ibid.
44. "Immediate Report No. 61 (Combat Observations)," Headquarters 12th Army Group, 22 September 1944.
45. "Penetration of the Siegfried Line by the 16th Inf. Regt." Combat Interviews, 1st Infantry Division, National Archives.
46. Ibid.
47. First United States Army, Report of Operations, 1 August 1944–22 February 1945, 49.
48. Engel, "The First Battle Near Aachen, 16 September to 22 September 1944."
49. First United States Army, Report of Operations, 1 August 1944–22 February 1945, 49.
50. Engel, "The First Battle Near Aachen, 16 September to 22 September 1944."
51. Collins, 271.
52. Engel, "The First Battle Near Aachen, 16 September to 22 September 1944."
53. Alex Buchner, *Das Handbuch der Deutschen Infanterie, 1939–1945* (Wölfersheim-Berstadt: Podzun-Pallas-Verlag GMBH, not dated), 36ff. Hereafter Buchner.
54. Hans Martens, "Deployment of III./RJG Platoon of 13/09 Between 09/17 and 09/20/44," My War, www.faem.com/mywar. Hereafter Martens.
55. Köchling.
56. Combat Interviews, 3d Armored Division, Maj. Samuel Adams, S-2, CCA, National Archives.
57. Combat Interviews, 3d Armored Division, Lt. Col. E. F. Driscoll, CO, 1st Battalion, 16th Infantry Regiment, 1st Infantry Division, National Archives.
58. *Gefechtsbericht Stolberg*, 9th Panzer Division, records of *LXXXI Armee Korps*.
59. Combat Interviews, 3d Armored Division, Lt. Elton K. McDonald and Lt. Col. E. F. Driscoll, National Archives.
60. Combat Interviews, 3d Armored Division, Lt. Elton K. McDonald, National Archives.
61. Combat Interviews, 3d Armored Division, Maj. H. M. Mills, National Archives.
62. *Spearhead in the West*, 99.
63. *Gefechtsbericht Stolberg, Anlage 1*, 9th Panzer Division, records of *LXXXI Armee Korps*.
64. Engel, "The First Battle Near Aachen, 16 September to 22 September 1944."
65. *Gefechtsbericht Stolberg, Anlagen 1 und 2*, 9th Panzer Division, records of *LXXXI Armee Korps*.
66. *Fernschreiben*, Model to Rundstedt, 27 September 1944, *Heeresgruppe B, Ia, Lagebeurteilungen, Wochenmeldungen*, National Archives.
67. *Kriegstagebuch*, Supreme Command West, cited by Guderian, 180.
68. "3rd Armored Division, Penetration of the Siegfried Line, 12–25 September 1944."
69. First United States Army, Report of Operations, 1 August 1944–22 February 1945, 50.
70. Ibid., 49.
71. Straube.
72. Mittelman, 250–51.
73. Engel, "The First Battle Near Aachen, 16 September to 22 September 1944." "Penetration of the Siegfried Line by the 47th Inf. Regt." Combat Interviews, 9th Infantry Division, National Archives.

74. MacDonald, *The Siegfried Line Campaign*, 324. Collins, 269. *Rhineland*, CMH Pub 72-25 (Washington, DC: U.S. Army Center of Military History, not dated), 17. Hereafter *Rhineland*. Gerald Astor, *The Bloody Forest, Battle for the Huertgen, September 1944–January 1945* (Novato, CA: Presidio Press, Inc., 2000), 37. Hereafter Astor.

75. Collins, 271.

76. Von Gersdorf, "The Battle of the Hürtgen Forest, Nov–Early Dec 1944," 9.

77. Collins, 273.

78. First United States Army, Report of Operations, 1 August 1944–22 February 1945, 47.

79. Schmidt, "*3. Teil. Kämpfe in Nordfrankreich.*"

80. First United States Army, Report of Operations, 1 August 1944–22 February 1945, 47.

81. *Generalleutnant* Hans Schmidt, "*4. Teil. Kämpfe im Rheinland der 275. Infanterie-Division*," MS # B-373, 17 February 1947, National Archives. Hereafter Schmidt, "*4. Teil. Kämpfe im Rheinland der 275. Infanterie-Division.*"

82. First United States Army, Report of Operations, 1 August 1944–22 February 1945, 47. Houston, 279. Guderian, 222.

83. *Generalleutnant* Wolfgang Lange, "183d Volksgrenadier Division (Sep 1944–25 Jan 1945)," MS # B-753, not dated, National Archives, 1–2. Hereafter Lange. Schmidt, "*4. Teil. Kämpfe im Rheinland der 275. Infanterie-Division.*" *Kampf um Aachen, Ia KTB, LXXXI Armee Korps.* Hubert Gees, "Memories of Hubert Gees," My War, www.faem.com/mywar. Hereafter Gees.

84. First United States Army, Report of Operations, 1 August 1944–22 February 1945, 47. Houston, 280–81.

85. Ibid., 47.

86. Ibid.

87. Bradley, 422. Wilmot, 483.

88. Wilmot, 533–34. Bradley, 419, 422.

89. Letter from Bradley to Hodges, 23 September 1944.

90. "Defense of the West Wall." Schramm, 189.

91. First United States Army, Report of Operations, 1 August 1944–22 February 1945, 57.

92. Schramm, 192–93.

93. Charles B. MacDonald, *The Battle of the Bulge* (London: Guild Publishing, 1984), 62. Hereafter MacDonald, *The Battle of the Bulge.*

94. First United States Army, Report of Operations, 1 August 1944–22 February 1945, 55.

CHAPTER 3: AACHEN AND BEYOND

1 Griess, 362.

2. Köchling.

3. Collins, 271.

4. First United States Army, Report of Operations, 1 August 1944–22 February 1945, 54.

5. AAR, 2d Armored Division. Harmon, 206–7. Houston, 285.

6. Opns Memo 101, Headquarters VII Corps, 1 October 1944.

7. Opns Memo 102, Headquarters VII Corps, 5 October 1944.

8. *Generalmajor* Gerhard Engel, "12th Infantry Division, 22 Sep–22 Oct 1944," MS # B-415, 12 April 1947, National Archives. Hereafter Engel, "12th Infantry Division, 22 Sep–22 Oct 1944." *Ia, Zustandsberichte, 10.10.–17.12.1944, LXXXI Armee Korps.*

9. Lange, 1–2. *Kampf um Aachen, Ia KTB, LXXXI Armee Korps. Ia, Zustandsberichte, 10.10.–17.12.1944, LXXXI Armee Korps.*

10. *Kampf um Aachen, Ia KTB, LXXXI Armee Korps.*

11. First United States Army, Report of Operations, 1 August 1944–22 February 1945, 57. Engel, "12th Infantry Division, 22 Sep–22 Oct 1944."

12. *Ia, Wochenmeldungen, LXXXI Armee Korps. Ia, Zustandsberichte, 10.10.–17.12.1944, LXXXI Armee Korps.* Macholz.

13. "Casualty Information," memorandum dated 1 November 1944, Office of the Registrar, 41st Evacuation Hospital, contained in the miscellaneous records of the Adjutant General's Office, Box 24130, National Archives.

14. Engel, "12th Infantry Division, 22 Sep–22 Oct 1944." *Ia, Zustandsberichte, 10.10.–17.12.1944, LXXXI Armee Korps.*
15. Griess, 361.
16. First United States Army, Report of Operations, 1 August 1944–22 February 1945, 52–53.
17. Ibid., 55.
18. Lt. Col. H. E. Hassenfelt, Division G-3, Combat Interviews, 30th Infantry Division, National Archives. Engel, "12th Infantry Division, 22 Sep–22 Oct 1944." Köchling. Lange, 6.
19. Maj. Gen. Leland S. Hobbs, commanding general, 30th Infantry Division, Combat Interviews, 30th Infantry Division, National Archives. Lt. Col. Robert E. Frankland, Combat Interviews, 30th Infantry Division, National Archives.
20. Lt. Col. Robert E. Frankland, Combat Interviews, 30th Infantry Division, National Archives. Narrative of Operations, 117th Infantry Regiment. Robert L. Hewitt, *Workhorse of the Western Front, the Story of the 30th Infantry Division* (Washington, DC: Infantry Journal Press, 1946), 110. Hereafter Hewitt. Maps and overlays, *Kampf um Aachen, Ia KTB, LXXXI Armee Korps.*
21. Letter dated 2 October 1944, Pfc. Richard Lowe Ballou, Combat Interviews, 30th Infantry Division, National Archives.
22. Narrative of Operations, 117th Infantry Regiment.
23. *Kampf um Aachen, Ia KTB, LXXXI Armee Korps.* Lt. Col. Robert E. Frankland, Combat Interviews, 30th Infantry Division, National Archives. Hewitt, 115.
24. Lange, 6–7. Macholz. *Kampf um Aachen, Ia KTB, LXXXI Armee Korps.* "Breaching the Siegfried Line," XIX Corps, 12 January 1945.
25. First United States Army, Report of Operations, 1 August 1944–22 February 1945, 58. Capt. Wayne Culp and Lt. Orrin Cooley, Combat Interviews, 30th Infantry Division, National Archives. Hewitt, 120. Macholz.
26. First United States Army, Report of Operations, 1 August 1944–22 February 1945, 58. Donald E. Houston, *Hell on Wheels, The 2d Armored Division* (Novato, CA: Presidio Press, 1977), 287. Hereafter Houston.
27. Interview with officers of 1st Battalion, 41st Armored Infantry Regiment, CCB, 2d Armored Division, contained in Combat Interviews, 30th Infantry Division, National Archives. "Operation of Combat Command 'B,' 3 October–8 October, 1944, Part II," 2d Armored Division Report of Operations. Hewitt, 120.
28. Interview with officers of 1st Battalion, 41st Armored Infantry Regiment, CCB, 2d Armored Division, contained in Combat Interviews, 30th Infantry Division, National Archives. AAR, 2d Armored Division. MacDonald, *The Siegfried Line Campaign*, 263ff.
29. Köchling. Status reports, *LXXXI Armee Korps. Kampf um Aachen, Ia KTB, LXXXI Armee Korps. Op.-Befehle, Band 3*, Army Group B, National Archives.
30. *Kampf um Aachen, Ia KTB, LXXXI Armee Korps.*
31. First United States Army, Report of Operations, 1 August 1944–22 February 1945, 58. AAR, 2d Armored Division. Houston, 290–91.
32. First United States Army, Report of Operations, 1 August 1944–22 February 1945, 58ff. Lt. Col. Robert E. Frankland, Combat Interviews, 30th Infantry Division, National Archives. Interview with officers of Company L, 3d Battalion, 117th Infantry Regiment, Combat Interviews, 30th Infantry Division, National Archives. Lt. Col. William D. Duncan, CO, 743d Tank Battalion, Combat Interviews, 30th Infantry Division, National Archives. Hewitt, 122.
33. Houston, 291–92.
34. Ibid., 293.
35. Interview with officers of Company L, 3d Battalion, 117th Infantry Regiment, Combat Interviews, 30th Infantry Division, National Archives. G-3 Report of Operations, 1st Infantry Division. Hewitt, 122–23. Houston, 291. *Kampf um Aachen, Ia KTB, LXXXI Armee Korps.*
36. Hewitt, 124. Lt. Col. Robert E. Frankland, Combat Interviews, 30th Infantry Division, National Archives. Interview with officers of Company L, 3d Battalion, 117th Infantry Regiment, Combat Interviews, 30th Infantry Division, National Archives. Narrative of Operations, 117th Infantry Regiment. Macholz.

NOTES

37. First United States Army, Report of Operations, 1 August 1944–22 February 1945, 58ff. *Kampf um Aachen, Ia KTB, LXXXI Armee Korps.* Macholz. Schneider, entry for 7 October 1944.
38. Engel, "12th Infantry Division, 22 Sep–22 Oct 1944."
39. Engel, "12th Infantry Division, 22 Sep–22 Oct 1944." *Divisions-Befehl für dan Angriff zur Wiedergewinnung des Nordrandes Alsdorf,* 49th Infantry Division, 8 October 1944, records of *LXXXI Armee Korps. Kampf um Aachen, Ia KTB, LXXXI Armee Korps. Bericht über den Einsatz des II./Gren. Rgt. 351 (183. Volksgren. Div.) in der Zeit vom 7.–9. Okt. 1944 im Abschnitt der Division,* 9 October 1944, 49th Infantry Division, records of *LXXXI Armee Korps. Gefechtsbericht über den Einsatz der 2./(Stu.Gesch.) Pz.Jg.Abt. 12 im Verband der 49. Gren.Div. am 7. und 8.10.1944, 9 October 1944, Panzerjäger-Abteilung 12,* records of *LXXXI Armee Korps.* Lt. Col. Robert E. Frankland, Combat Interviews, 30th Infantry Division, National Archives. Lt. Col. S. T. McDowell, Combat Interviews, 30th Infantry Division, National Archives. Interview with officers and NCOs of Company I, 3d Battalion, 117th Infantry Regiment, Combat Interviews, 30th Infantry Division, National Archives. Lt. Col. William D. Duncan, CO, 743d Tank Battalion, Combat Interviews, 30th Infantry Division, National Archives. Capt. Robert Sinclair, 803d Tank Destroyer Battalion, Combat Interviews, 30th Infantry Division, National Archives. Hewitt, 128. Tommy Maurice Löwenzahn-Nilsson, letter to author, August 2003.
40. Collins, 272.
41. G-3 Report of Operations, 1st Infantry Division.
42. Engel, "12th Infantry Division, 22 Sep–22 Oct 1944."
43. "Battle of Aachen—18th Infantry Regiment," Combat Interviews, 1st Infantry Division, National Archives.
44. G-3 Report of Operations, 1st Infantry Division.
45. *Kampf um Aachen, Ia KTB, LXXXI Armee Korps.*
46. Memorandum from Bradley to Hodges, 8 October 1944.
47. Hewitt, 129. Macholz.
48. *Kampf um Aachen, Ia KTB, LXXXI Armee Korps.* Capt. Ross Y. Simmons, Combat Interviews, 30th Infantry Division, National Archives. Maj. Laney and Capt. Hardaway, Combat Interviews, 30th Infantry Division, National Archives. Journal, 119th Infantry Regiment. Hewitt, 130–31. Guderian, 210.
49. "Battle of Aachen—18th Infantry Regiment," Combat Interviews, 1st Infantry Division, National Archives. G-3 Report of Operations, 1st Infantry Division.
50. G-3 Report of Operations, 1st Infantry Division.
51. Maj. Gen. Leland S. Hobbs, commanding general, 30th Infantry Division, Combat Interviews, 30th Infantry Division, National Archives. Brig. Gen. W. H. Harrison, Combat Interviews, 30th Infantry Division, National Archives.
52. First United States Army, Report of Operations, 1 August 1944–22 February 1945. Guderian, 209. *Generalmajor* Fritz Krämer, "*Das I. SS-Pz. Korps im Westen 1944 [9.9.1944–20.10.1944],*" MS # C-048, not dated, National Archives. Hereafter Krämer, 12.
53. History, AAR, summaries of medal citations, 823d Tank Destroyer Battalion.
54. *Kampf um Aachen, Ia KTB, LXXXI Armee Korps. Tagesmeldungen, Ia, H.Gr.B,* National Archives. Guderian, 211.
55. "Battle of Aachen—18th Infantry Regiment," Combat Interviews, 1st Infantry Division, National Archives.
56. AAR, 26th Infantry Regiment, 1st Infantry Division. Drew Middleton, "Offer Handed Foe," *New York Times,* 11 October 1944, 1,3.
57. G-3 Report of Operations, 1st Infantry Division.
58. G-2 periodic report, First U.S. Army, 12 October 1944.
59. First United States Army, Report of Operations, 1 August 1944–22 February 1945. *Gefechtsbericht des I.SS-Btl. (Kampfgruppe Rink) für die Zeit vom 9.–22.10.44, Ia KTB, LXXXI Armee Korps,* National Archives. Guderian, 211–12. Whiting, *Bloody Aachen,* 115.
60. History, AAR, summaries of medal citations, 823d Tank Destroyer Battalion.
61. Hewitt, 134.
62. History, AAR, summaries of medal citations, 823d Tank Destroyer Battalion. Hewitt, 134–35.

63. Hewitt, 135.

64. Ibid., 136–37.

65. Whiting, *Bloody Aachen*, 118. Hewitt, 137.

66. Hewitt, 137.

67. Engel, "12th Infantry Division, 22 Sep–22 Oct 1944." Drew Middleton, "Counter-Attack Fails," *New York Times*, 13 October 1944, 1,4.

68. First United States Army, Report of Operations, 1 August 1944–22 February 1945.

69. AAR, 26th Infantry Regiment, 1st Infantry Division.

70. *Rhineland*, 15.

71. First United States Army, Report of Operations, 1 August 1944–22 February 1945, 59.

72. G-3 Report of Operations, 1st Infantry Division. AAR, 26th Infantry Regiment, 1st Infantry Division.

73. Joseph Balkoski, *Beyond the Beachhead, The 29th Infantry Division in Normandy* (Mechanicsburg, PA: Stackpole Books, 1999), 24–25. Hereafter Balkoski.

74. Hewitt, 137–38. First United States Army, Report of Operations, 1 August 1944–22 February 1945, 59. Houston, 297. Guderian, 214.

75. Hewitt, 138.

76. Guderian, 218.

77. "Battle of Aachen—18th Infantry Regiment," Combat Interviews, 1st Infantry Division, National Archives.

78. G-3 Report of Operations, 1st Infantry Division.

79. Engel, "12th Infantry Division, 22 Sep–22 Oct 1944."

80. G-3 Report of Operations, 1st Infantry Division.

81. *Generalmajor* Walter Denkert, "The 3d Panzer Grenadier Division in the Battle for Aachen," MS # A-979, 10 July 1950, National Archives. Hereafter Denkert, "The 3d Panzer Grenadier Division in the Battle for Aachen." *Handbook on German Military Forces*, 86–87.

82. *Op.-Befehle, Band 3*, Army Group B, National Archives.

83. Hewitt, 139.

84. Guderian, 218. *Op.-Befehle, Band 3*, Army Group B, National Archives.

85. Dr. F. M. Von Senger und Etterlin, *German Tanks of World War II* (New York, NY: Galahad Books, 1969), 203. Hereafter Von Senger und Etterlin.

86. G-3 Report of Operations, 1st Infantry Division.

87. G-3 Report of Operations, 1st Infantry Division. Engel, "12th Infantry Division, 22 Sep–22 Oct 1944." Denkert, "The 3d Panzer Grenadier Division in the Battle for Aachen." *Erfahrungsberichte, 23.10–30.12.44, LXXXI Armee Korps.*

88. Tommy Maurice Löwenzahn-Nilsson, letter to author, August 2003.

89. G-3 Report of Operations, 1st Infantry Division. Macdonald, *The Siegfried Line Campaign*, 291–92. Denkert, "The 3d Panzer Grenadier Division in the Battle for Aachen." Engel, "12th Infantry Division, 22 Sep–22 Oct 1944."

90. Hewitt, 139–41. G-3 Report of Operations, 1st Infantry Division.

91. Engel, "12th Infantry Division, 22 Sep–22 Oct 1944." First United States Army, Report of Operations, 1 August 1944–22 February 1945, 59. *Infanteristische Kamfstärken*, 3d Panzergrenadier Division, records of *LXXXI Armee Korps*.

92. "Breaching the Siegfried Line," XIX Corps, 12 January 1945.

93. "The Fall of Aachen," Combat Interviews, 1st Infantry Division, National Archives.

94. Köchling. Whiting, *Bloody Aachen*, 119–20.

95. Köchling. "The Fall of Aachen," Combat Interviews, 1st Infantry Division, National Archives. Undated memo reporting losses and battle strength of the 12th Infantry and 246th Volksgrenadier divisions, records of *LXXXI Armee Korps*.

96. "Clearing Area South of the Rail Road Tracks," Combat Interviews, 1st Infantry Division, National Archives.

97. Clifton Daniel, "City is 85% Ruined," *New York Times*, 13 October 1944, 1.

98. Drew Middleton, "First Storms City," *New York Times*, 14 October 1944, 1, 3.

99. "Clearing Area South of the Rail Road Tracks," Combat Interviews, 1st Infantry Division, National Archives.

100. Ibid. MacDonald, *The Siegfried Line Campaign*, 310.
101. "Clearing Area South of the Rail Road Tracks," Combat Interviews, 1st Infantry Division, National Archives.
102. Desmond Hawkins, ed., *War Report, D-day to VE-day* (London: British Broadcasting Corporation, 1985), 212–13. Hereafter Hawkins.
103. Drew Middleton, "Germans Prolong Agony of Aachen," *New York Times*, 19 October 1944, 1, 5.
104. Hawkins, 215–16.
105. "Aachen Fighting Fantastic," *New York Times*, 16 October 1944, 5.
106. "Clearing Area South of the Rail Road Tracks," Combat Interviews, 1st Infantry Division, National Archives. AAR, 26th Infantry Regiment, 1st Infantry Division. Whiting, *Bloody Aachen*, 149–53. MacDonald, *The Siegfried Line Campaign*, 313.
107. "Clearing Area South of the Rail Road Tracks," Combat Interviews, 1st Infantry Division, National Archives. AAR, 26th Infantry Regiment, 1st Infantry Division. AAR, 634th Tank Destroyer Battalion.
108. *Fernspruch von Kampfkommandant Aachen*, 15 October 1944, records of *LXXXI Armee Korps*.
109. *Kampf um Aachen, Ia KTB, LXXXI Armee Korps*.
110. *Gefechtsbericht des I.SS-Btl. (Kampfgruppe Rink) für die Zeit vom 9.–22.10.44, Ia KTB, LXXXI Armee Korps*, National Archives.
111. Denkert, "The 3d Panzer Grenadier Division in the Battle for Aachen."
112. Untitled memorandum, Headquarters, 3d Battalion, 18th Infantry Regiment, 1st Infantry Division, 24 October 1944.
113. Denkert, "The 3d Panzer Grenadier Division in the Battle for Aachen." Untitled memorandum, Headquarters, 3d Battalion, 18th Infantry Regiment, 1st Infantry Division, 24 October 1944.
114. Bradley and Blair, 340.
115. First United States Army, Report of Operations, 1 August 1944–22 February 1945, 60.
116. Bradley and Blair, 337.
117. Maj. Gen. E. N. Harmon with Milton MacKaye and William Ross MacKaye, *Combat Commander, Autobiography of a Soldier* (Englewood Cliffs, NJ: Prentice-Hall, Inc., 1970), 216. Hereafter Harmon.
118. Krämer, 14.
119. G-3 Report of Operations, 1st Infantry Division.
120. "Clearing Area South of the Rail Road Tracks," Combat Interviews, 1st Infantry Division, National Archives. *Gefechtsbericht des I.SS-Btl. (Kampfgruppe Rink) für die Zeit vom 9.–22.10.44, Ia KTB, LXXXI Armee Korps*, National Archives. *Rhineland*. 15.
121. *Kriegstagebuch, Kampfverlauf, 22.10–31.12.44, LXXXI Armee Korps. Befehle Gen. Kdo. An Div. vom 1.–31.12.44, LXXXI Armee Korps*.
122. "Clearing Area South of the Rail Road Tracks," Combat Interviews, 1st Infantry Division, National Archives. AAR, 26th Infantry Regiment, 1st Infantry Division. Knickerbocker, et al., 277. P. F. Gorman, "Aachen 1944, Implications for Command Post of the Future," Institute for Defense Analyses, not dated but probably 2000, 1. Hereafter Gorman.
123. Hewitt, 141.
124. Engel, "12th Infantry Division, 22 Sep–22 Oct 1944." Guderian, 227.
125. G-3 Report of Operations, 1st Infantry Division.
126. SHAEF/17100/18/Ops(A), "Decisions reached at Supreme Commander's Conference on 18 October 1944," 22 October 1944.
127. AAR, Ninth Army. *Conquer, The Story of the Ninth Army* (Washington, DC: Infantry Journal Press, 1947), 55, 65. Hereafter *Conquer*.
128. Bradley, 436–37.
129. Bradley and Blair, 340. Bradley, 422.
130. Harmon, 212.
131. AAR, Ninth Army.
132. Ibid.
133. Ibid.
134. 475 GNMDC, 15 November 1944.

135. *General der Panzertruppen* Hasso-Eccard Von Manteuffel, commanding general, Fifth Panzer Army, "Statement by General von Manteuffel," MS # A-857, not dated, National Archives. Hereafter von Manteuffel.

136. Von Gersdorf, "The Battle of the Hürtgen Forest, Nov–Early Dec 1944," 1ff. Von Manteuffel.

137. Von Gersdorf, "The Battle of the Hürtgen Forest, Nov–Early Dec 1944," 1ff.

138. *Stärkemeldungen vom 20.10.44, LXXXI Armee Korps. Ia, Wochenmeldungen, LXXXI Armee Korps.*

CHAPTER 4: THE NOVEMBER OFFENSIVE BEGINS

1 MacDonald, *The Siegfried Line Campaign*, 390–92.

2. AAR, Ninth Army.

3. Bradley, 439.

4. Ninth United States Army, Operations, IV, *Offensive in November*, February 1945, 1–3.

5. MacDonald, *The Siegfried Line Campaign*, 406.

6. *Conquer*, 85.

7. Bradley, 439.

8. MacDonald, *The Siegfried Line Campaign*, 409.

9. First United States Army, Report of Operations, 1 August 1944–22 February 1945, 65.

10. Collins, 274–75. William H. Stoneman, "104th Division a Winner for Maj Gen Allen, Too," *Chicago Daily News*, copy in history of 415th Infantry Regiment, not dated.

11. First United States Army, Report of Operations, 1 August 1944–22 February 1945, 71.

12. Ibid., 72.

13. Ibid.

14. Ibid., 72–73.

15. AAR, Ninth Army.

16. Ibid.

17. Ibid. *Conquer*, 74–75.

18. Ninth United States Army, Operations, IV, *Offensive in November*, February 1945, 1–3.

19. Lt. Gen. Sir Brian Horrocks, *A Full Life* (London: Collins, 1960), 233. Hereafter Horrocks.

20. Ninth United States Army, Operations, IV, *Offensive in November*, February 1945, 11.

21. Ibid., 5.

22. Ibid., 2.

23. AAR, Ninth Army.

24. Ninth United States Army, Operations, IV, *Offensive in November*, February 1945, 2.

25. 475 GNMDC, 15 November 1944.

26. Von Manteuffel. Köchling.

27. *Generalmajor* Carl Wagener, Chief of Staff, Fifth Panzer Army, "The Action of the Fifth Panzer Army During the American November Offensive," MS # A-863, 12 December 1945, National Archives. Hereafter Wagener.

28. Köchling. *Tagesmeldungen, LXXXI Armee Korps. Ia, Zustandsberichte, 10.10.–17.12.1944, LXXXI Armee Korps.*

29. *Tagesmeldungen, LXXXI Armee Korps.*

30. *Kriegstagebuch, Kampfverlauf, 22.10–31.12.44, LXXXI Armee Korps. Tagesmeldungen, LXXXI Armee Korps.* Karl Schacht, "The Diary of Karl Schacht," My War, www.faem.com/mywar. Hereafter Schacht. *Historishes Kalendarium—April,* www.gubenergeschichte.de/german/index.html. *Ia, Zustandsberichte, 10.10.–17.12.1944, LXXXI Armee Korps.* Tommy Maurice Löwenzahn-Nilsson, letter to author, August 2003.

31. Köchling. *Ia, Wochenmeldungen, LXXXI Armee Korps. Tagesmeldungen, LXXXI Armee Korps. Ia, Zustandsberichte, 10.10.–17.12.1944, LXXXI Armee Korps.*

32. *Generalleutnant* Max Bork, "47th Volks Grenadier Division at the Western Front," My War, www.faem.com/mywar. Hereafter Bork.

33. Headquarters 1st U.S. Infantry Division, Intelligence Activities (1 Nov 1944 to 30 Nov 1944), 1 December 1944.

34. *Kriegstagebuch, Kampfverlauf, 22.10–31.12.44, LXXXI Armee Korps. Tagesmeldungen, LXXXI Armee Korps.*

35. Schacht.

36. Bork.

37. *Conquer*, 84. MacDonald, *The Siegfried Line Campaign*, Map VII. *Kriegstagebuch, Kampfverlauf, 22.10–31.12.44, LXXXI Armee Korps. General der Panzertruppen* Heinrich Von Lüttwitz, "The 47. Pz Corps in the Rhineland from 23 Oct–5 Dec 1944," MS # B-367, 11 January 1947, National Archives, 1. Hereafter Von Lüttwitz.

38. *Generalleutnant* Hans Schmidt, "275th Infantry Division (3 Oct–21 Nov 1944)," MS # B-810, 15 December 1947, National Archives, passim. Hereafter Schmidt, "275th Infantry Division (3 Oct–21 Nov 1944)."

39. Von Gersdorf, "The Battle of the Hürtgen Forest, Nov–Early Dec 1944," 1ff. Schmidt, "275th Infantry Division (3 Oct–21 Nov 1944)," appendix 6.

40. G-3 Report of Operations, 1st Infantry Division.

41. Bradley, 440.

42. Ibid.

43. Leo A. Hoegh and Howard J. Doyle, *Timberwolf Tracks, The History of the 104th Infantry Division, 1942–1945* (Washington, DC: Infantry Journal Press, 1946), 115. Hereafter Hoegh and Doyle.

44. Guderian, 271.

45. Albert Trostorf, "Zusammenfassung der Kriegsereignisse im Raum Merode," Merode 2000, www.merode.com/. Hereafter Trostorf.

46. "Operations 'Q,'" Headquarters, Ninth Army, 23 January 1945. *Conquer*, 81ff. First United States Army, Report of Operations, 1 August 1944–22 February 1945, 73.

47. Schacht.

48. *Kriegstagebuch, Kampfverlauf, 22.10–31.12.44, LXXXI Armee Korps.* Köchling.

49. G-3 Report of Operations, 1st Infantry Division. MacDonald, *The Siegfried Line Campaign*, 413.

50. First United States Army, Report of Operations, 1 August 1944–22 February 1945, 74.

51. Schacht.

52. Ibid.

53. Hoegh and Doyle, 115, 121.

54. *Southern France*, CMH Pub 72-31 (Washington, DC: U.S. Army Center of Military History, not dated), 7. Hereafter *Southern France*.

55. Stan Zimmerman, letter to author, April 2003.

56. First United States Army, Report of Operations, 1 August 1944–22 February 1945, 72–73.

57. *Spearhead in the West*, 103.

58. George Forty, *Tank Warfare in the Second World War, An Oral History* (London: Constable and Company Ltd., 1998), 169–70. Hereafter Forty, *Tank Warfare in the Second World War, An Oral History*.

59. AAR, 3d Armored Division. Cooper, 148. Forty, *Tank Warfare in the Second World War, An Oral History*, 166ff. MacDonald, *The Siegfried Line Campaign*, 422ff. *Hauptmann* a.D. Hans Zeplien, "Reorganization of GrenReg 89 after arrival of reserves, and creation of a new main line of resistance," My War, www.faem.com/mywar. Hereafter Zeplien.

60. Combat Interviews, 1st Infantry Division, Lt. Col. Edmond F. Driscoll, National Archives.

61. Ibid.

62. Combat Interviews, 9th Infantry Division, Lt. Col. James D. Allgood, National Archives.

63. Ibid.

64. Ibid. Schacht.

65. Schacht.

66. Sgt. Mack Morriss, "In the Huertgen Forest," originally published in *Yank*, reprinted in Don Congdon, ed., *Combat, European Theater* (New York, NY: Dell Publishing Co., Inc., 1958), 245. Hereafter Morriss.

67. AAR, 4th Infantry Division. Astor, 212–13.

68. AAR, 4th Infantry Division. Schmidt, "275th Infantry Division (3 Oct–21 Nov 1944)," 28–29.

69. Narrative History, 4th Infantry Division.

70. *Conquer*, 89.

71. Ibid., 79–80.

72. Ibid., 89.

73. Ibid., 86.

74. Ninth United States Army, Operations, IV, *Offensive in November*, February 1945, 36–37, 48ff.

75. Lange, 10, 13. *Kriegstagebuch, Kampfverlauf, 22.10–31.12.44, LXXXI Armee Korps.* Houston, 309.

76. Ninth United States Army, Operations, IV, *Offensive in November*, February 1945, 36–37, 48ff. Journal, 29th Infantry Division. Balkoski, 44ff.

77. AAR, 29th Infantry Division. Ninth United States Army, Operations, IV, *Offensive in November*, February 1945, 35ff.

78. Ninth United States Army, Operations, IV, *Offensive in November*, February 1945, 41.

79. Journal, AAR, 29th Infantry Division.

80. Ninth United States Army, Operations, IV, *Offensive in November*, February 1945, 12. Hewitt, 145.

81. Ninth United States Army, Operations, IV, *Offensive in November*, February 1945, 18–19.

82. Hewitt, 146.

83. *Conquer*, 89.

84. Ninth United States Army, Operations, IV, *Offensive in November*, February 1945, 55–56.

85. *Kriegstagebuch, Kampfverlauf, 22.10–31.12.44, LXXXI Armee Korps. Tagesmeldungen, LXXXI Armee Korps.* Wagener.

86. *General der Infanterie* Gustav von Zangen, "Fifteenth Army (22 Nov 44–9 Mar 45), Defense Battles at the Roer and Rhine," MS # B-811, 15 November 1947, National Archives, 2ff. Hereafter von Zangen, "Fifteenth Army (22 Nov 44–9 Mar 45), Defense Battles at the Roer and Rhine." *Kriegstagebuch, Kampfverlauf, 22.10–31.12.44, LXXXI Armee Korps.* MacDonald, *The Siegfried Line Campaign*, 417.

87. Deutsche Geschichte, "Gustav Adolf von Zangen," balsi.de/biozangen.

88. First United States Army, Report of Operations, 1 August 1944–22 February 1945, 74–76.

89. Ibid., 76.

90. MacDonald, The Siegfried Line Campaign, 424ff.

91. Stan Zimmerman, letter to author, April 2003.

92. AARs, 750th Tank Battalion.

93. Stan Zimmerman, letter to the author, April 2003.

94. Collins, 275.

95. First United States Army, Report of Operations, 1 August 1944–22 February 1945, 76. *Tagesmeldungen, LXXXI Armee Korps.*

96. History, 415th Infantry Regiment.

97. First United States Army, Report of Operations, 1 August 1944–22 February 1945, 76.

98. *Tagesmeldungen, LXXXI Armee Korps.*

99. 104th Infantry Division, National Timberwolf Association, www.104infdiv.org.

100. First United States Army, Report of Operations, 1 August 1944–22 February 1945, 77.

101. Schacht.

102. First United States Army, Report of Operations, 1 August 1944–22 February 1945, 77–78.

103. AAR, 3d Armored Division. First United States Army, Report of Operations, 1 August 1944–22 February 1945, 76. Schacht.

104. Schacht.

105. AAR, 3d Armored Division.

106. First United States Army, Report of Operations, 1 August 1944–22 February 1945, 76. Bork.

107. Combat Interviews, 9th Infantry Division, Lt. Col. James D. Allgood, National Archives.

108. Combat Interviews, 1st Armored Division, Lt. Col. Wallace Nichols and seven other 745th Tank Battalion officers, National Archives. G-3 Report of Operations, 1st Infantry Division.

109. Combat Interviews, 1st Infantry Division, Lt. Col. Edmond F. Driscoll, National Archives. Headquarters 1st U.S. Infantry Division, Intelligence Activities (1 Nov 1944 to 30 Nov 1944), 1 December 1944.

110 Bork.

111. First United States Army, Report of Operations, 1 August 1944–22 February 1945, 76.

112. Combat Interviews, 9th Infantry Division, Lt. Col. James D. Allgood, National Archives.

113. Schacht. *Kriegstagebuch, Kampfverlauf, 22.10–31.12.44, LXXXI Armee Korps. Erfahrungsberichte, 23.10–30.12.44, LXXXI Armee Korps. Tagesmeldungen, LXXXI Armee Korps.* Guderian, 137, 274.

114. Combat Interviews, 1st Infantry Division; Lt. Col. Henry Davisson, Maj. Karl Herd, Capt. James Armstrong, Lt. Norman Bays, Lt. Sam Daniels, National Archives. G-3 Report of Operations, 1st Infantry Division. *Kriegstagebuch, Kampfverlauf, 22.10–31.12.44, LXXXI Armee Korps.*

115. Headquarters 1st U.S. Infantry Division, Intelligence Activities (1 Nov 1944 to 30 Nov 1944), 1 December 1944. First United States Army, Report of Operations, 1 August 1944–22 February 1945, 76. MacDonald, *The Siegfried Line Campaign,* 418.

116. Combat Interviews, 1st Infantry Division, Lt. Col. Edmond F. Driscoll, National Archives. Headquarters 1st U.S. Infantry Division, Intelligence Activities (1 Nov 1944 to 30 Nov 1944), 1 December 1944.

117. Combat Interviews, 1st Infantry Division; Lt. Col. Henry Davisson, Maj. Karl Herd, Capt. James Armstrong, Lt. Norman Bays, Lt. Sam Daniels, National Archives.

118. Combat Interviews, 1st Infantry Division, Lt. Col. Edmond F. Driscoll, National Archives. Astor, 188–89.

119. First United States Army, Report of Operations, 1 August 1944–22 February 1945, 76. MacDonald, *The Siegfried Line Campaign,* 418.

120. *Tagesmeldungen, LXXXI Armee Korps.*

121. Headquarters 1st U.S. Infantry Division, Intelligence Activities (1 Nov 1944 to 30 Nov 1944), 1 December 1944. Schacht. *Tagesmeldungen, LXXXI Armee Korps.*

122. Combat Interviews, 1st Infantry Division, Capt. Fred W. Hall, National Archives. Combat Interviews, 1st Armored Division, Lt. Col. Wallace Nichols and seven other 745th Tank Battalion officers, National Archives.

123. Combat Interviews, 1st Armored Division, Lt. Col. Wallace Nichols and seven other 745th Tank Battalion officers, National Archives. G-3 Report of Operations, 1st Infantry Division. G-3 journal, 16th Infantry Regiment. *Kriegstagebuch, Kampfverlauf, 22.10–31.12.44, LXXXI Armee Korps.* Guderian, 277. Astor, 193.

124. Headquarters 1st U.S. Infantry Division, Intelligence Activities (1 Nov 1944 to 30 Nov 1944), 1 December 1944. *Tagesmeldungen, LXXXI Armee Korps.*

125. Bork. MacDonald, *The Siegfried Line Campaign,* 418.

126. *Kriegstagebuch, Kampfverlauf, 22.10–31.12.44, LXXXI Armee Korps.*

127. First United States Army, Report of Operations, 1 August 1944–22 February 1945, 72–73.

128. Ibid., 76.

129. Astor, 201.

130. First United States Army, Report of Operations, 1 August 1944–22 February 1945, 78. Schacht. G-3 Report of Operations, 1st Infantry Division. Guderian, 278.

131. First United States Army, Report of Operations, 1 August 1944–22 February 1945, 78.

132. MacDonald, *The Siegfried Line Campaign,* 480. Bork.

133. First United States Army, Report of Operations, 1 August 1944–22 February 1945, 78.

134. Combat Interviews, 1st Infantry Division; Capt. James Libby, Capt. Besor Walker, Capt. Gilbert Fuller, and Lt. Ray Smith, National Archives.

135. Astor, 198. First United States Army, Report of Operations, 1 August 1944–22 February 1945, 78.

136. Bork.

137. First United States Army, Report of Operations, 1 August 1944–22 February 1945, 76. AAR, 4th Infantry Division. Astor, 204–6.

138. Schmidt, "275th Infantry Division (3 Oct–21 Nov 1944)," 28–29.

139. Ibid., 30.

140. Guderian, 274. Von Gersdorf, "The Battle of the Hürtgen Forest, Nov–Early Dec 1944," 13.

141. First United States Army, Report of Operations, 1 August 1944–22 February 1945, 76. AAR, 4th Infantry Division.

142. Narrative History, 4th Infantry Division. Morriss, 246.

143. *"Soixante-Dix," A History of the 70th Tank Battalion,* records of the 70th Tank Battalion, 11.

144. Morriss, 246.

145. Von Gersdorf, "The Battle of the Hürtgen Forest, Nov–Early Dec 1944," 14.

146. AAR, 4th Infantry Division. Schmidt, "275th Infantry Division (3 Oct–21 Nov 1944)," appendix 8.

147. Schramm, 253.

148. First United States Army, Report of Operations, 1 August 1944–22 February 1945, 78.

149. Narrative History, 4th Infantry Division. AAR, 4th Infantry Division.

150. Cited in Morriss, 249.

151. *Tagesmeldungen, LXXXI Armee Korps.*

152. First United States Army, Report of Operations, 1 August 1944–22 February 1945, 78.

153. Ibid.

154. Ibid.

155. Ibid.

156. Hoegh and Doyle, 127.

157. First United States Army, Report of Operations, 1 August 1944–22 February 1945, 78.

158. Zeplien.

159. Stan Zimmerman, letter to the author, April 2003.

160. AAR, 750th Tank Battalion.

161. First United States Army, Report of Operations, 1 August 1944–22 February 1945, 78.

162. Bork. Headquarters 1st U.S. Infantry Division, Intelligence Activities (1 Nov 1944 to 30 Nov 1944), 1 December 1944.

163. First United States Army, Report of Operations, 1 August 1944–22 February 1945, 78. Headquarters 1st U.S. Infantry Division, Intelligence Activities (1 Nov 1944 to 30 Nov 1944), 1 December 1944.

164. Schacht. *Kriegstagebuch, Kampfverlauf, 22.10–31.12.44, LXXXI Armee Korps.*

165. Narrative History, 4th Infantry Division.

166. Astor, 213–14.

167. AAR, 4th Infantry Division.

168. Schmidt, "275th Infantry Division (3 Oct–21 Nov 1944)," 31–33.

169. Ibid., 31.

170. First United States Army, Report of Operations, 1 August 1944–22 February 1945, 79.

171. Ibid., 67.

172. Ibid., 79.

173. Ibid.

174. Schacht.

175. First United States Army, Report of Operations, 1 August 1944–22 February 1945, 79. Schacht.

176. Schacht.

177. Ibid. Bork.

178. Combat Interviews, 9th Infantry Division, Lt. Col. James D. Allgood, National Archives. Collins, 276.

179. First United States Army, Report of Operations, 1 August 1944–22 February 1945, 78.

180. Mittelman, 264.

181. First United States Army, Report of Operations, 1 August 1944–22 February 1945, 79.

182. Bork. *Kriegstagebuch, Kampfverlauf, 22.10–31.12.44, LXXXI Armee Korps.*

183. First United States Army, Report of Operations, 1 August 1944–22 February 1945, 79.

184. Narrative History, 4th Infantry Division.

185. AAR, 4th Infantry Division.

186. Ibid.

187. Schmidt, "275th Infantry Division (3 Oct–21 Nov 1944)," 35.

188. Von Gersdorf, "The Battle of the Hürtgen Forest, Nov–Early Dec 1944," 14. Schmidt, "275th Infantry Division (3 Oct–21 Nov 1944)," 36. *Generalmajor* Eugen König, "272d Volks Grenadier Div. (13 Dec 1944–Mar 1945) and 91st Airborne Division (15 Sep–13 Dec 1944)," MS # B-171, 8 October 1950, National Archives. Hereafter König.

189. First United States Army, Report of Operations, 1 August 1944–22 February 1945, 79.

190 Journal, 415th Infantry Regiment. Schacht.

191. First United States Army, Report of Operations, 1 August 1944–22 February 1945, 79–80.

192. Ibid., 80.

NOTES

193. Ibid.

194. AAR, 4th Infantry Division.

195. Ninth United States Army, Operations, IV, *Offensive in November*, February 1945, 60. *Tagesmeldungen, LXXXI Armee Korps.*

196. *Tagesmeldungen, LXXXI Armee Korps.*

197. Journal, 29th Infantry Division.

198. Ninth United States Army, Operations, IV, *Offensive in November*, February 1945, 82ff.

199. Ibid., 20ff. Hewitt, 149. *Tagesmeldungen, LXXXI Armee Korps.*

200. MacDonald, *The Siegfried Line Campaign*, 530. Jack Bell, "Second Armored Drove Back Massed Tigers, Panthers in Roer River Battle," *Chicago Daily News Service*, 24, included in *Second Armored Division*, 2d Armored Division, 1945. Hereafter Bell.

201. MacDonald, *The Siegfried Line Campaign*, 530.

202. Von Senger und Etterlin, 200–201.

203. Von Manteuffel. AAR, 2d Armored Division.

204. Ninth United States Army, Operations, IV, *Offensive in November*, February 1945, 68.

205. Ibid., 69. Wolfgang Schneider, *Tigers in Combat I*, errata posted at J. J. Fedorowicz Publishing, Inc.'s website, www.jjfpub.mb.ca/tigers_in_combat_i.htm, entry for 17 November 1944.

206. Houston, 310–13. MacDonald, *The Siegfried Line Campaign*, 531. Bell, 24ff. Ninth United States Army, Operations, IV, *Offensive in November*, February 1945, 67ff.

207. Houston, 314–16. AAR, 702d Tank Destroyer Battalion.

208. History, AAR, 771st Tank Destroyer Battalion. Medal citations for Lt. George F. Killmer Jr. and Sgt. Walter F. Nedza.

209. *Conquer*, 93.

210. Bell, 25–26.

211. *Conquer*, 90.

212. AAR, 747th Tank Battalion.

213. Homer D. Wilkes, *747th Tank Battalion* (Scottsdale, AZ: self-published, 197/?), 45–46. Hereafter Wilkes.

214. Ibid., 48.

215. *Conquer*, 93.

216. Köchling.

217. *Conquer*, 92.

218. Ninth United States Army, Operations, IV, *Offensive in November*, February 1945, 25–26.

219. *Tagesmeldungen, LXXXI Armee Korps.*

220. Ninth United States Army, Operations, IV, *Offensive in November*, February 1945, 28. Köchling. *Tagesmeldungen, LXXXI Armee Korps.*

221. Ninth United States Army, Operations, IV, *Offensive in November*, February 1945, 69. Hewitt, 154. *Tagesmeldungen, LXXXI Armee Korps.*

222. Köchling. *Oberstleutnant iG* Hans-Hubert Voigt, "The 340th Volksgrenadier Division in Combat in the Rhineland (2 September–25 December 1944," MS # B-462, 1952, National Archives, 1. Hereafter Voigt. *Kriegstagebuch, Kampfverlauf, 22.10–31.12.44, LXXXI Armee Korps. Handbook on German Military Forces*, 142. *Tagesmeldungen, LXXXI Armee Korps.*

223. *Kriegstagebuch, Kampfverlauf, 22.10–31.12.44, LXXXI Armee Korps.*

224. Ninth United States Army, Operations, IV, *Offensive in November*, February 1945, 181–85. *Kriegstagebuch, Kampfverlauf, 22.10–31.12.44, LXXXI Armee Korps. Erfahrungsberichte, 23.10–30.12.44, LXXXI Armee Korps. Tagesmeldungen, LXXXI Armee Korps.*

225. *Conquer*, 93. Ninth United States Army, Operations, IV, *Offensive in November*, February 1945, 161–62. Journal, 29th Infantry Division.

226. The following account follows Ninth United States Army, Operations, IV, *Offensive in November*, February 1945, 166ff. See also Wilkes, 49, and *Erfahrungsberichte, 23.10–30.12.44, LXXXI Armee Korps.*

227. Except where noted, the following account follows Ninth United States Army, Operations, IV, *Offensive in November*, February 1945, 162ff. See also Wilkes, 49, and the AARs of the 29th Infantry Division and 175th Infantry Regiment.

228. Voigt, 8.
229. Ibid.
230. *Kriegstagebuch, Kampfverlauf, 22.10–31.12.44, LXXXI Armee Korps.*
231. Ninth United States Army, Operations, IV, *Offensive in November*, February 1945. 171. *Kriegstagebuch, Kampfverlauf, 22.10–31.12.44, LXXXI Armee Korps.* Hewitt, 157.
232. Hewitt, 156.
233. *Conquer*, 92.
234. Horrocks, 234.
235. *Conquer*, 82–83. MacDonald, *The Siegfried Line Campaign*, Map VII.
236. *Conquer*, 83, 91.
237. Horrocks, 235.
238. Lange, 9. Ninth United States Army, Operations, IV, *Offensive in November*, February 1945, 91ff.
239. Ninth United States Army, Operations, IV, *Offensive in November*, February 1945, 95ff.
240. Ibid., 109–10.
241. Ibid., 111.
242. America's Greatest Generation Living Their Finest Hour: World War II—1941–1945, "Gene's World War II Diary," http://carol_fus.tripod.com/army_hero_ggreenburg.html. Hereafter America's Greatest Generation Living Their Finest Hour: World War II—1941–1945, "Gene's World War II Diary."
243. Ninth United States Army, Operations, IV, *Offensive in November*, February 1945, 185.
244. Lange, 13.
245. Von Zangen, "Fifteenth Army (22 Nov 44–9 Mar 45), Defense Battles at the Roer and Rhine," 2ff.

CHAPTER 5: GERMAN RESISTANCE HARDENS FURTHER

1. First United States Army, Report of Operations, 1 August 1944–22 February 1945, 80. Opns Memo 119, Headquarters VII Corps, 22 November 1944. Collins, 277.
2. Collins, 276–77.
3. First United States Army, Report of Operations, 1 August 1944–22 February 1945, 80.
4. 104th Infantry Division, National Timberwolf Association, www.104infdiv.org.
5. AAR, 750th Tank Battalion.
6. *Kriegstagebuch, Kampfverlauf, 22.10–31.12.44, LXXXI Armee Korps. Tagesmeldungen, LXXXI Armee Korps.*
7. First United States Army, Report of Operations, 1 August 1944–22 February 1945, 80.
8. Ibid.
9. History, 3d Armored Division. Bork. Zeplien.
10. First United States Army, Report of Operations, 1 August 1944–22 February 1945, 81–82. AAR, 4th Infantry Division.
11. First United States Army, Report of Operations, 1 August 1944–22 February 1945, 82. AAR, 4th Infantry Division.
12. *The Victory Division in Europe, Story of the 5th Armored Division* (Gotha, Germany: 5th Armored Division, 1945), 14–15. Hereafter *The Victory Division in Europe.*
13. Morriss, 246.
14. Marvin Jensen, *Strike Swiftly, The 70th Tank Battalion from North Africa to Normandy to Germany* (Novato, CA: Presidio Press, 1997), 252.
15. AAR, 4th Infantry Division.
16. Von Manteuffel.
17. *Kriegstagebuch, Kampfverlauf, 22.10–31.12.44, LXXXI Armee Korps.*
18. First United States Army, Report of Operations, 1 August 1944–22 February 1945, 81–82.
19. Journal, 413th Infantry Regiment.
20. Zeplien. AAR, 750th Tank Battalion.
21. First United States Army, Report of Operations, 1 August 1944–22 February 1945, 81–82.
22. *Kriegstagebuch, Kampfverlauf, 22.10–31.12.44, LXXXI Armee Korps.* Heinz Schnelle, "Yesteryear," My War, www.faem.com/mywar. Hereafter Schnelle. *Handbook on German Military Forces*, 107.
23. Schnelle.

24. History, 3d Armored Division. *Spearhead in the West*, 104–5.
25. First United States Army, Report of Operations, 1 August 1944–22 February 1945, 82. *Kriegstagebuch, Kampfverlauf, 22.10–31.12.44, LXXXI Armee Korps.*
26. First United States Army, Report of Operations, 1 August 1944–22 February 1945, 82.
27. Zeplien.
28. Schacht.
29. The American perspective is drawn from Combat Interview, 9th Infantry Division, Capt. William L. McWaters; MacDonald, *The Siegfried Line Campaign*, 485ff; and Astor, 273ff. Astor, in turn, based his account on an unpublished manuscript written by Chester Jordan. The German perspective is based on several separate accounts posted at My War, www.faem.com/mywar/. As one might imagine, the accounts on both sides are riddled with inconsistencies. The reports at times differ even regarding dates. This version follows the dates in MacDonald's official U.S. Army history.
30. Headquarters 1st U.S. Infantry Division, Intelligence Activities (1 Nov 1944 to 30 Nov 1944), 1 December 1944. *Meldungen, Gen. Kdo. An Armee, vom 23.10–31.12.1944, LXXXI Armee Korps.*
31. First United States Army, Report of Operations, 1 August 1944–22 February 1945, 82.
32. Headquarters 1st U.S. Infantry Division, Intelligence Activities (1 Nov 1944 to 30 Nov 1944), 1 December 1944. *Kriegstagebuch, Kampfverlauf, 22.10–31.12.44, LXXXI Armee Korps.*
33. First United States Army, Report of Operations, 1 August 1944–22 February 1945, 82. AAR, 4th Infantry Division.
34. First United States Army, Report of Operations, 1 August 1944–22 February 1945, 82.
35. Ibid.
36. AAR, 4th Infantry Division.
37. Ibid.
38. Bork. *Kriegstagebuch, Kampfverlauf, 22.10–31.12.44, LXXXI Armee Korps.*
39. Schnelle.
40. *Generalmajor* Walter Denkert, "The 3d Panzer Grenadier Division During the Defensive Combat for the Inden Bridgehead," MS # A-976, December 1945, National Archives. Hereafter Denkert, "The 3d Panzer Grenadier Division During the Defensive Combat for the Inden Bridgehead."
41. "The Fights at the Inde," My War, www.faem.com/mywar. Hereafter "The Fights at the Inde."
42. Denkert, "The 3d Panzer Grenadier Division During the Defensive Combat for the Inden Bridgehead." "The Fights at the Inde." *Kriegstagebuch, Kampfverlauf, 22.10–31.12.44, LXXXI Armee Korps.*
43. Denkert, "The 3d Panzer Grenadier Division During the Defensive Combat for the Inden Bridgehead." "The Fights at the Inde." *Kriegstagebuch, Kampfverlauf, 22.10–31.12.44, LXXXI Armee Korps.* Journal, 413th Infantry Regiment. "The Battle of Inden," Combat Interviews, 104th Infantry Division, National Archives. Hoegh and Doyle, 149–51.
44. Denkert, "The 3d Panzer Grenadier Division During the Defensive Combat for the Inden Bridgehead." "The Fights at the Inde." Journal, 413th Infantry Regiment. *Meldungen, Gen. Kdo. An Armee, vom 23.10–31.12.1944, LXXXI Armee Korps.*
45. First United States Army, Report of Operations, 1 August 1944–22 February 1945, 83. Journal, 413th Infantry Regiment. "The Fights at the Inde." "The Battle of Inden," Combat Interviews, 104th Infantry Division, National Archives.
46. Denkert, "The 3d Panzer Grenadier Division During the Defensive Combat for the Inden Bridgehead." "The Fights at the Inde." Journal, 413th Infantry Regiment.
47. *Kriegstagebuch, Kampfverlauf, 22.10–31.12.44, LXXXI Armee Korps.*
48. Denkert, "The 3d Panzer Grenadier Division During the Defensive Combat for the Inden Bridgehead." "The Fights at the Inde."
49. Ibid.
50. "The Battle of Inden," Combat Interviews, 104th Infantry Division, National Archives.
51. Trostorf.
52. Combat Interviews, 1st Infantry Division; Capt. James Libby, Capt. Besor Walker, Capt. Gilbert Fuller, and Lt. Ray Smith, National Archives.
53. Trostorf.
54. Combat Interviews, 1st Armored Division, Lt. Col. Wallace Nichols and seven other 745th Tank Battalion officers, National Archives.

55. Otto Krannich, "Reported by Captain Otto Krannich," My War, www.faem.com/mywar. Hereafter Krannich.
56. Astor, 286.
57. Combat Interviews, 1st Infantry Division; Capt. James Libby, Capt. Besor Walker, Capt. Gilbert Fuller, and Lt. Ray Smith, National Archives.
58. Trostorf. First United States Army, Report of Operations, 1 August 1944–22 February 1945, 82. "The Fight of 3rd ParaDiv Between 11/27 and 11/30/1944," My War, www.faem.com/mywar. Hereafter "The Fight of 3rd ParaDiv Between 11/27 and 11/30/1944."
59. First United States Army, Report of Operations, 1 August 1944–22 February 1945, 82. "The Fight of 3rd ParaDiv Between 11/27 and 11/30/1944." Bork. Trostorf.
60. Journal, 26th Infantry Regiment, 1st Infantry Division.
61. Combat Interviews, 1st Infantry Division; Capt. James Libby, Capt. Besor Walker, Capt. Gilbert Fuller, and Lt. Ray Smith, National Archives.
62. Trostorf.
63. Ibid.
64. AAR, 4th Infantry Division.
65. Ibid.
66. First United States Army, Report of Operations, 1 August 1944–22 February 1945, 83.
67. AAR, 4th Infantry Division.
68. Ninth United States Army, Operations, IV, *Offensive in November*, February 1945, 204.
69. Von Lüttwitz, 15.
70. Ibid., 13–14.
71. Ninth United States Army, Operations, IV, *Offensive in November*, February 1945, 196ff. *Tagesmeldungen, LXXXI Armee Korps.*
72. Ninth United States Army, Operations, IV, *Offensive in November*, February 1945, 200–201. Wilkes, 50. *Kriegstagebuch, Kampfverlauf, 22.10–31.12.44, LXXXI Armee Korps. Meldungen, Gen. Kdo. An Armee, vom 23.10–31.12.1944, LXXXI Armee Korps.*
73. Ninth United States Army, Operations, IV, *Offensive in November*, February 1945, 201–2.
74. Hewitt, 158–59.
75. Ninth United States Army, Operations, IV, *Offensive in November*, February 1945, 213.
76. Ibid., 204–5.
77. Ibid., 205.
78. Ibid., 205–6.
79. *Kriegstagebuch, Kampfverlauf, 22.10–31.12.44, LXXXI Armee Korps.* Voigt, 11.
80. Wilkes, 52.
81. Ninth United States Army, Operations, IV, *Offensive in November*, February 1945, 214–19. Voigt, 12.
82. Ibid., 220ff.
83. SHAEF Mémo, "Discussion of the immediate prospects on the Western front, chiefly of the 1st and 9th Armies," 28 November 1944.
84. Ninth United States Army, Operations, IV, *Offensive in November*, February 1945, 206.
85. Ibid., 239–48. *Kriegstagebuch, Kampfverlauf, 22.10–31.12.44, LXXXI Armee Korps. Erfahrungsberichte, 23.10–30.12.44, LXXXI Armee Korps.*
86. Voigt, 15–17.
87. Ninth United States Army, Operations, IV, *Offensive in November*, February 1945, 233ff. Journal, 29th Infantry Division.
88. Hewitt, 161.
89. *Kriegstagebuch, Kampfverlauf, 22.10–31.12.44, LXXXI Armee Korps.*
90. Ninth United States Army, Operations, IV, *Offensive in November*, February 1945, 255.
91. Ibid., 256. Von Lüttwitz, 16–17.
92. Ninth United States Army, Operations, IV, *Offensive in November*, February 1945, 256.
93. Ibid., 256ff.
94. Von Lüttwitz, 20.

95. Von Zangen, "Fifteenth Army (22 Nov 44–9 Mar 45), Defense Battles at the Roer and Rhine," 15ff. Von Lüttwitz, 21.

96. Ninth United States Army, Operations, IV, *Offensive in November*, February 1945, 296ff.

97. Ibid., 256ff.

98. America's Greatest Generation Living Their Finest Hour: World War II—1941–1945. "Gene's World War II Diary."

99. Ninth United States Army, Operations, IV, *Offensive in November*, February 1945, 272ff.

100. Von Lüttwitz, 24–25.

101. Von Zangen, "Fifteenth Army (22 Nov 44–9 Mar 45), Defense Battles at the Roer and Rhine," 15ff.

102. Schnelle.

103. Engel, "12th Infantry Division, 22 Sep–22 Oct 1944."

104. Bork. *Ia, Wochenmeldungen, LXXXI Armee Korps.*

105. Schacht.

106. Ibid. *Ia, Wochenmeldungen, LXXXI Armee Korps.*

107. Köchling. Voigt, 18. *Kriegstagebuch, Kampfverlauf, 22.10–31.12.44, LXXXI Armee Korps. Ia, Wochenmeldungen, LXXXI Armee Korps.*

CHAPTER 6: A DEFENSIVE VICTORY

1. David Eisenhower, 543–46.

2. Butcher, 720.

3. David Eisenhower, 547–48.

4. First United States Army, Report of Operations, 1 August 1944–22 February 1945, 83.

5. G-3 Report of Operations, 1st Infantry Division.

6. Collins, 276.

7. First United States Army, Report of Operations, 1 August 1944–22 February 1945, 82–83, 88–89.

8. Collins, 277.

9. First United States Army, Report of Operations, 1 August 1944–22 February 1945, 84.

10. *Befehle Gen. Kdo. An Div. vom 1.–31.12.44, LXXXI Armee Korps.*

11. History, 415th Infantry Regiment. "Battle of Lucherberg, Germany, 2–5 Dec. 1944," Sgt. Leon Marokus, Combat Interviews, 104th Infantry Division, National Archives. Periodic G-2 reports, 104th Infantry Division. *Befehle Gen. Kdo. An Div. vom 1.–31.12.44, LXXXI Armee Korps.*

12. First United States Army, Report of Operations, 1 August 1944–22 February 1945, 85. Journal, 413th Infantry Regiment. Hoegh and Doyle, 159. "The Fight of 3rd ParaDiv Between 11/27 and 11/30/1944." *Kriegstagebuch, Kampfverlauf, 22.10–31.12.44, LXXXI Armee Korps. Befehle Gen. Kdo. An Div. vom 1.–31.12.44, LXXXI Armee Korps.*

13. Emil Weiss, "Report of Emil Weiß, soldier in 6th Company, GrenReg 404 of 246th VGD," My War, www.faem.com/mywar. Hereafter Weiss.

14. First United States Army, Report of Operations, 1 August 1944–22 February 1945, 85. "The Fight of 3rd ParaDiv Between 11/27 and 11/30/1944."

15. History, 415th Infantry Regiment. Lt. Harry Goldberg, T/Sgt. James Kelly, and Pfc. Robert Jones, Combat Interviews, 104th Infantry Division, National Archives. Weiss.

16. Weiss.

17. Capt. W. D. Beard, Combat Interviews, 104th Infantry Division, National Archives.

18. History, 415th Infantry Regiment. AAR, 750th Tank Battalion. *Kriegstagebuch, Kampfverlauf, 22.10–31.12.44, LXXXI Armee Korps. Befehle Gen. Kdo. An Div. vom 1.–31.12.44, LXXXI Armee Korps.* Köchling.

19. History, 415th Infantry Regiment. Letter from Collins to Allen, 26 December 1944, records of the 415th Infantry Regiment.

20. First United States Army, Report of Operations, 1 August 1944–22 February 1945, 84.

21. Ninth United States Army, Operations, IV, *Offensive in November*, February 1945, 325ff.

22. Ibid., 334. AAR, 29th Infantry Division.

23. *Kriegstagebuch, Kampfverlauf, 22.10–31.12.44, LXXXI Armee Korps. Erfahrungsberichte, 23.10–30.12.44, LXXXI Armee Korps.* Köchling.

24. Ninth United States Army, Operations, IV, *Offensive in November*, February 1945, 334–35. *Kriegstagebuch, Kampfverlauf, 22.10–31.12.44, LXXXI Armee Korps.* Köchling.

25. Ninth United States Army, Operations, IV, *Offensive in November*, February 1945, 313ff. Von Lüttwitz, 27.

26. Von Zangen, "Fifteenth Army (22 Nov 44–9 Mar 45), Defense Battles at the Roer and Rhine," 15ff.

27. Ninth United States Army, Operations, IV, *Offensive in November*, February 1945, 274.

28. Von Zangen, "Fifteenth Army (22 Nov 44–9 Mar 45), Defense Battles at the Roer and Rhine," 15ff.

29. Ninth United States Army, Operations, IV, *Offensive in November*, February 1945, 337. AAR, Ninth Army.

30. Bradley and Blair, 347.

31. Ibid., 349–51.

32. First United States Army, Report of Operations, 1 August 1944–22 February 1945, 89.

33. Ibid., 90.

34. Ibid. AAR, 83d Infantry Division. *The Thunderbolt Across Europe, A History of the 83d Infantry Division 1942–1945* (Munich, Germany: 83d Infantry Division, 1945), 60ff. Hereafter *The Thunderbolt Across Europe.*

35. First United States Army, Report of Operations, 1 August 1944–22 February 1945, 89.

36. Ibid. Combat Interviews, 9th Infantry Division, Lt. Col. Frank L. Gunn and Capt. John H. Whitmore, National Archives. History, 3d Armored Division. *Spearhead in the West*, 105–06.

37. Mittelman, 273.

38. Schnelle.

39. Von Zangen, "Fifteenth Army (22 Nov 44–9 Mar 45), Defense Battles at the Roer and Rhine," 15ff. Wagener.

40. First United States Army, Report of Operations, 1 August 1944–22 February 1945, 90. *Kriegstagebuch, Kampfverlauf, 22.10–31.12.44, LXXXI Armee Korps.* Köchling. *Befehle Gen. Kdo. An Div. vom 1.–31.12.44, LXXXI Armee Korps.*

41. First United States Army, Report of Operations, 1 August 1944–22 February 1945, 90.

42. Ibid.

43. Ibid. AAR, 83d Infantry Division.

44. Bork. *Kriegstagebuch, Kampfverlauf, 22.10–31.12.44, LXXXI Armee Korps.* Köchling.

45. AAR, 83d Infantry Division.

46. Opns Memo 130, Headquarters VII Corps, 13 December 1944.

47. Von Zangen, "Fifteenth Army (22 Nov 44–9 Mar 45), Defense Battles at the Roer and Rhine," 15ff.

48. 104th Infantry Division, National Timberwolf Association, www.104infdiv.org.

49. Journal, 413th Infantry Regiment.

50. First United States Army, Report of Operations, 1 August 1944–22 February 1945, 91. *The Thunderbolt Across Europe*, 61–62. AAR, 83d Infantry Division.

51. Schacht.

52. First United States Army, Report of Operations, 1 August 1944–22 February 1945, 91.

53. Ibid.

54. *Kriegstagebuch, Kampfverlauf, 22.10–31.12.44, LXXXI Armee Korps. Befehle Gen. Kdo. An Div. vom 1.–31.12.44, LXXXI Armee Korps.* Köchling.

55. MacDonald, *The Siegfried Line Campaign*, 594.

56. Ibid., 593–94.

57. *Conquer*, 113.

58. Ibid., 112.

59. AAR, Ninth Army.

60. Ibid.

61. Dwight Eisenhower, 323.

62. Bradley, 441, 444.

63. Von Zangen, "Fifteenth Army (22 Nov 44–9 Mar 45), Defense Battles at the Roer and Rhine," 31–33.

CHAPTER 7: THE DAMS OF PERDITION

1. Hewitt, 162.
2. "Military Geography Study No. 8," Engineer Headquarters, Ninth Army, 25 October 1944.
3. Ninth United States Army, Operations, IV, *Offensive in November*, February 1945, 4.
4. First United States Army, Report of Operations, 1 August 1944–22 February 1945, 67.
5. MacDonald, *The Siegfried Line Campaign*, 324ff.
6. Ninth United States Army, Operations, IV, *Offensive in November*, February 1945, 205–06.
7. Collins, 274. *Rhineland*, 18.
8. *Rhineland*, 18.
9. Von Gersdorf, "Questions for Consideration and Reply."
10. Ninth United States Army, Operations, IV, *Offensive in November*, February 1945, 207.
11. AAR, Ninth Army.
12. First United States Army, Report of Operations, 1 August 1944–22 February 1945, 88.
13. Von Gersdorf, "Seventh Army; Siegfried Line—Defense of the Siegfried Line," 6.
14. Von Gersdorf, "The Battle of the Hürtgen Forest, Nov–Early Dec 1944," 8.
15. Köchling.
16. Von Gersdorf, "The Battle of the Hürtgen Forest, Nov–Early Dec 1944," 26–27.
17. Von Zangen, "Fifteenth Army (22 Nov 44–9 Mar 45), Defense Battles at the Roer and Rhine," 23ff.
18. Ibid.
19. Von Zangen, "Fifteenth Army (22 Nov 44–9 Mar 45), Defense Battles at the Roer and Rhine," 26–28.
20. AAR, Ninth Army.
21. First United States Army, Report of Operations, 1 August 1944–22 February 1945, 97–98.
22. Von Zangen, "Fifteenth Army (22 Nov 44–9 Mar 45), Defense Battles at the Roer and Rhine," 43–44.
23. AAR, Ninth Army.
24. Von Zangen, "Fifteenth Army (22 Nov 44–9 Mar 45), Defense Battles at the Roer and Rhine," 45.
25. Bradley, 495–97.
26. Memorandum for the Record, 20 January 1945.
27. Willam L. Shirer, *The Rise and Fall of the Third Reich* (New York, NY: Fawcett Crest, 1983), 1424–25. Wilmot, 622–23, 663–64. Guderian, 322ff.
28. Hitzfeld, 10–11.
29. Von Zangen, "Fifteenth Army (22 Nov 44–9 Mar 45), Defense Battles at the Roer and Rhine," 53ff.
30. *General der Infanterie* Karl Püchler, commanding general, LXXIV Corps, "The Rhineland—74. Armeekorps—The Periods from 2 to 27 Oct. 1944 and 16 Dec. 1944 to 23 Mar. 1945," MS # B-118, 26 July 1946, National Archives. Hereafter Püchler. Ralf Anton Schäfer, "*Die 62. Volksgrenadier Division*," www.62vgd.de/. Hereafter Schäfer.
31. "Operations of the 78th Infantry Division, 30 January to 4 February," undated manuscript contained in Combat Interviews, 78th Infantry Division, National Archives. Lt. Col. Robert C. Wilson, G-2, Combat Interviews, 78th Infantry Division, National Archives.
32. Von Zangen, "Fifteenth Army (22 Nov 44–9 Mar 45), Defense Battles at the Roer and Rhine," 53ff. Püchler. Schäfer.
33. *Oberstleutnant* Horst Wangenheim, "The 277th Volks Grenadier Division, 26 Jan–9 Mar 1945," MS # B-754, not dated, National Archives, 2ff. Hereafter Wangenheim. Hitzfeld, 4.
34. Schäfer.
35. Wangenheim, 2ff.
36. Memorandum, "Notes on conference with General Bradley on his return from SHAEF, this date," 1 February 1945. First United States Army, Report of Operations, 1 August 1944–22 February 1945, 150–54.
37. Mittelman, 300.
38. First United States Army, Report of Operations, 1 August 1944–22 February 1945, 150. Lt. Col. Jack Houston, G-2, Combat Interviews, 9th Infantry Division, National Archives.
39. *The Victory Division in Europe*, 34–35.

40. "Operations of the 78th Infantry Division, 30 January to 4 February," undated manuscript contained in Combat Interviews, 78th Infantry Division, National Archives. AAR, 78th Infantry Division. First United States Army, Report of Operations, 1 August 1944–22 February 1945, 150. Schäfer. Charles B. MacDonald, *The Last Offensive: United States Army in World War II, The European Theater of Operations* (Washington, DC: Office of the Chief of Military History, Department of the Army, 1993), 72. Hereafter MacDonald, *The Last Offensive.*

41. "Operations of the 78th Infantry Division, 30 January to 4 February," undated manuscript contained in Combat Interviews, 78th Infantry Division, National Archives. First United States Army, Report of Operations, 1 August 1944–22 February 1945, 151. Schäfer.

42. First United States Army, Report of Operations, 1 August 1944–22 February 1945, 152.

43. Ibid. Püchler.

44. First United States Army, Report of Operations, 1 August 1944–22 February 1945, 152. Lt. Col. Robert L. McKinney, G-3, Combat Interviews, 78th Infantry Division, National Archives. AAR, 78th Infantry Division.

45. Von Zangen, "Fifteenth Army (22 Nov 44–9 Mar 45), Defense Battles at the Roer and Rhine," 57–58. Püchler. First United States Army, Report of Operations, 1 August 1944–22 February 1945, 152. "Operations of the 78th Infantry Division, 30 January to 4 February," undated manuscript contained in Combat Interviews, 78th Infantry Division, National Archives. Wagenheim, 31. Schäfer.

46. Mittelman, 304. First United States Army, Report of Operations, 1 August 1944–22 February 1945, 153. AAR, 78th Infantry Division.

47. Mittelman, 308. Lt. Col. Robert C. Wilson, G-2, Combat Interviews, 78th Infantry Division, National Archives. First United States Army, Report of Operations, 1 August 1944–22 February 1945, 153.

48. First United States Army, Report of Operations, 1 August 1944–22 February 1945, 155.

49. Lt. Col. Robert L. McKinney, G-3, Combat Interviews, 78th Infantry Division, National Archives. Püchler.

50. First United States Army, Report of Operations, 1 August 1944–22 February 1945, 156.

51. Von Zangen, "Fifteenth Army (22 Nov 44–9 Mar 45), Defense Battles at the Roer and Rhine," 57–58. First United States Army, Report of Operations, 1 August 1944–22 February 1945, 152.

52. Lt. Col. Floyd Call and other officers, 3d Battalion, 309th Infantry Regiment, Combat Interviews, 78th Infantry Division, National Archives. Püchler.

53. Gen. James G. Gavin, *On to Berlin* (New York, NY: Bantam Books, 1984), 265.

54. Von Zangen, "Fifteenth Army (22 Nov 44–9 Mar 45), Defense Battles at the Roer and Rhine," 57–58. First United States Army, Report of Operations, 1 August 1944–22 February 1945, 152.

55. First United States Army, Report of Operations, 1 August 1944–22 February 1945, 157. AAR, 78th Infantry Division. MacDonald, *The Last Offensive,* 79.

56. Mittelman, 309. MacDonald, *The Last Offensive,* 81.

57. Col. John G. Van Houton, Combat Interviews, 9th Infantry Division, National Archives.

58. Mittelman, 312. Col. John G. Ondrick, CO, 309th Infantry Regiment, and Lt. Col. Robert L. McKinney, G-3, Combat Interviews, 78th Infantry Division, National Archives. First United States Army, Report of Operations, 1 August 1944–22 February 1945, 159.

59. AAR, Ninth Army.

60. Von Zangen, "Fifteenth Army (22 Nov 44–9 Mar 45), Defense Battles at the Roer and Rhine," 59.

CHAPTER 8: ACROSS THE ROER

1. H. Essame, *The Battle for Germany* (New York, NY: Charles Scribner's Sons, 1970), 126. Hereafter Essame.

2. Von Zangen, "Fifteenth Army (22 Nov 44–9 Mar 45), Defense Battles at the Roer and Rhine," 52.

3. Ibid. Lange, 17–18.

4. Whiting, "Siegfried," 143.

5. Peter White, *With the Jocks* (Stroud, UK: Sutton Publishing, 2001), 60ff. Hereafter White. Patrick Delaforce, *Monty's Marauders* (London: Chancellor Press, 2000), 197. Hereafter Delaforce, *Monty's Marauders.*

6. White, 64ff.

7. Von Zangen, "Fifteenth Army (22 Nov 44–9 Mar 45), Defense Battles at the Roer and Rhine," 52.

8. Delaforce, *Monty's Marauders*, 197–98. White, 82.

9. Patrick Delaforce, *The Fighting Wessex Wyverns* (Phoenix Mill, UK: Sutton Publishing, 2002), 242–43.

10. White, 108.

11. White, 110ff. Essame, 127–28.

12. Essame, 128.

13. Von Zangen, "Fifteenth Army (22 Nov 44–9 Mar 45), Defense Battles at the Roer and Rhine," 52.

14. AAR, Ninth Army. *Conquer*, 135ff. Bradley, 504. MacDonald, *The Last Offensive*, 136, 140. Wilmot, 664–65.

15. Von Zangen, "Fifteenth Army (22 Nov 44–9 Mar 45), Defense Battles at the Roer and Rhine," 58, 95.

16. AAR, Ninth Army. *Conquer*, 135ff. Bradley, 504. MacDonald, *The Last Offensive*, 136, 140.

17. Bradley, 499, 504–5. *Conquer*, 146.

18. Langhauser.

19. AAR, Ninth Army. *Conquer*, 162.

20. Ibid., 158.

21. AAR, Ninth Army.

22. Ibid. *Conquer*, 167. Hewitt, 215. AAR, 29th Infantry Division.

23. *Conquer*, 170. Undated summary manuscript, Combat Interviews, 102d Infantry Division, National Archives.

24. *Conquer*, 170. Chronology, Combat Interviews, 84th Infantry Division, National Archives. MacDonald, *The Last Offensive*, 153ff.

25. Hewitt, 212.

26. Ibid., 216ff. "Across and Beyond, the 30th Infantry Division Crosses the Roer River," undated manuscript, Combat Interviews, 30th Infantry Division, National Archives.

27. Journal and AAR, 29th Infantry Division. *Generalleutnant* Walter Poppe, "The Commitment of the 59. Inf Div in Rheinland from 3 Dec 44 to 28 Feb 45," MS # B-152, May 1946, National Archives, 11–12.

28. *Generalmajor* Rudolf Langhauser, "12 VGD (Volksgrenadier Division), Defensive Battle Between Roer and Rhine, 23 Feb–27 Mar 45," MS # B-080, 15 June 1946, National Archives. MacDonald, *The Last Offensive*, 157.

29. Collins, 299. MacDonald, *The Last Offensive*, 159ff.

30. 104th Infantry Division, National Timberwolf Association, www.104infdiv.org.

31. Ibid.

32. Hoegh and Doyle, 231.

33. Collins, 299.

34. *Conquer*, 171. MacDonald, *The Last Offensive*, 162.

35. AAR, Ninth Army.

36. *General der Infanterie* Gustav von Zangen, "Fifteenth Army (22 Nov 44–9 Mar 45), Anglo-American large-scale attack across the Roer and Rhine," National Archives, 3. Hereafter Von Zangen, "Fifteenth Army (22 Nov 44–9 Mar 45), Anglo-American large-scale attack across the Roer and Rhine."

37. Ibid., 4–5. *Generalmajor* Wolf Ewart, "The Engagement of the 338th Inf Div in the Rhineland, Part II," MS # B-531, not dated, National Archives, 2.

38. AAR, Ninth Army.

39. Langhauser.

40. AAR, Ninth Army.

41. *Conquer*, 175ff.

42. Collins, 301.

43. Langhauser.

44. Von Zangen, "Fifteenth Army (22 Nov 44–9 Mar 45), Anglo-American large-scale attack across the Roer and Rhine," 28.

45. AAR, Ninth Army. *Conquer*, 180.

46. AAR, Ninth Army.

47. Collins, 303.

BIBLIOGRAPHY

ARTICLES AND INTERNET PAGES

104th Infantry Division, National Timberwolf Association. www.104infdiv.org.

"Aachen Fighting Fantastic," *New York Times*, 16 October 1944, 5.

America's Greatest Generation Living Their Finest Hour: World War II—1941–1945. "Gene's World War II Diary." http://carol_fus.tripod.com/army_hero_ggreenburg.html.

Bell, Jack. "Second Armored Drove Back Massed Tigers, Panthers in Roer River Battle," *Chicago Daily News Service*, included in *Second Armored Division*. 2d Armored Division, 1945, 24–26.

Bork, *Generalleutnant* Max. "47th Volks Grenadier Division at the Western Front." My War, www.faem.com/mywar. This document is an independent English translation of the German-language report that served as the basis for Bork, *Generalleutnant* Max, former commander of the 47th Volksgrenadier Division. "The 47th Volksgrenadier Division in the West." MS # B-602, June 1947. National Archives.

Deutsche Geschichte. "Gustav Adolf von Zangen." http://balsi.de/biozangen.

"The Fight of 3rd ParaDiv Between 11/27 and 11/30/1944." The anonymous German author states that the account follows the records of the *5th Fallschirmjäger Regiment*. This may be part of an account written by *Generalleutnant* Friedrich Sixt. My War, www.faem.com/mywar.

"The Fights at the Inde." The anonymous author was a soldier in the 3d Panzergrenadier Division. My War, www.faem.com/mywar.

Gees, Hubert. "Memories of Hubert Gees." My War, www.faem.com/mywar.

Gorman, P. F. "Aachen 1944, Implications for Command Post of the Future." Institute for Defense Analyses, not dated but probably 2000.

Krannich, Otto. "Reported by Captain Otto Krannich." My War, www.faem.com/mywar.

Martens, Hans. "Deployment of III./RJG Platoon of 13/09 Between 09/17 and 09/20/44." My War, www.faem.com/mywar.

Middleton, Drew. "First Storms City." *New York Times*, 14 October 1944, 1, 3.

———. "Offer Handed Foe." *New York Times*, 11 October 1944, 1, 3.

Miller, Michael, Jeff Chrisman, et al. Axis Biographical Research, www.geocities.com/%7Eorion47/.

Schacht, Karl. "The Diary of Karl Schacht." My War, www.faem.com/mywar. This document mixes the personal experiences of Schacht, a soldier in the 47th Volksgrenadier Division, with material extracted verbatim from other German sources not directly available on the Internet. These include the text of the paper covering the period of the November offensive written for the Foreign Military Studies series by *Generalmajor* Gerhard Engel (MS # B-764).

Schäfer, Ralf Anton. "*Die 62. Volksgrenadier Division*." www.62vgd.de/.

Schneider, Wolfgang. *Tigers in Combat I*, errata posted at J.J. Fedorowicz Publishing, Inc's website, www.jjfpub.mb.ca/tigers_in_combat_i.htm.

Schnelle, Heinz. "Yesteryear." My War, www.faem.com/mywar.

Stoneman, William H. "104th Division A Winner for Maj Gen Allen, Too." *Chicago Daily News*, copy in history of 415th Infantry Regiment, not dated.

Trostorf, Albert. "Zusammenfassung der Kriegsereignisse im Raum Merode." Merode 2000, www.merode.com/. Trostorf's account is unique in that it relies in part on eyewitness reports from the civilian population in Merode during the battle there.

Weiss, Emil. "Report of Emil Weiß, soldier in 6th Company, GrenReg 404 of 246th VGD." My War, www.faem.com/mywar.

Zeplien, Hans. *Hauptmann* a.D. "Reorganization of GrenReg 89 after arrival of reserves, and creation of a new main line of resistance." My War, www.faem.com/mywar.

BOOKS AND BOOKLETS

Ambrose, Stephen E. *Citizen Soldiers*. New York, NY: Touchstone, 1997.

The American Arsenal. London: Greenhill Books, 2001. The Greenhill volume is essentially a reprint of the U.S. Army's *Catalog of Standard Ordnance Items* of 1944.

Astor, Gerald. *The Bloody Forest, Battle for the Huertgen, September 1944–January 1945*. Novato, CA: Presidio Press, Inc., 2000.

Balkoski, Joseph. *Beyond the Beachhead, The 29th Infantry Division in Normandy*. Mechanicsburg, PA: Stackpole Books, 1999.

Bishop, Chris, and Adam Warner, eds. *German Weapons of World War II*. Edison, NJ: Chartwell Books, Inc., 2001.

Bradley, Omar N. *A Soldier's Story*. New York, NY: The Modern Library, 1999.

Bradley, Omar N., and Clay Blair. *A General's Life*. New York, NY: Simon and Schuster, 1983.

Buchner, Alex. *Das Handbuch der Deutschen Infanterie, 1939–1945*. Wölfersheim-Berstadt: Podzun-Pallas-Verlag GMBH, not dated.

Butcher, Capt. Harry C. *My Three Years with Eisenhower*. New York, NY: Simon and Schuster, Inc, 1946.

Collins, J. Lawton. *Lightning Joe, An Autobiography*. Baton Rouge, LA: Louisiana State University Press, 1979.
Conquer, The Story of the Ninth Army. Washington, DC: Infantry Journal Press, 1947. This volume was written by the staff of Ninth Army and is, for practical purposes, the army's official history.

Cooper, Belton Y. *Death Traps, The Survival of an American Armored Division in World War II*. Novato, CA: Presidio Press, Inc., 2000.
Delaforce, Patrick. *The Fighting Wessex Wyverns*. Phoenix Mill, UK: Sutton Publishing, 2002.

———. *Monty's Marauders*. London: Chancellor Press, 2000.

Eisenhower, David. *Eisenhower at War 1943–1945*. New York, NY: Random House, 1986.

Eisenhower, Dwight D. *Crusade in Europe*. Garden City, NY: Doubleday and Company, Inc., 1948.

Essame, H. *The Battle for Germany*. New York, NY: Charles Scribner's Sons, 1970.

Forty, George. *Tank Warfare in the Second World War, An Oral History*. London: Constable and Company Ltd, 1998.

———. *US Army Handbook 1939–1945*. Phoenix Mill, UK: Sutton Publishing Ltd., 1998.

Gavin, General James G. *On to Berlin*. New York, NY: Bantam Books, 1984.

Green, Michael. *M4 Sherman*. Osceola, WI: Motorbooks International Publishers & Wholesalers, 1993.

Griess, Thomas E., ed. *The West Point Military History Series, The Second World War, Europe and the Mediterranean*. Wayne, NJ: Avery Publishing Group Inc., 1984.

Guderian, Heinz Günther. *From Normandy to the Ruhr, With the 116th Panzer Division in World War II*. Bedford, PA: The Aberjona Press, 2001.

Handbook on German Military Forces. Baton Rouge: Louisiana State University Press, 1990. This is a reprint of a massive U.S. War Department study by the same title published on 15 March 1945.

Harmon, Maj. Gen. E. N., with Milton MacKaye and William Ross MacKaye. *Combat Commander, Autobiography of a Soldier*. Englewood Cliffs, NJ: Prentice-Hall, Inc., 1970.

Hawkins, Desmond, ed. *War Report, D-day to VE-day*. London: British Broadcasting Corporation, 1985.

Hewitt, Robert L. *Workhorse of the Western Front, the Story of the 30th Infantry Division*. Washington, DC: Infantry Journal Press, 1946. The book was published under division auspices and is, for practical purposes, its official history.

Hoegh, Leo A., and Howard J. Doyle. *Timberwolf Tracks, The History of the 104th Infantry Division, 1942–1945*. Washington, DC: Infantry Journal Press, 1946.

Horrocks, Lt. Gen. Sir Brian. *A Full Life*. London: Collins, 1960.

Houston, Donald E. *Hell on Wheels, The 2d Armored Division*. Novato, CA: Presidio Press, 1977.

Jablonski, Edward. *Wings of Fire*. Garden City, NY: Doubleday & Company, 1971.

Jensen, Marvin. *Strike Swiftly, The 70th Tank Battalion from North Africa to Normandy to Germany*. Novato, CA: Presidio Press, 1997.

Knickerbocker, H. R., et al. *Danger Forward, The Story of the First Division in World War II*. Washington, DC: Society of the First Division, 1947.

Liddell Hart, B. H. *History of the Second World War*. New York, NY: G. Putnam's Sons, 1970.

BIBLIOGRAPHY

MacDonald, Charles B. *The Battle of the Bulge*. London: Guild Publishing, 1984.

———. *The Last Offensive: United States Army in World War II, The European Theater of Operations*. Washington, DC: Office of the Chief of Military History, Department of the Army, 1993.

———. *The Siegfried Line Campaign: United States Army in World War II, The European Theater of Operations*. Washington, DC: Office of the Chief of Military History, Department of the Army, 1993.

Mittelman, Capt. Joseph B. *Eight Stars to Victory, A History of the Veteran Ninth U.S. Infantry Division*. Washington, DC: The Ninth Infantry Division Association, 1948.

Montgomery, Bernard Law. *The Memoirs of Field-Marshal the Viscount Montgomery of Alamein, K. G.* New York, NY: The World Publishing Company, 1958.

Morriss, Sgt. Mack. "In the Huertgen Forest." Originally published in *Yank*, reprinted in Congdon, Don, ed. *Combat, European Theater*. New York, NY: Dell Publishing Co., Inc., 1958.

Northern France. CMH Pub 72-30. Washington, DC: U.S. Army Center of Military History, not dated.

Rhineland. CMH Pub 72-25. Washington, DC: U.S. Army Center of Military History, not dated.

Shirer, Willam L. *The Rise and Fall of the Third Reich*. New York, NY: Fawcett Crest, 1983.

"Soixante-Dix," A History of the 70th Tank Battalion. Soixante-Dix is an informal history contained in the 70th Tank Battalion's official records.

Southern France. CMH Pub 72-31. Washington, DC: U.S. Army Center of Military History, not dated.

Spearhead in the West. Frankfurt, Germany: 3d Armored Division, 1945.

The Thunderbolt Across Europe, A History of the 83d Infantry Division 1942–1945. Munich, Germany: 83d Infantry Division, 1945.

The Victory Division in Europe, Story of the 5th Armored Division. Gotha, Germany: 5th Armored Division, 1945.

Von Senger und Etterlin, Dr. F. M. *German Tanks of World War II*. New York, NY: Galahad Books, 1969.

White, Peter. *With the Jocks*. Stroud, UK: Sutton Publishing, 2001.

Whiting, Charles. *Bloody Aachen*. New York, NY: Stein and Day, 1976.

———. *Siegfried, The Nazis' Last Stand*. London: Pan Books, 2003.

Wilkes, Homer D. *747th Tank Battalion*. Scottsdale, AZ: self-published, 1977?

Wilmot, Chester. *The Struggle for Europe*. Ware, England: Wordsworth Editions Limited, 1997.

"Defense of the West Wall." Interview with Major Herbert Büchs, aide to *Generaloberst* Alfred Jodl. ETHINT-37, 28 September 1945. National Archives.
Denkert, *Generalmajor* Walter. "The 3d Panzer Grenadier Division During the Defensive Combat for the Inden Bridgehead." MS # A-976, December 1945. National Archives.

————. "The 3d Panzer Grenadier Division in the Battle for Aachen." MS # A-979, 10 July 1950. National Archives.

"Employment of Panzer Forces on the Western Front." Interview with *Generaloberst* Heinz Guderian. ETHINT-39, 16 August 1945. National Archives.
Engel, *Generalmajor* Gerhard. "The First Battle Near Aachen, 16 September to 22 September 1944." MS # A-971, 27 March 1946. National Archives.

————. "12th Infantry Division, 22 Sep–22 Oct 1944." MS # B-415, 12 April 1947. National Archives.

Ewart, *Generalmajor* Wolf. "The Engagement of the 338th Inf Div in the Rhineland, Part II." MS # B-531, not dated. National Archives.

Hitzfeld, *General der Infanterie* Otto, commanding general, LXVII Corps. "Rhineland, Combat Operations (15 September 1944 to 21 March 1945) of LXVII Corps for the Period From 26 January 1945 to March 1945." MS # B-101, 19 September 1950. National Archives.

Köchling, *General der Infanterie* Friedrich, Commanding General, LXXXI Corps. "The Battle of the Aachen Sector." MS # A-989 to MS # A-998, series begins 16 December 1945. National Archives.

König, *Generalmajor* Eugen. "272d Volks Grenadier Div. (13 Dec 1944–Mar 1945) and 91st Airborne Division (15 Sep–13 Dec 1944)." MS # B-171, 8 October 1950. National Archives.

Krämer, *Generalmajor* Fritz. "*Das I. SS-Pz.Korps im Westen 1944 [9.9.1944–20.10.1944]*." MS # C-048, not dated. National Archives.

Lange, *Generalleutnant* Wolfgang. "183d Volksgrenadier Division (Sep 1944–25 Jan 1945)." MS # B-753, not dated. National Archives.

Langhauser, *Generalmajor* Rudolf. "12 VGD (Volksgrenadierdivision), Defensive Battle Between Roer and Rhine, 23 Feb–27 Mar 45." MS # B-080, 15 June 1946. National Archives.

Macholz, *Generalleutnant* Siegfried. "*Die Kämpfe der 49. I.D. von derMaas bis an Den Westwall Nördlich Aachen und um den Westwall (2.9.–10.10.44)*." MS # B-792, 26 February 1948. National Archives.

Mahlmann, *Generalleutnant* Paul. "353d Infantry Division (9–18 Sep 1944)." MS # B-232, not dated. National Archives.

Neitzel, *Oberst* Hasso. "89th Infantry Division (13 Sep–1 Oct 1944)." MS # B-793, not dated. National Archives.

Poppe, *Generalleutnant* Walter. "The Commitment of the 59. Inf Div in Rheinland from 3 Dec 44 to 28 Feb 45." MS # B-152, May 1946. National Archives.

Püchler, *General der Infanterie* Karl, Commanding General, LXXIV Corps. "The Rhineland—74. Armeekorps—The Periods from 2 to 27 Oct. 1944 and 16 Dec. 1944 to 23 Mar. 1945." MS # B-118, 26 July 1946. National Archives.

Schmidt, *Generalleutnant* Hans. "275th Infantry Division (3 Oct–21 Nov 1944)." MS # B-810, 15 December 1947. National Archives.

————. "*3. Teil. Kämpfe in Nordfrankreich.*" MS # B-372, not dated. National Archives.

————. "*4. Teil. Kämpfe im Rheinland der 275. Infanterie-Division.*" MS # B-373, 17 February 1947. National Archives.

Schramm, *Major* Percy Ernst. "OKW War Diary (1 Apr–18 Dec 1944)." MS # B-034, not dated, National Archives. The "war diary" was an unofficial compilation (circa March 1945) of notes and summaries based on meetings and original documents, many of which were destroyed.

Straube, *General der Infanterie* Erich. "*Einsatz des Generalkommandos LXXIV. Armeekorps (Sept. bis Dez. 1944).*" MS # C-016, not dated. National Archives.

Voigt, *Oberstleutnant iG*, Hans-Hubert. "The 340th Volksgrenadier Division in Combat in the Rhineland (2 September–25 December 1944)." MS # B-462, 1952. National Archives.

Von Gersdorf, *Generalmajor* Rudolf Christoph, Freiherr, Chief of Staff, Seventh Army. "The Battle of the Hürtgen Forest, Nov–Early Dec 1944." MS # A-891, 12 December 1945. National Archives.

————. "Questions for Consideration and Reply." MS # A-892, not dated. National Archives.

————. "Seventh Army; Siegfried Line—Defense of the Siegfried Line." ETHINT 53, 24 November 1945. National Archives.

Von Kahlden, *Oberst iG*, Chief of Staff, Fifth Panzer Army. "Fifth Pz Army (15 Sep–15 Oct 44)." MS # B-472, not dated. National Archives.

Von Lüttwitz, *General der Panzertruppen* Heinrich. "The 47. Pz Corps in the Rhineland from 23 Oct–5 Dec 1944." MS # B-367, 11 January 1947. National Archives.

Von Manteuffel, *General der Panzertruppen* Hasso-Eccard, Commanding General, Fifth Panzer Army. "Statement by General von Manteuffel." MS # A-857, not dated. National Archives.

Von Schwerin, *Generalleutnant* Gerhard Graf, Commanding General, 116th Panzer Division. "116th Panzer Division from the Seine to Aachen." ETHINT 18, October–November 1945. National Archives.

Von Zangen, *General der Infanterie* Gustav. "Fifteenth Army (22 Nov 44–9 Mar 45), Anglo-American large-scale attack across the Roer and Rhine." National Archives.

————. "Fifteenth Army (22 Nov 44–9 Mar 45), Defense Battles at the Roer and Rhine." MS # B-811, 15 November 1947. National Archives.

Wagener, *Generalmajor* Carl, Chief of Staff, Fifth Panzer Army. "The Action of the Fifth Panzer Army During the American November Offensive." MS # A-863, 12 December 1945. National Archives.

Wangenheim, *Oberstleutnant* Horst. "The 277th Volks Grenadier Division, 26 Jan-9 Mar 1945." MS # B-754, not dated. National Archives.

INDEX

INDEX

Engel, Oberst Gerhard, 42–48, 50, 51, 58–60, 71, 74, 76, 81, 107, 108, 112, 113, 116, 117, 127–129, 131–133, 141, 162, 167, 173, 175, 177, 198, 244, 249, 269, 271, 290, 294

Engineer Combat Group, American, 1106th, 74, 77

Erft River, 34, 229, 256

Erkelenz, 123, 155, 254, 255

Erman, Technical Sergeant John, 191

Eschweiler, 3, 9, 11, 12, 25, 27, 28, 39, 43, 45, 62–64, 71

Essen, 101

Euchen, 75, 122

Euskirchen, 234

Ewald, Captain William, 175, 176

Falaise Pocket, 31

Feind, Oberst, 110

Felix, Francis, 213

First Allied Airborne Army, 27

Flossdorf, 195, 197, 246

Foote, Lieutenant Theodore, 64, 65

Frankland, Lieutenant Colonel Robert, 61, 62, 65, 70, 153, 154, 272, 273

Frenz, 163, 167, 172

Frenzerburg Castle, 173, 174

Friealdenhoven, 149

Fronhoven, 155

Fuller, Captain William, 92

Gaab, Wes, 125, 177

Garcia, Private Marcario, 177

Gavin, Major General James, 237, 288, 292

Geilenkirchen, 53, 61, 68, 69, 77, 99, 101, 104, 105, 107, 158–160, 162, 186

Gemmenich, 14

Gemünd, 40

Gereonsweiler, 120, 148, 151

Gerhardt, Major General Charles, 57, 120, 146, 156, 193

Gevenich, 254

Gey, 144, 210, 212, 215

Gillem, Major General Alvan Jr., 104, 186

Gladbach, 109, 247

Gleason, Captain Ralph, 179–181

Göbbels, Dr. Joseph, 243

Gomes, Lieutenant Colonel Lloyd, 160

Göring, Hermann, 24, 54

Graeber, Second Lieutenant Robert L., 191

Granville, 54

Gray, Captain Robert, 121, 157, 158

Gressenich, 45, 51, 103, 117, 129, 133

Gropp, Sergeant, 165

Grosshau, 40, 136, 142, 163, 166, 167, 170, 176, 177, 185, 201

Grosswald Forest, 132

Gubel, 42

Guderian, General Heinz Günther, 17, 37, 226, 267–271, 273–275, 277–279, 287, 292, 294

Haaren, 74, 79

Halder, Generaloberst Franz Halder, 88

Hamich, 103, 115, 117, 128–133

Harmon, Major General Ernest, 58, 69, 72, 82, 98, 119, 120, 146, 156, 275, 292

Harris, RAF Air Chief marshal Sir Arthur, 222

Harrison, Brigadier General W. H., 77 273

Harscheidt, 237

Hasenfeld Gut, 193, 207

Hasenfeld, 201, 237, 238

Hasselt, 54

Havighorst, Oberleutnant Ludwig, 175, 176

Hehlrath, 111, 139

Heinsberg, 34, 111, 124, 195, 209, 225, 239, 240, 241, 242

Heinz, Oberst (984th Grenadier Regiment), 110, 112, 178, 198

Heistern, 134, 139, 140, 144

Herbach, 68

Herford, Leutnant (29th Grenadier Regiment), 180

Herhan, 234